The Man Everybody Knew

The Man Everybody Knew

BRUCE BARTON AND THE
MAKING OF MODERN AMERICA

Richard M. Fried

Ivan R. Dee

CHICAGO 2005

www.ivanrdee.com

Library of Congress Cataloging-in-Publication Data:
Fried, Richard M., 1941–
  The man everybody knew : Bruce Barton and the making of modern America /
Richard M. Fried.
    p. cm.
  Includes bibliographical references (p.   ) and index.
  ISBN 1-56663-663-9 (cloth : alk. paper)
    1. Barton, Bruce, 1886–1967. 2. Legislators—United States—Biography. 3.
United States. Congress. House—Biography. 4. Advertising executives—New York
(State)—New York—Biography. 5. Authors, American—Biography. 6. Political
consultants—United States—Biography. I. Title.
E748.B264F75 2005
328.73'092—dc22

                                                                    2005011373

To McRae, Maddy, Max, Kevin, and Eli

Contents

Preface

BRUCE BARTON (1886–1967) was famous in his day. His best-selling book *The Man Nobody Knows* and other claims to celebrity made him "the man everybody knows" over some four decades. He was a cultural icon; a business idol; a political figure as both a public relations adviser and, later, a candidate and congressman; an editor; and the co-founder of a prominent advertising agency. People sought audiences with him for jobs, advice, his latest wisdom, or a boost for various projects. Con artists claimed they *were* Bruce Barton. It would be hard, from the 1920s into the 1950s, not to know who Bruce Barton was. Yet somehow, as a subject of full-length biography, he has slipped through the cracks, receded nearly to the status of a punchline in history textbooks. His life warrants biographical salvaging.

This lapse in coverage would have astounded his contemporaries, for the name of this much-quoted, much-noted American tripped off many tongues and graced a profusion of articles, editorials, and even jokes. He became the point of reference for all sorts of "——nobody knows" constructions as a result of his most famous book, which was a 1920s publishing phenomenon. Hell (or, for others, church) became "the place nobody goes." Celebrated editor Maxwell Perkins shepherded to press the works of Ernest Hemingway and F. Scott Fitzgerald, but Bruce Barton's book—more widely read at the time than *Gatsby* or *Farewell to Arms*—evaded his fold.

Barton became part of the cultural currency of his heyday. His name popped up in gossip columns and in hard news of business, politics, and religion. He was one of those people who warranted being interviewed whenever he alighted from a train in Atlanta or Phoenix or disembarked from a liner in New York or Hong Kong. Batten, Barton, Durstine & Osborn, or BBDO, became a shorthand reference to Madison Avenue, an exemplar of the emerging field of advertising as a whole, and even an endlessly repeated gag on Jack Benny's hit radio comedy show. Jimmy Cagney in a 1933 movie told his cronies he had to leave to lunch with Bruce Barton. In real life, when Barton squired "America's Sweetheart" Mary Pickford into the House dining room in 1938, congressional jaws stopped chewing. Years later, retired President Harry S. Truman would fulminate against Republican party publicity devices as the product of "Bunko, Bull, Deceit & Obfuscation."

Via several avenues Barton offered advice to Americans on how to adjust as they navigated a "transitional" period. He formally entered the field of advertising in 1919. He prospered particularly with institutional advertising for corporate behemoths like General Motors and General Electric, for American capitalism itself, and for the business of advertising. He enabled Americans in an era of flux to conceive of these mega-businesses on a human scale, through comforting images of an earlier, less troubled day. His most widely known book reassuringly linked the realms of religion and business. Critics dismissed it as a sappy Valentine to business and advertising. It was more than that: it aimed to make businessmen more spiritual, not simply to outfit them with halos. In any case, buyers outnumbered critics. He succeeded in harnessing the virtues and consolations of an earlier day—the work ethic, the simple life—to the imperatives of the modern age—high mass consumption, city living—and in fortifying his readers in the view that a kindly God smiled upon such developments.

He also achieved prominence in politics. He advised candidates who became president—Calvin Coolidge and Herbert Hoover—as well as some who did not (notably Thomas E. Dewey). He was thus an early "spin" artist, helping waft the methods and insights of Madison Avenue into the smoke-filled room. He could spin himself as well.

Elected twice to the House of Representatives, he won multiple mentions as a presidential dark horse but lost a race for the U.S. Senate. His political career ended after, and partly as a result of, a famous litany that President Franklin D. Roosevelt included in a speech belittling Republicans as the party of "Martin, Barton and Fish." The irony that he was done in by a clever ad-like gibe was not lost on him.

His prominence peaked in the 1920s and 1930s, but it was on the rise in the latter teens and still high after 1940. Newspaper references faded a bit once he left electoral politics and thinned out as he aged, but he retained his iconic status. BBDO remained a proxy for "Madison Avenue" even though a younger generation was now running it. People still remembered and treasured Barton's writings, and *The Man Nobody Knows* stayed in print during his lifetime—and beyond.

Historians came to use Barton to represent the soul of the 1920s. His identification as the boardroom bard of the "age of wonderful nonsense" or the epitome of the Coolidge era when "the business of America [was] business" began early. Hardly a textbook fails to mention Barton's utterances coupling business and religion. Most offer a brief quotation from *The Man Nobody Knows*, usually the line that Jesus "picked up twelve men from the bottom ranks of business and forged them into an organization that conquered the world."

Barton did write as quoted, did intertwine business and religion as indicated, but more of his life than this one snippet merits attention. Although he will never be studied in American Lit classes, he achieved popularity as an author in a variety of formats. He edited a weekly magazine, which anticipated the layout and appeal of Henry Luce's *Life*. He wrote ads that won prizes and became models for his maturing profession—and were taught at universities. Corporate magnates insisted that *he*, not merely his agency, write their advertising copy. He interviewed prime ministers. He hobnobbed with presidents. His pithy editorials appeared in national magazines and in newspapers across the land.

Bruce Barton is surely the most prominent American of the twentieth century without a biography. This book attempts to correct that striking oversight.

Acknowledgments

BOOKS HAVE scores of fathers and mothers. This one is no exception. I have benefited from the help of friends, colleagues, archivists, librarians and family, and from the kindness of strangers. The following is a partial list.

My chief archival debt is to the Wisconsin Historical Society, especially Director Harry Miller and the staff of its Manuscript Reading Room, where the Bruce Barton Papers reside along with other collections that illuminate the history of advertising and mass communications. Also invaluable were the records retained in the library of BBDO–New York. There I profited from the support of Linda Clarke, Mary Muenkel, Mariel Urena, and others in the agency. At Amherst College's Robert Frost Library I received assistance from Head of Archives Daria D'Arienzo. Robert Park at the Franklin D. Roosevelt, Randy Sowell at the Harry S. Truman, Dwight Miller at the Herbert Hoover presidential libraries, Jessica Steytler at the Congregational Library and Archives (Boston), Rod Ross at NARA, Kay Peterson at the National Museum of American History, and their colleagues all eased my research.

The generous aid of the staff of the Richard J. Daley Library at the University of Illinois at Chicago was indispensable. Dr. Stephen Wiberley was especially helpful in unblocking futile searches, finding ways to bring Bartoniana to my doorstep. The Interlibrary Loan Department and Ana Lopez performed magic on many occasions. The

College of DuPage Library and Glen Ellyn Public Library also provided assistance. Caribou Coffee of Glen Ellyn supplied no books but made possible a continuum of space, time, and cappuccino.

I am grateful to the trustees of the University of Illinois for a sabbatical which expedited this project and to the UIC Humanities Institute and the Office of the Vice Chancellor for Research for two research grants which made possible travel to various collections.

Many colleagues at UIC bestowed encouragement, ideas, research and bibliographical tips, and even "stuff" that ended up in the book. These include Jim Sack, Richard John, the late Peter D'Agostino, Perry Duis, Burt Bledstein, Eric Smith (who did some remote-control manuscript acquisition for me), and Bob Hunter. Sara Rose was an admirable and essential research assistant. Elizabeth Tieri lent help as an Honors College undergraduate research assistant.

Ivan Dee has been both a source of encouragement and support as a publisher and sound advice and an unerring eye as an editor.

Prof. James L. Baughman of the University of Wisconsin–Madison provided ideas, expertise in the field of mass communications, hospitality on my many trips to Badgerland, and cherished invitations to the renowned Friday evening "seminar" at that institution of learning. Nina and Dick Rieselbach also opened their home to me. Many other scholars variously supplied stimulation, ideas, and research suggestions and materials, among them William E. Leuchtenburg (as often before), Jackson Lears, Leo Ribuffo, David Farber, Pamela Walker Laird, Michael T. Carroll, John E. Miller, Margaret Bendroth, Justus Doenecke, James Kenneally, Edrene Montgomery, John Morello, and William "Larry" Bird. Mark Cherrington of Amherst College kindly sent alumni data about Barton.

I was fortunate to speak or correspond with a number of people who either knew Bruce Barton or could share their experiences at the advertising agency that bears his name. I wish to express my thanks to Robert D. Barton (Bruce's nephew), Allen Rosenshine, Richard Detwiler, Jeannette Paladino, Alphonse Normandia, John R. Osborn (Alex

Osborn's grandson), Marilyn Ellman Buel, Ed Brody, Lou Pringle, Marcia Kamien, and my college roommate Richard Joslin.

This book would have been unthinkable without the support of my family. Our son Rocky and daughter Gail provided perspectives on mysteries of the business world—terra incognita to this academic—and also some internet wizardry. They (along with Lycia Carmody Fried and Kevin Patrick Scannell) also furnished the book's five dedicatees.

My wife Barbara, as with earlier books, has made the enterprise possible by covering for my absence on research junkets, tolerating (or tuning out) my prattle about the topic, dodging slag heaps of books and papers, reading drafts, and offering valued criticism. In numberless other ways she has made the book a reality. Ordinarily I would dedicate the book to her. But in deference to Bruce Barton's own emphasis on the importance of youth—and to build readership—it is dedicated to our five precious grandchildren.

R. M. F.

Glen Ellyn, Illinois
June 2005

The Man Everybody Knew

1

A Son of the Manse

WHEN BRUCE BARTON was born in Robbins, Tennessee, August 5, 1886, his father's family had been established on American shores for a little more than a century. On his mother's side, his line could be traced to early colonial Connecticut, to Francis Bushnell, signer of the Guilford, Connecticut, covenant, to John Davenport, founder of New Haven, to Governor Robert Treat, who had hidden Connecticut's charter in the famous Charter Oak, and to the first president of Yale.[1]

Barton's paternal great-great-grandfather was William Barton (1754–1829), son of a British soldier James Barton, who was killed in the French and Indian War. After also joining the British army, William was sent to North America during the Revolution. He pulled out of Boston with General William Howe, fought on Long Island, and campaigned up the Hudson River. But he came gradually to sense that he was enlisted in "the wrong army," one which his descendant Bruce Barton later described as pursuing "a mission of Bureaucratic Uplift." Grabbing a bucket on the pretext of fetching water one day, Barton strode toward the river. An officer ordered him back to camp; his refusal earned a nasty sword swipe that would leave a scar across his face. Striking back with his bucket, Barton unhorsed his superior, seized his sword and made his way across the Hudson. Welcomed into the Continental Army, he rose to the rank of lieutenant. While manufacturing cannon shot for the Americans in New Jersey, he met Margaret Henderson and married her after three weeks' courtship. The British officer's sword that William Barton made off with would become a treasured family heirloom.[2] Archibald M. Willard, the artist whose *Spirit of '76* later became the central iconic representation of the patriot cause, also painted a canvas depicting the bucket-wielding Barton's confrontation with the redcoat officer.[3]

The Bartons' son Eleazar lived in New Jersey, but when two of his sons returned from the West with tidings of the prosperous hinterland, the family packed its belongings, took a ferry up the Hudson, traversed the Erie Canal, crossed the Great Lakes by steamboat, and arrived in Chicago. From there they headed west, in three days reaching Knox Grove, Illinois. There in 1846 the extensive Barton family settled.

Among Eleazar's ten sons was Jacob B. Barton (1834–1912), who had made the trip west as a boy. At sixteen Jacob suffered a severe case of pneumonia. A doctor's role in his recovery stimulated an interest in the healing arts and led Jacob to read medicine at this village practitioner's office. He returned to Knox Grove where he taught school, practiced medicine, and compounded remedies that he sold from his wagon to farmers in the surrounding countryside. Moving to Sublette, just four miles away, he opened a drug store. As other doctors came into the area, they asked Jacob Barton to fill their prescriptions; in turn, he all but gave up practicing medicine. Neither of these pursuits enriched him. In his own prime, Bruce Barton recalled his grandfather as "a kindly old country doctor and druggist, who brought babies into the world for whose arrival he was never paid, and passed out his healing drugs to the suffering but could never quite bring himself to insist that his bills be promptly met." To make ends meet, Jacob also took on the postmastership and installed two printing presses. Soon his store was crammed with drugs, printing gear, arriving and departing mail, and many of Sublette's 350 or so townspeople who were looking for one or another of these services.

In 1860 Jacob Barton married Helen Methven. Her father, a farmer and preacher, had emigrated from Scotland in 1837, the rest of his family soon following. In a room above the store, William Eleazar Barton was born on June 28, 1861. William, who became Bruce Barton's father, would have a powerful influence on his famous son and no small fame of his own. Although it would not be long before William left his rural youth behind, it would carry well into the next generation. Bruce Barton had little actual experience in such circumstances, but he would always idealize his adolescence as that of a "small-town boy." Other observers noticed the pattern this distant past had etched on Barton. In an obituary, Alistair Cooke, the astute English observer of the American scene, called Barton "a rampant individualist and frontier Republican to the day he died."

By the mid-nineteenth century the frontier had passed the town of Sublette. Once scene of a skirmish in the Blackhawk War, now it was "civilized" though still raw. Its homespun generosity was evidenced near the end of the Civil War, when the Barton family cow died. The Baptist preacher took up a subscription to replace it—even if the Bartons attended the Methodist church. Yet when the worm of politics turned and the Democrats took over, neighborliness did not prevent Jacob Barton from losing his postmastership and, amid the ravages of the Panic of 1873, with it the underpinnings of his store's and his family's prosperity, such as it was. Foresightedly he had bought thirteen acres of fertile land, which saw the Bartons through on a reduced scale.

Perched above the watersheds of the Rock and Illinois rivers, the town had a railroad running through it, though it never became a major way point. The railroad meant progress, but the rough-and-tumble was seldom far away. As a young lad William himself had once leaped aboard a runaway boxcar, tightening down the brake wheel before the car plunged down the sloping track into an oncoming locomotive. In 1877 a secretive couple summered in Sublette; afterward William Barton wondered if this might have been the bandit Frank James, recuperating after the Northfield, Minnesota, raid, and his wife.

Sublette's social and intellectual life centered in its surfeit of churches. In tiny congregations, their members stretched to acquire missing skills. William Barton's sister learned to play a "little cabinet organ" as a child, and he himself was of tender years when he "began taking, in emergencies, the place of an absent Sunday School teacher." The church was so often without a minister that sometimes his uncle or father filled in with a sermon, "usually one by Henry Ward Beecher." His father held a license to preach, and though he did not pastor a church, he sometimes conducted small neighborhood services and funerals.

Despite thin academic resources, learning was cherished in Sublette, acquired through personal effort more than institutional matriculation. Jacob Barton often "mourned" the limits of his formal education. He was interested in religion and history and owned books on law. (He was also a notary public.) His family read novels and poetry aloud together. Books traveled much from hand to hand, and townspeople often disputed theological and other topics. Outside lecturers and performers passed through. The Bartons opposed theatergoing but, as foes of slavery, made an exception when *Uncle Tom's Cabin* was staged. Despite Sublette's rough finish, William Barton's memoir offers tastes of simple sweetness that dominate more tart and painful rural experiences. Barton reminisced of one deep childhood friend: "Seraphine, you happy, resourceful, versatile girl; we liked each other and that was all there was of it." At her death "it was your long-time friend who conducted your funeral service." Small-town life peeps through in a far less gothic manner than from the pages of *Spoon River Anthology*, Edgar Lee Masters's bittersweet poetic evocation of another Illinois town.[4]

Yet for the long term Sublette would not do for William Barton. When he finished high school in 1878 at age sixteen, the prospect he saw ahead was a life in farming, the family's current mainstay. The limits of this horizon and a yearning for more education stirred quiet revolt in a youth who thought of himself as "saucy" but whose makeup was far from rebellious. Still, in June 1878 he packed his few belongings in a pair of boots and stole forth as a "tramp." He walked and hitchhiked a mere forty miles and one county north, to Stillman Valley. His whereabouts unknown to his family, he supported himself with farm work. Attending school through the winter, he dreamed of college. Uncle Bruce Hunting, from the Methven side, who was minister of Sublette's Congregational church (which William had joined in his teens), had told him about the school at which he taught, Berea College. The Kentucky institution, geared to the needs of poor students of its mountain surroundings, enabled them to work their way through by performing tasks in the college's upkeep.

William returned to Sublette. His father, reconciled and supportive of his ambition, sent him off with his sister Mary to Berea. They arrived in December 1880 with $16 between them. Tuition was only $3 a term, but even with work by spring they were $15.65 in debt. William taught school over the summer, trekking seventy miles into the mountains. He did well, though one parent, recoiling from young Barton's teaching that the Earth was round, pulled his son from school. There would be more summer and Sunday school teaching, two summers spent selling books, and some preaching as a "lay brother." At Berea, William also met a primary school teacher named Esther Treat Bushnell, from Ohio. They shared literary interests, spent increasing amounts of time together, and in July 1885 were married. Casting up the simplicity of his parents' lives, their nobility of mind and religious faith, their son Bruce would later declare: "I regard them as the happiest and most successful people I have ever known."

In his senior year William E. Barton, who had envisioned himself as a lawyer and statesman, changed his mind and decided to enter the ministry. He had an invitation to preach as a home missionary employed by the American Missionary Association. Although he had been a funloving undergraduate, Barton's seniors and contemporaries thought him a good fit for the ministry: he took some rushed lessons in theology and accepted the call. The president and other Berea faculty laid on hands in June 1885, and so he was ordained. Berea would continue to occupy an important place in the Barton family's affections.[5]

The Bartons embarked for Robbins, Tennessee, where William was to ride circuit and conduct mission work on a salary of $800 a year, thus launching a lifetime of preaching. He rode a white mare to visit seven churches in mountain country. On August 5, 1886, William and Esther's first child, Bruce, was born. Robbins was home for two happy, rewarding years, but William felt the need for deeper theological training: in 1887 the family departed for Ohio's Oberlin Theological Seminary. Robbins had provided two more additions to their household. At a sawmill, Reverend Barton chanced upon an abandoned mulatto boy of undetermined years (they assigned an age of twelve). They took Webster Beatty in, raised him as a member of the family, and provided an education that led him into the dental profession. They also were joined by Rebecca, a young African-American girl whose mother asked them to raise her. From the train station to their little house in Oberlin in the fall of 1887, they formed an eye-turning procession: Webster leading the horse on which Esther rode cradling Bruce, Becky leading the cow, and William following on the sidewalk.

In Oberlin they stayed until William Barton received his degree in May 1890. Their family gained a second son, Charles William Barton, in 1887, and a daughter, Helen, in 1889. William preached at a small church and lectured to support his growing family. After graduation he accepted a call from a church in Wellington, Ohio. Another son, Frederick Bushnell Barton, was born during the three years spent there. Reverend Barton's career soared in 1893 when he received a call to become minister of Boston's Shawmut Church. (In Boston in the following year their fourth son Robert Shawmut Barton was born.)[6]

Boston was a long way from Sublette. The pastor of a prominent Congregational church in the city that spawned many of the nation's good causes and much of its intellectual life in the nineteenth century, Barton associated with a range of notables and numbered as friends Thomas Wentworth Higginson, Edward Everett Hale, and Julia Ward Howe, each a figure touched with Civil War–era renown. He became a vice president of the American Peace Society. At the close of a heated public debate before the American Board of Commissioners for Foreign Missions over a fine point of disputed religious doctrine, Barton made a brief conciliating speech that won applause, publicity in the local papers, and renown for the young minister. It showed Barton's characteristic impatience with doctrinal quarrels.

Although the expenses living in Boston imposed on a minister's salary were high, the Bartons managed to buy a cottage in nearby Foxboro, which, after repairs and the addition of more buildings and acreage, eventually included a small lake and became the family's summer vacation home for many years. The Bartons soon webbed themselves into the hamlet's life. Reverend Barton would offer the memorial address on the town common marking the death of President Warren G. Harding in 1923. Foxboro was an antidote to the stresses and costs of city living, which proved wearing on Barton; his son Fred recalled that in Boston his father was sometimes "nervous and unwell." Bruce would later share these symptoms and claimed similar relief in communing with nature as Foxboro defined it.

William Barton's growing reputation brought the offer of several new pulpits (including the one Jonathan Edwards had held in Northampton, Massachusetts). The call to become pastor of the First Congregational Church of Oak Park, Illinois, proved more attractive. Barton was not eager to move but was persuaded that he could solve the challenge of reuniting a riven congregation. In Boston he had acquired some repute as a scholar of history. He lectured widely and his writings included stories as well as small historical contributions. When he announced his departure for Oak Park, some of his Shawmut congregants were moved to tears. The redoubtable Edward Everett Hale joked at his pleasure in not having to play "second fiddle" now that this rival authority on the history of Boston and New England was leaving.[7]

When the Bartons moved to Oak Park in 1899, they arrived not in a village, for the political subdivision of that name would not be established for another two years. Oak Park was a locality whose name was attached officially only to a post office and a railroad station; it also had a school district. But the area was still a political dependency of Cicero Township, with a population of nine thousand. Well supplied with rapid rail transport, building lots, and busy housing developers, the community was blossoming as a bedroom suburb just west of Chicago. It became a place of middle-class (and sometimes higher) comfort, though at least as late as 1907 the community was vexed by a scare over typhoid. By the end of Reverend Barton's twenty-five-year pastorate, it would grow to encompass nearly sixty thousand souls.

Like similar communities at the turn of the twentieth century, Oak Park faced a number of challenges. It often identified itself as a residential and moral sanctuary from the social problems and moral laxity of the Windy City. The community's early nickname was "Saints' Rest." When the Bartons arrived, Oak Parkers were struggling to set themselves apart from the Gomorrah to their east. In a series of elections they managed to achieve separation from Cicero, incorporation as a village, and the expulsion of Austin, their unloved neighbor to the east, into the maw of Chicago. They also managed to maintain temperance, prevent the showing of movies on Sunday (until 1932), and constrain the building of apartments in favor of single-family homes, even as the population of their village doubled from 1900 to 1910 and doubled again in the next decade.[8]

Conflicts between the forces of restraint, both self-imposed and mandated by the community, and those pressing for release and hedonism were playing out in thousands of localities and millions of individual minds in early-twentieth-century America. Oak Park was a way station not only between the metropolis and the great agricultural hinterland but between an older, small-town, individualistic, church-led, producer-oriented ethos and a metropolitan, consumption-driven, corporate society. Alert to the changes roiling their world, Oak Park parents sought to bring up their children to cope with them. They spun a dense network of institutions in which to shape their offspring: schools, churches, the YMCA, and local clubs to afford wholesome leisure activities for their children and socialize their sons into a corporate world. Bruce Barton, who remembered his Oak Park years fondly, had little to say about the impress of the more elaborate of these institutional niches, the clubs.[9] His own lively home, the extended family of his father's congregation, his high school, and his youthful work experiences were the formative frame he identified. Clearly he imbibed the modern, corporate sociability that fathers sought to hand on to their sons, and also the reasserted (and redefined) masculinity cultivated in the suburb. Yet in his memory home was something simpler, a typical small town—"a country town," as he once put it.[10]

As a much-heeded clergyman, Reverend Barton prominently addressed these cultural changes. He often endorsed when he did not lead his neighbors' efforts to reconcile old values and new conditions. A prime booster of his village, he waxed evangelical on the moral stewardship and example this and similar suburbs must offer. "The righteousness of the suburb," he said, "must reinforce that of the city." He even noted in a 1911 sermon that in his Jerusalem years Jesus "was a suburbanite." He supported most efforts to sustain the community's moral standards against the growing pressures of hedonism, commercialism, and secularism. He opposed Sunday movies as an intrusion on the Sabbath. He warned against the excesses of materialism, exalting the "sunbonnet" of old over "this season's adaptation of the Merry Widow hat," and the "little prairie home with a chromo on the wall" over contemporary houses "whose shining mahogany is the mere coffin of all ideas save vulgar display." Sometimes the quest for lifeways rooted in the past had an element of quaintness. Barton was struck by the contrast between the clean currency he saw at the Treasury in Washington and the "filthy money" circulating in Chicago. Considering it a matter of morality as well as sanitation, he catalyzed a campaign to have local merchants accept and circulate only "clean money" from banks. Bruce, too, would profess some ambivalence toward money. He maintained that "the only reason for having plenty of it is to be able never to have to think about it or talk about it."[11]

Yet Reverend Barton suggested that Oak Parkers could have their suburban cake and eat it too. His liberal theology held that Christianity was not a dour religion of Puritanism. Money and pleasures were tolerable if not the objects of idolization and excess. Comfort was desirable; materialistic excess was not. He shunned pointed theological disputation, was never a stickler about doctrine, and tended, at least within the realm of Protestantism, to be ecumenical. He led a delegation to a conference in Lausanne to explore a world federation of Protestant churches. Like other Protestant leaders of his community, he sought to reconcile the earlier Calvinist, producer-oriented, republican moral strictures of the nineteenth century with the corporate, consumption-driven, bureaucratic world that supplanted it. One former parishioner remembered for years a parable that Reverend Barton offered about how a "very penurious individual" traveling on a Mississippi River steamboat brought along his own lunch. At the end of the trip he learned that meals were included in his fare. The lesson? The good things in life "went along with the ticket of living." In the 1920s one of the tasks and achievements of Bruce Barton in his prime would be to mediate between these two vast and usually motley armies facing off along this cultural divide.[12]

Taking hold of a sorely divided congregation, Reverend Barton urged his parishioners not just to forgive but to forget their past strife. So intent was he on burying this unpleasant history that he refused to be briefed on the nature of these conflicts even by the most well-meaning and dispassionate informants. It took a while, but eventually his strategy succeeded in reknitting First Congregational. Edgy passivity gave way to communal vigor. When Barton arrived, the church and parsonage were in poor shape, a large debt burdened the congregation, and his salary was none too generous. In time these problems yielded to the congregation's renewed energies. The church building was remodeled and expanded, and the premises soon hummed with different activities to attract its members. A bolt of lightning in 1916 gutted the church, but within a year and a half it was rebuilt and ready for dedication.[13]

In theological matters Reverend Barton was a staunch liberal, to the point that he roused the hostility of conservatives who would soon come to be labeled fundamentalists. In a 1898 speech, in terms compatible with the intellectual outlook of the Progressive Era, he declared that modern believers might "modify the form in which they phrase their faith, and that they should interpret Christ in the light of the twentieth century's experience." This did not mean that the church was to retire from active engagement. Prefacing a publication promoting his suburb, he pridefully told how one teamster replied to his mate's query about how they would know they had reached Oak Park: "when the saloons stop, and the church steeples begin." He suggested that the village's ban on liquor sales might be "the very cornerstone of Oak Park's intellectual and moral supremacy." Yet, he added, Oak Park was no "oppressively religious town." He was also impatient with denominational hairsplitting. Generally the Protestant churches of Oak Park, striving mutually to keep their community afloat in a sea of urban temptations, took a more cooperative than competitive tack with one another.[14] Reverend Barton's religious beliefs had a marked impact on his son Bruce, who freely acknowledged his intellectual debt. For Bruce, said his brother Fred, religion was a "simple, rational, reasonable and pleasant part of life."[15]

First Congregational lay at the hub of Oak Park's tight-knit, self-conscious middle-class world. That culture has had its critics. Most famously, its native son Ernest Hemingway would dismiss the place as one of "broad lawns and narrow minds." The Barton and Hemingway orbits occasionally intersected. The novelist's father was the Barton family doctor. Bruce later recalled Ernest as a "tough little boy," and Hemingway once reminisced to one of Bruce's business colleagues that "the Barton brothers were always shooting at one another with twenty-two rifles."[16] Although the story carries a scent of apocrypha, the Barton offspring seldom radiated the sanctity of the parsonage. One tradesman remembered having to replace the glass front of a shoulder-high bookshelf, a casualty of the boys' roughhousing. (One of Bruce's younger brothers had thrown a shoe, and the intended target ducked.) He also reminded Bruce that his parents were sometimes "at their wits' end" to know how to make the boys "control yourselves."[17]

The Barton manse hummed with more than flying brogans. Bruce's brother Fred later recalled that at a given moment the Bartons might host parishioners, one of their many relatives, "maybe a visiting college

professor, maybe a missionary home from Africa to fatten up" before returning abroad. There were lecturers, writers, college presidents. Once
"a struggling artist," his wedding performed in the Barton parlor, offered
a painting, allegedly of a ship, in lieu of a cash fee.[18] Presiding over this
genial-managed chaos was Esther Bushnell Barton, an ideal minister's
wife, beloved of her congregation and all who knew her. She brought
several hundred dollars into the marriage, and, since the fund was periodically replenished from sources that came Reverend Barton's way to
further his work, it never ran out and was a reservoir that watered many
growing projects of charity and goodwill. Thus the assembly hall of a
mission compound in Madura, India, was named in her memory, as
was an Esther Barton Hospital in China.[19]

For the Bartons the Oak Park years were rewarding and, by Bruce's
recollection, idyllic. Although, like his father, he would leave the cozy
locale of his youth for a theater that more fully engaged his ambitions,
Bruce Barton never saw his as the sort of forceful break with his boyhood environment that his father's had been. In his writings Bruce
would often marvel at the inner spark that had driven exceptional
small-town boys, including both the young Jesus and many captains of
American industry, to sense that their destinies must be fulfilled in a
wider, more cosmopolitan world than the comfortable hamlets in
which they grew up. Barton himself identified with this podunk-to-
metropolis dynamic, though it fit his father better.

Reverend Barton probably stood near the top end of the ministe-
rial salary scale, but at the turn of the century that was none too high.
The Barton kids were comfortable but well short of spoiled. They did
not feel themselves deprived. "No one ever talked about money at our
house," Bruce's brother Fred recalled. Still, there were creature com-
forts. When the children "longed so for a pony," their father, who
wrote voluminously on the side, sold a "boy's story" to a magazine and
came home leading the pony. Reverend Barton never owned a car, but
with a telephone call to a well-to-do parishioner one would material-
ize, along with a chauffeur, for an afternoon of pastoral calls. Bruce
later generalized that one of the advantages preachers' sons carried

into life was the "high respect" yet corresponding "high disregard" for money, as well as other attributes that led to achievement.[20]

The boys' story that leveraged the pony was no one-time thing. Reverend Barton had an ease with the written word that led to numerous avenues of publication. Favored sermons often appeared as pamphlets. He wrote articles, both historical and fanciful. He took over a failing Congregational magazine and, among other insertions in its pages, created a character named Safed the Sage. The whimsical adventures and ruminations of Safed and his circle, depicted in quasi-biblical language, appeared in numerous stories, which were syndicated to a number of other church papers. One even dealt with an ethical question raised by a golf game—the issue of whether to count a ball knocked into the cup by an earthquake. In his prime Reverend Barton took an abiding interest in Abraham Lincoln. He often retraced the Rail Splitter's historical movements, examined several of the myths that gathered about that legendary figure, and wrote numerous articles and books, including a respected biography. In 1930, the final year of his life, his publications list was so extensive that his was the third-longest entry in that year's edition of *Who's Who*.[21]

Later in life Bruce often enlarged upon the blessings of being a preacher's son. He noted that a disproportionate number of those who made the pages of *Who's Who* grew up in the manse. He recalled fondly that a preacher's son "has the enormous advantages of poverty. He learns early what it means to have to work hard and live on little" yet to enjoy a life built on "good books . . . serious conversation and high thinking. We were poor," he said with some exaggeration, "but we never thought of ourselves as poor." With this background, Bruce learned early how to turn a dollar and was a textbook case in youthful hustle. In Boston at age nine he had a paper route. Later he took a liking to the maple syrup produced on an uncle's farm and successfully tested his hypothesis that his neighbors would like it too, obtaining the informal franchise for Oak Park and making as much as $600 a year peddling the syrup door to door and then passing the enterprise on to his brothers. Soon the uncle was forced to buy from farm neighbors to meet demand. Barton would boast later of having "the biggest business in maple syrup around Chicago."[22] He also was a reporter, both for his high school paper (which he edited) and for the local *Oak Leaves*, which paid him $3 to work three afternoons a week plus evenings.[23]

He was a busy striver. His brother Charles ascribed to him "the boyish determination to make good for the sake of his father and mother." He did well at Oak Park and River Forest High School. His scholastic performance is not well documented, but intellectually he was well primed. Fred Barton recalled that "Bruce always seemed grown up to the rest of us," with "a sober, serious way about him which marked him as a boy who intended to get somewhere." At the family dining table there was rapid-fire give-and-take. Fred recounted that each of the children would read verses of the Bible at family worship. Bruce read his in Greek. Throughout his career Bruce was a voracious reader, and that habit seems to have taken root early. He was also an effective talker. He won the high school's annual oratory contest with "an eloquent arraignment of municipal corruption" (based presumably on reportage by the likes of the muckraking crusader Lincoln Steffens). These were good years, filled with activities both remunerative and character-building, along with academic achievement and youthful joys. The only shadow was a sometimes frail constitution. Charles recalled that his brother "suffered with poor health as a boy" and consequently "began taking extra good care of himself," exercising regularly.[24]

When Bruce decided to go to Amherst College, his father prevailed on him to spend his first year at his own alma mater, Berea, where every student worked to put himself through and to sustain the college itself. It was also the only college south of the Mason-Dixon line that admitted both black and white students. Reverend Barton declared his motive: "I want your sympathies always to be on the side of the boys and girls who have to struggle for their education." Somewhat grudgingly, Bruce acceded. At Berea he worked in the print shop, learning to set type and proofread, skills that later proved useful. Life was not all grindstone at Berea: Bruce was also one of the principals behind a magazine filled with innocent humor, *The Josher*.[25]

He transferred to Amherst College as a sophomore. Firmly within the orbit of Congregationalism, Amherst had been founded in 1821 to combat the "wicked Unitarian heresy" of Harvard. It had enjoyed growth and rising stature; some of its graduates would earn renown as Barton himself rose to prominence. Yet his first year at Amherst was so unhappy, he recalled, "that I seriously thought of quitting college and going to work." He felt insecure. He "arrived on the Amherst campus in a twelve-dollar suit marked down to eight dollars." But he received invitations from two fraternities and decided to join Alpha Delta Phi. Not always in good health, Bruce found himself "a very poor boy in a fraternity house where there were a good many rich boys; I felt useless and awkward, and generally futile."[26]

This would not be Barton's last experience of rising doubt and ebbing self-confidence. An uncertainty about direction would occasionally translate itself into physical maladies. He also suffered a crisis of faith in his college years. His father, sensing something amiss when Bruce returned home one Christmas, escorted him into his study. Bruce "blurted out" his yawning doubts about the existence of God or heaven. Without reproach or scriptural fulmination, his father calmly coaxed him back to belief with the argument "that if there be no Intelligence behind the universe then the universe has created something greater than itself; for it has created us, and we *know* that we have intelligence." This syllogistic approach to religion would undergird Barton's faith, beleaguered as it often was, throughout the years. As he put it twenty years later: "If there is a God he must be good; for we are good. And He could not have made us better than Himself. And if He is good there must be something after death; for none of us . . . would ever have planted love, and hope and courage in human souls only to snuff it out."[27]

In the next two years his college life improved. Barton played some football, showed talent as a debater, became a campus leader, and served as a grader for the history department. He was elected to the senior society, and then as its president. Over two summers Barton helped finance his education by selling aluminum pots and pans door to door, and before his senior year he was placed in charge of thirty salesmen. He noted that college men, averse to "intimate contact with irate old men and bulldogs," not to mention dragging a ponderous sample bag down dusty lanes, seldom sought work as salesmen, but he found his own experience as a drummer "an unexcelled opportunity for observing human nature." Despite these triumphs, Barton remembered, "I wasn't very well at Amherst, and was too poor to be particularly happy."

In his senior year his class voted him most likely to succeed. He was graduated Phi Beta Kappa, the youngest member of his class, just shy of twenty-one. The *Chicago Record Herald* ran a picture of Barton captioned "one of the best all-around men in Amherst." He was a good fit. The paper's correspondent reported that in Barton's class Republicans outnumbered Democrats fifty to four (with one independent); that nearly half the class planned to enter business and only four the ministry. Amherst's president called '07 "just an average lot of fellows—intelligent, practical, useful, well-rounded men who are likely to make good citizens and succeed in life, but there are no geniuses among them, and he does not expect to hear that any of them have set the Connecticut River on fire."[28]

But physically and mentally Bruce was not out of the woods. His senior year was also marked by reversals, notwithstanding his achievements and duties—and perhaps induced by their burden. That winter he came down with a severe case of influenza. After release from the infirmary he was afflicted by "a terrible case of insomnia and was thoroughly frightened" that by losing so much sleep "I might lose my mind." Bruce, his brother Fred recalled, was "always a nervous, hardworking, driving sort of worker, he could easily have worn himself out before 30 and ended in a sanitarium." He completed all his coursework in the fall semester and so could go to the family summer place in Foxboro, where he hoped the exercise of outdoor work would tire him enough to win some sleep at night. The therapy failed; he returned to Amherst unrecovered. That his classmates had voted him "most likely to succeed" was "the crowning touch of irony." He had no job, no rest, was despondent and "on the edge of a nervous break-down."[29]

Barton was also at loose ends for a career. Since boyhood he had assumed he would join the ministry, imagining himself alongside his father, but in his last year in college he "finally abandoned the idea." He jettisoned part of his "bundle of beliefs," but mostly, he realized, "as I came to know myself . . . never under any possible conditions could I be as successful in it as my father had been." He lacked his father's energy, reserve of emotional stamina, and bottomless wellspring of love. Throughout his life he would express wistful second thoughts about the road not taken, often in published paeans of admiration for his father.[30]

Bruce gave thought to teaching history. The department head at Amherst told him that if he took a year of graduate training, he could come back to teach at his alma mater. The University of Wisconsin offered him a fellowship in history—the offer came to him from Frederick Jackson Turner, the nation's most renowned historian.[31] But a chance encounter with a visiting journalist, William E. Curtis, whom he befriended during graduation week, left Barton with the notion that he might have a future in journalism. He wrote an article on fraternities for Curtis, who also featured him in a piece in the *Chicago Record Herald*; a publisher who happened to read that paper—and that article, rather than his usual morning *Tribune*—would eventually give him a job. Barton was a believer in the importance of luck and often referred to this contingent chain of events to make his case.[32]

Barton investigated jobs in publishing, but the business slump of 1907 deferred that as an immediate option. Questions about his health and the absence of other choices prompted him to take a job, offered to him by a member of his father's church, as a timekeeper with Bates Rogers Construction at a Montana construction camp engaged in building railroad bridges across the Missoula River. He was still experiencing "a period of very great distress," lacking ambition, focus, and certainty about his direction. He may even have taken the job as part of a half-baked plan to get "started around the world."[33]

In any event, Montana proved restorative. The railroad construction camp teemed with roughnecks, some on the lam from the law or
unwanted wives, and they were apt to have little patience with a college kid. Hiring a cook who would not poison this unruly population
proved to be one of the labors Barton was called on to perform: at one
point a delegation of men informed him that they would kill the current cook if he were not replaced. Barton explained that he had hired
a replacement, upon whose arrival he would fire the incumbent chef.
Until then the latter was not to be harmed. "I am the boss," Barton asserted, emphasizing the point by carrying a sawed-off pick handle to
the next meal. He was gratified by the "undercurrent of respect" that
flavored the crew's "sullen silence." "I made good at that job," he recalled. Another drama developed the day the banks, beset by the 1907
panic, could not cash the construction workers' paychecks. These
"Montenegrins, to whom the financial situation could not be explained, built a huge bonfire" in front of the office, threatening an attack; Barton and other managers sat the night inside "with loaded
shotguns across our knees." More commonly, long days of hard work
brought him sound sleep, and the surroundings and challenges re-
stored his frayed faith and self-confidence too, a spiritual pilgrimage he
described in an article in *Christian World* which recounted the experience in the words of an "eye witness."[34]

But timekeeping was not to be Bruce Barton's career. After a job as
a reporter with the *Daily Missoulian* evaporated in the recession, with
his father's help he was invited to return to Chicago to work for a magazine publishing company. The construction superintendent rode out
from headquarters in Spokane to offer Barton a raise and the prospect
of promotion, but this was an opportunity the recent college graduate
was not about to turn down. He returned to Chicago and began what
became a long career in writing, publishing, sales, and advertising. He
had acquired learning, work experience, and social skills that would
serve him well in that cluster of vocations. An excellent student, he
had attained a first-rate education. He particularly valued Greek and
mathematics for the training they brought to the mind, and came to

consider himself a "frank reactionary" for holding these educational preferences. One of his later pieces of writing praised Amherst for sending forth men who "were creators, not merely consumers" (a somewhat ironic formulation, given his career path).[35] He had the makings of an appealing writer—he would credit the Barton family's endless immersion in the King James Bible for much of his facility with the language.[36] He had met people from numerous walks of life— striving fellow students at Berea, well-off classmates at Amherst, Montenegrin construction workers in Montana, the sources he had questioned as sole reporter for the *Oak Leaves*—and he had already begun to understand what made them tick. He had had several successful experiences in salesmanship, an art to which, in one form or another, he would devote the rest of his life. Starting in 1908, his life took an upward trajectory. There would be more blind alleys in his career, some reversals, and many doubts, but as he boarded the train from Montana to Chicago, he was on his way.

2

Wordsmith

IN HIS PRIME Bruce Barton would reminisce that he had graduated from college jobless into the teeth of an economic depression, yet persevered and made his way. For one collegiate readership he wrote: "We stepped out of our friendly fraternity houses into a panic," in which "hundreds of thousands of jobless walked the streets." Looking to work in publishing, the best he could do was his timekeeper's job in Montana. This saga, with its implicit testimony of his own prowess, he often cited as a lesson for other young strivers who confronted later hostile business environments.[1] In fact, Barton left school during the run-up to the 1907 economic slump. As he was fitted for his cap and gown in late spring 1907, overspeculation in Wall Street securities, followed by the dumping of shares and reinvestment in less liquid assets, and complicated by an arthritic credit and banking system, was causing audible creaks and groans in the American economy. But the slump "officially" began only the next October, when a large New York bank failed and runs on others threatened a broader collapse. Timely U.S. Treasury deposits in these banks, as well as President Theodore Roosevelt's willingness to wink at Wall Street magnate J. P. Morgan's scheme to restore stability by having U.S. Steel acquire the Tennessee Coal and Iron Company, may have prevented a deeper plunge. While 1907 was described as a rich men's panic, like others of that ilk, its waves shook humbler foundations, and economic hardships rippled ahead into 1908.

Barton made his first stab at a livelihood during the onset of the "high" Progressive era. Within the religious community there were many, clergy and laity, who argued that believers had a social as well as a theological duty to their fellow humans. In his unfolding career, and through his manse connections, Barton became familiar with many efforts of Social Gospel reformers. Muckraking journalists were also at the peak of their visibility in 1907. TR was president, and while his coinage of the term "muckraker" for these adversarial journalists was invidious, in the last two years of his presidency his own rhetoric against "malefactors of great wealth" grew more radical as he adopted some of the more pronounced Progressive remedies for economic instability and injustice. The malefactors themselves blamed journalism and a government hostile to capitalism for the economy's continuing fluctuations.[2]

In this harsh setting, Barton could be considered lucky. Even if his first job was beneath his talents and station, any job in the overbuilt railroad system was a fortunate find. His next berths in the field of magazine publication, though they taught him much that he put to later use, were not impervious to the business cycle. Barton was always endowed with the gift of coping, hustling, working hard, and succeeding, and he would eventually find his way. His longer-term problem was not so much surviving or finding something to do but rather defining and justifying it to himself. In his parade to success, doubt often occupied a front seat in the lead vehicle.

When Barton had first looked for work in publishing, he had been offered a job soliciting ads for a small Chicago magazine. But the panic benumbed the advertisers, and for the near term the job evaporated. In less than six months he gave up the Montana timekeeper's job when a position opened up with a Chicago company owned by one of his father's parishioners. It published "household magazines," including "a news weekly, a religious journal, and a farm paper." Barton seized the new opportunity that materialized at the end of 1907. He was hired to sell space in the *Home Herald*, but in the depressed economy few were advertising, so he threw himself into the work of

the editorial department. He took on a variety of responsibilities, writing articles and editorials for each of the magazines, reading proof and
pasting up dummies, answering mail and soliciting subscription re-
newals. He wrote "lead articles, editorials, farm articles, comments on
the Sunday-school lessons, letters to the editor, answers to letters to the
editor. . . . I did literally everything there is to be done in the editorial
or business office of a magazine." He soon became managing editor of
Home Herald. He wrote articles for the magazine, including numerous
interviews. For the approaching 1908 election, Barton oversaw a series
of articles on ten presidential possibilities and wrote seven of them, including the one on William Howard Taft, the eventual winner.[3]

Before long he was managing editor of two other magazines, a
monthly and a farm journal. In his early career, however, Barton had
a penchant for joining crews of ships that were about to founder.
Pleading a shortage of capital, his publisher persuaded Barton to draw
only $10 of his weekly salary and "let the other $30 accumulate"; because he lived with his parents in Oak Park, he could manage on this
sum. After about two years of hard work and skimpy cash rewards, Barton was shocked on reporting for work one morning to find the sheriff
occupying the premises. The business was bankrupt.

Dextrously Barton now turned catastrophe to advantage. He strode
into the office of the court-appointed receiver and declared himself a
creditor whom the magazines owed $1,600 in back pay. He offered to
settle by taking this amount in advertising in these death-bound publications—plus his old typewriter. The receiver, considering advertising
space in such "one-horse magazines" to be worthless, gladly agreed.
But Barton made ingenious use of this concession. He went to a travel
agency that organized excursions to the Oberammergau Passion Play
in Germany and persuaded a friend to grant him a $75 commission for
every traveler he signed up. He then composed an ad for the tour to
run in the religious weekly. The notice stirred interest, and Barton ca-
joled his respondents with information and encouragement until he
saw their ship off. The result was a substantial profit. Barton learned a
precious lesson in converting this loss to gain: ". . . so long as a man

keeps his health and his courage, there is hardly any experience, no matter how unpleasant, that can't be turned to a profit." The typewriter became a charm, reminding him for over two decades of his ability to make his way in business.[4]

Valued lessons aside, Barton had no job. But his work in Chicago had won favorable notice and eventually prompted job offers. He moved on to New York to become managing editor of *Housekeeper*, jointly published by Robert J. Collier and Conde Nast, the publisher of *Vogue*. With Nast he developed a mail solicitation of advertising for *Vogue*. He first lived at the Twenty-third Street YMCA and poured long hours into *Housekeeper*, but that religious weekly closed shop shortly after his arrival. The publisher of *The Continent*, a Presbyterian journal, hired him to run his New York office and to build circulation. While connected with *The Continent* and for a few years after, Barton wrote a number of articles about religious, missionary, and social uplift efforts. In fact he began at this stage of his life to write for a number of outlets, a practice that he continued his entire working life. He was also acquiring the knack of writing the snappy editorials for which he later became noted.[5]

THIS PHASE of Barton's career coincided with the zenith of the Progressive Era. Historians have long puzzled over the nature of Progressivism, but most would agree that it embraced a sense that conditions in American society called for reform and an optimism that progress, sustained by advancing science and its methods of inquiry, an informed citizenry, and expert administrators, was within human reach. Genially rather than insistently, Barton imbibed the spirit of Progressivism in his early years in publishing, and certainly until about 1915. He was no radical. Eventually—probably no single event precipitated it—he would come to repose greater hope for progress in businessmen and would grow skeptical of the efforts of political reformers. The noted historian of Progressivism Arthur S. Link has suggested that in the 1920s the middle class generally shifted their faith in improvement from political to business leadership; Barton (who identified himself militantly with the middle class) anticipated this shift, as is evident in the editorials he wrote in the period 1915—1918.[6]

Later Barton would recall, with some exaggeration, having left college a firebrand, "a reformer with definite convictions on everything." He would even claim he made "a pilgrimage to Washington" after graduation to talk to Senators Robert M. La Follette and William Borah, seeking their counsel on his pipedream of moving to one of their states, buying "a little newspaper and fight[ing] the battle of the free West against the 'entrenched wealth' and 'special privilege' of the effete East." He also avowed that his earliest writings favored women's suffrage, the popular election of U.S. senators, and railroad regulation—three darlings of progressivism. But reform was a young man's game, and by the 1920s Barton styled himself an "ex-reformer." For a time he espoused the single-tax scheme of Henry George, but he later concluded that the movement for this startling change in the political economy had no chance of success.[7]

From 1910 to 1915 Barton wrote eighteen articles for *The Continent*. Several fell within the limits of Social Gospel advocacy, but in its mildest precincts. They tended less to charge religion with catalyzing drastic social reform than to see it, in some of its current manifestations, as already achieving social and spiritual uplift. Improvement accreted less from structural change than from individual reform and redemption. Thus one piece described Chicago's Pacific Garden Mission, located on Van Buren Street, Chicago's "dead line" dividing "respectability" from the zone where "poor, hopeless bits of human wreckage are tossed about from bar to bar, empty bottles on the sea of life." From a roomful of derelicts, Barton singles out one battered soul whose previous life in railroad construction camps had consisted of "work and drink" in endless cycles, but who, having been saved a year earlier, had not had a drink since, had begun to put money aside, and now looked forward to domestic contentment. Barton emphasized the spiritual over the socioeconomic service the mission performed, though he made it clear that the prospect of a meal had drawn his once-despairing protagonist there in the first place.[8]

Barton did not ignore social conditions. One article dispassionately laid out the views of Joseph Ettor, a fiery leader of the Industrial Workers of the World, and Jeff Davis, self-styled chief of America's hoboes, on the cause and cure of the unemployment that gripped swelling ranks of workers in 1915. These agitators were "unimportant in themselves; but the great surging, inchoate movements of which they are the expression are about the most important thing in the country today," Barton warned. He never outlined a solution to this or other socioeconomic problems. He did commend those mission keepers and alley preachers who got down in the muck. He applauded one New York pastor who took his message to prisons, found beds for the homeless, and was "chaplain of the sockless, confessor of the unshaved." Barton searched for caring, vigorous, masculine men of God to write about. He refuted the denigratory inference of a "Man at the Club" who marked "the average missionary" a second-rater who earned more than he would have in business, since "the real leaders" among college men did not go into the mission or the YMCA. As counterexamples he cited a former football hero doing mission work in China and a successful engineer ministering to front-line troops in Asia.[9]

After *The Continent* folded, Barton wrote similar sorts of religious reportage for *The Congregationalist*. In a cool-eyed appraisal of the famed revivalist Billy Sunday, he termed the former baseball player "scarcely more than two-thirds a Christian, for to his faith and hope he adds singularly little charity." Barton revisited the site of one of Sunday's revivals and talked with his fans as well as detractors. He concluded that while there were many "backsliders" in the wake of the six-week revival, and while critics complained that the community was too "'burned over'" to support further spiritual ventures, still "some results . . . remain even after five years."[10] Barton brought a similar sangfroid to his report on a textile strike spearheaded by the IWW in New Bedford, Massachusetts. He managed to be both appalled by the IWW's obdurate combativeness and understanding of the conditions that invited it. Its vision of laying siege to the owners' mansions dominating the company town appealed, Barton warned, to "the hollow-cheeked father whose pay envelope grows no heavier as the years of his strength grow less, and the gaunt, unlovely woman who hurries the baby from her breast because she must be back at the mills." Barton also wrote for *The Advance*, a tiny Congregationalist publication for which his father had assumed responsibility. One piece lauded the efforts of women trained in foreign tongues at a humble mission school in Cleveland to do missionary work among "the horde of foreigners . . being poured out on us," selflessly "civilizing" these masses and saving them from anarchism.[11]

In 1912, after his editorial stints with two doomed publications, Barton finally found steady work as assistant sales manager of P. F. Collier & Son, publishers of books and a magazine. He supervised more than a thousand salesmen, operating out of thirty-one branch offices, who sold their products house to house. Barton's job entailed a great deal of travel. Already experienced in sales from his days of pitching maple syrup and kitchen utensils, he did well with Collier. After he was famous, some of the junior employees he met in the branch offices wrote him fond notes of "I-knew-you-when," and his replies suggest that he had found this work rewarding. Through trial and error he learned something about managing employees—and that this was a responsibility he would just as soon delegate to others. He discovered some devices that improved prospects for success in the difficult task of canvassing door to door. When his sales force in a Western city found it impossible to get past the maids and butlers in the wealthier homes, he outfitted them with "natty walking sticks" which made them "feel like regular gentlemen." They were able to convey an aura that melted the defenses of the domestics who barred their way.[12]

The position with Collier gave Barton the financial foundation he needed to marry. (By this time, he later recalled, he was making $12,000 a year.)[13]At a party in Chicago for members of Alpha Delta Phi, the national fraternity he had joined at Amherst, he had met Esther Randall. He had impressed her by "taking her in my arms and lifting her over the puddles" of a rainy evening. She too had gone to Oak Park High, but, a mere freshman when he was a senior, had not come to his notice. Intelligent, attractive, artistic, athletic, and popular among her peers, she was the only daughter of Mr. and Mrs. Charles Randall. Her father had been a member, and later a director, of the Chicago Board of Trade. A health problem had prompted him to move his family to Colorado, where for five years they ran a fruit ranch. Esther rode to school on a burro petulant enough to throw her every so often, but she thrived on the hardy, outdoor life. The Randalls were able to return to Oak Park, and Esther went on to Wellesley College. She was president of the Class of 1910 (and reelected to that office for the next twenty years). Bruce and Esther were married at her parents' home on October 2, 1913. They took a "little apartment on 11th Street" in Manhattan. Esther sometimes accompanied Bruce on his travels for Collier's, staying in "second-rate hotels all over the country."[14]

At Collier he also composed his first significant ad, one of many, and one of a number that won fame. Word came up from the press room one day of a quarter-page of blank space in a magazine, and only a few minutes before press time to fill it. Barton went to Dr. Eliot's Five Foot Book Shelf, a compendium of great books under the aegis of Harvard University's noted president; he ripped out a picture of the condemned Marie Antoinette in a tumbril and captioned it: "This Is Marie Antoinette Riding To Her Death." Did the reader know her "tragic story? How the once beautiful queen of France, broken and humbled, her beauty gone, was jostled through the bloody streets of Paris to the guillotine?" And what about Burke's writings on the French Revolution, or other notable works? Barton certified that Eliot "has picked the few *really worth while books out of the thousands of useless ones.*" The ad, which he called his "first major operation," quickly became legendary. It prompted eight times as many readers to send in coupons as any previous advertisement for the set. It was reused repeatedly. It rejuvenated sales of the fifty-volume Harvard Classics. The ad showed, according to a senior colleague at BBDO, that Barton had managed to transcend the "cut-and-dried appeals that had previously been used in so-called mail-order advertising." One retelling of the triumph explained that it was "radically new in 1912" to advertise books with ads topped "with an interesting picture, and a headline taken right out of the book itself." This improvised invention later earned membership on a list of the hundred greatest ads.[15] Barton had, consciously or not, taken one of the two approaches that members of the advertising profession would debate in the ensuing decades, choosing the "story" approach which enwreathed the reader in a scenario in which the product was a carefully placed prop, as against simply detailing the product's virtues with straightforward descriptive prose. Barton also advertised the set with the tag line: "Let Dr. Eliot of Harvard give you the essentials of a liberal education in only fifteen minutes a day." This device also became part of the Barton legend.[16]

The work was interesting, but Barton had aspirations beyond sparking sales. In his years at Collier he also wrote busily. Moving beyond church publications, he contributed to magazines with broader audiences, particularly *Collier's*, the *American Magazine*, *Woman's Home Companion*, and *Farm and Fireside*, the last three issued by the Crowell Publishing Company. Mark Sullivan, the famed journalist who then edited *Collier's*, persuaded Barton to write for magazines while he continued to handle the sales promotion of Collier's books. The first three magazines especially had important roles in Barton's life as a writer and journalist. He would publish throughout his career in *Collier's*. *Woman's Home Companion* was another favorite outlet, and its editor Gertrude B. Lane was a close friend and adviser. Collier's president was Thomas H. Beck, a man Barton came to revere and to whom he credited much of his tutoring in matters of sales and publishing. Barton was able to crank out magazine pieces in off-hours, on weekends, and in other spare moments. He even wrote articles during his honeymoon.

While Barton was at Collier, John M. Siddall, the editor of *American Magazine* from 1915 on, took a liking to his work and decided he had a talent for conducting and writing interviews. Siddall and his magazine, Barton would later recall, "were two of the biggest influences in my life." He helped Siddall put out the magazine and wrote incessantly for it, under his byline, anonymously, and sometimes as a ghostwriter for others. He sat down with a number of eminent figures, including Woodrow Wilson and David Lloyd George. Siddall shaped his magazine in a manner characteristic of Barton's own orientation and seems to have reinforced Barton's penchant for positive thinking. He filled it with "close-ups of great and successful men who have backgrounds of struggle, of the man . . . who has succeeded, despite handicaps that are akin to our own shortcomings." He aimed it "straight to the individual. It carrie[d] no gloom. . . . It [was] not hitched to any cause." It prized brevity and fizz. "What we do in this magazine," Siddall declared, "is to stand at the hard places in the road and cry, 'you *can* come through. You can win.'"[17]

Barton produced all manner of articles for *American Magazine*, especially after World War I. He interviewed the famed British novelist/historian H. G. Wells, who listed the "six greatest men in history" (a list Barton would repeatedly cite in his writings) and whose assessment of Jesus coincided closely with the views Barton would famously communicate. One of his articles, "How I Found Health in a Dentist's Chair," prosaically touted root-canal work and described how it cleared up his mysterious bout with ill health. Another set forth "What I Have Learned About Writing Letters." Another, under a pseudonym, empathized with the ambitious toolmaker who despaired that his boss never noticed his drive. This, Barton suggested, would soon end once psychology's new "tests of trade skill and intelligence" (such as the army had used during the war) were widely adopted. He even wrote a piece, "Has My Money Been a Hindrance to My Husband?" signed by "a wife whose father is rich." An anonymous short story traced the frustrations of a man whose ambitions were thwarted by obligations first to his parents, then to his wife and children. Swallowing his disappointments, the man concentrated on parenthood and found his ambitions satisfied by being known as the "Father of the Harding Boys." Long, short, signed, unsigned and pseudonymous, fiction or fact, advice or speculation—Barton could knock out articles to meet any demand.[18]

His contacts as a writer and publishing executive dramatically widened his circle of acquaintances and friends. He came to admire the achievements of the leaders of business he was meeting and the talents and character that made their feats possible. In turn they appreciated his bankable journalistic skills and his reassuring admiration. Frederick Lewis Allen, the great chronicler of 1920s America, hints at the kinds of connections that were webbing Barton into the world of movers and shakers. He describes a day, probably in 1916, when Charles E. Mitchell and Bruce Barton "were standing together by a window in the Bankers' Club in New York, looking down upon the city." On his way to becoming "one of the mightiest powers in American banking," president-to-be of the National City Bank, Mitchell regaled Barton with a story about how he energized his salesmen at the National City Company (an affiliate of National City Bank) to go and sell bonds by showing them the same view while telling them to visualize the millions of people down below with dollars to invest who were "just waiting for someone to come and tell them what to do with their savings. Take a good look, eat a good lunch, and then go down and tell them." This was typical Bartonian anecdote: the skilled mobilizer of men with the deft touch to offer a simple pep talk that advanced a cheering perspective on how to tackle a challenge.[19] Such experiences of being shown the view from the steel-and-glass mountaintops of Gotham may have done much to erase what was left of Barton's youthful "radicalism."

While much of his writing dealt with secular topics, he never relinquished the realm of religion. In 1914 Barton published a book titled A Young Man's Jesus. This slim volume prefigured later writings (most notably The Man Nobody Knows). Barton wanted to reclaim Jesus for manly young strivers of his own age. "It is time," he wrote, "for those of us who are this side of thirty-five to unite and take back our Jesus." The false impression of "a tired, unhappy martyred Jesus who lived without a real laugh and looked forward to dying in a sort of fanatical eagerness" had become fixed in the public mind. "He had our bounding pulses, our hot desires. . . . He is our Jesus, and we have surrendered Him to priests and to women, to hospitals and monasteries. . . ." This Jesus (as in Barton's later writings) was manly, strong, courageous, sociable, quick-witted, dynamic, charismatic, exuding vigor, teaching that religion was a matter of spirituality, not ritual. This early book reflected Barton's immersion in the world of the Social Gospel—religion oriented toward reform—far more than did his writings a decade later. Jesus was "on the side of the poor" and often criticized the rich. In 1914 he would have opposed child labor and the "exploitation" of women workers. His teachings were democratic and egalitarian; he often raised his voice against the rich. Yet having gone this far toward locating Jesus in the current reform ethos, Barton also placed the insurgency more on a spiritual than a political plane. And despite copious attention to Jesus' condemnation of the rich, Barton praised several anonymous corporate leaders who claimed to be inspired by Christ's teachings. The book was no breakthrough volume, but it received commendatory notes in a number of church publications, all of which appreciated the emphasis on Jesus' manliness.[20]

Barton tried his hand at fiction too. Anonymously he published a serialized story in *American Magazine* that then appeared as a novella. Thornton, a go-getter businessman from Millersville, is raised by a strict grandmother who unwittingly teaches him to hate God. Working hard, he takes over a derelict cutlery factory and prospers rather unfeelingly until forced to visit his office boy's deathbed. The attending doctor makes it clear that this and similar cases could be laid to harsh working conditions. Getting "religion" in the most secular sense, Thornton remodels the plant, brings in light and air, and shortens the work day and week. Now his employees confide in him. "I was becoming a sort of father to the whole three hundred of them." He finds some religion in their sturdy lives but more in communing with nature. A flash of religious belief arrives: "the world couldn't have created something greater than itself." So Thornton, like Barton in and after college and in many of his later religious writings, reasons his way to belief. He also discovers it in service. *Finding God in Millersville* lays out Barton's most extended elaboration of the Social Gospel and also illustrates the limits of his conception of it: Thornton changes through personal experience, not through any state intervention, and his religious calling is highly social and imposes no heavy theology. His is a kindly God (unlike his grandmother's) who "really needs me as a working partner."[21]

Barton also published a novel, *The Making of George Groton*, first as a serial beginning in late 1917 in the *American Magazine*, then as a book. It has elements of a Horatio Alger tale: it wraps the plot around unlikely turns of fate, and its focus (and target) is young people—an audience that Barton often aimed to reach over his life as a writer. Pitching for hometown Merwin in the big game against Hortonville, young George stars; after the game he saves the umpire by intercepting a bottle heaved by an irate fan. This burst of Algerine luck secures his future, for the man in black is none other than Merode Juergens, a Merwin boy who has struck it rich, runs a Wall Street brokerage, and has returned to ump the big game. A grateful Juergens tells George he is "too good for this town," hands him money, invites him to New York, and hires him. He rises quickly, from clerk to the boss's personal secretary, performs tasks ably, shares in profitable deals, and is on his way.

But Groton, not surprisingly, shares some of Barton's misgivings. He witnesses the underside of securities speculation: Juergens's company falls below the standard of more respectable Wall Street firms. Moreover, the city is alienating—so many anonymous souls who care nothing for their fellow New Yorkers; so many humans packed in apartments, "every family walking above some other family's head"; so much loneliness. George's spiritual compass swings loosely in this moral vacuum. He grows apart from Merwin, his parents, and his virtuous girlfriend Betty, the daughter of his hometown minister. He treats with disdain her calling to work in a New York settlement house.

His attempt to convince Juergens to follow a more ethical path brings instant dismissal, but George catches on with a more upright firm, and his rise continues. With a friend he launches an enterprise on the side. One of their speculative market plays backfires and wipes

them out. But this financial disaster matters not at all, for another som-
ersault of fortune wins George back the woman of his life, Betty Wilson. Her saintly minister father, on his deathbed in Merwin, reunites
them. Laughing off his financial ruin, George now sees what is important, and Betty sees his true and sterling character. In this new,
wholesome frame of mind, he gets a job from a good-hearted banker,
who instructs him with the biblical lesson that "service" is "the secret
of all success." Once more he prospers. If less lucrative, the new job
offers stability and uplift. Engaged in foreign trade, the bank helps "to
open the dark places of the earth to civilization." He has found goodness in the wicked city, and George and Betty presumably live happily
ever after.[22]

   Barton allowed that both his novels were "pretty punk." Offering
excessive internal monologue and relying on improbable circumstances, *George Groton* is no jewel in the tiara of modern American literature. Yet it had its admirers. One of Barton's friends noted that its
final installment brought his wife to tears and that the novel offered
much to an America that "must learn the lesson of 'service.'" It praises
the existential struggle of good people enmeshed in the world of business; it suggests that the homely virtues can and do survive in such a
world. One review called it a "classic picture" of the "minister in the
small town who lives his life according to his ideals." And it dealt with
a topic to which Barton often turned: the dilemma of ambitious boys
from the sticks who hied to the city to address their ambitions but
found that they missed the neighborliness of small-town life. On several levels the novel was autobiographical.[23]

   During his brief phase as a novelist, Barton was meanwhile moving up the publishing ladder two rungs at a time. In 1914 Crowell hired
him as the editor of *Every Week*, which had begun life as a newspaper
Sunday supplement. With the coming of the world war, many newspapers, under economic pressure, began canceling their contracts for
it. But Joseph Knapp, whose American Lithograph Company printed
the supplement, devised the idea of augmenting it with more fiction
and a weekly editorial by Barton and selling it separately as a magazine

in places whose papers did not carry it. The publishers marketed it at newsstands as "the first three-cent weekly in America," assuming that a buyer paying two cents for a paper would pop for a magazine with the rest of his nickel. Knapp, who headed Crowell Publishing Company, later persuaded P. F. Collier & Son to take over *Every Week*.[24]

Every Week was a successful, innovative venture. Driven in part by the demands of a publication schedule that precluded the late-breaking coverage of a daily newspaper, Barton had to emphasize less timely, if also less perishable, contents. He later recounted that "our formula for *Every Week* was Youth, Love, Success, Money and Health—all things in which people are vitally interested." He solicited short stories, at least some of which aspired to quality. He published some of Edna Ferber's earliest work. He bought short fiction by Sinclair Lewis, who was momentarily disenchanted with the slim earnings of his early novels. But *Every Week* specialized in a photo-driven layout, often in two-page spreads, in which the pictures carried the story; Barton excelled in providing punchy captions that maintained narrative flow. He was something of a pioneer in this, and when he turned to the field of advertising the technique would propel some of his most effective work. William H. Johns, who would become a leading executive in Barton's eventual advertising agency, emphasized the importance of Barton's innovations at *Every Week*—namely the technique of creating "interesting pictures with the text presented as captions"—to his talents as an advertising man. The last letter dictated by the renowned novelist Jack London before his 1916 death lauded Barton's "new picture-caption technique." Later, Barton noted banteringly, when Henry Luce was hauled into court and accused of having stolen the format for his *Life* magazine, he borrowed Barton's bound copies of *Every Week* to prove that the idea of "picture-caption articles" had originated not with the litigants but in Barton's magazine.[25]

Barton also made himself a master of the editorial homilies that became an *Every Week* staple. These short pieces featured messages of "uplift" which appealed to a wide audience.[26] Barton had a knack for crafting columns short on words but long on evocation, presenting an optimistic and smiling mien. One column exalted the spiritual value of gardening, arguing that "God was the first gardener: he started the human race in a garden." Barton also lauded gardening's value as a psychological fillip: someone who feels depressed should "go into [his] back yard and dig and plant something." Another piece that stressed the power of appearances asked the reader to query himself, "What kind of an advertisement am I for myself?" It cited the "experiment" of two men Barton knew who first dressed well and were received "deferentially" at a top hotel restaurant, then returned in shabby attire and were ill-treated. These pieces were very much in the emerging vein of cheerful, therapeutic advice columns that would festoon American newspapers for much of the century. Edgar Guest met a similar demand with his catchy rhymes. In fact, the title of one of Barton's columns—"Do You Live in a Home or Only in a House?"—suggests a parallel to one of Guest's most remembered couplets.[27] The headline of another piece captured one of his favorite cracker-barrel philosophies: "Cut down your necessities, and you will be able to afford a few luxuries."[28]

Barton's short pieces (then and later) prompted enough interest to warrant publishing four anthologies of them: *More Power to You: Fifty Editorials from Every Week* (1917), *It's a Good Old World* (1920), *Better Days* (1924), and *On the Up and Up* (1929). Themes found in Barton's more prominent writings, including his best-known book, *The Man Nobody Knows*, made early appearances in these short pieces. He wrote of the tug-of-war ambitious men faced between their small-town origins and the lure of the city's larger stage for enterprise. Thoreau remained a frequent totem in his writings for the joys and virtues of the simple life; Napoleon, who with Lincoln was probably the mortal who most interested Barton the amateur historian, could find triumph only amid urban multitudes. A number of pieces from *Every Week* were also reprinted in other periodicals and business house organs. For the next half-century Barton's office fielded requests to reprint material he had written.[29]

By the spring of 1918, as the war ground on, inflation pushed the price of newsprint to inordinate levels, and "the bankers" warned

Joseph Knapp that it was time to terminate *Every Week*—which was not
returning a profit—since the fighting might go on for years. When the
publication expired in May 1918, it was widely mourned. One reader
confessed a "feeling of aching loss." Another said, "A death in my immediate family wouldn't mean much more than the loss of dear old
Every Week." Still another compared the magazine's demise to the recent loss of his infant daughter. Professional journalistic sources were
more dry-eyed, one calling the magazine too "preachy," another saying
it had run out of ideas, and a third charging that it had "insisted on doing all the thinking for its readers."[30] In later years readers wrote to express their fond recollection of Barton's pieces and to seek help in
finding copies of them. On several occasions Barton, who never
ceased to write for newspapers and magazines, would commit himself
to produce a regular column. His short, often inspirational articles,
written in punchy prose with an eye for the crackling moral of the
story, continued to find an audience. He often recycled articles from
an earlier into a later series.[31]

FOR BARTON, however, a contingency in Sarajevo altered the trajectory
of his life, as it did—often far more drastically—for many people around
the globe. Had a Serbian nationalist not assassinated the heir to the
throne of the Austro-Hungarian Empire, Barton might have continued
a career in the business of mass-circulation magazines and to further innovation in that medium's methods and format. Instead of giving us the
advertising man we know as Bruce Barton, his career might have more
closely resembled that of, say, the publisher Henry Luce.

World War I was unprecedentedly bloody. It was noisy as well, a
Great War of words, to whose vast volume the adolescent American
advertising industry added heroically. The Committee on Public Information, created by President Wilson, was charged with proclaiming
America's war aims. George Creel, the erstwhile newspaperman, reformer, and *Collier's* editor who headed the Committee, called his task
"in all things, from first to last, . . . a plain publicity proposition, a vast

enterprise in salesmanship, the world's greatest adventure in advertising." Numerous figures later prominent in the field of advertising and public relations, including Edward L. Bernays and Carl Byoir, worked for the CPI, which even had an advertising division. Barton, however, was not among them.

Barton did not work for the CPI, nor was he yet officially an advertising man, but his duty in the Great War was heavily promotional. In 1918, after the demise of *Every Week*, he attempted to enlist in the armed forces but was rejected. Barton said little about this episode: a *New Yorker* profile suggested that being passed over "was a real disappointment" to him. The prospect of joining the army came up once more: Barton weighed the idea of enlisting in the fall of 1918, but the war-related project he was working on got delayed, and, estimating that the war was nearing an end, he did not like the idea of being newly in uniform after a cease-fire, when "the last in will probably be the last out."[32] Barton first devoted his wartime energies to fund-raising for the Salvation Army, in the course of which he interviewed the Army's commandant Evangeline Booth. During their talk he coined what was to become its slogan: "A man may be down, but he's never out." Booth liked the line and "appropriated it." It became one of many creations on which Barton's fame was grounded.[33]

Barton also handled publicity for the Young Men's Christian Association (YMCA) as it geared up for its ballooning role in the nation's military training camps.[34]As the campaign unfolded, the War Department decided to combine the appeals of six other agencies—the Salvation Army, the YWCA, the National Catholic War Council, the Jewish Welfare Board, the War Camp Community Service, and the American Library Association—with the YMCA's into a single effort. Often complaining that their respective interests were suffering in the merged appeal, these groups received the nickname of the "Seven Sobbing Sisters." Barton headed the publicity committee of this United War Work Campaign in a nationwide drive to raise funds to subsidize canteens and other amenities for American soldiers at training camps and bases in the United States and France. There would be wholesome pastimes: Americans must be made and kept "fit to fight." There would be no taking up of the French government's offer to let Americans share the system of licensed, inspected bordellos established for their own *poilus*. In a famous interchange, when Raymond D. Fosdick, in charge of camp activities, showed the French offer to Secretary of War Newton Baker, the latter exclaimed: "For God's sake, Raymond, don't show this to the president or he'll stop the war."[35]

Under Barton, the United War Work Campaign became a massive and ecumenical effort to gather funds. His work was *gratis*; he supported himself by writing magazine articles on the weekends. The entire fund-raising crusade was scheduled to take place during the week of November 11–18, 1918. The timing could not have been less fortunate: the campaign's opening day turned out to be Armistice Day. Nevertheless an effort consonant with the hullabaloo of the Great War went off as scheduled. The drive was one of the projects given the strenuous support of Creel's organization, whose famous Four Minute Men, some 75,000 strong, made it the subject of their enthusiastic oratory, and the CPI produced five posters geared to the crusade. With a goal of $170 million, the drive brought in more than $205 million.[36]

Barton made one further contribution to the war effort, yet another prose confection. In 1919, for the national Victory Loan bond drive aimed at defraying the war's costs, Barton drafted a pamphlet, "I Am New York and This Is My Creed." The brochure depicted a storm-buffeted Statue of Liberty from behind, set against a backlit sky wreathed in smoke. Barton described New York as the Gotham of disparate peoples, travelers from over the ocean and "clean-hearted, clear-eyed boys and girls" from American farms, but also as a New Jerusalem. New York's fame was painted of "luxury or pleasure; sometimes of gold. But my faith—who is there that has measured it?" Those who had "mingled with my people in their work, and sacrifice and suffering" knew "how human, and how responsive and how unswerving is my heart." The polyglot denizens of the city "have laid my foundations on Faith, and fashioned my greatness with Honor and the Plighted Word." (The prose included both the quasi-biblical cadences that were to make Barton's work memorable and themes that recall the famous Emma Lazarus poem "The New Colossus.") For decades, "at least once a year, and sometimes more often," someone sought permission to reprint "I Am New York." The Victory Loan was oversubscribed; and during World War II the committee charged with selling war bonds in New York cited the flier as a winning model. Barton was "a little touchy" about getting all the credit for this appeal. Someone down the line had decided to put Barton's authorship on the poster. "You can imagine my feelings as a struggling young ad man when I had to pass forty or fifty of these damn things [in poster form] on my daily trips to and from Pennsylvania Station."[37]

Although he often rummaged through his life to find grist for his writings, Barton was reticent in later years about his wartime experience. He did at the time write an article that reflected his experience: The biblical David, about to meet the Amalekites in battle, tells some of his men to "tarry by the stuff," to protect the supplies during the fighting; they too get to share in the booty. Barton wrote the piece having in mind those men who wanted to go to war but couldn't, those who were compelled to "tarry by the stuff."[38]

More often the war's narrative importance to him lay in the events to which it led—the founding of his advertising agency. Still, the United War Work Campaign, and certainly the war experience in general, seem to have set him on the road to an anti-militarist, even pacifist point of view which he expressed vigorously and frequently in his prominent years. Many Americans adopted such views later in the 1920s and '30s, as "revisionist" history began to sprinkle public discourse and politicians braced to prevent a recurrence of the late war. Barton arrived at this position early.

The war had barely ended when Barton reflected on it in a piece in the December 14, 1918, *Collier's* entitled "And they shall beat their swords into—Electrotypes." In the wake of the sacrifices the war had exacted, he predicted that the world's people would no longer passively accept things-as-they-are. Businesses would shape up, seeking not just profit but "the progress of the race." Advertising had proven

itself so essential in the war that Barton proposed harnessing it to secure peace. He would write into the peace treaty a clause obligating
every signatory nation to spend annually "at least 1 percent of its present war costs in international advertising, explaining to the rest of the
world its own achievements and ideals. . . ." He would flesh out this
campaign with wholesale exchange programs sending newspeople,
clergy, professors, and other shapers of public opinion to work in
other countries and thus add to mutual understanding. The appeal
more fully expressed the newfound potency of advertising—the field
to which Barton had recently committed himself—than the urgency
of peace. In fact, Barton's new firm reproduced the article as a pamphlet, probably more in the interest of self-promotion than pacifism.[39]
But Barton would soon return to the horrors of war.

The war's carnage itself might explain Barton's, or anyone's, disillusionment, but his next writing on the subject suggests a deeper connection with personal experience, far though it was from the trenches.
For Memorial Day 1921 he wrote a *Collier's* editorial enjoining readers
to avoid the sloppy thinking that came with war, to avoid fuzzy gener-
alizations ("All Germans were murderers"). War, he warned, "is the
patron of extravagance; it is the patron of over-organization as well.
The individual is destroyed in the mass; personal responsibility is swal-
lowed up in organized effort. . . ." Citizens needed to give up their reliance on Washington, on the collectivity, and to relearn the
"ennobling gospel of hard work." World War I probably played a critical role in orienting Barton's political views toward a more conservative individualism. Thanks to the war, he concluded—mostly with
regret—that "individualism, as we used to understand it, is dead." And
he saw the war as a consuming, sapping experience, one to whose
"months of strain" he attributed the untimely deaths and "physical
breakdowns" of a number of fellow war workers. "Not all the lives by
which the war was won were sacrificed on the battle-fields of France,"
he wrote in a letter to the editor to mark the passing of one of his co-
workers in fund-raising. "Men were wounded in offices also, and have
died of their wounds."[40]

Barton may have served as his own best example of war-induced "extravagance." In 1916 *Every Week* carried his "A Personal Letter to the Kaiser." Its mock-familiar, condescending paragraphs were not an unadulterated indictment: they likened Kaiser Wilhelm to TR, praised Prussia's welfare state, but warned that the innate Prussian proclivity to arrogance and force was imperiling the likelihood of any future rapprochement. Barton included a reminiscence of a boyhood escapade, a snowball fight with two Prussian coachmen who worked for his neighbors; they took unseemly pleasure in pummeling the smaller, ten-year-old Barton with iceballs. This episode sprang back to mind when a German U-boat sank the liner *Lusitania* and, along with other barbarities, demonstrated the stark difference between Prussian and American culture.[41] That he himself had succumbed to the wartime delirium was something Barton soon came to regret. He recalled in sadness "the speeches all of us were making in 1914 and 1915," which placed all the blame on Germany and none on England. He would come to deplore the "romantic" view of war. General John J. Pershing, leader of the American Expeditionary Force, was no more romantic than Henry Ford. Both had engaged in mass production— Ford "making automobiles, and Pershing making mass destruction at long range."[42]

Distaste for war was no one-time thing for Barton. As early as 1909 he had written of the waste—"four dollars for every man, woman and child in the United States"—that went into spending on defense and was thus diverted from worthier causes; this was "our tribute for the privilege of shooting our fellow men." For *Good Housekeeping* in 1922 he drafted an indictment of war's futility. Depicting the burial of the Unknown Soldier from the last war, Barton imagined, once the mortal captains and kings had departed, a convening of the shades of other Unknowns who had fallen at Thermopylae, Tours, and Waterloo. Each had listened to testimonies that his death had been both noble and meaningful, but none of them could see any good stemming from his sacrifice. "The real inscription" such unknown soldiers deserved, said Barton, would come in a future dictionary that defined war as "an armed contest between nations—now obsolete." This homily enjoyed a long afterlife: for years people requested copies, and Barton himself recycled the story when he resumed column-writing in the 1950s.[43]

Speaking in 1937, Barton would reflect that his generation "was born in one of the golden eras of American life," the late nineteenth century, when the Civil War was receding from memory and wealth and technology were blooming. It was "a time when it was easy to believe in God, in the eternal importance of human life, in a not-too-far-removed millennium." But with the world war's sudden advent, "all the hidden ugliness of human nature sprang into ghastly view. Human life that had seemed so indefinitely precious became cheap as dirt." Both sides prayed that God "destroy their brothers across the lines. Our faith reeled." Nor did the postwar boom and bust "restore our morale."[44]

War also came, for Barton, to reside beyond the outer bounds of what he considered acceptable rhetoric and propaganda. He had already sailed the seas of publishing, selling, and advertising and would assert that "truth" was the ultimate harbor to which these voyages were bound. This was the claim of all spokesmen for advertising. But truth was an elastic commodity. Barton would find many ways to describe its dimensions so as to include advertising, but war, for him, seemed to be an abuse of the skills of his trade.

ARMISTICE DAY left Barton at loose ends, uncertain where to hang out his shingle—or indeed, what shingle to hang. Certainly magazine writing would have a place in his career plans. He had been prolific before the war, and during the fighting such work was his only source of income. Of one thing he was sure: he would not "go back on anybody's pay-roll." His past jobs had given him ample experience of being bossed by others and of laboring for doomed enterprises. He thought of renting space for a "Literary Blacksmith Shop," which would gratefully execute "orders for articles, poems, plays and novels."

He would continue to write books, columns, and articles, but, however conscious of it, he had already assembled fragments of a career in activities that fell under the labels of advertising, publicity, and public relations. Whether he used these classifications to define himself or not, others were doing so. As early as 1910 he had had the inside track on a job of handling "the literary end [presumably copywriting] of one of the best advertising agencies in the country." E. E. Calkins, a noted advertising consultant and expert, attempted to lure Barton into joining the firm of Calkins and Holden after the war.[45]

But Calkins was too late. Two men who had worked with Barton on the United War Work Campaign got to him first. One of them, Alex F. Osborn, Barton had hired on the recommendation of a mutual acquaintance.

The principals who founded the advertising agency of Barton, Durstine and Osborn imbued the circumstances of its creation with an aureole of myth. The most commonly repeated legend had Barton and Osborn eating dinner soon after the Armistice at the Grand Central Oyster Bar. Barton asked Osborn what he should do next in life. Osborn suggested editing a magazine, but Barton no longer hankered for such work. "Well," Osborn offered, "go into the advertising agency business. You're a natural for it." That seemed unappealing: Barton said he would "hate to have to hire and fire and to keep track of money and all that." Osborn suggested that he bring in another veteran of the United War Work Campaign, Roy Durstine, to carry out those tasks. Durstine, a onetime newspaper reporter, had been a partner in a small New York ad agency, Berrien-Durstine, before the war. As he stepped off the boat from an assignment in Europe, Durstine learned that his partner wanted to shutter the firm.

Barton, Osborn, and Durstine had gotten along well in the United War Work Campaign and came to respect one another's abilities. At a storied lunch, now in the Grand Central Station lunchroom, Osborn sketched out the three men's complementary talents. Osborn suggested that if Barton teamed up with Durstine, Osborn would go back to Buffalo to mend his similarly neglected agency and then in six months join them. The men who would supply the "D" and the "O" to the new firm had experience in advertising and would provide the "technical-creative" energies, relying on Barton to write copy and hoping his "wide acquaintance would make [him] a big business getter."[46] He had, after all, a reputation for his "amazing ability to meet, interest and satisfy important men."[47] He would provide the firm's public face for the next forty years.

Some such inspirational meal may have taken place, but the demands of good narrative seem to have skewed the date, for Barton had determined to go into advertising with Roy Durstine at least as early as late summer 1918. In the same letter to his parents in which he declared that he would not join the army, Barton swore them to secrecy about his revelation that he was "going to open an office of my own on January first [1919] where I will do writing, lit'ry [sic] and commercial. I shall have with me Roy S. Durstine, one of the finest and ablest young fellows in the advertising business. . . ."[48]

The alliance may have come to include Osborn at the later date, which became part of the standard account. The three men reportedly solemnized their new affiliation over a dinner at the Athens Hotel. Barton pledged himself to the enterprise, but did so with the proviso that he would commit perhaps fifteen years to it, leaving open the option to move on to another calling at the end of that time.[49] In fact Barton never pigeonholed himself into a single line of work. He had written and edited in his early years after college, and he would continue to write columns, articles, and books while engaged in advertising; he wrote about religion as well as commerce; and he took a hand in politics as well.

After the three men agreed to team up, Osborn went back to Buffalo, promising to become part of the new firm the next summer. Barton and Durstine placed an announcement of their partnership in the papers eight days after the Armistice. Each of the founders brought distinct abilities to the enterprise. Barton's was a facility in meeting and befriending people and in spinning printer's ink into gold. Durstine, at least in the early years, proved adept in management and in seeing the vast potential of the new gadget radio. Osborn turned out to be proficient in both management and advertising and was wrestling with the problems of how to routinize and channel innovation. The Barton, Durstine, and Osborn agency would play a conspicuous role in the emergence of Madison Avenue and the transitions that would mark American life in the 1920s.[50]

3

A New Name on Madison Avenue

WHEN BRUCE BARTON co-founded BDO in 1918, he was too late to be a true pioneer in the advertising business. Already over the past half-century it had taken on many of the dimensions of its modern shape, outgrowing its rough-hewn antebellum origins. In the mid-nineteenth century only patent medicine vendors and impresarios of entertainment spectacles like circuses had advertised in any sense recognizable to the twentieth century. Merchants who publicized their available goods did so with little reference to their distinctiveness. Brand names lay in the future—the later nineteenth century. As larger stores, department stores, and mail-order houses emerged, they began to advertise heavily. It took the development of particular types of products (complicated musical instruments, for example, or farm machinery) and an increasingly national market rather than merely local markets for such products to stimulate sustained advertising efforts. Similarly, companies engaged in the mass production of consumer goods resorted to advertising to sustain a level of demand that matched their increased capacity. Advertising became—though proof was hard to ensnare—a more efficient means of making known the availability of cheaper, mass-produced goods. Before 1900, advertising slogans like the Kodak camera's "You press the button and we do the rest" were becoming part of the culture. Only a few years later, the pictorial linkage of Prudential Insurance with the Rock of Gibraltar had become fixed in the public mind. Barton may have set the standard for dashing off the telling phrase, the pithy parable, but he did not invent the genre. Advertising had already barged obtrusively into American life. By 1920 neon-lighted signs selling dental cream, autos, Coke, two cigarette brands, and other products chased away the night in New York's Times Square.

The first known enterprise engaged exclusively in advertising had opened in 1849, and in its early life the ad business had mostly involved brokering between producers with goods to sell and the media—that is, newspapers—in unfamiliar, distant markets. The early adman was a buyer of space in newspaper columns. He held down his market niche thanks to his presumed knowledge of out-of-town newspapers and by vouching for his advertising clients to the publishers. In the half-century before 1900 the number of American dailies grew ninefold, the number of weeklies fourteenfold. By the second decade of the twentieth century, advertising had found its primary home in newspapers and magazines (and accounted for two-thirds of their revenues), which had come to supersede billboards (still very much present) and quainter media like trade cards and posters at the point of sale.

From the 1890s advertising agencies had placed growing emphasis on a broad array of "service" to the client. ("Service" would become a mantra for Barton in several of his roles—as an advertising executive and spokesman, as a preacher to and for business, and as a popularizer of religious views.) Agencies were taking increasing control over the content of ads; as large, bureaucratic enterprises arose, advertisements were no longer the lengthened shadow of an owner-proprietor, with pictures of his plant, his home, even his children. Agencies began to study the consumer as well as the products their clients produced. Even so, the arrogation of expertise by advertising agencies took time. When Daniel Lord, an early Chicago adman, made bold to offer advice about a client's ad, the latter replied: "You may know a lot about advertising, but you know very little about the furniture business."[1]

By the early twentieth century, advertising was well launched toward professionalization. Agencies were taking over the task of writing

ad copy; correspondingly, it was less frequently produced by copywrit-
ers attached to the manufacturer or operating freelance. By 1910 agencies were more likely to have an art department and even some
employees engaged in market research. Some agencies were substantial businesses: by 1910 New York's George Batten agency had 100 employees; N. W. Ayer had 298 and would employ 496 within a decade.
By 1917 "some 95 percent of national advertising was handled by agencies." Admen (and overwhelmingly they were men) had elaborated a
number of industry organizations, whose members gained respect and
whose activities included efforts to police the industry to discourage
practices that brought ill-repute upon it. In 1913 the National Association of Advertisers met and approved a code of ethics promising
straightforward ad copy; over their conference site a large electric sign
spelled out "TRUTH." In 1917 the American Association of Advertising
Agencies (AAAA) was established to set and maintain standards for the
profession. By 1915 *Printers' Ink*, a leading trade journal, could pontifi-
cate that historians might well label the twentieth century "The Age of
Advertising." Yet at the same time advertising strategists were coming
to see the need to understand the mentality of the would-be consumer, to exploit the truths and tricks to be borrowed from the emerging field of psychology.[2]

   Not surprisingly, the growth of advertising was almost matched by
the propagation of its faultfinders. Advertisers often shilled for dubious
products—patent medicines in particular—and some made extravagant
claims. Some admen were also noted for playing both ends against the
middle. Looking back on his twenty-five years in the business, George
Batten recalled: "In those days it was common practice for an Agency
to send an order to a newspaper for 10 lines, a cut measuring 12, and
bill the advertiser for 14 lines." Admen aspiring to respectability labored
to cleanse their calling of its sharper operators. This effort at self-regu-
lation came, not surprisingly, during the reformist Progressive Era. A
central theme of the broader reform impulse was a quest for honesty—
in politics and in business—and the advertising industry's more for-
ward-looking segments marched in that direction. Spurred on by the

Associated Advertising Clubs of America, local advertising clubs established vigilance committees and, more commonly, Better Business Bureaus to respond to complaints about devious advertising. Like other
industries, advertising sought to minimize state regulation and amplify
its own, often informal, powers of self-rule. One of Bruce Barton's
chief and valued roles as an adman was to confer further respectability
upon his colleagues, a task he performed both with uplifting rhetoric
defending his line of work and by coming, through his varied public
activities, to occupy an esteemed place in public life. More than two
decades after BDO's founding, one of his associates attested that "Barton's identification with advertising made many people think more
highly" of people in that business.[3]

Advertising had an odorous reputation to overcome. Its past linked
it to patent medicines and carnivals. Bruce Barton's generation was
both sensitive to this recent lurid history and insistent in claiming respectability. Barton often referred to the bad old days, Chicago in the
1890s, where one office building posted a sign saying "No beggars, peddlers or advertising solicitors allowed." Everyone in the business had a
similar story. Barton's partner Osborn told of hearing his father say,
"Well, I see that McCutcheon is *advertising* again. Mother, I want you
to promise me never to shop in *that* store again!" Thanks partly to Barton's efforts, the ad business climbed toward integrity. As Helen Woodward, a writer with a career in advertising, saucily but aptly put it: "In
1905 advertising had no class. Its chief sport was poker. In 1914 it was
golf. And today [1938] it is getting to be polo."[4]

In the teens and later, critics claimed that advertising added nothing to goods but a higher cost, that it relied on exaggerated sales
pitches, and that it sought to inspire people to buy things they didn't
need—less by outlining a product's utility and merit than by appealing
to the buyer's sense of self-worth and gauzier dreams. A classic response from spokesmen for advertising was to note that products available to the consumer had so proliferated that he—or more often she,
since Madison Avenue quickly discerned that women were the most
active consumers—was often ignorant of their existence or uncertain

which best filled his needs. Advertising came to the perplexed buyer's rescue by providing "education," that magic commodity so valued in the Progressive Era. Indeed, Alex Osborn, four years before BDO existed, wrote a piece extolling advertising as "part of the present day educational systems." It taught by creating "new and better tastes" and contributed more to "the development of the American mind than all the schools in the country." It was "the usual person's high school," offering continuing education in "mechanical and scientific progress" and providing much of the average person's entree to art.[5]

As the 1920s opened, advertising had a crucial role in American life—"educational," but not in quite the sense Osborn meant. It taught the multitudes thronging to the cities the ways of modern urban life, "new urban habits of hygiene, dress, and style consciousness." It "facilitated the exchange of goods and services between multitudes of strangers. . . ." Advertising had begun to change the focus of its appeals, from "reason-why" argumentation that was product-centered (singing the virtues of the particular product) to a more psychologically oriented appeal. As Roland Marchand described it, ads sold "prestige instead of automobiles, sex appeal instead of mere soap." *Printers' Ink* asserted that advertising in the 1920s had switched from "the factory viewpoint" to emphasize "the mental processes of the consumer." Admen constructed sermonettes that offered Americans a means to conquer "the complexities of an increasingly urbanized, specialized, interdependent mode of life." BDO stood in the ranks of agencies that practiced the newer forms of advertising, but Barton himself was particularly adept in building bridges of prose between tradition and modernity.[6]

Barton had joined the roster of a profession muscling into prominence. "Madison Avenue" was about to become a metaphor to describe an activity that was becoming a conspicuous part of American capitalism. A number of New York agencies moved to the area around Grand Central Station, clustering heavily on Madison Avenue. According to an internal BBDO memo, the first reference to "Madison Avenue," based on this emerging geography, appeared in *Advertising & Selling* in May 1923. Ads were increasingly becoming animating topics of conversation. The advertising world made room, however briefly, for such literary luminaries as Sherwood Anderson, John P. Marquand, Stephen Vincent Benet, Sinclair Lewis, and F. Scott Fitzgerald. Some wrote effective copy. They—and all the frustrated novelists who stayed longer on Madison Avenue—nonetheless excoriated the agencies as houses of ill repute.

Admen would soon meet and master new media that took them beyond the printed word. The first radio station went on the air in 1920, barely a year after BDO opened its doors. Television loomed on the horizon, and in less than three decades, while Barton was still active in his firm, it would take a leading role in bringing advertising to TV, as it had in the twenties to radio. (BBDO had predicted great things for television in the early thirties and began experimenting with the medium in cooperation with Westinghouse.) Madison Avenue's concrete also met some of the rubber of the discipline of psychology. John B. Watson, the "father" of behavioral psychology, hired on at the J. Walter Thompson agency and brought his knowledge to the aid of the advertising profession. E. L. Bernays, a nephew of Sigmund Freud, pioneered in the theory and practice of public relations.[7]

ON THE DAY after New Year's 1919, Barton and Durstine opened an office with fourteen employees at 25 West 45th Street. They were not exactly neophytes. Whatever Barton's various job titles in the past ten years, his work had included sales, promotion, and advertising. Durstine had similar experience. A 1908 Princeton graduate, he had worked as a reporter for the *New York Sun*. Briefly he had written copy for the Street Railways Advertising Company, but with so little zest that he jumped at an offer to head the press bureau for Teddy Roosevelt's 1912 Bull Moose presidential campaign. That assignment too involved advertising, even though TR was a product that largely advertised itself. Durstine then worked for the Calkins & Holden agency and in 1916 co-founded the small advertising firm of Berrien-Durstine. The "struggling" status of the partnership, the war's interruption, and the connection with Barton encouraged Durstine to make the switch. Barton and Durstine each had borrowed $10,000 to launch the agency. Initially Barton took no salary, intending to support himself by continuing to write for the magazines, and Durstine drew only $100 a week. Durstine's political, not to say Republican, experience, along with Barton's developing associations ensured that the firm started with a wealth of connections, political as well as commercial. Durstine would be what one advertising journalist called an "organization man. He thinks of the hive, not the bee."[8]

On August 1, 1919, the two men were formally joined by Alex F. Osborn. Although born in the Bronx, Osborn had spent most of his working life in Buffalo. Forty-one years old, a graduate of Hamilton College, he, like Durstine (and many others who gravitated into advertising in that era), had been a newspaper reporter. He had also worked for the Buffalo Chamber of Commerce; as sales manager of the Hard Manufacturing Company, which, somewhat incongruously, made beds; and as business manager of the E. P. Remington advertising agency. Now, with five co-workers from that agency, he opened BDO's office in Buffalo, where he would continue to live, commuting to Manhattan by train for main-office business. His most notable contribution to advertising—to both its substance and mythology—would spring from his interest in promoting "creative" thinking; he was the father of "brainstorming": colleagues sitting around a table, concentrating on a problem and spontaneously spouting out streams of ideas—not to be criticized or examined until the process was completed and the suggestions compiled. Osborn's firm would first try brainstorming in 1939. The device soon spread to other major agencies, which were careful to brainstorm different names for the practice so that they would "not be following BBDO." Osborn would be a steadying influence for continuity at the agency and a close friend of Barton's. He would name his son Russell Barton Osborn.

BDO came into the world with a logo that had a B and D attached like ears to the top half of Osborn's O. It took little time for the young firm to muscle into the front rank of American advertising agencies.

The same ad that announced the three-way partnership also listed the firm's thirty-three clients. Some were companies of note: Dennison Manufacturing (tags and labels), the publishers Doubleday Page & Company and McGraw-Hill, Conde Nast Publications, Scribner's Magazine, and Wildroot hair tonic. Osborn brought in the business of the General Baking Company. Barton's wide acquaintance after a decade of writing, selling, and editing probably accounted for the presence of the clients in publishing. The fact that he "knew everyone" served as one of the main assets he brought to the partnership. Barton had worked with many people in publishing, had interviewed many more, and had a broad circle of friends. The friendship of older men "has always been stimulating to me," he would note, and these were the sort who ran vast corporations.[9]

The first weeks in business were hardscrabble, with Osborn still in Buffalo and Durstine laid up with pneumonia. Barton was left in charge. He recalled that, by some calculus, the firm lost $60 the first week. He scrambled to get McGraw-Hill to hire him as a consultant for a half-day a week. However dicey the winter months of 1919 looked, success would flower early. Durstine had projected a first year's loss of a mere $20,000, but at the end of 1919 the directors were able to vote a 3.5 percent dividend. This, Barton recalled, was "far in excess of anything we had dared to hope," and for the first time he "knew what it would be like to feel rich." In July 1920, not even a year after they had imprinted BDO on their stationery, the principals voted themselves salaries of $25,000 each. A year later the partners gave themselves a 30 percent increase in salary, retroactive six weeks, and in the meantime the dividend had shot up. Neither BDO nor its successor agency would have a losing year until 1932, the nadir of the Great Depression.[10]

Although it was a small shop, BDO moved up fast. In 1920 it added four more clients, including the Equitable Trust Company and the Edison Lamp Works, and ranked twenty-third in size among American agencies. It was tenth in 1921 (four new accounts), eighth in 1922 (adding General Motors and the National Biscuit Company),

fifth in 1923 (seven new clients, including Macy's and General Electric), and fourth in 1924 (five new clients, including Union Carbide).
Another gauge, number of lines of advertising placed in *Good Housekeeping* magazine, also indicated BDO's growth. The agency stood
twenty-first on the list in 1921; sixth in 1922, and fourth in 1923 (behind
N. W. Ayer, J. Walter Thompson, and Lord and Thomas, all well-
established agencies).

Life with BDO in those days had a lot of fizz. As a 1923 letter from
Barton to Durstine suggests, good things were coming in bunches. Barton wired congratulations to BDO's Boston office on a recent triumph,
meanwhile hailing Durstine for his "faith" in that outpost; he reported
on a "very satisfactory meeting" with GE and "quite a wonderful meeting in Detroit," as a result of which Barton anticipated an advertising
budget of $600,000 to $750,000 from GM. More business looked to be
in the works. By 1923 or 1924, BDO concluded that it lost money on
"any job that was not the equivalent of a hundred thousand dollar account, that is, which did not provide a gross revenue of about fifteen
thousand dollars." Barton thus found himself in the position of having
to decline a lesser project proposed by Marshall Field & Company in
Chicago. (Field's would up the ante.) By 1926 he told a friend that
their business was "going like a house afire."[11]

To keep its best employees from striking off in their own agencies,
in its early years BDO began to issue stock to its key people. This policy may have been a response to an early symptom of growing pains
signaled by the departure of two employees who left to form the Ped-
lar & Ryan agency, taking six clients with them. By mid-1923 BDO
had to find larger quarters, moving to 383 Madison Avenue, "a new office slightly smaller in area than the Polo Grounds," according to a jo-
cose announcement in *Sparks*, the BDO newsletter, which went on
to explain the new building's complex elevator system: "three are just
decoys."

The bantering in the newsletter suggests the easy informality with
which the BDO office functioned. Eventually this atmosphere would
become common, even legendary on Madison Avenue, but older firms,

working against their profession's uneasy reputation, more commonly cultivated rows of starched collars and fields of propriety. Barton opted for looseness and open doors. He claimed, in this connection, that "our greatest necessity is to keep in ourselves the spirit of youth, to build youth into the organization." For in youth lay the "market." One outside observer years later told Barton that his agency, uniquely, had "the great capacity for delegating authority" so that "your younger men take responsibility, go ahead and work with us without having to go to the top to get permission to do this or that. It's a wonderful spirit you have, and different from anything in the business."[12]

To stay at the top, BDO felt compelled to offer clients a widening variety of services. While earlier buyers of its institutional advertising seem to have been "attracted by the reputations of Barton, Durstine and Osborn, all of whom were skilled writers," over the long haul the agency acquired clients who valued "research and merchandising." BDO paraded its full-service assistance. One admirer recalled a lunch with Barton and Durstine at which one of them declared, "If we make it our business to give a client about ten per cent more in work and effort than anybody else will give him, we will not only hold that account, but it will grow, and it will help us attract new business of the kind we want." Thus BDO produced a motion picture for General Baking Company. For United Fruit it coined a name for a subsidiary responsible for selling bulk bananas; invented a device to stamp this trademark on every banana; devised the carton; plotted delivery routes; held cooking demonstrations; designed delivery trucks and drivers' uniforms; "and much more," as advertisers are wont to say. BDO prompted Hills Brothers (a client since 1921) to market a new product—canned grapefruit. It ran various contests, including one in bread baking. It put an Electrolux refrigerator in the Philadelphia zoo's monkey house and photographed a woman feeding a baby chimp in front of it. In 1932 it built a mock-up of a gasoline station in its rear office to figure out how to restyle such facilities. One executive subbed in a tennis tournament for a client's injured doubles partner. The agency ran an ad—for itself—telling the story of how one of its principals (perhaps Barton) was traveling with a client's sales executive. En route they ran into four other men from the agency, all on errands to provide various forms of assistance to other clients. The impressed sales executive declared, "I never knew you dug so deep into your clients' sales problems." Although the agency culture placed a high value on this eagerness to throw down capes over obstructing puddles large and small, in 1926 the management committee found that the practice was getting out of hand. A memo warned against "over-anxiety to serve clients," reminding employees that "it's not our province to do odd jobs for clients, such as hiring stenographers or typists," to run "errands" unrelated to advertising work, or "to buy 'fight' tickets."[13]

Nevertheless BDO marched along with the trend among advertising agencies to institutionalize a broad array of services for clients. In 1930 it installed a kitchen to test recipes that exploited its clients' food products. It would leap into new media and shape the programs that provided clients with the vehicles that carried their commercial messages. In 1927 it hired John Caples, who became a "world authority on copy testing" as well as mail-order advertising. With another agency, Caples had written the famous music correspondence-school ad, "They Laughed When I Sat Down at the Piano."

From the beginning, by agreement (under which he also declined any role in management), Barton split his workday between his home and the agency. He worked at home from 8 A.M. to noon, by when he "finished all the creative work—whether it be advertising copy or magazine stuff—that I expect to get done that day." "[T]hen I go to lunch with somebody. Then I come to the office and see people and dictate mail. . . ." The agency acquired ninety-eight clients within four years, and so many wanted their copy written by Barton that BDO, according to one in-joke, ran out of space for all the "Bruce Bartons" supplying copy. By 1926 he had backslid, coming to the office each morning. "It requires much more courage to stay at home," he confessed. Meanwhile he continued to be active in areas unrelated to the agency. Quantities of magazine articles continued to pour from his pen.

When Barton was in his office, his door remained resolutely open. He was available to co-workers at the agency for advice, encouragement, and general cheer. He also was welcoming to people in off the street, especially "all young people and all applicants for jobs," for he never knew, he claimed, where inspiration might originate, and "the young chap out of a job today is likely as not to show up in three years as the advertising manager of a big company with a large contract to place."[14] The efficiency of his own office improved in 1925 when Louise MacLeod became his secretary. She managed nearly everything for Barton, staying with him and BBDO through the rest of his life. She once boasted of herself, "She goes back to the Ark, as do most of her files."[15]

While Barton's approach might seem casual, he contributed mightily to BDO's rapid success. An agency history noted that in the early years Barton "not only served as an account executive," managing the delicate relationship with clients, "but wrote a great deal of the copy for many of the clients." It soon acquired a reputation for quality. Barton reported in 1929 that Colonel Frank Knox, then with the Hearst newspapers, told him that his agency "can handle our advertising if you personally will agree to write the copy."

Barton's energies helped lift the agency to rapid success. He had a central role in winning two giant concerns as bellwether clients: General Motors and General Electric. Agency lore had it that Barton acquired these clients in one miraculous week, and, indeed, one account had BDO garnering the business of GM, GE, and National Biscuit Company in "one fateful week." Other in-house chronologies suggest that GM and GE came aboard in December 1922 and January 1923.

Barton was a virtuoso in the boardrooms of prospective clients. One journalist labeled him the epitome of "master performers before executive groups," combining "the finesse of a Richelieu with the cunning of a Benjamin Franklin, with the persuasiveness of a Daniel Webster and with the fighting sincerity of a St. Paul."[16] He was also nimble in proposing novel campaigns. He admonished the head of Socony Vacuum Oil that his own and all other gasoline company advertising was "in a rut." He urged Socony to buy six double-page spreads in the

Saturday Evening Post, which would tout the touristic appeal of New England. The impact on gas sales was unclear, but the reward in goodwill in the region, to a tentacle of the hitherto excoriated Standard Oil octopus, was enormous.[17]

Barton composed some of the new agency's most admired ads. One client for whom he did important work was the Alexander Hamilton Institute, which offered business training by correspondence. A 1921 pitch offered the sort of storytelling prose for which he became celebrated and the pictorial linkage singled out by Johns. Under a cut illustrating a father with his growing family pointing to the uphill road ahead, Barton described "The Glory of the Upward Path." It had a typical Barton opener: "Two paths begin at the bottom of the hill of life." One "winds about the base, thru years of routine and drudgery," a "slow and difficult" route "bordered with monotony." The other mounts rapidly "into positions where every problem is new and stirring, where the rewards are comfort, and travel and freedom from all fear." The ad was garnished with testimonials from happy clients. "In the past eight years my income has increased 750%," wrote one. Another announced his election to his company's board of directors. "The day when I enrolled with the Alexander Hamilton Institute was the turning point in my career." The ad later earned inclusion in *The 100 Greatest Advertisements*.[18] Another of Barton's treasured ads for the Institute lamented "The Years the Locust Hath Eaten." He applied this biblical line to the "year after year [when] men go along feeding their lives to the locust" of indecision, laziness, or fixation on petty detail. The Institute learned weekly of such "tragedies" from men reporting career roadblocks they might have skirted had they subscribed earlier to the Modern Business Course and Service. Instead they could only rue "the years the locust hath eaten."[19] Barton's lengthy connection with the Alexander Hamilton Institute had begun even before BDO was founded. He was a consultant; he wrote one of its first advertising texts; his brother Fred was a member of its advertising department.[20]

Barton led the campaign to win General Electric's advertising business. BDO first "got into the GE picture" when Barton showed its president, Owen D. Young, a proposed two-page spread for the *Satur-day Evening Post*. Crudely pasted together, it sought to connect GE "in the public mind with research, invention and progress." Soon after Gerald Swope became president of GE, he invited several agencies, each of which had handled a part of the company's advertising, to appear before a large body of GE executives at a Schenectady golf club, each agency given an hour and a half for its pitch. After two days of this, the officers voted roughly 80 percent in favor of BDO. Obtaining this account was "literally a bombshell in the agency business, and unquestionably hastened our rise to major stature," Barton later recalled.[21]

Barton helped turn General Electric into a household word. He wrote the first ad carrying GE's logo—the two letters in fancy script inside a curlicued circle—and captioned these "the initials of a friend." The symbol was something Barton "came up with." Agency lore had it that it came from a design glimpsed on a manhole cover or perhaps a trolley car. The ad's prose credited GE with making "big motors that pull railway trains" and "tiny motors that make hard housework easy." Perhaps Barton's most famous turn of phrase on GE's behalf came in an ad that first appeared in the August 7, 1926, *Saturday Evening Post*, asserting that "Any woman who does anything which a little electric motor can do is working for 3 cents an hour!" The ad won a Harvard Award, in an annual competition that occurred from 1924 to 1930, and Barton's line was remembered in at least one of his obituaries.[22] BDO's campaign was also meant to supply a sort of internal corporate advertising, which would forward Swope's aim of achieving closer unity among the multiple components brought together into the sprawling GE empire.[23]

General Motors also got the Barton touch. The public initially had little sense of the identity of this rickety assemblage of auto- and parts-making firms pulled together by William Crapo Durant in 1908, then rescued with Du Pont money after the war. Again Barton furthered the corporation's need to create a unified identity from disparate units. He designed a series of ads that were not so much explicit descriptions of the quality of GM cars as parables about their use, emphasizing, as the president of his agency later put it, how the company was "performing their duty as servants of the public." One two-page sociodrama entitled "That the Doctor Shall Arrive *in Time*" pictured a dying girl, her grief-ridden mother, and the doctor, whose trusty GM car had enabled him to deliver artificial respiration in the nick of time. "The little girl would never have seen another sunrise had it not been for the automobile." The ad went on to note that "probably one in every five" physicians in North America drove GM cars. General Motors offered the ad "as an inspiration," suitable to be hung "in every factory and plant, in every showroom and service station. May it be a reminder that the service of the automobile is a part of the most sublime service that any human being is privileged to render to another. . . ." This ad too won a Harvard Award. The story in another ad in the series depicted how, thanks to his "little car," a minister had motored among the widely scattered denizens of the countryside and webbed them together into a church—something skeptics had told him "can't be done."[24]

These ads were designed to "knit the organization more closely, and to make the public more friendly to the Corporation as such." Barton sought to portray General Motors as a "family." This would make that automotive empire into something more than an abstraction to consumers; it also meshed with the strategy of GM's leader, Alfred P. Sloan, to build greater coordination and collective identity among the diverse, sometimes warring parts of that empire. Barton was an excellent salesman for such institutional advertising, but here he had an advantage in that Sloan required no persuasion to see the need for public relations and advertising. Even so, Sloan's biographer notes that Barton, "like the great romantic poets, knew how to imbue bloodless entities with great human emotion and spirituality." In a more practical vein, Barton expressed delight that a survey of GM car dealers found that nearly nine of ten believed "that the institutional campaign is helping mightily in the actual sale of cars."[25]

Barton conducted another noteworthy institutional ad campaign on the seventy-fifth anniversary of Marshall Field & Company. Like some other great emporia (notably Wanamaker's in Philadelphia), Field's conducted its business with a strong tone of evangelical Protestantism.[26] The ad series employed a number of themes, including the prominence of women in Field's management. (Barton's first ad had been dismissive of their role, some of them had complained, and so another was written to rectify the error.) Field's not only closed its store on Sundays but even covered the display windows. An ad titled "The Things Unseen" made capital of this spiritual stand. The store then sent out over ten thousand copies of the ad, many to religious bodies. More than twenty-five ministers used it as a sermon topic.[27]

Barton's skills became so legendary that he received credit even for advertising innovations that were not his. In some circles he became known as the inventor of Betty Crocker, the imaginary, matronly recipe dispenser for General Mills food products. In fact she was invented by the in-house advertising department of a General Mills predecessor company, her signature adorning letters responding to requests for recipes and advice.[28] Sometimes Barton's contributions to advertising were more mundane. Seeking a novel way to advertise petroleum products, he won the advertising business of the Standard Oil Company of New York with the phrase "Clean Rest Rooms."[29]

Barton's latchkey could open corporate portals. An in-house pep-up message urging BBDOers not to slacken in their service to clients specified Barton's public persona as an asset in winning business, jocularly quoting the president of the imaginary Automatic Shoe Lacing Corporation of America: "I have been captivated by Bruce Barton's personality. My wife reads his stuff in the magazines. An hour in his book-lined office and I feel that I've become 'the man who knew Coolidge' and an industrial blood-brother to Owen D. Young." His partner Osborn would later flatter him by saying, "This good-will of ours, packaged in the name of Bruce Barton, is a tremendous thing." He was an excellent envoy for the agency, good at impressing audiences of corporate leaders. To potential clients, to friends, even to foes, he glistened with "sincerity." Yet there was more to Barton's contributions than hit-and-run charisma. For General Motors he attended every meeting of its institutional advertising committee, saw Sloan every other week, and made numerous trips to Detroit. In their minds, GM—and Sloan—were dealing with Barton, not with BDO.[30]

Barton also continued to apply his skills to matters of public welfare. He raised funds for Berea College, his father's alma mater and venue of his freshman year, writing a series of letters which argued the merit of these descendants of the "pure blooded English folks who settled in Virginia" and then ventured west; making the case that no donation got more bang for the buck, he wrote twenty-four men soliciting $1,000 from each (committing the same amount himself), enough to underwrite ten students per donation.[31]

In the 1920s he drafted a parable about generosity and selfishness, which had a long afterlife. The text, "There Are Two Seas," had a biblical provenance.

> "There are two seas in Palestine," it began. "One is fresh, and fish are in it." Trees grew and children played along its banks, birds and humans thrived nearby. This was the Sea of Galilee. But downstream lay another sea, without fish, song, laughter—or life. While the River Jordan fed both, the Sea of Galilee took the Jordan's waters but sent them on. "The giving and receiving go on in equal measure." The other sea, "shrewder," hoarded every drop.
>
> "The Sea of Galilee gives and lives. This other sea gives nothing. It is named The Dead."
>
> "There are two kinds of people in the world."
>
> "There are two seas in Palestine."

"There Are Two Seas" appeared in *McCall's* in 1928. It lay fallow until John D. Rockefeller, Jr., asked to include it in a speech to support the 1945 USO drive; the *Readers' Digest* then reprinted it. The Community Chest took it up in 1946 and used it for years on the national radio broadcast launching that charity's annual campaign. It adorned Christmas cards and graced a publication edited by the Reverend Norman Vincent Peale, whose sunny religious message in the 1950s resembled Barton's in the 1920s.[32] Throughout his life Barton's pen would prove a valuable ally in various fund-raising causes.

Barton also served as an ornament to both the advertising profession and his own firm. He often supplied *le mot juste* in defense of advertising; over a long career he gave numerous speeches vindicating the profession to the public and to advertisers. In 1923, for example, his speech before the National Electric Light Association (NELA) was called "Which Knew Not Joseph." It summarized Joseph's "remarkable career" but stressed the denouement: when Pharaoh died, "there arose in Egypt a new King which knew not Joseph." So in 1923 a new generation was emerging that would know none of the current commonplaces but needed constant education. Corporate reputations thus demanded constant tending. This sermon struck a chord with businessmen. Barton's agency would for decades thereafter receive about twenty-five requests annually for a copy of the speech, and "countless organizations" reprinted it. Barton also recycled it as an editorial.[33]

By some tastes, Joseph's PR machine was overdoing it, especially in the electric power industry. In the 1920s Americans were all fully awake to the wonders of electricity—which needed no advertising—but some were underserved or overcharged. Many found attractive the idea of municipally owned utilities. Both camps energetically debated the future of the power available from waters rushing along the Niagara frontier and down the Tennessee River, on which, at Muscle Shoals, the government had begun during the war to build a dam to power a nitrate plant and now looked to dispose of it. But to whom? The issue pitted Progressives like Senators George Norris and Thomas Walsh, who wanted such power sources operated by and for public interests, against utility companies, which clearly did not. Critics of the "power trust" claimed that profit margins as well as the rates of the utility companies were exorbitant. In 1929 Americans paid on the average nearly six times as much per kilowatt-hour as did citizens of Ontario.[34]

In 1925 Barton helped produce some of his trademark sermonettes at the behest of privately owned utilities. One pamphlet addressed proposals "that the government should enter the electric light and power business and furnish 'service at cost.'" Utility companies operated under government regulation and were "*already* furnishing service at cost," he wrote. Utility holding companies—another hot topic—were logical consolidations "to promote efficiency and economy." Another leaflet reported that the cost of living had risen 65 percent (1914–1925) while electric rates had stayed fairly level. Another pictured cartoon orators whose windy "'Talk Talk" seemed to be levitating the globe.[35] These pithy pieces argued for the profit motive (and the reasonable returns that utilities supposedly earned), lauded the service provided by privately owned companies, and denigrated municipally owned utilities. The mail that brought the utility bill into homes also carried as many as nine million of these "envelope stuffers" with Barton's "honeyed articles," part of a campaign that cost the NELA some $175,000. Thus customers who paid their light bills were being propagandized with their own money.[36]

The utility industry was guilty of still more heavy-handed suasion, including subsidizing favorable interpretations in textbooks and other still less subtle efforts to influence teaching at all levels of education. These pressures, as well as Barton's hired pen, were publicized in an investigation launched in 1928 by the Federal Trade Commission. Evidence presented to the FTC indicated that Barton had received $5,000 for his efforts; he took pains to correct the impression that the money was his personal fee, insisting that it was meant for BBDO (to whom he endorsed the checks). Barton's role as an advocate for the Power Trust paled when set in the overall picture of utility arrogance and did no important damage to his or BBDO's reputation, though it surely reinforced the inclination of those on the political left to think ill of the advertising industry and to see in Barton a hired gun for special interests.[37]

Barton persistently lectured corporations on the need for attention to their public relations, using such occasions to burnish his own industry's reputation. At the Bok Award banquet in 1931, preaching perhaps to the choir, he brought the ad industry into the company of architects, surgeons, teachers, and ministers as a calling: "We build of imperishable materials, we who work with words." He then one-upped the architects by suggesting that the words of the Gettysburg Address would live long after the Lincoln Memorial had crumbled.[38]

Those Bok Awards provided another gauge of BDO's success. The Publisher Edward Bok had endowed a set of annual awards for advertising; admen juried and the Harvard School of Business administered the competition. Of the 1924 awards, announced in 1925, BDO won three of nine, in the categories "national advertising, local advertising and market study." Barton emphasized that these campaigns had succeeded in terms of sales, not just aesthetics. In 1925 no BDO ad was entered in competition because Barton served on the jury. In 1926 BDO's institutional ads for GE and its research for Johnson & Johnson were awarded prizes, and in 1927 its advertising text for Marshall Field & Company and its local campaign for Macy's received awards. In 1929 its local campaign in New York for Lewis & Conger's "carriage trade" pots and pans was recognized. The firm's institutional advertising for the B & O Railroad was a winner for 1930, when it also won an award for its headline on an Electrolux Refrigerator ad ("As Silently as Nature Makes Ice"). In the seven years the award was conferred, BDO or its successor won eleven of them, more than the next two winning agencies combined.[39]

Barton knew that advertising had its blemishes. An early defense on his part was his claim that it was a young business, prone to some of the follies of youth, and so it needed "time" to mature. Given his belief that business, more often than not, was beneficent, it should be no surprise that he thought the same of advertising. He upheld the general honesty of his profession as well as that of his own firm. As he put it to a colleague on Madison Avenue after a quarter-century in his agency, "I am constitutionally against dishonest advertising of any sort. That's one reason why our agency has always been a little weak in the kind of advertising that tells men that if they change from one cigarette to another their throats will feel better" or women if they switch toothpastes "they will have more telephone calls."[40]

At times he had doubts about advertising and its social utility. In drafting a speech for an advertising convention in 1926, he sought moral and intellectual support from a friend who taught at NYU's Business School. Some advertising was called for, Barton knew, because people "will never do what is good for them until a great deal of persuasion has been used." Thus undeniably valuable products like the sewing machine or life insurance had languished until they were advertised. Yet, he feared, much current advertising embodied "the most wasteful phases of the competitive system." The automobile required publicizing when it was a new product, but now it needed advertising no more than "the multiplication table." Advertising seemed mostly designed "to steal each other's customers . . . switching people from . . . William's Shaving Soap to Colgate's Shaving Soap." He wondered whether, given the saturation of the "home market," American advertisers might not take a portion of their ad budget "and invest it in developments abroad, in helping those countries which have no purchasing power to acquire purchasing power." While Barton defended his profession, according to one historian of advertising, he "embrac[ed] the trade in public while keeping his distance in private." In a 1928 speech he boasted that advertising was "coming to be recognized for what it really is, a tremendous educational force." In another he conceded "the cruelties of competition, and the dishonesty that still stains too many business operations." But he defended advertising because it was "the power which keeps business out in the open, which compels it to set up for itself public ideals of quality and service and to measure up to those ideals." A year later he linked his profession with the nation's mission: "We live in a democracy, and when you make the world safe for democracy you automatically make it safe for advertising."[41]

Barton most often kept his doubts to himself.[42] For the profession he served as a potent free lance. He answered critics like Stuart Chase, who argued that advertising was wasteful. In 1927 Chase and F. J. Schlink's *Your Money's Worth* appeared, prompting a stir and a number of reprintings. The book had nothing good to say about advertising but directed its main barrage against the shoddy if not worthless, over-priced, sometimes even lethal goods behind the ads. It aimed heavy fire on adulterated products and poisonous patent medicines, and instructed consumers that they could mix their own foods, cleansers, and remedies by buying the simple key ingredients and diluting them. Compared to smaller, ballyhooed, expensively packaged products on the market, the cost would be pennies on the dollar. The consumer needed, said the authors, a citizens' equivalent of the Bureau of Standards, which enabled the federal government to buy cheaply the high-quality products needed to paint its ships, feed its troops, and clean its hallways. They called for an institution to test all manner of products for strength, durability, and basic function (as Underwriters Labs did for electrical appliances) and give the hapless consumer the information he needed to choose among the flood of products shouting for his dollar.[43]

When earlier Chase had argued that advertising was wasteful, Barton conceded the point, but "all forms of competitive activity are wasteful." Were the government to control advertising, "instantly the wheels of industry would slow down," for producers, with no way to increase market share, would lose all incentive to innovate. Moreover, "far from being non-productive," advertising was the "driving force behind all production, and is the builder of civilization." A "savage tribe" has "no wants." But let an advertising man descend by plane on that tribe, laden with "red neckties and tan shoes . . . and automobiles and bicycles," and instantly "wants would be kindled" that would propel the savage to "voluntarily enlist himself in servitude to the creation of a civilization." When President Calvin Coolidge spoke to the American Association of Advertising Agencies in 1926, he made virtually the same point—no surprise, since he incorporated a number of Barton's suggestions into the speech.[44]

A year later Barton assured the convention of the AAAA that, just like medical doctors, who had progressed beyond having endlessly to prove that they cured more patients than they killed, their young profession was no longer on "probation" and need not answer "every half-baked criticism that is flung at us." If anything, criticism was a badge of honor, "a normal accompaniment to achievement," and muckraking was easy—until "you get all the facts." One could decry doctors, lawyers, even mothers. Barton argued that advertising created demand and so made possible "quantity production" with all its savings. Chase was asking Americans to return to a primitive state of "petty economies"—home-mixed or bulk-bought remedies in place of packaged conveniences. Consumer tastes for style and convenience were sovereign. Speaking up for the self-indulgent consumerism of the twenties, Barton exulted: "We have ceased to count our pennies in America. . . ." Advertising helped consumers differentiate their desires and resist "the standardization of modern life." While business was far from perfect, it had been in the saddle only a short time, and Barton placed his faith in "the gradual evolution of its ideals."[45]

A year later, in a radio talk carried nationally by NBC, Barton combined his various rationales for advertising. It encouraged the wider distribution of goods; by raising demand it made mass production feasible and thus products cheaper; it stirred "desire" and so led to "progress"; it improved the business world by making its doings and pledges public. Barton did not claim that business had reached the ultimate stage of evolution. Further progress, he noted more tentatively, would depend on "character" and humanity's ability to prevent war. As 1929 opened brightly, he wrote that "Business is the greatest ally and promoter of Honesty," and that at the apex of the business world, "nine times out of ten you will find an idealist."[46] Yet Barton knew his profession did not always measure up. In framing his advertising credo in 1930, he conceded that the trend marked by the emergence of pro-consumer institutions like the Good Housekeeping Institute and especially the U.S. Bureau of Standards (a favorite of Chase and Schlink) might "make many of the present purely competitive uses of advertising unnecessary or even obsolete." At its best, advertising educated. ("When does the last train run?" "What is on at the Rialto tonight?") At its worst, it abetted profit-obsessed retailers or manufacturers, but Barton himself professed not to "believe that either sales or profits are objects in themselves."[47]

Over time Barton raised the ante: at its best advertising also performed "service," a word bold-faced in Barton's lexicon. He offered several anecdotes to prove that advertising was capable of doing good. He recalled an early ad he had prepared for a life insurance company; it caused one young father to buy a policy and mail in the premium. When he soon died from an infected dental extraction, his family was provided for: prudence inspired by good magic had triumphed over bad magic. Beyond that, advertising, by stimulating desires, stirred ambition and thus improvement; it made manufacturers uphold their promises; it brought rationality and openness to pricing; it enabled the print media to flourish while keeping prices low; by the 1950s Barton could say that it had sustained "a system that has made us the leaders of the free world: The American Way of Life."[48]

Barton also addressed the broader question raised by advertising: the kind of life it promoted. While at times he endorsed the simple life (and told his archetypal stories about boys dragged by ambition from sweet small-town pleasures to the churning cities), he often spoke as a defender of the new values of consumption and hedonism. A 1928 editorial urged readers to "Cut Down Your Necessities." By eliminating his own "foolish necessities," he was able to buy "one big, wise luxury," in this case a car, which enabled him to square the circle by being able to motor to his own country cottage.[49] Extravagance thus begat simplicity—and Foxboro was just down the road from Walden Pond.

Barton was looking for an elusive moral balance in the 1920s, between "the lingering Puritan tradition of abstinence which makes play idleness and spending sin," as the sociologist Robert S. Lynd put it, "and the increasing secularization of spending and the growing pleasure basis of living." Similarly, the nation's leading philosopher, John Dewey, noted that "the old-fashioned ideal of thrift" had been rendered moot in an age when "speeded-up mass production demands increased buying," which had become "an economic 'duty.'"[50] Barton strove to align advertising with traditional virtues: honesty, rationality, economic efficiency. In the historian Warren Susman's phrase, he "found a way of bridging the gap between the demands of a Calvinistic producer ethic with its emphasis on hard work, self-denial, savings and the new, increasing demands of a hedonistic consumer ethic: spend, enjoy, use up."[51] Such efforts did not satisfy critics like Chase and Schlink, who preached a stronger, perhaps more old-fashioned, producer-oriented ethos that urged consumers to educate themselves about a product's ingredients and inherent, as opposed to ascribed, worth; to mix their own to save money; and to disdain the deceiving "magic" and "wizardry" of salesmanship with its accompanying "quackery." If Barton tried to hold a rhetorical straddle between Thoreau's Walden and the neon-lit 1920s, Chase and Schlink would leapfrog back to the virtues preached by Ben Franklin and the standardized products of Eli Whitney's gun factory. Barton's was probably the more astute reading of consumers' desires.[52]

Whatever his persisting qualms in identifying with his profession, Barton may have modulated them simply by making sure that advertising never became his entire life—even his working life. The finite time horizon to which he committed when he agreed to join BDO suggests his misgivings at the outset. His career never consisted solely of writing ads and persuading clients. Politics, writing for audiences beyond consumers or corporate advertisers, and lay moralizing absorbed a great deal of his energies. Even so, they were not fields so separate as to prevent him from importing into them the language and axioms of advertising.

BDO's success and fame stemmed more from the charismatic qualities of its principals than from its bureaucratic exactitude. Some thought that the agency's structural oddities, its "Rube Goldberg" arrangement, impeded its progress. Durstine, the "organization man" charged with administering the agency, believed that virtually every employee should be a jack-of-all-trades, an "all-around adman," not a specialist. Under his rule, there was no copy department. Everyone could write copy, just as everyone could be a contact man or provide whatever assistance a client needed. BDO sometimes boasted of this nonspecializing approach: one BDOer exclaimed that "just about the whole agency is the copy department." But it was a dubious assumption that everyone could do anything, and there were those who criticized Durstine's leadership on this account.[53] By 1928, reinforcements were on the way.

GEORGE BATTEN died in 1918 at age sixty-four, having founded, in 1891, and prospered with the agency that bore his name. He radiated respectability in a profession that hungered for it. When he became part of the business, Batten found that advertising men were held in lower esteem than a "life insurance solicitor or book agent," and he struggled to elevate the profession's standing. He placed much of his early advertising in religious journals, then expanded into the agricultural press. He opposed the use of the abbreviation "ad" as demeaning of his profession's dignity. Batten was a minister's son like Barton and like many others who came to advertising in its golden age. The porter at his agency told a young job applicant, "If you haven't got religion, get some right now!"

Batten held firmly to several axioms. "There is," he avowed, "some business we do not want." Proving the point, he once turned down $50,000 in commissions from an unworthy product. He claimed to have founded his business on a basic idea: "to make advertising pay the advertiser." He was a stickler on punctuality. When an employee, having moved his family from the city to a New Jersey suburb, used that circumstance to excuse his late arrivals at the office, Batten fixed him with a look and asked, "Has it ever occurred to you that if you had moved to Poughkeepsie you wouldn't have to come in at all?"[54]

After BDO moved to 383 Madison Avenue in 1923, they found the George Batten Agency settled in three floors above them. Batten's firm, with one clerk, had initially occupied a twelve-by-fourteen-foot office. It did $25,000 of business in its first year. Its first account, Macbeth's Lamp Chimneys, was still with it. Members of the two firms naturally rubbed elbows in the elevators. In 1925 they played each other in baseball. William E. Benton, a rising star at Batten, made bold to suggest a merger, stressing that Batten produced good ads but lagged in soliciting new clients, while BDO wrote "lousy" ads but hunted new business aggressively. Benton was fired in May 1928 for "disloyalty," even though the combine he proposed was only weeks away.[55] In fact, negotiations had begun in March. Others made similar assessments of the complementarity of the two agencies. Charles Brower, who much later would become president of the combined agency, recalled that while BDO had a knack for getting new customers, it fell short in providing "service." Batten, less aggressive in scouting out new accounts, provided better client support. The natural enough idea of a merger had also occurred to William H. Johns, yet another minister's son, who had led the Batten agency after its founder's death in 1918.[56]

Johns and Durstine, both former presidents of the AAAA, were attending that organization's 1927 convention when Johns asked his BDO counterpart, "Do you realize that our two agencies have not a single conflicting account?"

"Is that so?" replied Durstine. "Well, what do you mean by all this?"

Johns replied, "Not a thing in the world." But the idea percolated in both offices, conversations continued, and the merger came to pass on September 15, 1928. It was a union of equals (stock shares of each were valued equally, and there were no plans to prune staff). The two agencies were now roughly equal in size; at the turn of the year 1927, BDO had 215 employees while Batten had 212. In billings, BDO with $23 million, had moved well ahead of the Batten Agency with $8 million. At the time of the merger, Roy Durstine wrote a memo noting that fifty-four of BBDO's clients had come in with BDO, fifty-nine with Batten. Barton became chairman of the board, Johns was named president, and Durstine was vice president and general manager. There were eight other vice presidents, including Osborn. The agency now had offices in Chicago and Boston as well as Osborn's fiefdom in Buffalo.[57]

Johns had been an early George Batten hire, in 1891. He was fired (for misquoting Robert Burns in an ad), then rehired the next year. Johns was a staunch defender of the 15 percent commission (paid by

the media) to advertising agencies and a founder of the AAAA. His contributions to advertising history included the line "Hammer the Hammer," a challenge to test the safety of Ivor-Johnson revolvers; he
created the Dutch Boy in Dutch Boy cleanser ads; and he reputedly
thought up the expression "used cars" as preferable to "secondhand."
Johns found the merger attractive because it offered the prospect of
lightening his administrative load and allowing him to concentrate on
sales. "His forte is contact work," according to one author. As president
he was delighted to leave much of the administrative burden of running the agency to Durstine. He informed Batten employees that the
two offices complemented rather than competed with each other: "We
are adding two and two and making five."

There were some physical problems to resolve, what with one
agency housed on the seventh floor and the other on the ninth and
tenth. And some clashing cultural edges between the merged agencies
required chamfering. Reflecting its founder, the Batten Agency held to
greater formality, expressed moralism more freely, and acted in a pa-
ternalistic fashion toward its personnel. Management placed a rose on
each employee's desk to mark his or her hiring anniversary, or "Batten
Birthday." This practice ended hurriedly after a BDO man acknowledged his flower with doggerel: "When you gave me a rose instead of
a raise, you sure got a rise out of me!" The two agencies were not so
far apart in their understanding of the moral economy of advertising.
While Batten had proudly turned down unworthy clients, for at least
two decades BDO and its successor agency carried no hard-liquor account, though, Barton noted, "we have been offered several million
dollars' worth of such business."[58]

The new name was to be a stopgap until Barton thought up something shorter. Meetings to mull the matter consumed hours. Rapidly,
however, the moniker became a tag line in public banter and "a vaude-
ville joke" that brought the firm high name recognition. Even before
the merger, the BDO partnership had been subject to frequent mis-
spelling. Now a trade journal complained that it took nearly a column
to print the name of the new firm. On Jack Benny's popular radio

show, his "man" Rochester famously proposed that his boss's suggestions be run by "Batten, Barton, Durstine and Osborn." When Benny
phoned BBDO, the "receptionist" invariably answered, "Batten, Barton,
Durstine and Little ol' Osborn." (Eventually a BBDO client would sponsor Benny.)

One wag said the firm name sounded like a trunk falling down-
stairs. This line had a long shelf-life and was often attributed to Benny
or fellow comedian Fred Allen. The *New Yorker* carried an item about
a litter of five kittens named "Batten, Barton, Durstine, Osborn and
God."[59] A New York columnist asserted rhapsodically that the name "is
so waltzy and toe tingling that it could be played by a Viennese string
band. You can switch the four names all around and they will always
read in two-four time." BBDO even earned mention in a movie. In *Hard
to Handle* (1933), James Cagney has the line, "Well, so long, boys—I'm
lunching with Bruce Barton of Batten, Barton, Durstine & Osborn."
At the second Ad Man's Jazz Concert benefit in 1957, Helen Ward,
onetime chanteuse with Benny Goodman's band, sang a number that
included the refrain "I've got the Batten, Barton, Durstine—and Osborn blues."[60]

BDO and BBDO were quick to add radio to the media in which they
operated. In 1922 Barton visited a radio station for a broadcast by comedian Ed Wynn. The new medium's reach enraptured him—the notion that up to 250,000 listeners might be tuning in, their antennae
looped over tree branches or radiators and linked to cabinets whose
contents "I do not understand and you do not need to." Radio had the
potential to deliver "almost a liberal education" to every home.

Yet it was Roy Durstine who provided BDO's strongest push in this
direction and saw the pregnant future of commercial sponsorship.
Harford Powel, a frequent writer on advertising topics, observed: "The
radio made Durstine, and Durstine made the radio." It was the
medium that best harnessed his creative bent. In 1927 he established
BDO's radio department, the "first official advertising agency Radio
Department" and, said Powel, "the ablest." Brought in to head it was
Arthur Pryor, Jr., son of the noted bandleader. Atwater Kent, the radio

manufacturer, became a BDO client in 1925, and this connection linked the agency more closely to the medium. Durstine convinced the company, which already aired radio shows, to cast them with leading singers. He soon obtained them the sole right to broadcast the stars of the Metropolitan Opera. Another show, "Atwater Kent Auditions," ran for four years and pointed the way toward the "amateur hours" that soon filled the airwaves. Pryor directed "The March of Time," a news dramatization, and a GM-sponsored program that featured such stars as Kate Smith and Nelson Eddy. The march king John Philip Sousa made his radio debut on a BBDO sponsor's program. Soon such luminaries as the slugger Babe Ruth and the aviator Amelia Earhart were visiting BBDO's office to arrange their appearance on the radio program "The Inside Story."

Some saw radio as a public resource, not a commercial cat's-paw, and they cringed at the way American radio developed, pushed along by commercial sponsorship. Durstine had no such qualms. In the late 1930s, after more than a decade of activity in radio, he evangelized that Big Business was "now in show business" and, both with and without radio, part of "the quickened tempo of today." Durstine insisted that BBDO must generate and produce the client's programs, and he insisted that account executives become more active on the radio production side, to make them less ready to "join with the client in bemoaning what a poor program went on the air last night." Radio billings would come to constitute between one-fifth and one-quarter of the agency's billings. By 1938 BBDO advertising revenues from radio would outstrip those for magazines.[61]

BDO AND BBDO were strong partnerships. By no means did all their initiatives or energy come from Bruce Barton. Nor in fact could they, given his many other undertakings. He continued to write for magazines—prodigiously while BDO was getting off the ground, when the articles served as a major source of income at a time he was taking no salary. Many articles, sometimes two or three per issue, appeared in the *American Magazine*, with whose editor John M. Siddall he had a close relationship. Barton could convert almost any experience, intimate or vicarious, into the printed word—fiction or nonfiction, some signed, some ghosted, and some anonymous (a few attributed to orphans). Several articles of a religious bent were signed by "the author of 'Finding God in Millersville.'"[62]

During the 1920s he wrote opening homilies for *Redbook*. In 1926 he began writing a column for Sunday papers through the McClure Newspaper Syndicate. Some of these columns he recycled from earlier pieces, even from *Redbook*. McClure's boasted that these "inspirational editorial articles" were by "one of the highest-priced writers of the day," one who, like the famous English essayist Charles Lamb, "has the rare gift of making his readers feel that they are his personal friends." These articles continued their march into the gales of the depression, when newspapers, seeking to cut costs, pared such items. By 1932 McClure's was losing money on Barton, possibly because his cheeriness no longer matched the public mood, and Barton ended the connection.[63] When he offered his pen to other outlets, the *New York Herald Tribune* agreed to handle syndication. Soon that company too reported continuing woes—cancellations, demands for lower rates, negative returns—and asked to alter the arrangement. Barton persevered with his column for the *Herald Tribune* until early 1934, when a world tour prompted an end to it.[64]

Alex Osborn affirmed that Barton made $50,000 a year writing magazine articles. His writing career was obviously no secret; BDO's house newsletter even celebrated it. "Not a month passes without something from his pen"—actually his "veteran typewriter"—appearing in *Collier's*, *Red Book*, *Woman's Home Companion*, or the *American Magazine*. This creativity flowered, it was suggested, not in spite of Barton's busyness in advertising but because of it, for "experience" provided soil for effective writing, as it had for Nathaniel Hawthorne the customs clerk or Joseph Conrad the ship captain. Barton himself demurred at the thought of writing full-time. "Having a family, I have never felt that I wanted to risk their three meals a day on my capacity to turn out something that would please an editor." Also, he advised an aspiring writer, "I like to be in active life and I think that I should dry up pretty fast as a writer if I were to leave the stimulation of city life and practical affairs." He suspected too that he was a "second rater" as a writer; thus writing made a "very good advocation" but not a career. In fact, he enjoyed it. A colleague, speaking anonymously at his death, said Barton did not stew over "whether one cigarette won out over another. He had his most fun when he went home and wrote—yes, he was a writer rather than a marketing man."[65]

Although Barton sometimes harbored misgivings about aspects of the advertising game, he liked it. Unlike the early pioneers in the profession, to whom the term "game" was *infra dig*, Barton, who advised that all work ideally should have an element of play, expressed no qualms about this jargon. Advertising was where the action was. Business was currently the "greatest single influence" in life, and advertising was "the voice of business." It shaped public opinion, so crucial to democracies. It paid well. It was like golf: "No one is ever good all the time, yet at frequent intervals one is supremely good." Advertising "offers the thrills of pioneering and gold hunting. It affords the fun of running the locomotive."[66]

However good he was at the "game," through his ads, his defenses of his profession, and his outside activities Barton conferred a patina of respectability on advertising that his fellow practitioners valued highly. Harford Powel, a friend, sometime employee, and thus a biased source, made precisely this point in nominating his friend for a prestigious award. Barton had elevated advertising prose, propagating worthy messages on behalf of valuable products and causes. But most important, his career was "of incalculable benefit to the younger men who are now able to look upon advertising as a profession rather than as a 'game.' . . ." Barton "has borne himself at all times in a way that advances the standards and ethics of the profession." He was praised in a publisher's house organ as someone who "makes us proud to be advertising men" and "is the outstanding advocate of what might be termed, 'advertising statesmanship.'"[67]

Barton had an astute understanding of his field. In the foreword to a 1936 book by a colleague, he listed the three "significant developments" in advertising in the preceding fifteen years (essentially the life span of BBDO): the founding and "phenomenal success" of the tabloid *New York Daily News*; the use of "picture 'strip' treatment" in advertising, which resembled newspaper comics; and radio. The first two spoke to the young, who drew ideas "not from the printed page, but from a succession of pictures—either on the screen or in the press. They are not type-minded; they are picture-minded." Similarly, the radio offered access to the buyer's brain through a previously unused route. Barton allowed that these trends might not suggest "the race is growing intellectually," but for those with goods to sell the issue was irrelevant.[68]

In both his advertising work and his general writing, by age forty Barton had achieved striking success. He was renowned as a writer of copy, and his agency marched at the front of the Madison Avenue parade. He held forth effusively in his tony office, one wall of which was a photo mural of Coney Island with an inset of the bleachers at a country baseball game—Barton's effort to stay connected to the public that read his ads.[69] He had (as we shall see) achieved fame as the author of a best-selling religious book. He consorted with presidents. He had friends in high places—Washington and especially New York. He was famous. He was well off financially. After a number of ventures in investment during the 1920s that produced scattered results, he decided to invest most of his money with State Street Investment Corporation in Boston.[70]

Renown in this age of ballyhoo had its price. One or more men went about the country claiming to be "Bruce Barton" (or his nephew), leaving manuscripts to be typed or published, buying cars, staying at resorts, cashing false checks, renting houses, and doing other mischief. The true "Barton" became a lodestone for scores of importunate callers. They included such "cranks" as "people who want to borrow money or be financed for one thing or another; people who should be in insane asylums," according to his secretary who guarded his door and time.[71]

Still, for Barton the mid-twenties were ripe times. He joined select clubs, rubbing elbows with prominent New Yorkers. He lived at desirable Manhattan addresses, moving in 1929 to 117 East 55th Street. He steadily improved his summer home in Foxboro, including the addition of a separate cabin where he could write. He played golf. His favorite foursome included M. H. Aylesworth of the National Broadcasting Company, Kent Cooper of the Associated Press, and John Wheeler of the North American Newspaper Alliance.[72] He was among those who played the inaugural round in 1933 when the Augusta National Golf Club opened its new course, co-designed by the champion Bobby Jones. He kept a horse to ride mornings in Central Park. He attended the shows and sporting events with which life in the 1920s effervesced for New York's fortunate classes. His name sometimes garnished gossip columns. A book review cited his opinions as a point of comparison to those of the author in question. An essayist called the editor of *Forbes'* magazine a "Scotch disciple of Bruce Barton."[73]

His family thrived. Esther and he had three children. Their first-born, son Randall (bearing Esther's maiden name) arrived in 1915; Betsey Alice was born in 1917; and Bruce Jr., nicknamed "Pete," completed the family in 1921. The Bartons lived well. After their first child was born they moved to Great Neck, Long Island, and Bruce commuted to work. But the city's attractions drew them back and the trek home was a burden: there was "an accumulation of between-the-acts battles at the theater" over whether to leave early. Finally a storm that left them snowbound in Manhattan convinced them to move back. They took a house on East Tenth Street. In 1925 they bought a house previously owned by Harvard College, on Fifty-fifth Street between Park and Lexington. At this exclusive location Esther Barton, skilled in home design, remodeled and presided, with ample domestic help, over a gracious residence, which eventually received a spread in *Town and Country*.[74]

One blight on the rosiness of young middle age and a busy family was the palpable aging of Barton's beloved parents. Reverend Barton retired from his Oak Park pulpit in August 1924, having held it for a full twenty-five years. He and Mrs. Barton had enjoyed the affection of their parishioners and their neighbors. They were able to travel, once going around the world, and they settled in their summer home in Foxboro. Esther Barton was growing frail, however, and on a sunny fall day in Foxboro in 1925, she took her morning walk, collapsed en route of a cerebral hemorrhage, bade farewell to her husband who had rushed to her rescue, and died. Condolences poured in from around the world—the hospital in China and the mission in India that she had aided, and others her kindnesses had caressed.[75]

Her son—prosperous, widely known, in demand for his writings, owning a vast circle of friends—was on course for a happy life. Looking back over his career four decades later, Louise MacLeod recalled "the lighter, gayer side of his nature . . . he's never been at all serious" and had a "natural conviviality. He's always enjoyed and liked people. . . ."[76]

But some burr still irritated the ease of his otherwise enviable life. Insomnia continued to deprive him of rest. In the mid-twenties his father poured out advice on how Bruce might conquer his ailment: exercise, leisure reading, prayer, reciting poetry, positive thinking, daydreaming about future aspirations. Bruce went off to rest-cure camps, places for overstressed businessmen to gain respite from the corporate grind through exercise and relaxation. For at least a decade he frequented Bill Brown's Browndale in upstate Garrison, New York. In his own name and pseudonymously, he even wrote its praises using themes that appeared in other writings. One testimonial declared that Browndale battled against "the great city . . . full of treacherous wiles," which lured enterprising men with its "rich prizes" but stole their health. By restoring it to them, Brown made himself "a friend of 4,000 Wives." In 1924 Barton took a long vacation in Wyoming, hoping that fishing and riding would bring sleep. (His brother Charles published a newspaper in that state.) In 1927 insomnia forced him to interrupt work to go away for a rest. In 1928, afflicted with his worst case of sleeplessness yet, he packed himself off to a clinic in Canada that thought insomnia was related to problems of digestion (but treated him by extracting his tonsils).[77]

One might suspect overwork as the culprit. That emerged as a theme in his rest-spa testimonials (though the maladies of urban living occupied more space in these recommendations than did fatigue from too much work). In some respects Barton was a dynamo—a public speaker who seemed to live on trains, a rapid producer of varied writings, a fount of ideas for clients, a friend of magnates and bootblacks. No one could accuse him of slacking off. Yet his close associates did not reprove him for working too hard—not for the historical record, at least. Charlie Brower, who took over BBDO's helm in 1957, declared that "Bruce might have been a truly great man, except for a small prejudice against too much work and too many hours." A like comment from an anonymous colleague adorned his obituary: "Bruce was a trifle lazy. He didn't sweat very much in his life."[78] Barton's sermons urging his readers not to fixate solely on the bottom line but to leave time to dig in the earth or watch trees sway in the wind, his paeans to Thoreau and to life in Foxboro, the injunctions not to squander the whole of life at the office—these may have contained an element of self-justification for his own life, which left plenty of room for golf, vacations, and a flexible daily schedule.

A close friend of Barton's described another long-term health problem: he was a "hypochondriac," convinced he was "the battlefield of all the germs in creation." One article about Barton described his "hobby" of going through the medicine cabinet and downing all the medicinal remnants of bottles and vials.[79] He did spend much time in the 1920s at various clinics and health spas. How much ill health was objective, how much subjective remains murky. The insomnia seems to have been authentic.

Mentions of insomnia fell sharply after the 1920s, though Barton continued to visit sanitariums in the 1930s. But other hardships would enter his life. In the meantime, thanks to a spate of writings that ushered business close to the altars of religion, and escorted religion into the world of business and advertising, Barton came to occupy an altogether more prominent niche in American life than merely the cofounder of a famous advertising agency.

4

The Gospel According to Bruce

TO 1925 Bruce Barton, now in his late thirties, had achieved much. He had enjoyed success and repute at the helm of *Every Week*, but that vessel's decommissioning had abbreviated any long editorial tack his career might have followed.[1] He continued to write magazine and newspaper articles in abundance, even as his new ad agency gained prestige and business on Madison Avenue. As he rose in advertising, on a parallel track he was gaining prominence as a public relations adviser to illustrious Republicans, including the president. His influence with other Republican political figures would persist well beyond the 1920s. All these activities established and sustained his celebrity.

But lasting fame befell him only in 1925, when he published *The Man Nobody Knows*. Without this book he would have rated sentences and paragraphs in chronicles of the politics in which he figured, and paragraphs, perhaps even pages, in treatments of advertising. Now the book and he jointly became a defining sign of the 1920s. Historians have seized on *The Man Nobody Knows* primarily to epitomize the ascendancy of a "business civilization." It does underscore the triumph of business in the decade, but at the time it did more than that. It established Barton not just as a herald for the coronation of business but as a guide to the complexities of maintaining religious faith in an increasingly secular world. Linking as it did the domain of the boardroom with that of the pulpit, the things that were Caesar's with the things that were God's, the book did help canonize business in the 1920s. But Barton's purpose ran mainly in the opposite direction: he hoped with his book—and his aspirations for it were modest—to re-connect the realm of the spirit with the world of hustle and com-merce. He may have ended by sanctifying business, but he intended to show how religion could be made modern and relevant to contempo-rary life.

That a churchman's son should discourse on religious topics comes as no surprise. Barton had done so many times before. It is not entirely clear what drove him to write *The Man Nobody Knows*, but driven he was. While editing *Every Week* he had pondered composing such a vol-ume, and its argument and subject matter were closely related to the small book he had written in 1914, *A Young Man's Jesus*. Many of the themes in *The Man* also appeared in his magazine articles.[2] His venture into advertising might qualify as more surprising than his inclination to religion, but only slightly so. As he often maintained, sons of the manse were raised amid quantities of good reading and writing; many in his age cohort in the agencies had clergyman fathers.

On a symbolic level, the path between First Congregational and Madison Avenue may have been even more deeply trodden. One of the emphases in Jackson Lears's cultural history of advertising, *Fables of Abundance*, is the important role of mystery in human life. The Protes-tant Reformation was aimed in part against the carnivalesque, and self-discipline and sobriety became values dear to Protestant modernity. But ambivalence persisted.

Mystery had earlier inhabited the realm of religion. As parts of the world moved toward modernity, away from land-based modes of life, even away from the producer orientation of the early nineteenth cen-tury, mystery found other spaces in life. Part of Lears's provocative ar-gument suggests that one by-product of the Protestant Reformation's flight from the icons of Catholicism was to allow room for the baubles of consumerism to replace such graven images as loci of magic. (This was not a full reversal: Lears notes that commercial fairs and carnivals had been twinned since around 1500; "the market place remained part

of an animated world—a mix of the miraculous and the carnivalesque.") While the advertising profession of the twentieth century
tried to distance itself from its literally carnivalesque roots in the age of
P. T. Barnum, one way or another the boomerang kept coming back.
Its defenders argued that advertising was about education and was thus
the abode of rationality, but a century of ads show that illusion, sug-
gestion, and magic remain tightly linked with it.[3] The world of the
spiritual and that of the material were never far apart in Barton's professional life.

   That spiritual world was one of light and laughter, not cloistered
dimness or sackcloth. Congregationalism might have Puritan parent-
age, but Barton, a very modern, liberal Congregationalist, rejected
Puritanism in virtually any form. There were exceptions and thus
conflict among held values. In politics, for instance, a sometimes Puritan Barton stood in for the modern Barton of business and religion.
He appreciated—and publicized—the "Puritan" heritage of Calvin
Coolidge.[4] He valued the old republican virtues of New England; his
father and he were both culturally New Englanders, even though the
Barton side of the family had steered clear of the region until the
1890s, and Bruce frequently took inspiration from the writings of
Emerson and Thoreau, not those of Jonathan Edwards.[5] He did cherish the work ethic, so firmly linked to Protestantism and the Puritans.
But Puritanism, broadly interpreted, challenged the modern ethic of
Madison Avenue, which valorized the new, the desirability of consumption, the importance of one's neighbors' views as against the
mind of God.

   The 1920s witnessed a frontal assault by American intellectuals and
opinion makers upon Puritanism in all forms. A few years earlier H. L.
Mencken had defined the creed as a fear "that someone, somewhere,
may be happy." The historian Charles Beard wrote that Puritanism
had expanded to explain "anything that interfere[d] with the new freedom, free verse, psychoanalysis, or even the double entendre."[6] Barton
sometimes joined in the attack. Speaking at an art exposition at Macy's
department store, he argued that "American art has suffered from the

Puritan repression of beauty." He blamed that cast of mind for "our dreary factories" and took heart in the fact that "beauty is the most important factor in modern advertising, and it has both material and aesthetic value." Perhaps his most heartfelt indictment of Puritanism came much later, at the 1954 funeral of Grantland Rice, the famed sportswriter, but he had in mind this earlier period. Barton placed his friend in a time when "the harsh rule of the Puritan tradition" was on the wane. "Yet some vestige of that rigid, fun-denying code of our ancestors remained." Work reigned and play was still "for boys and for fools." Fortunately Rice "helped mightily to break down" that "austere tradition." He was "the evangelist of fun, the bringer of good news about games." For Barton, Puritanism lay across enemy lines from his world of advertising and the modern good life.[7]

While the world of business and advertising bloomed in the 1920s, the realm of the spirit met with what the scholar Robert T. Handy called a "religious depression." For American religion it was a clamorous age. Many Protestant denominations experienced a wearing battle between modernists and fundamentalists. The modernist strain had emerged in the nineteenth century, comprising religious spokesmen who accepted modern science (notably evolution) and sought to reconcile it with the sacred, and who embraced the new (chiefly German) "higher criticism" of the Bible, which sought to place that source in its historical context and not take it literally. Fundamentalists rejected this turn. They took their name from a series of booklets, *The Fundamentals*, published in 1910–1915, which excoriated Darwinism and asserted, among other beliefs, the Bible's inerrancy. In 1925, the year *The Man Nobody Knows* was published, modernism and fundamentalism faced off over the issue of evolution in a Dayton, Tennessee, courtroom in the Scopes "Monkey Trial."[8] Reinhold Niebuhr, on his way to becoming the leading American theologian of his century, argued in 1927 that both modernism and fundamentalism were symptoms of "a psychology of defeat" that "has gripped the forces of religion."[9] The columnist-philosopher Walter Lippmann titled the first chapter of *A Preface to Morals*, his influential elegy on the 1920s, "The Problem of Unbelief."

Standing at the center of unease amid the unmet cravings of an age when "Whirl is King," he argued, was "modern man who has ceased to believe, without ceasing to be credulous." Niebuhr had similarly lamented the "great many moderns who are emancipated from every kind of religious discipline without achieving any new loyalty which might qualify the brutal factors in human life."[10]

The shrinking world of believers, especially Protestants, was also being pounded by deep-running currents of change in the envisioning of Jesus. Christ had not, according to the historian Stephen Prothero, been especially central to the worship of the early English colonists. He obviously was essential, always, to Christian salvation, but New England Puritan thinkers had viewed Jesus largely in abstract terms while keeping their theology anchored more in the Old than the New Testament. From several causes, change would come. Thomas Jefferson razored out those portions of the Gospels in which he could believe, collating a volume of the teachings of Jesus that epitomized for him what was of value in Christianity. American evangelicals of the nineteenth century placed their emphasis on a more personal (less theological) Savior. In the same era, American women found their "separate sphere" in churchly activities, and this emphasis tended to produce a Jesus notably meek and mild. Around 1900 there came a reaction to a Jesus whom many men found too feminine. Different sorts of Christs entered the lists: a warrior come with the sword, a carpenter to lead the working class. Bruce Barton stood squarely with those Christians who insisted on a masculine Jesus. He was not the first to deliver such a Christ, but his may have been the most strongly figured of the genre.[11]

Barton did not plunge into these doctrinal battles and often waved them aside, but his allegiance was clear. He marched with the modernists, like his father, from whom he continued to draw guidance for his religious views and writings. Both Bartons were theological liberals. Reverend Barton was impatient of disputes over dogma within and between denominations and worked to blur the boundaries between them. In a sequel to *The Man Nobody Knows*, Bruce reviewed the New

Testament and found no support on Jesus' part for fine points of doctrine. Such views could hardly endear him to articulators of fundamentalism.[12] Neither did his beliefs put him in good grace with
Calvinists, or even with Arminians. "We are all going to Heaven," he
would declare at a later time. When a Catholic priest "chided" him for
his theological shortcuts, Barton shrugged off controversy but asked this
priest of "the Infallible Church": "Will there be any good eighteen-
hole golf courses in Heaven?" The reply: "My son, I think there will be,
and I shall meet you there."[13]

   Although it had been more than a decade since he had labored for
church weeklies, Barton never deserted the religious fold. His writings,
including his *Every Week* editorials and contributions to other magazines, continued to chew at religious topics. Many themes and homilies found in *The Man Nobody Knows* appeared first in these articles.
As early as 1914 Barton had written that "the preacher is really a salesman," conflating the pulpit and sales counter as he would in the 1920s.
His war-related work had encompassed the YMCA and the Salvation
Army. In the early twenties, as he was winning clients to BDO, he was
also communicating with spiritual leaders. He queried the prominent
liberal divine, Reverend Harry Emerson Fosdick of Union Theological Seminary, about various questions that would figure in his writings.
(Was there "a distinction between business and social service?" "Does
it do any good to pray?" "What can I believe?")[14]

   These probings led ultimately to *The Man Nobody Knows*. Barton
marveled at his own "temerity" in writing it. Both his father and he had
long addressed the need for a Jesus fit for their age—a loving, manly
Jesus. Reverend Barton had a pivotal influence on the project: he encouraged Bruce to pursue it, drafted an outline, and furnished the theology and sense of Jesus that informed the book.[15] As an editor, Bruce
had approached "several well-known authors" with the idea, but none
took it up. Eventually he broached the notion to Gertrude B. Lane,
editor-in-chief of *Woman's Home Companion* and a close friend, while
she was visiting him in Foxboro. She urged him on, gave continuing
editorial advice, and ultimately published the book first as a serial in

the *Companion*. Barton completed a first draft in 1923 and a revision
by late March 1924. He had much help and encouragement from his
father, who had written an earlier life of Christ.

Anticipating its capacity to offend, Barton had his manuscript
carefully vetted. He gave it to his mother, saying he would "burn it up
and forget it" if she found it "irreverent" in any way—but both his parents approved it. He also welcomed advice from Professor George B.
Hotchkiss, an authority on advertising at NYU, who could see why
some thought the work "radical." Hotchkiss suspected it would "pro-
voke a lot of controversy" and might "make a few enemies," and urged
Barton to remove the discussion of Jesus' manly qualities. Similarly,
Harford Powel, a sometime BDO employee, found it inoffensive but
urged caution in the portrayal of Jesus as a salesman. But Barton had
written the book "distinctly to men," having had doubts as to whether
it would appeal to women readers. And so salesmanship remained in
the book.[16]

Barton had next to select a publisher. The choice came down to
the International Book Company, Scribner's, and Bobbs-Merrill. He
had promised a good friend at International a chance to see the book.
Well connected with the publishing industry, Barton had dealt with
Scribner's over a book of President Coolidge's speeches timed for the
1924 election. There he negotiated with Maxwell Perkins, the famed
editor who groomed the work of Ernest Hemingway, F. Scott Fitzgerald, and other luminaries. Perkins saw the book's sales potential, but
Charles Scribner himself, "with his long background of serious religious publishing," was appalled and ordered it rejected. Perkins re-
gretfully told Barton the book was "too advanced for us." *The Man* was
"in reality reverent" but would "shock" many of Scribner's clientele.
(The year would still be good to Perkins: in 1925 he published Fitzgerald's *The Great Gatsby*.)[17] Bobbs-Merrill, a less prestigious house,
nonetheless made a sturdy run at Barton's book. Its vice president,
D. L. Chambers, learned of the project from Gertrude Lane, thought
it a "thunderingly good idea," and saw a strong market for it. One of
his editors bubbled that Barton had "taken Jesus out of the stained

glass window and made Him a man." Despite being "hard-boiled" from twenty-five years in the business, the editor confessed he was "as nervous as a debutante" awaiting Barton's decision. "I must publish that book." No one else, he guaranteed, "could center the force of his drive on one title—your title—as could we." Barton gave his book to the Indianapolis publisher.[18]

Written in sometimes biblical cadence but in modern language, and with the terse sentences and dramatic flourish of his advertising copy, Barton's book enthralled readers. The preface, "How It Came to Be Written," depicted a "little boy," obviously himself, and his "hour of revolt" in Sunday school—against the tedium but even more against "the pale young man with flabby forearms and a sad expression" who passed for Jesus in these surroundings. He preferred "winners" like Daniel, "standing off the lions," or David with his sling. "He wondered if David could whip Jeffries" (Jim Jeffries, the onetime heavyweight boxing champion). The Sunday school Jesus was "sissified" and for girls. This cankered depiction of Sundays appears to have matched reality: years later a contemporary wrote to reminisce about a pencil "duel" that Barton and another bored classmate had conducted. Lead that broke off from Barton's weapon had left a blue mark still visible on the other lad's skin.[19] The boy of the introduction, now a "businessman," in maturity discovered that Jesus was no "physical weakling" nor "Kill-Joy." Far from "a failure," Jesus "picked up twelve men from the bottom ranks of business and forged them into an organization that conquered the world." And so the grown-up little boy, Bruce Barton, wrote the book.

Chapter One called Jesus a modern "Executive." Tellingly for Barton, when the disciples urged Jesus to rain fire on a village that turned them away, He responded simply with eloquent silence and led them elsewhere. Like other famous leaders ancient and modern (Barton interspersed modern mortal examples in his story), Jesus came from a rural village and exemplified "the eternal miracle . . . the awakening of the internal consciousness of power" that often came to small-town boys and made them realize the limits of their surroundings. So too,

Jesus "knew that he was bigger than Nazareth." But during the forty days in the wilderness and at other times, Jesus, like other leaders, knew doubt but conquered it. He came to command through "personal magnetism." He knew how to choose and keep disciples, often from unlikely sources. He had infinite "patience."

Chapter Two, "The Outdoor Man," disposed of the Jesus on Sunday school walls. He swung an adze in Joseph's carpenter's shop, lived in the open air, fasted forty days in the wilds, had the strength to scourge the money changers from the temple, and embodied vibrant health, curing by charismatic example. Barton chided the church for dwelling on Mary and ignoring Joseph. "The same theology which has painted the son as soft and gentle to the point of weakness, has exalted the feminine influence in its worship, and denied any large place to the masculine." Men accepted Jesus as a leader with strength, and women too; "and women are *not* drawn by weakness."

Chapter Three depicted a "Sociable Man" who "loved to be in the crowd." Jesus conversed, joked, and dined with high and low, virtuous and fallen. He attracted young and old, lepers and centurions. He was "the most popular dinner guest in Jerusalem." It was false that he never laughed. A sad Savior, Barton explained, was conveyed by the early theologians, who "lived in sad days." No Puritan, Jesus enforced no code. "His God was no Bureau, no Rule Maker, no Accountant" but rather "a happy God, wanting His sons and daughters to be happy." The chapter's defining event was the wedding feast of Cana, where Jesus changed water into wine "to keep a happy party from breaking up too soon, to save a hostess from embarrassment." At the Last Supper he said, "Be of good cheer."

Barton outlined Jesus' "Method" in a chapter that linked Christianity and democracy. Treating religion as a product (for which, like all others, supply preceded demand), Barton said that what Jesus had added to it was to invite humanity "to stand upright and look at God face to face! He called upon men to throw away fear. . . . It is the basis of all revolt, all democracy. For if God is the Father of all men, then *all* are his children. . . . No wonder the authorities trembled."

That Jesus delivered his message to all sectors of society, Pharisee or Samaritan, and spoke to listeners in their own language, in terms they could understand, clinched Barton's point.

Jesus communicated effectively by "His Advertisements." Perhaps no chapter irritated Barton's critics more than this one, which seemed on its face self-serving and self-referential. But Barton argued that as the doctor focused on the miracles of healing, the preacher on the Sermon on the Mount, the "agitator" on how Jesus "denounced the rich," the Communist on the disciples' "common purse," why should the advertising profession hang back? "The first four words ever uttered, 'Let there be light,' constitute its charter." Jesus grasped "that all good advertising is news." Everything he did or said translated into punchy headlines; Barton filled the chapter with might-have-been headlines from the *Capernaum News*. Today Jesus would preach in the marketplace, but the modern marketplace, said Barton, was the daily or magazine, the latter "a bazaar filled with the products of the world's work." The parables provided models of modern advertising: terse, dramatic, in the idiom of the auditors. "Jesus hated prosy dullness."

Chapter Six hailed Jesus as "The Founder of Modern Business." To confirm this claim, Barton quoted Jesus, adding his own italics: "Wist ye not that I must be about my father's *business?*" Jesus' business ethic chiefly stressed "service." "'Whosoever will be great among you, shall be your minister,' he said, 'and whosoever of you will be the chiefest, shall be servant of all.'" Here followed Barton's fullest apologia for modern business: when it succeeded, it was because ambitious businessmen provided better service than their competitors. Contemporary examples—George W. Perkins (New York Life), Henry Ford, and Theodore N. Vail (AT&T)—thrived not by fixating on the bottom line but by losing themselves in their calling, in "service." The ultimate service involved self-denial, as when Jesus refused the crown. "In that hour of crisis he proved his right to be the silent partner in every modern business. . . ." For years Barton had been acclaiming successful businessmen as people who understood that "service" was their mission; if they pursued it single-mindedly rather than grubbing for dollars, the dollars would naturally follow. He often quoted such a corporate leader: "Did you ever notice that the man who starts out with the deliberate intention of making a lot of money seldom makes very much?" But "render a real service" and money took care of itself.[20] In *The Man Nobody Knows*, Barton attributed a variant of the remark to Ford.

The book's final, bittersweet chapter depicts Jesus as rejected by his hometown, doubted even by his family, deserted by the crowds, surrendering to the soldiers, accepting a known fate. It does not discuss doctrine so much as underscore calm heroism. Those who pictured Jesus "as weak, as a man of sorrows, uninspiring, glad to die" were wrong and should consult the final scene, when a crucified thief "looked into his dying eyes and saluted him as king."

The Man Nobody Knows stressed the humanity of Jesus. Its admirers lauded Barton for that; critics ridiculed it. Barton strove to illustrate his case with the achievements of mortals. He invoked Lincoln frequently. Other statesmen, business leaders, even athletes made cameo appearances. Historians ever since have remarked at how Barton moved Jesus into the pantheon of business and, conversely, supplied sanctification to statesmen of industry. They have noted Barton's transubstantiation of Jesus into the corporate boardroom, the emphasis on "service" as the halo crowning the good businessman. They less often point out that Barton did criticize corporate types (generic ones) who did not live up to these standards—those who squinted nearsightedly at only the bottom line or their own salaries and promotions. (Barton placed Judas in these ranks: not an evil man, merely one of limited vision—a bookkeeper mentality.) True success was found only by those who lost themselves in service.

Other leitmotifs surface in the book which reflect enduring elements of Barton's thinking. There is a fixation on the dilemma of ambitious small-town boys, sensing their own powers and the limits of the boonies, who must seek their destinies in the city. Jesus did so in *The Man Nobody Knows*. George Groton did so in Barton's novel, and in other writings Barton pointed to this demographic shift as a central dynamic of modern life. (One might think from such allusions that Oak Park, ten miles from Chicago's Loop and well connected by rail, was a hick town.)

Barton disdained controversy over dogma. He often said that many of the issues most disputed by religious doctrinaires were not issues to Jesus, who said nothing, for example, about the Virgin Birth. Despite this anti-sectarianism, his Jesus is, not surprisingly, mainline Protestant. The book conveys aromas of displeasure with Catholic doctrine and practice, notably the heavy presence of incense and ceremony, the emphasis on Mary at Joseph's expense, and the weak, pallid image of Jesus in sacred art. The book also contains slighting remarks about Jews. Zacchaeus is a "little Jew," the Pharisees lost the spirit for the letter, the rabble demanded a political rather than a spiritual savior. In other corners of his life, Barton made occasional allusions to Jewish stereotypes, but they were tame compared to those of some of his friends and mild for the era. Although his father published an article in Henry Ford's anti-Semitic *Dearborn Independent* that may have been occasioned by the fact that he was temporarily filling a Detroit pulpit. Barton himself censured Ford in a 1928 speech. He admired the man's prowess in making cars but termed him a fanatic and "almost a fool" in other regards, notably his anti-Semitism.[21] For his day, Barton ranks toward the high end on tolerance. Later events in his life would confirm this evaluation. Not that he was perfect.

The Man Nobody Knows also ascribed rather traditional roles to women. Mostly their job was to follow and adore strong men. Barton's Jesus had sex appeal, and he meant his book as a corrective to an overly feminized Christ. The author found himself in crowded company among those who regretted that American Protestantism, since early in the nineteenth century, had adapted to the growing influence of women, and its Jesus had become less manly. In the context of World War I, Theodore Roosevelt had rejected the notion of a pacifist Savior, stressing how (in a scene much as Barton had described) Jesus "armed himself with a scourge of cords and drove the money-changers from the Temple."[22]

Barton also attributes to Jesus a sort of "grace under pressure"—a quality often ascribed to the heroes of the novels of his fellow Oak Parker Ernest Hemingway. The book's politics are democratic, mildly Progressive perhaps, but not socialist. Its villains tend to be bureaucrats, rule worshipers, a priesthood chained to formalism, rituals, and codes. Jesus and the book's other heroes, while taught by experience, seem to be natural leaders with vast personal magnetism. There may be some tension between the theme of democracy and that of inborn leadership. (Both apparently go naturally with small-town boys.) While the book maintains Barton's rejection of "Puritanism," its canonization of "service" brings it close to the Puritan doctrine of "calling" which rang out from many a seventeenth-century New England pulpit. All this analysis may exceed what so feathery a book ought to bear, but since so many people read it—more than read much of the literature we now deem emblematic of the 1920s—one might argue that the attitudes it expressed received circulation at least as wide as those of Fitzgerald's Nick Carraway.

In its message, *The Man Nobody Knows* resembles *A Young Man's Jesus* of a decade earlier. Both books emphasized the same particulars: Jesus' strength (work as a carpenter, life outdoors), sociability, rejection of Puritanism, formalism and the depredations of the priestly caste (banquets are fine, gouging widows in the temple court is bad), natural executive ability, courage under duress. The earlier book, the product of a twenty-eight-year-old, may make a bit more of the fact that Jesus was a young man. The latter book offers more detail about Jesus' executive abilities—and the talk of "His Advertisements" is entirely novel. *The Man* is also more snappily written and briefer, and it is more empathetic to the modern man of business.

Reviews and notices of Barton's book were largely positive. The *Boston Herald* lauded his boldness in humanizing Jesus. The *New York Times* weighed in with a positive assessment (shocking but "reverent," novel, written in "crisp advertising English"), though it took issue with Barton's felt need to stress Jesus' "success" in what could be termed business. The *New York Sun* declared: "Not more than two people since Matthew, Mark, Luke and John, have known equally well how to reach the heart with the real story of the Christ."[23]

The Man Nobody Knows owed its vast appeal to something more than reviewers' praise. It anchored news items in other parts of the paper—about sermons based on it, visits by Barton to the city in question, even references in gossip columns. Word-of-mouth played a large role. A New York Central Pullman porter told Barton that he had seen as many as six copies of the book being read in his car on a single trip. A rider on the Long Island Railroad reported a conversation during one trip in which a fellow commuter was eulogizing the book. One admirer spoke of the peregrinations of her now-lost copy and told Barton, "Your book is going the rounds in the way similar to a 'chain letter.'"[24]

A number of notable readers expressed their appreciation. The president of Yale wrote with huzzahs for Barton's "sorely needed" emphasis on "the masculine character" of Jesus. Frank Buchman, future founder of Moral Rearmament, called the book one of the "three outstanding contributions to my life and work." Frank Crane, a prominent clergyman and another author noted for uplift, offered praise. Liberal Christians naturally applauded the book. Years later, the Methodist G. Bromley Oxnam recounted his "high esteem" for its author.[25]

Ordinary readers wrote in gratitude. Some suspected divine inspiration had played a role in the book's writing—one surmised that Jesus had dictated it to Barton. A woman testified that the book "touched me profoundly." Another woman, raised in a framework of stern belief, came so to fear the Second Coming that she lay awake nights, "dreading every sound in case it was the return of Christ." But Barton's book (and a sequel) taught her that "God does not give us Fear—but Power—and Love—and a sound mind." A letter to a church periodical chided a critical reviewer: if he "has done one thousandth as much good in his entire ministry as Bruce Barton . . . he is a remarkable and unusual minister." During World War II a soldier wrote that *The Man Nobody Knows* cleared the fog shrouding his religious path and "made my outlook on life and religion a happy one."

Barton, his publisher, even BDO co-workers and clients promoted *The Man Nobody Knows* energetically. Bobbs-Merrill printed brochures laden with blurbs. Partner Alex Osborn passed along an account of a Buffalo bookstore's campaign to persuade business executives to purchase the book for gifts. President Calvin Coolidge received two copies; the book made the rounds of his official family, and after his wife and he spoke kindly of the book to Barton's father, D. L. Chambers of Bobbs-Merrill had hopes that Coolidge "would say something that we could quote." Nothing came of this effort.[26] The publisher also hunted up endorsements from religious leaders. Dean of the University of Chicago's Divinity School, Shailer Mathews, offered kind words that were duly exploited, and Bobbs-Merrill detailed a man to attend Dr. S. Parkes Cadman's meetings in the hope of questioning him about the book and then spreading the news. Eventually, they obtained an endorsement from Cadman, who was president of the Federated Council of Churches of Christ. This and other approving comments by clergy were paraded across promotional materials. By summer 1926 the book was being serialized in newspapers, stimulating further sales.[27]

Barton attempted to spice up the promotion of his book. He drafted an appeal to ministers that *The Man* (and its sequel) be used in Sunday school classes and asked them to ponder the point that "the Christian Church is the greatest business organization the world has ever had." He suggested that "every employer in the United States ought to send a copy of this book for Christmas to the ten most valuable men in his organization" to give them "a new thrilling conception of modern business." A number of admirers did give away multiple copies. An executive of the National Mazda Lamp company who invited 125 Detroit manufacturers to his summer place put a copy of the book at each guest's seat at the table. A businessman in Philadelphia sent copies to twenty friends. The head of Ralston Purina intended to give one hundred copies as Christmas presents. When Barton's sequel was published, a four-page brochure was printed connecting the two books, but especially aimed at recapping some of the pivotal points in *The Man* (the little Sunday school prisoner impatient with the "meek

and lowly" Jesus, Jesus as a "real executive") and displaying the testimonials of prominent divines.[28]

Despite all the positive comments and mushrooming sales, the
book encountered withering criticism from across the theological
spectrum. Catholics reacted hotly to the earlier serialized version in
Woman's Home Companion, its editor Gertrude Lane reported. Barton
worked out a form letter to turn away their wrath. He was, said his partner Durstine, "a very sensitive guy," and reviews in Catholic—and
other—circles "really got under his skin."[29]

Reactions from fundamentalist ranks were savage. One reader
called it "one of the worst books published in recent years."[30] Dr. Arno
C. Gaebelein said the book "has no marked literary value nor has it a
true spiritual message." In modernizing and secularizing Jesus, Barton
"stabs, whenever he can, at the very heart of Christianity" by taking
"the Cross of Christ and His substitutionary sacrifice" and resurrection
out of Christianity.[31] A pamphlet by Amos H. Gottschall argued that
Barton's title and subtitle (*A Discovery of the Real Jesus*) "require prodi-
gious audacity, even for an advertising man. . . . If conceit, imagination, and the use of catchy phrases constituted true wisdom, then
Mr. Barton might be considered wise and a safe teacher." Gottschall
quoted a number of theological authorities who were offended by Barton's proposition that Jesus was hitherto unknown. Scripture posited a
known Jesus. So did faith, through which "millions of Christians . . .
know Christ well and savingly." This was the genteel part of the ob-
jection, which moved on to reprove Barton for sacrilege, to counter his
portrait of a sociable, muscular, non-"meek" Jesus with New Testament text, to call one of Barton's claims worthy of a "rank infidel."
This was not black news to Barton; one of his promotional ideas was
to have the famous fundamentalist radio preacher John Roach Straton
"roast it."[32]

Not only fundamentalists but sober traditionalists reached a negative verdict. Reverend C. E. Wagner of New York's West Side Methodist
Episcopal Church fulminated that Barton epitomized the modern dis-
pensation to turn religion into "sanctified commercialism." Wagner

located *The Man* with such symptoms of the disease as the "Rotarian pastors" who guaranteed "grit and *gold*" to those who vowed to attend church regularly or called Moses "a real estate man." Parts of Wagner's argument echoed secular critics of Barton's apology for business, but his concern was more fully directed against mingling the things of Caesar with those of God. Borrowing from Wagner, in a sermon accompanied by slides, a New York City Presbyterian pastor charged that "Rotarian preachers throughout the country inspired by" Barton's writings were "making of religion a sanctified commercialism with Jesus a Big Business Man and Christianity a Babbitt cult." A similar criticism from the side of religious belief was entitled "The Rotarian Nobody Knows." The rejection of Barton's alignment of Jesus with business also arose in religion's liberal wing. A leader of New York City's Society for Ethical Culture, while sympathetic to the tedium of "the old Sunday schools" and "droning organ music," found little gained "by turning the Heavenly Choir into a 'sing' by a Rotary club." The speaker knew of no book "so shamelessly out of harmony with its subject." In an unsigned review titled "Jesus as Efficiency Expert," Detroit pastor Reinhold Niebuhr flayed the book for its smug sermon about "service."[33]

By the same token, those of secular bent, the "smart set" of the 1920s who criticized the small-mindedness of "Main Street" (as in Sinclair Lewis's novel of that title), saw Barton not as a liberator of religion from fundamentalism or doctrinal hairsplitting but as an apologist for business, for the "Rotarian" mind, for the nation's Babbitts whom Lewis had etched so sharply. H. L. Mencken, the debunking columnist and smartest of the smart set, referred cryptically to *The Man Nobody Knows* in a piece on the banality of the typical businessman's daily life. It took its fun at the expense of those who "argue that John the Baptist was the first Kiwanian."[34] The author of the chapter on literary achievements in a yearbook covering 1926 dismissed *The Man* as "of no permanent value." In the *New Republic*, Gilbert Seldes called Barton facile and "ignorant of the history of Christianity." He did credit Barton with "seriously trying to sell Jesus to America because Jesus was businesslike," but concluded that the author "is so interested in making him a companionable and energetic Son of Man (read Brother Rotarian) that he must despoil him of all the attributes of the Godhead."[35] Later still, news correspondent William Henry Chamberlin, a supporter of the Bolshevik Revolution turned critic, poked fun at this "amusing" book, which he deemed "impregnated with the spirit of the time." It sought to "'sell' Jesus as a pioneer Rotarian to the contemporary generation of back-slapping, slogan-shouting salesmen" exemplified by Sinclair Lewis's Babbitt.[36] Some of these criticisms Barton took to heart. When a new edition was being planned ten years later, he wanted to remove the chapter on advertising, which had attracted the bulk, Barton believed, of all the criticisms and was "not important to the general theme."[37]

Despite a cacophony of criticism, a larger group of readers and reviewers applauded the book. Max Ascoli, the refugee from Mussolini's Italy who went on to edit *The Reporter*, recalled that *The Man Nobody Knows* was "one of the first books he had read upon reaching the free soils of America after escaping . . . the ire of Mussolini. . . ." It was "part of his psychological introduction to America," and he "enjoyed it thoroughly." A number of servicemen encountered the book in a cheap military edition during World War II and wrote Barton in appreciation. In 1950 a woman wrote to thank the author. Until four years before, even though schooled in a convent, she had been an agnostic. It was only after reading *The Man* that "a whole spiritual illumination came." One clergyman/educator surmised three decades later that the book "rendered a significant service in the renewed awakening of the laity in the affairs of our churches and the religious life of our country."[38]

Assailed from the religious right and the cultural left, Barton's book would seem to have needed armor-plated covers to survive. Yet if its author cried on the way to the bank, he had numerous occasions for tears. The book sold, and sold well. It made the nonfiction best-seller list for 1925 (fourth place) and 1926 (number one). After it passed its second anniversary, one story marveled at this "third year of its career as a best seller," proof that it was "not . . . a flash across the sky, but an inspirational, understandable book for long time to come."[39] At the time it outsold most of the books later defined as central to the culture of the age, including F. Scott Fitzgerald's *The Great Gatsby*. It remained on *Publishers Weekly*'s best-seller list for eighty weeks.

In treating religion, *The Man Nobody Knows* was no novelty. Books of its kind were published and sold in numbers in the "decadent" twenties. In 1921 Robert Keable's *Simon Called Peter* ranked fifth among fiction best-sellers. (Sinclair Lewis's *Babbitt*, thought to represent and skewer the age, lagged in tenth place; it moved to third a year later.) Giovanni Papini's *The Life of Christ*, a perspective at variance with Barton's, made the list from 1923 through 1925 (though in the latter year it ranked behind *The Man*). Edgar Guest's *The Light of Faith* stood ninth in the nonfiction category in 1926, the year *The Man* was first. The next year, when Barton's book had fallen from the heights, Sinclair Lewis's corrosive novel about an evangelist, *Elmer Gantry*, was number one in fiction sales—a very different perspective on religion. In 1928 the biographer Emil Ludwig published *The Son of Man*; it spent some weeks on the list but had less impact than his other studies of men like Napoleon and Goethe.[40]

Multiple editions of *The Man Nobody Knows* made sales over the years a bit hard to track. The book sold more than 250,000 copies in the first eighteen months. By 1944 nearly 487,000 copies had been printed, between Bobbs-Merrill (186,000) and others put out by Review of Reviews, Grosset and Dunlap, Triangle Books, and Pocket Books. In 1938 Grosset and Dunlap produced an edition that combined *The Man* and *The Book*. By 1959, when a new edition was being readied, sales figures totaled 726,890, if not more, in nine different editions.[41] The book also had an international life. It sold well in England, and, in translation, Germany and Scandinavia; there were also editions in Italian and Japanese.[42] For the rest of the twentieth century, *The Man* was in print more often than not—in whole, in part, in combination with other works.

Why, ultimately, did *The Man Nobody Knows* cut such a swath through a secularizing age? Part of the answer lies in the fact that

Barton escorted it to market with canny public relations touches, a task made easier by the fact that he was already a prince of Madison Avenue and a prominent figure. But the book had more than adept PR going for it. It filled a broadly felt need. Walter Lippmann's comment that Americans had cast aside some of their beliefs but not their need to believe, that they still felt a "vacancy," was astute. Like prisoners set free, they "stagger out in trackless space under a blinding sun." Church attendance had fallen, in Lippmann's view, because Americans doubted "that they were going to meet God when they go to church."[43] Barton was hardly anti-church, but his gospel suggested that God could be found elsewhere. Indeed, his Jesus preached in the marts and in the byways of daily life. He offered a way to hold a faith to those distracted or unsettled by the cannonading between fundamentalists and modernists. It was an easy, fun-loving, sociable, sunlit gospel that allowed space for religion but did not crowd out "progress."

The book also helped launch Barton's "career" in movies. In the 1920s film was boisterously elbowing other media aside in the contest for public attention. Barton had a couple of bit parts in the story of the emergence of this medium. Plans were afoot for him to assist the renowned director D. W. Griffith on a religious picture to be made in the Famous Players–Lasky studios. He came up with several ideas, including a treatment that presented the biblical version and a modern updating of the story of Saul, David, and Bathsheba that would run parallel through the movie. These projects fell through, but rumors and stories about supposed Barton motion picture products persisted, often to his embarrassment; still, he ended $5,000 the richer for his unfilmed contributions.[44]

He did get to Hollywood. With his penchant for filming biblical extravaganzas, Cecil B. DeMille wanted to use *The Man Nobody Knows* as a basis for his film *King of Kings*, and to have Barton's advice. Barton agreed to be a consultant in 1926, but only if he could bring along his wife and if his father were hired too. He accepted because it was crucial that "the modern world . . . rediscover Jesus not as the sad unhappy figure of the artists but as the strong young carpenter[,] the friend of little children[,] the happy sharer in all life's normal activities and pleasures[,] the great companion." These Hollywood days were exciting. At times the set was zoolike: DeMille's secretary gushed at how well "the leopards behaved." There was some arm wrestling over DeMille's itch to script a "love affair between Mary Magdalene and Judas, for which there is no authority whatever." Reverend Barton wrote about this contretemps in Henry Ford's *Dearborn Independent,* in an article otherwise rhapsodic about the experience. DeMille agreed to "soften" the plot device and wished ruefully that Dr. Barton had seen the final cut before writing the piece. The Bartons all seemed to have enjoyed their Hollywood interlude and emerged from it unscandalized and uneaten by camera-savvy wildlife.[45]

With Roy Durstine, Barton had created a film company, Better Day Pictures, in 1922. They made a handful of short silent films, apparently of an "editorial" nature, for which Barton wrote scenarios, but they lost money and the company remained in limbo until it was dissolved, along with Barton's $5,225 investment, in 1931. *The Man Nobody Knows* also served as the basis for a six-reel silent film of the same name (produced by Pictorial Clubs in 1925), for which Barton wrote the titles. The film was an atmospheric travelog, without actors, showing "the places where Jesus lived and worked and the same kind of people he knew."[46]

The Man Nobody Knows took little time to move from being the object of praise or polemic to the symbol for an age—an age that was assuming its recognizable character swiftly, if not concurrently. Critics of *The Man* sometimes belittled it as a product of its time, and its time was one of rampant business dominance. The *New York Herald Tribune* headlined a year-end review "Big Business Leads in Events in United States During 1925." It cited President Coolidge's speech arguing that business "is the work of the world" and "has for its main reliance truth and faith and justice," and then the high points of Barton's portrait of Jesus.[47] Soon Barton's book became a byword for various trends located in the 1920s.

Variants of the phrase "The———Nobody Knows" became a running wisecrack and parlor game. Remarking on the growing season, the humorist Frank Sullivan wrote gratuitously of people who "'know their eggs' or 'know their onions,' but nobody seems to know the potato, with the possible exception of Bruce Barton." Another columnist referred to Barton's Oak Park as "the Suburb Nobody Knows." Barton himself encouraged the fad by suggesting that the McClure Syndicate publicize his newspaper column with the label "The Man Everybody Reads." The author of a *New Yorker* piece on Texas Guinan, the famed speakeasy proprietress, wanted to introduce her to Barton so he could title his next book "The Girl Everybody Knows." A well-wisher suggested another book, to be titled "The Place Nobody Goes." An article about him was headlined, "The Man Every One Knows." (One of the decisions Barton made as the book was nearing publication was to drop the title "The Man *Whom* Nobody Knows.") Barton dubbed his next offering *The Book Nobody Knows* and considered naming the one that followed *The Religion Nobody Knows.*[48]

Barton became an icon of the popular culture. With *The Man* he had won prominence in a third field, religion, as well as in politics and business. He did not segregate them: as he brought the macho drama of business into the realm of religion, so he expounded frequently on the importance of morality and character in business and politics. And the media acknowledged his competence to minister in all three. His books and articles, his speeches, his random observations became grist for public comment. To launch their own articles, columnists snapped up his sayings like chum tossed to porpoises. His statement that "the world is owned by men who cross bridges [i]n their imaginations miles and miles in advance of the procession" prompted a letter to the editor stressing the importance of vocational choice in high school. The *Atlantic Monthly* asked him to review Ernest Hemingway's classic-to-be, *The Sun Also Rises.* Skipping over his slight connection with the author, Barton praised the book mightily, calling its characters "amazingly real and alive." He called Hemingway "the freshest new voice since Frank Norris, excepting [Ring] Lardner and [Sinclair] Lewis," but hoped he might turn his talents to a book about "more respectable people."[49]

Barton himself inspired a character in a novel. Written by his friend Harford Powel, Jr., *The Virgin Queene* opens on "Barnham Dunn, high priest of modern advertising" and "preacher of uplift," tapping out twelve ads for a magazine, all pegged to readers' letters. The thirteenth of these, plus the cumulative weight of sheaves of "optimistic messages, with genial commands to let some public-spirited corporation solve the problems of the reader" and other vexations, drives him round the bend. He hurls his typewriter to the floor, sacks his Early American office, and takes indeterminate leave of his agency, fleeing to England. There he buys a manor dating from Henry VIII and hires a charming and able factotum, Major Grey. Dunn settles in, shudders as his prep-school daughter develops a crush on his majordomo, and writes a play (one of Barton's true ambitions) that brilliantly mimics Shakespeare. Grey transcribes the typescript into a mock period manuscript, to which he forges the Bard's name, then buries it. Soon it is accidentally "discovered" and universally attributed to Shakespeare; Dunn's lark becomes an international sensation and triggers litigation and hoopla. In despair, Dunn burns the manuscript, but the play is a best-seller brought to Broadway with three of the famed Barrymores in the cast. The book has a happy if chastening ending. Daughter Ann and the Major are engaged. Able to convince no one that he wrote the play (nor even get a ticket to see it), Dunn slips cheerfully back into his agency, resuming work on the very ad that drove him away in the first place.[50]

Barton's prominence transcended obscure novels. He became a lasting representative of his age. The pattern was set in 1931, after the current of 1920s prosperity plummeted into the long lightless shaft of the depression. When the popular historian Frederick Lewis Allen published *Only Yesterday*, his tongue-in-cheek inquest into the fads and foibles of the 1920s, his chapter on "Coolidge Prosperity" noted the "new veneration" accorded to business, in which church and counting house virtually swapped places. His standout evidence of this merging of worlds was *The Man Nobody Knows*, which argued Christianity's "resemblance to business." He quoted from it, including the line that became obligatory, that Jesus "picked up twelve men from the bottom ranks of business and forged them into an organization that conquered the world."[51]

Allen's interpretation etched deep channels in the historical landscape.[52] Most subsequent treatments of the 1920s might query details of the course but often followed the same route. James W. Prothro's critical monograph on business values of the decade quotes Barton several times, emphasizes his conflation of "work and *religious* work," repeats the salvaging of the twelve down-and-outer apostles, and uses the book's popularity as proof "that business and religion offered stout support to one another during the Dollar Decade."[53] William E. Leuchtenburg's *Perils of Prosperity*, a sweep of the era written with greater perspective, seriousness, and evidence than *Only Yesterday*, takes in much of the same terrain. It finds in *The Man Nobody Knows* "the classic statement of the secularization of religion and the religiosity of business."[54] Probably two-thirds of all American history textbooks, which typically are organized to allot a chapter to the 1920s, mention Barton as an emblematic figure, and most of those use his line about the twelve disciples.[55]

While Barton did indeed defend business as a source of economic progress and social and even moral improvement, he did not simply confect a spiritual gloss for pro-business propaganda. Religion comprised the book's core. Several historians, notably Leo Ribuffo, Warren Susman, Lynn Dumenil, and Otis Pease, have understood that religion in it must be taken seriously, not just lampooned, and that Barton was disapproving of aspects of the "business civilization" of the 1920s. If the message was sometimes superficial, the same could be said for the way some of his critics have read it.[56]

The Man Nobody Knows made Barton a hot literary property. It stirred the market for his magazine pieces, and other publishers, including

Doubleday and Putnam, murmured "sweet nothings" in his ear about his next book. *Collier's*, with whom he had had a long relationship, announced that as of August 1925 he would be a monthly contributor.[57]

When *The Man* was published, Barton had more ideas for religious publications. He received a great deal of mail about the book from businessmen and wanted to write for them a piece perhaps titled "What Can a Man Believe?" (*The Book Nobody Knows* would come first, before his third book in the twenties, which bore the suggested title.) In it he hoped to lay out his positivist religious philosophy, built on the reassurances of his father, which had gotten him through his college doubts: "If there is a God he must be good; for we are good. And He could not have made us better than Himself." The publisher and editor of *Collier's* urged him to write a sequel (which first came out as a serial in *Collier's*). Bruce relied on paternal suggestions for "much of the material" in it.[58]

In 1926 Bobbs-Merrill brought out *The Book Nobody Knows*. Offering a quick and friendly tour of the Bible, Barton swept through the Old Testament in two chapters, the four Gospels in another, and the rest of the New Testament in a fourth. He gave a chapter each to "Ten Great Men of the Bible" and "Ten Famous Women," one to how we got the Bible (it was a human product—God did not dictate it), and one to its influence (vast and good). The interpretation is relentlessly modernist. Thus Genesis can be reconciled with the science of evolution; its "creative Spirit" dovetails with the scientists' "First Cause." Barton shuffles through the interesting human characters, dwells briefly on Cain's positive side, praises Joseph as an economist, Moses as a lawgiver (and an expert on taxation), and David, despite his one sin, for his psalms and other deeds. He derides the notion that the Song of Songs was an "allegory of Christ and the Church": it sang "the triumph of virtuous love over all the riches that a king can offer." He lauds Jews for having struggled through many tribulations to discover a lone God who did not require sacrifices and who evolved in their understanding from terrible to kind.

Barton's New Testament coverage, not surprisingly, offers a Jesus similar to *The Man*'s. He led an exemplary life from which modern humankind could draw endless inspiration. Significantly, Jesus did not dwell on many of the doctrinal issues that convulsed modern Christianity. Barton waves aside the issue of virgin birth as unmentioned by Mark, John, or Paul. His Jesus was more tolerant than his modern interpreters. He came from a family with six siblings. He was (again) sociable, democratic, decidedly unmeek and un-puritanical, and endowed with executive skills.[59]

The Book also had good sales, though less robust than *The Man*'s, but for a giddy period in 1926 they were both on the best-seller list simultaneously. They were jointly promoted. A Los Angeles bookstore mounted a window display of both books, complete with candelabras, linen-draped lectern, and Gothic-window-shaped signs. *The Book* stayed on *Publishers Weekly*'s best-seller list for thirty-six weeks (in the number one position for eight). Sales generally ran ahead of reviews, some of which applauded the book while others thought it skimpy fare.[60]

Bruce again relied closely on his father's advice. He acknowledged this help by splitting royalties on articles and books.[61] Reverend Barton and his son were always close, more so after the death of Bruce's mother, and they encouraged and collaborated in each other's writing. The father sent the son notes and drafts for numerous projects. They began work on a history of business, which never came to completion.[62] William Barton's interests had always included history, and in his later years he became an able and prolific Lincoln scholar. He deflated several Lincoln myths, ran his scholarly épée through a reworking of the Lincoln–Anne Rutledge legend based on fraudulent letters, and published shoals of books and articles on Lincoln.[63] He helped Bruce on many publications and seems to have derived some benefit in the reverse direction. While Bruce authored *What Can a Man Believe?* in 1927, in 1930 Reverend Barton (who received a share of royalties on it) delivered a series of sermons titled "What Can a Modern Man Believe?"[64]

Barton had tentatively titled his third book with Bobbs-Merrill "Should Religion be Abolished?" but it appeared in 1927 as *What Can a Man Believe?* The book claimed to answer a business executive and friend of Barton's who challenged him to address basic practical questions for modern business types like himself. Barton presented a history-driven, modernist interpretation of Christianity. Thus, he wrote, though Moses may have believed the Ten Commandments "were handed to him direct from God . . . he had learned most of them as a lad in Egypt." He offered comments on the psychology and sociology of belief: dwellers on the land tended to be religious; prosperity and religiosity were antithetical. He offered a trial balance on whether the church had "done more harm than good." The Catholic church had resorted to torture and suppressed science, but so had other religions; and for St. Francis and that ilk it could be forgiven these enormities. It had kept the light of "civilization" flickering after Rome fell. It gave poor people faith and hope. Barton also made a tolerant comparative analysis of the major religions, seeking the virtues of all but finding more in Christianity. In answering the question in the book's title, Barton, as he had often, argued the reasonableness of believing in God—starting with himself, and reasoning from his own intelligence to God's greater intelligence and from human goodness to the necessarily greater goodness of the Creator. He agreed with William James that human experience was unlikely to be the highest form in the universe.

He made a positive case for religion. If, as was true, many churches seemed unable to hold their audiences, the same could be said of political parties. But as institutions, churches must adapt. Barton foresaw a church with a stronger social-welfare dimension (with preachers using generous discretionary funds to help people out). Their buildings would be open around the clock for whoever needed their services, and whenever. Denominational boundaries would be erased and congregations merged. Some of his predictions were astute: he foresaw prayer being broadcast over television. Ultimately Barton rested his case for religion on the assumption that "faith" was a universal need.[65]

What Can a Man Believe? sold not as well as its predecessors. Even so, it resided on the best-seller list for twelve weeks. For sympathetic readers, it lacked the novelty of Barton's earlier books. Positive reviews tended to be polite more than enthusiastic. The *New York Times* declared Barton open-minded, with "his feet on the ground and his mind on the needs and benefits of this world and its daily life." Still, the noted divine Dr. S. Parkes Cadman thought *What Can a Man Believe?* better even than *The Man Nobody Knows*. A review in an Oregon paper said it was "a virile, brainy discussion." *The Times Literary Supplement* also found virtue in it.[66]

The theologically inclined were dismissive. Reviews in Catholic outlets were fierce. *The Catholic World* dismissed the book as an anecdotal hodgepodge penned by an "amateur logician, as well as an amateur theologian," who also showed "reckless disregard for historical truth." Barton was just another of the erroneous "anti-Catholic controversialists." (Barton actually cautioned, after reviewing instances of Catholic suppression and persecution, that Protestant authorities were no less bigoted.) All this led the reviewer to a rant about a New York exhibit of "horrible paintings of the Spanish Inquisition," whose timing seemed more than accidental, given the prospect of an approaching Al Smith presidential campaign. *The Church Militant* (London) thought it an "exceedingly interesting book," in parts, but one that showed "ignorance" of the Catholic church.[67]

One might have expected a less hostile perspective from the precincts of liberal Protestantism, but Reverend John Haynes Holmes pegged it as "the most superficial book on religion that I have ever read," and the *Yale Divinity Review* said that, in the "best Rotary Club style," it threw "little or no light" upon its subject and deferred too tamely to the Catholic church! The liberal journalist Elmer Davis carved with a rapier in the *Saturday Review*. He liked Barton's prescription for the future church—nondenominational and service-oriented—but thought it an unlikely outcome. As for Barton's theology, Davis allowed that since Christianity had sent apostles to everyone else, why not one "to the Luncheon Clubs," bearing a Gospel of the "Everlasting Yea"? Writing for "the Divine Average," Barton might find buyers for the common stock of his "Cosmos Development Corporation."[68]

Barton's last religious book, *He Upset the World*, appraised St. Paul. He originally "did not like Paul" because of his abrasiveness and theology but came to discover his "personality and power" and to sympathize with "his ups and downs of temperament and circumstance." He found Paul strikingly human in contemporary terms—"combattive," assailed by doubts—once to the verge of a "nervous breakdown." Paul fought with valor against the "formalizing and ritualizing" that began soon after Jesus' crucifixion. He stood against "dogma and ritual" and for "love, joy, long suffering, kindness, meekness, self-control." He preached not "creed" but "good news—news that God had come near to man in Christ," creating a natural, rational religion. In a very modern way, Barton suggested, Paul prefigured the other-directedness that was coming to inform American society. He would adapt practice to his audience, following Jewish law when it would forward his agenda, putting it aside among Gentiles. He was "an artist who played upon humanity as on a pipe organ. . . ." Barton also liked in him the fact that "he *forgot the past*" and "moved fearlessly toward the future untrammeled by any dead hand."[69]

Both author and publisher hoped the book would be "a real tonic for the times." Barton thought Paul, "a failure at forty," might appeal to depression-raddled Americans. And, like Barton and his contemporaries, Paul lived in "an irreligious time." (Barton repeated with respect the viewpoint that lack of faith and depression were linked.) But selling into the teeth of the depression, the book lacked the impact of its predecessors.[70] Some reviews described it as a useful antidote for hard times. *Forbes* suggested that those who saw themselves as losers would find encouragement in it. It came out at about the same time as a book on Paul by Albert Schweitzer, the famed author and medical missionary, which some reviewers found more praiseworthy.[71]

FOR DECADES (with brief interludes), some of Barton's religious writings stayed in print. Whatever critics might say, demand—especially for

The Man Nobody Knows—proved persistent.[72] In various formats (cheap reprints, paperback, a combined edition with *The Book*), *The Man* remained available through Barton's life and beyond. Bobbs-Merrill produced new editions of *The Man* and *The Book* in the 1950s. Many readers wrote Barton over the ensuing decades to say how his writings had reinforced their faith, or asking where to find copies of them. Viewed from the perspectives of these correspondents, clearly Barton had performed the sort of "service" he had defined in *The Man Nobody Knows* and elsewhere as the secret of all success.

All of Barton's writings on religion and morality, but especially *The Man Nobody Knows*, established him as a pundit in this realm and a name in "seen on the street" gossip columns. A news summary of a 1928 radio talk described him as a "publicist and philosopher." In 1931 an Atlanta editorialist called him "proof that an advancing civilization provides its own human balance-wheels"; that between the humor of Will Rogers and the shrewd identification of "the essentials of our shifting dilemma" provided by Barton, a world in flux would remain on an even keel.[73] His reputation as a teller of terse and witty truths made him a popular speaker and a continuing asset to BBDO, for whom he continually traveled, bucking up the troops in branch offices, cajoling clients, giving newspaper interviews in the cities he visited, and addressing business groups. After 1945 he increasingly adopted the role of elder statesman, and his writings, particularly *The Man*, enhanced his continuing eminence. They also reinforced his gravitas as a political figure, another prominent role he assumed.

5

The Tents of the Mighty

TO CAREERS as adman and author, Barton added that of political *spinmeister*. These activities brought contacts, visibility, and clout and thus augmented rather than diminished his value to the agency. He had never been nonpolitical; as a young journalist he had interviewed politicians. His inheritance was Republican and, however reformist his youthful impulses may have been, by 1920 he had lost sympathy for the Woodrow Wilson variety of activism. He found traditional blowsy campaign rhetoric wearisome. As the 1920 election neared, he lamented that "for no sins of our own" his fellow voters and he stood "condemned to five solid months of campaign oratory." They now realized that the panaceas politicians offered brought little benefit, that "human nature is not changed by statute."

Before long Barton would tease himself about his youthful fling with reformism and offer mild, though barbed criticisms of what was increasingly being called liberalism. By 1928 he styled himself an "ex-reformer." At other times he labeled himself "one of the last remaining true democrats and Progressives in the world," but he did not flock with "Professional Progressives" because "they give me a severe pain in the neck." After 1906 or 1907, he argued, "Property has been on the run in the United States, and to be one of those who were tying a can to its tail has required not only no courage but has almost always resulted in a cheap kind of reward." In one of his homilies, he recalled once living in an apartment house with "a professional Idealist," full of talk about revolution, "economic readjustment, and other matters which I do not understand." But the great Idealist fell short in "supporting his wife and child" or paying his bills and, when he departed for his summer haunts, he left the cat behind—for Barton to feed. To those who aspired to be his "preceptor and guide," Barton insisted: "first feed your cat." In another article he maintained that "business itself . . . is making a fairer, more healthful and more comfortable world." Those who discounted it were "casting aside the most powerful tool of reform."[1]

Although from 1920 onward Barton could most often be found on the conservative side of a given issue, he was never a standpatter, still less a reactionary. His loathing of the Soviet experiment showed in his approving interview, published after the Red Scare had ebbed, with the ex-socialist John Spargo, who pictured Soviet communism as a "nightmare." Barton declared his preference for the American system, which he likened to "a great motor truck on which rich and poor alike ride the bumps through life. The view from the back seats is not as good as it should be; and there are no shock-absorbers on the rear springs. These matters should be attended to, and will be before very long." But it beat the "ox cart" that was the Soviet alternative.[2] Later, when the Democrats embraced Franklin D. Roosevelt's New Deal, Barton would argue in his most active political phase that the Republican Party needed to show a liberal face to the electorate.

As Barton came to favor only guarded change in the realm of public policy, in the technique of electoral politics he was a more willing innovator. He advised candidates to avoid strenuous, extensive campaigning and long orations. These were both old-hat and ineffective. Not surprisingly, such counsels dovetailed with emerging theory and practice on Madison Avenue, where it was discerned that, amid the velocity and clangor of modern life, consumers had limited attention spans. He also argued, consonant with current advertising belief, that "emotions affect votes much more than logic." For voters (especially in a radio audience, which "tires quickly") as much as consumers, Barton suggested, short was better than long. In 1924 he advised Calvin Coolidge to keep his speeches brief, to give them at regular intervals, and to use radio, which "has made possible an entirely new type of campaign." Let old-fashioned politicos harangue: if Coolidge, through radio, "will only talk to the folks (not address them), he will re-elect himself." Later he gave like advice to Herbert Hoover: "brief and simple."[3]

College ties drew Barton into his first important venture into politics. In the run-up to the 1920 presidential election, he joined a small group striving to "draft" Calvin Coolidge as the Republican presidential nominee. Coolidge, the governor of Massachusetts, was a graduate of Amherst College, and the effort to advance his cause was a project of Amherst alumni led by Frank Stearns, the Boston department store magnate.

The Coolidge persona always embraced both the authentic and the antic. Cherishing the former, Stearns came to respect and revere Coolidge. The story of their first contact became a foundational legend in the Coolidge mythology. Stearns went to ask Coolidge, then a state senator, to offer a bill to push forward a link between their alma mater's sewer system and that of the town of Amherst. By one account, Coolidge sat wordless; another version had him utter delphicly, "It's too late."[4] Either way, he did maneuver such a bill through the next legislative session and, said Stearns, never brought up the matter in order to solicit a reward or even gratitude. This quirky independence earned Stearns's unstinting loyalty, and the older man devoted money and life force to making Coolidge president.

In 1918 he was elected governor of Massachusetts. The next year he won renown and admiration with his blunt response to a request that he mediate a strike launched by Boston's police: "There is no right to strike against the public safety by anybody, anywhere, any time." Boston's crisis occurred as the Red Scare was unfolding. Radicals (not that the police fit that category) had few defenders. As one anonymous poem sent to Coolidge scolded them: "Get up and get out if you've got any doubt about this U.S.A. If you don't like it here why the ocean is clear, there's a boat going home every day."[5]

The no-right-to-strike comment put Coolidge on the board in the handicapping for the 1920 presidential nomination, but against long odds. Other Amherst eminents joined with Stearns, notably Coolidge's classmate Dwight Morrow. Having tired of his work—successful though it was—in corporate law, in 1914 Morrow had become a partner at the famed Wall Street banking house of J. P. Morgan & Company. He performed deftly several tasks in the higher reaches of American business, arranged for loans to the Allies in World War I, expedited wartime transport, and after the war busied himself in delicate diplomatic chores and efforts to unkink the constricted channels of international finance. Morrow stood squarely in the ranks of what would later come to be called the Power Elite. He threw himself into the Coolidge campaign while keeping a low profile for himself and, more pointedly, his Wall Street connections. He brought Barton into the junta, which campaign insiders labeled "the cabinet in New York." After Coolidge won reelection as governor in 1919, Stearns so bombarded Barton with suggestions and requests that the latter jestingly suggested to Morrow that "you and I better begin to close up our business and get ready to go to work."[6]

It was a simpler day and less intricate campaign than later-twentieth-century models, and it took place while the candidate publicly feigned lack of interest in the presidency. Politicking meant talking up Coolidge with friends and acquaintances (including Amherst grads) and publishing and disseminating to Republican activists a book of Coolidge speeches titled *Have Faith in Massachusetts*.[7] Barton pitched in on these and related tasks. He wrote the first national magazine article about Coolidge for *Collier's*. The governor was pictured behind a plow and also fully suited: rooted in the land (wearing his grandfather's work smock) but in tune with the modern world. The piece stressed his "picturesque" and "Yankee" qualities. Barton also characterized him as "a man who kept his own counsel, a novelty when most prominent politicians freely gave advice on everything."[8] Barton was hardly the first to sculpt a candidate's "image," but his work came relatively early. His image-making would take him into two new media—radio and television. Coolidge's first national campaign came at the end stage of the print media's monopoly on political communication. (Moving pictures had already begun elbowing for space.)

Barton positioned Coolidge's name and face before many audiences. He wrote a piece for *The Outlook* describing Coolidge as a workhorse, not a show horse, who turned down distant speaking invitations because "the people of Massachusetts have employed me to act as Governor of the State." On fresh-cut BDO letterhead he wrote Stearns in late 1919 that he had persuaded the editor of the *Woman's Home Companion* to run an article on Coolidge the next spring; he asked Stearns to wheedle from the governor a "message to the women of the United States" to go with it. He ended up constructing the statement himself, partly from Coolidge's earlier utterances. He suggested that Coolidge could be sold as a man "who can work with Congress," something then impossible because of the enmity between Wilson and Capitol Hill. Coolidge later remarked that of all the articles that were written about him, he liked this one the most.

Barton would fill other demands for biographical material on Coolidge, would encourage and broker journalists' requests for interviews, would perform such tasks as drafting a pamphlet about Coolidge's record on education for the nation's teachers, and would labor generally to get publicity for him. Among his ideas was a scheme to get Coolidge invited to speak at New York City's Cooper Union, where Lincoln had once made himself known to a wider, more cosmopolitan audience. He also placed $15,000 worth of small ads in newspapers in those places that hosted state caucuses to choose delegates to the GOP's convention.[9]

The Coolidge campaign had on its hands a man of simplicity, and it strove to merchandise that quality. As governor, the candidate lived in two rented rooms in Boston, retaining the Northampton home—half a double house—that he rented. For exercise he walked—he had golfed a total of twice in his life. The nickname "Silent Cal" and the linkage to the New England "Puritan" tradition had been affixed in his Massachusetts years, and Barton busied himself in giving these national circulation as the convention drew near. He wrote a pamphlet touting Coolidge as a "real American"—descended from Puritan stock, New England farm folk, a family noted for silence.[10]

The leading GOP candidates in 1920, General Leonard Wood and Governor Frank Lowden, found themselves deadlocked at the convention, an ideal situation for a dark horse like Coolidge. But another candidate, more to the liking of the Senate conservatives who gained control of the convention, would profit from the stalemate. By legend, Senator Warren G. Harding was chosen in the famous "smoke-filled room" at Chicago's Blackstone Hotel. (The *Boston Herald* had earlier classed Harding among first-tier compromise candidates; Coolidge among the "second compromises.") The group that maneuvered Harding's nomination tried to balance the ticket with a tame Progressive, Senator Irving Lenroot of Wisconsin, but many delegates, tired of being dictated to, flocked instead to the standard of Coolidge, who was placed in nomination by an Oregon delegate who refused to follow the script. The Republican journalistic icon William Allen White, the "Sage of Emporia," described the backlash as a "revolt of the mob." It was a mild mob and an ironic revolt, which crowned the efforts of Stearns, Morrow, Barton, and their group with partial success. But the outcome astonished them. All of the "Coolidge group" but Barton were off the floor when the vice-presidential nomination took its surprising turn. In fact, Barton's roommate at the convention claimed Harding's agents had earlier offered second place on the ticket to Coolidge, but his lieutenants, Senator Murray Crane and Dwight Morrow, initially refused it.[11]

During the nineteenth century and after, a vice president's likeliest career move was to become a former vice president. The odds of succeeding to the presidency improved with the factoring-in of the possible death of the incumbent—five men had so advanced before 1920—but the vice presidency otherwise had become something of a political cul-de-sac. Wilson's vice president, Thomas Riley Marshall, liked to tell the tale of two brothers: one ran away to sea, the other became vice president, and neither was heard of again. Nonetheless for Coolidge it was a job. He could eat, and his friends could keep their fingers crossed. Barton informed him after his nomination that the "Coolidge Committee" had decided to stay together. "We think it has important work to do four years or eight years from now."[12]

The Republicans' fall campaign signaled a shift toward more modern electioneering techniques, prominently characterized by methods of the emerging advertising profession. Albert Lasker, principal of the Lord and Thomas advertising agency of Chicago, counseled the Republican high command and introduced the new techniques. This was not the first time "advertising" or "public relations" had figured in electoral politics—all political publicity is advertising. Nor was Lasker even the first adman to play a role in a national campaign. Indeed, the George Batten agency had placed advertising for Republican presidential candidate Charles Evans Hughes in 1916. Ancient lore that survived in the combined firm of BBDO had it that the Batten Company had decided not to buy any advertising in California's newspapers; the state, whether for this or other reasons, went narrowly to Wilson, deciding the election.[13]

In 1920 party leaders determined that a "front porch campaign" like William McKinley's in 1896 would keep the second-rate Harding under control and out of rhetorical trouble. The campaign, in the form of representative groups of voters, could come to him rather than vice versa. Charged with projecting the Harding persona to the broad nation, Lasker did so in innovative ways. Harding, his family, and his visitors became the focus of folksy photo opportunities, and Lasker shipped fifteen million pictures out to newspapers at a cost of $200,000. He also exploited the new medium of motion pictures. When party figures expressed distress that some newsreel clips showed Harding playing the snooty sport of golf, Lasker organized a junket by the Chicago Cubs (of which he was part-owner) to Marion, Ohio, where they played a local nine, and where candidate Harding threw the ball game's first three pitches. The Democrats, engaged in a more traditional campaign of extensive travel and speechifying, complained, but futilely. Harding—and Coolidge—won in a landslide.[14] While Barton had made canny use of the media and his advertising skills in pressing Coolidge's cause on GOP delegates, Lasker's general election campaign used the new communication technologies with more sophistication. Perhaps Lasker was more adept in these technologies; but perhaps, too, they did not mesh as well with the politics of nostalgia with which Coolidge's friends sought to saturate their candidate.

The Harding campaign's innovations revealed an acceleration of the pace of politics, but galloping technology was altering the entire fabric of public life. Harding's Inaugural offered portents of the coming rattling changes to the way Americans lived. The *New York Times* Inaugural commemorative issue was sped to Washington by airplane; the Inaugural speech was for the first time carried on a public address system; at the festivities the Marine Band performed a jazz number. Presidents Harding and Wilson were whisked to the ceremony in an automobile.[15]

The Harding campaign pointed toward the modern, and Harding the candidate promised a reprieve from the moral agitation and crusading zeal of the Wilson years. Coolidge offered something else. As morally unyielding but more minimalist in oratory than Wilson, he was less inclined than Harding to go-along-and-get-along. In an article about Frank Stearns, Barton described Coolidge as one who "simply cannot and will not conform." Barton put his finger on a quality in Coolidge that the famed sociologist David Riesman would later mark as the old America of "inner-directed" personalities, people who responded to inward urgings originating in religion and morality. Increasingly—and the 1920s, according to Riesman, were a stage of transition—Americans would adopt "other-directed" personalities, responding less to the "gyroscope" of their internal guidance systems and more to the signals of the "radar" of messages received from other people. To Stearns and Barton, it was his older standards and ways of being that made Coolidge so attractive. But neither as adman nor political engineer could Barton survive on a diet of straight Coolidge. In his politics as in his career in advertising, Barton functioned as a mediator between ebbing but cherished values of a passing era and the allure of the modern.[16]

As vice president, Coolidge held a position which its previous occupants, from John Adams to the most recent, Thomas Riley Marshall,
had dismissed derisively. He was now a "Puritan in Babylon" amid
Warren Harding's Washington. Endless jokes about his awkward fit in
capital society made the rounds. Perhaps the most famous was his al-
leged response to a dinner partner who told him she had wagered that
she could pry three words out of him during the party. "You lose," he
replied. No social lion, neither was Coolidge able to strengthen his political standing while he served as vice president. From several sources
came indications that Republicans were casting about for a new vice-
presidential candidate on the 1924 ticket. Bruce Barton later recalled
hearing similar stories. As early as 1922 Coolidge had indications that
"the President and his group have decided to put me on the shelf."[17]

But Coolidge's friends had not disbanded their group, and Barton
continued to work to keep his name in the news and his supporters
mobilized. Even in the becalmed seas of Coolidge's vice presidency,
Frank Stearns persisted in believing that he would, if all went well, "be
the one great leader of the American people" and took "no stock in the
theory that fate cannot be helped along to do its duty." Barton provided
aid on some of the vice president's speeches.[18]

When Harding's weakened heart gave out on August 2, 1923, destiny did hammer, in the middle of the night, on Coolidge's door—or
the door of his father's farm in Vermont. "Colonel" John Coolidge, a
justice of the peace, administered the presidential oath to his son by
lantern light in that rustic setting. While Coolidge offered an antidote
to the sleaze of the Harding years, his friends, Barton very much
among them, rallied to ensure the certainty of his nomination for president in 1924. In fact, during Harding's illness, Morrow had even recommended Barton as a candidate for the vital post of secretary to the
president, should Coolidge succeed to that office. Morrow even offered to "make some arrangements to carry on your advertising business while you are away."[19]

Coolidge never made any such proposition, and Barton continued
to labor gratis on his behalf. He quickly published an article about

Coolidge as his friends knew him, again highlighting his "silence" and modesty. It made a point about service that found parallel emphasis in *The Man Nobody Knows*: in this case Coolidge was one "to do the job and let the credit take care of itself. . . ." In December 1923 Barton traveled to Chicago on an errand "in the interests of my friend in Washington." After checking out the Coolidge operation there, he agitated for an early start to the campaign to profit from the fact that the Democrats did not yet have a standard-bearer; urged placement of ads in strategic publications and the positioning of human-interest stories in the magazines; and proposed to launch a contact and tracking system focused on delegates to the coming convention.[20] In 1924 Barton saw to the publication of a book of more Coolidge speeches. He offered advice and drafted campaign materials, including a pamphlet titled "The Farmer Boy, The Public Servant, The President."[21]

Barton had a sharpened sense of how politics was changing; voters were moving away from identifying with a party and toward a candidate's "personality." "Emotions affect votes much more than logic." So it was crucial to "build up a wonderful Coolidge legend in the country." Eerily prefiguring the political magic of Franklin D. Roosevelt, he suggested that Coolidge tap the new medium of radio, for "it enables the President to sit by every fireside and talk in terms of that home's interest and prosperity."[22] Whatever Barton's influence, and whatever its effect, Coolidge won a stunning victory, amassing more votes in 1924 than his Democratic opponent John W. Davis and the Progressive candidate Robert M. La Follette combined.

Barton's labors did not go unrewarded. Coolidge was sensible of his debt before he became vice president. Barton's proximity to the White House redounded to the advantage of BDO. The payoffs came in visibility and reflected glory. Barton received various invitations to the White House, including a Cabinet dinner in 1926.[23] He visited the White House, and so did his father, prominent both as a church leader and as a Lincoln scholar. Although presidents—and Coolidge especially—dispatched messages of greeting and felicitation liberally to public meetings and celebrations, it was a feather in Barton's cap that the president sent a message to a conference of the Associated Advertising Clubs of the World at which Barton made a major address. Barton continued to aid various White House projects—the publication, for instance, of another book aimed at purveying a favorable picture of the president.[24]

Barton's crowning triumph was an exclusive interview with the president, syndicated by the Associated Press. Barton had long had a sterling reputation for his interviews, many of which the *American Magazine* had published. His procedure was subject-friendly: the interviewee had leverage to shape the end product. He often sent possible questions in advance, as he did this time. (In some cases the magazine paid both interviewer and interviewee an honorarium.) He told one prospect that the result would be "dignified and restrained, and that you will, of course, have a chance to see the manuscript and make any changes or suggestions." To Coolidge, Barton sketched the interview's shimmering possibilities. Other nations viewed America "as a huge cash register, and the President is pictured as the man behind the cash register—cold, impersonal, interested only in collecting the money due." By conveying a different, "human, friendly picture—we are doing one of the best things that can ever be done for the United States." From the White House perspective, Barton was the best choice for the job because, as Coolidge's secretary wrote him, "your name carried a conviction of sincerity which was absolutely essential." In politics as in advertising, "sincerity" was becoming Barton's stock-in-trade.[25]

Coolidge was savvy about his own publicity. Belying his "silent" reputation, he averaged two press conferences a week, and the telegraph from White Pine Camp in the Adirondacks, Coolidge's 1926 vacation retreat, poured forth 1.6 million words to the media. Indeed, the *New Republic* observed that "no ruler in history ever had such a magnificent propaganda machine." But contrary to procedure in his press conferences, he allowed Barton to quote him directly. As the price of this direct attribution, the interview could treat only the "human story," not issues of political relevance. Barton's questions, posed just before Coolidge departed for Washington, were cleared ahead of time; Barton even suggested answers to some, gleaned from previous conversations with the president. The AP covered the footprints of all these careful preparations with a wire story revealing that, as Coolidge broke camp to return to the White House, his "final house guests" (among many, it was noted) would be Mr. and Mrs. Barton.[26]

The interview showed the president at his most homey, Yankee best. He soliloquized about the influence of his family, the simple joys of the autonomous life in his Vermont home, the stimuli of modern life. There were queries about his boyhood ambitions (he had hoped once to "keep store"). He explained the importance of restraining presidential activism. "I try to remember that there is only one ex-President living." The interview blended the astute, the banal, and the ludicrous. For a girl who wanted to enter politics, "the best thing . . . is to get married and bring up a family." Then again, "there have been many excellent executives, both men and women, who have lived a single life." Why didn't he ride a horse? "It takes too long to change your clothes." The president's human side revealed itself in his declaration of the happiness of his marriage and Barton's description of how his two collies planted muddy pawprints on the presidential vest. Coolidge corrected a transcript of the interview in his own hand. In fact, he later recalled that he "wrote" most of the interview himself, "in response to [Barton's] questions," but that many questions came bundled with suggested answers; he noted snappishly that "it was put out and taken in such a way as to be mostly Barton and little of myself."[27]

The interview caused a sensation. In many quarters it won praise. David Lawrence, soon to acquire veteran status as a pundit, applauded its revelation of Coolidge's "human" qualities, naively assuming the interview was "not prearranged" but a spontaneous product of Barton's casual visit and awed reaction to Coolidge's personality. Others picked up on how it humanized a president often seen as austere, and this feature of the interview prompted speculation that it was the opening salvo in a campaign for reelection two years off. Democrats were quick to see it as the opening gun of the 1928 campaign.[28]

Many newsmen grumbled. The White House Correspondents Association protested that a writer "foreign to our organization" won permission to quote Coolidge directly, while they all had to attribute remarks to an "official spokesman." It breached the understanding between president and press. The White House responded that Coolidge had not violated their trust because the interview dealt not with "news matter," only "human interest." The episode occasioned ribbing at the Washington correspondents' annual Gridiron Dinner, and one columnist noted how Coolidge let "an out-of-town magazine writer scoop" faithful reporters who had hung around his camp "all summer writing fish stories." Some commentators derided the interview as an exercise in Coolidgean banality. One spoofer declared the president's private life exciting enough to warrant a movie: When the collie jumped on Coolidge, "Down, down, he commanded. I hastened to jot down these memorable words." The *Baltimore Evening Sun* dismissed the interview's "creamy blandness."[29] But clearly the pluses overwhelmed the minuses. The *New York Evening Post* editorialized that while "the 'intellectuals' may satirize it," most found it an "inspiration to faith in the old moralities." One piece of news copy called the interview a "high tide in publicity and [it] should be worth to Republican candidates far more than any direct campaign appeals" by Coolidge; Barton "never wrote a better advertisement and never placed one better." Their anguish suggested that Democrats agreed with that conclusion. Democratic Senator Thomas Bayard termed it a transparent effort to distract voters from the "complete failure of the so-called 'Presidential program.'"[30]

The dividends of loyalty kept flowing to Barton. He had a hand in Coolidge's address to the 1926 convention of the Association of American Advertising Agencies, the AAAA. His partner Durstine was president of the organization; getting Coolidge to speak was a coup. Coolidge had ideas of his own to express but included many Barton had laid out for him—and in Bartonian turns of phrase. Barton wrote that advertising should be thought of as "education"; so did Coolidge. Barton took on critics who stressed "the economic wastes of advertising"; Coolidge said, "advertising is not an economic waste." Barton argued that America's lead in productivity stemmed from "mass production" made possible only because of "the mass demand created by advertising." Coolidge concurred in this causal chain. "The savage has no wants and makes no progress," wrote Barton. Coolidge glossed this as: "The uncivilized make little progress because they have few desires." Coolidge's own peroration that "advertising ministers to the spiritual side of trade," and his point that Americans were learning to see in large corporations "their most faithful servants," could not have been better put by Barton, nor more consonant with views he expressed in the pages of *The Man Nobody Knows* (which Coolidge had read and appreciated). Barton hailed the speech as "the finest tribute that has ever been paid to advertising." It was a source of personal pride that it punctuated the close of Durstine's leadership of the AAAA.[31]

By the end of the Coolidge years, such favors and flourishes gave Barton a reputation as an insider. One news service picked up rumors that after 1928 Coolidge and Barton planned to travel around the world together. The two were neither that close nor that migratory, but Barton did operate virtually as Coolidge's literary adviser and helped him place his writings. He visited him in his Northampton retirement and entertained him in New York. He was able to schedule an interview with the retired president, and articles about Coolidge continued. Barton appears to have drafted the text of a full-page ad that ran in sixteen big-city newspapers calling on Republicans to draft Coolidge for vice president on the Hoover ticket so as to "restore confidence" and end fear in 1932. This he did despite his knowledge that Coolidge found the job of president wearing upon his health, remarking in 1932 in the words of Falstaff in *Henry IV* that he was "a shotten herring."[32]

Barton now had a reputation for political astuteness that attracted other GOP leaders. Seamlessly he shifted his energies to the disposition of the next Republican chieftain, Herbert Hoover, beginning in 1927, the year Coolidge said he did not "choose to run." Barton performed various chores for the Hoover campaign. He headed an effort to solicit campaign funds among New York advertising agencies. He gave advice on strategy and campaign themes. As an example, he counseled that the wives of the GOP candidates be pictured with them: however "sad" a "reflection on our democracy . . . thousands of women who vote against Al Smith will really be voting against Mrs. Smith." He urged Hoover to "do some fishing or tree-chopping, something that shows him a human being. . . ." He drafted messages (and sometimes the responses) and provided speech material. Some contributions Hoover used, some he discarded, such as Barton's proposal for a speech with "some ringing paragraphs about the obligations of big business and of great wealth." He did use significant portions of Barton's draft for his August 11 speech accepting the nomination.[33]

Hoover valued Barton's contributions enough to ask him to attend the Republican convention. He called frequently on Barton for advice; if he did not always follow it, he assured him, "you have been of much more help than you may think." After his election victory Hoover reiterated that he "had much more inspiration from your suggestions than was perhaps evident from the actual terms I used, and I am deeply grateful to you."[34]

Barton also wrote pro-Hoover pieces for publication. Perhaps his sharpest challenge was to answer H. L. Mencken, the nation's most acerbic pundit, who came out for Democrat Al Smith. Mencken told an interviewer that he required a president to be "amusing," and Smith, whom he termed—positively, in that age of Prohibition—a "cocktail," fit the bill while Hoover was "a dose of aspirin." "Lord Hoover" he labeled a "fat Coolidge." Barton was asked to make the rejoinder. He waved away the idea that leaders must amuse as more appropriate to an age of kings, for whom Mencken "would have made a grand court jester." Barton "would rather go fishing with Mencken than with the President. But I'd much rather have Coolidge in the White House." Mencken was an "actor," an "amusing fellow" offstage but probably tired of his role. "Mencken and his boys are always wrong and always licked. They are the sad voices crying in the wilderness and singing 'Sweet Adeline' in the speakeasies." (Barton said he had opposed the Eighteenth Amendment on libertarian grounds, but since

Prohibition was the law, it merited a chance.) Trying to convey his well-read and philosophical side, he quoted Emerson in response to the call for entertaining rulers, as saying that "history will continually grow less interesting as the world grows better." Who won the exchange could not be calculated, but Heywood Broun, another columnar giant of the age, scored the bout to Mencken. On the other hand, an editor at the *Telegram* reported to Barton the delight of his fellow staffers in the effective reply to Mencken.[35]

Barton's candidate thrashed Mencken's anyway. After Hoover's victory there was speculation that "the new administration will have a strong Bruce Bartonish and [George] Barr Bakerish flavor, that it will be saturated with uplift publicists or at least unpolitical intellectuals, that it will be all cluttered up with 'Boy and Girl Scouts.'" That did not ensue, as more practical considerations intervened, but Barton maintained access to the president. He was invited to White House banquets and to Hoover's rustic Rapidan River vacation retreat in Virginia. He sent Hoover suggestions ranging from appointments, to the recommendation (disregarded) that Hoover veto the Smoot-Hawley tariff bill, to ways to combat the economic disaster and the thickening gloom wrought by the bottomless Great Depression, which turned Hoover's administration into a nightmare. He advised on themes to emphasize in speeches, but more pointedly he sought to prod Hoover to *act* in ways that would alter the public's deteriorating estimate of their president. Thus he proposed that Hoover use the visit by France's premier as the "occasion for changing the present defeatist psychology of the nation and the world" by assembling congressional leaders of both parties to meet with him. He even passed "Hoover" jokes along to their target. He sent confidential political intelligence, such as the prediction that Al Smith would not run for president but would veto Franklin D. Roosevelt's nomination and so open the way for the nomination of Newton D. Baker, President Wilson's secretary of war. A few months later he revised his view of FDR's prospects but termed his nomination "the best luck the President could have." On his side, Hoover looked forward to Barton's visits, from which he expected "my usual crop of useful ideas from you."[36]

Hoover seemed out of touch with the public mood, but Barton sometimes read the climate little more accurately than did the president. For example, his advice on handling the Bonus Army, the veterans who poured into Washington in the summer of 1932 to demand early payment of the annuities due them for their war service, misfires in hindsight. Barton suggested that Hoover issue a dramatic statement like Coolidge's famous utterance during the Boston police strike. Noting that army intelligence tests showed that many doughboys "had the intelligence of a twelve year old child," he said: "These children must be dealt with as children—kindly, tolerantly, but firmly." Echoing Coolidge in 1919, Barton wrote, for Hoover's use: "There is no right by any group to attempt to intimidate the Congress of the United States." He thought that since Hoover was "going to lose all the pro-bonus votes anyway," he would do better if he "shook this subject to its roots" and sided with "us paying-voters," who outnumbered "receiving-voters."

Soliciting Barton's suggestions for his speech accepting renomination, Hoover used his first paragraph but ignored the second, in which Barton would have him admit, "I have made mistakes."[37] Barton suggested a short speech, but Hoover thought it better to make an oration "of some length." Barton wanted Hoover to use rhetoric gesturally—to transform words into acts, acts that would demonstrate empathy. Thus he proposed that Hoover tell an audience of New York's rich at the Union League Club that "the farm problem is their problem," that the farmer made "their very existence" possible. Such a speech could convey "plenty of the sincere emotion of a man on whose heart lies the burden and the suffering of millions of inarticulate people." Then he should go tell Iowans how he had spoken "to Wall Street about the farmer" and now came to explain to them the problems of banks and insurance companies—"'about how we are all bound together,' etc."[38]

There were reports that Hoover's campaign managers wanted Barton to serve as "a sort of adviser-in-chief with regard to publicity, . . . a sort of high strategist in New York in the campaign to sell Mr. Hoover

to the country." Barton gave advice liberally in 1932, but the connection remained informal. His political antennae were sufficiently at-
tuned to sense the dimness of Hoover's prospects. Even as gossip about
his centrality in Hoover's campaign circulated, he was subtly hedging
his bets in the spring of 1932 by seeking to advance the prospects of
Newton Baker in the Democratic party. Baker did not declare as a candidate but had admirers in both parties, and he made a fine alternative
to Franklin D. Roosevelt, whom Barton had come to distrust. Barton
encouraged his friend Roy Howard (of the Scripps-Howard newspapers), who labored to coax Baker into greater visibility and to encourage a draft movement.[39] While Barton continued to advise and support
Hoover and his allies, he increasingly suspected that FDR would win
and did not find that prospect "necessarily calamitous." Years later he
confided that, before either party's convention, he had decided to vote
Democratic "for the first time in my life," though preferring either Al
Smith or Baker to Roosevelt.[40]

Not political tips such as these, nor Hoover's profound sense of his
own correctness, could save him from a trouncing at the hands of
FDR. Hoover and his entourage were now wandering in the political
wilderness. Barton sustained a friendship with him that, if anything,
grew closer as the years passed. One of Barton's greatest talents was
comradeship extended to a wide circle of business, political, intellectual, and social familiars. As one of his confidants declared, "You have
a gift for friendship, Bruce." Dale Carnegie, author of *How to Win
Friends and Influence People*, wrote of Barton's "tremendous capacity
for friendship."[41]

Barton maintained affectionate ties with the Hoovers and encouraged the ex-president with compliments on his speeches and writings.
He also gave Hoover advice and aid in his publishing projects. Hoover
sent him a draft of his first major literary effort in exile, which became
The Challenge to Liberty (1934). Barton thought the writing "heavy and
difficult to understand," and likely to draw negative comparisons with
"the clear, simple language" of FDR. He and Gertrude Lane urged
the former president to hire a "collaborator." Hoover dismissed the

counsel: "if I did not love you both I would break off relations right now for we are too far apart in ideas." The differences stemmed, he sighed, from the fact that "you live in New York." Hoover did agree that the manuscript needed pruning. Barton helped negotiate with Scribner's, which would publish *The Challenge to Liberty*, and with the Book-of-the-Month Club, which selected the book.[42]

Despite their differences, the two men remained close. On their way around the world, the Bartons visited the Hoovers in Palo Alto in 1934 (after which Barton, though enjoying their time together, remarked that Hoover was "a trifle querulous" and still "bitter" about Roosevelt). Advice, felicitations, and favors flowed back and forth; Hoover invited Barton several times to join in the fellowship of the Bohemian Grove, the famous California summer camp for the rich and powerful. He attended Mrs. Barton's funeral. The two men were friends into their final years.[43]

Barton's political counseling extended beyond Hoover. His next presidential project might well have been Dwight Morrow, his co-worker in the Coolidge boom. After a well-regarded tour of duty as U.S. ambassador to Mexico, Morrow had enlarged his national prospects by winning election as a senator from New Jersey. Barton, who visited him in Mexico, had written a highly laudatory article, "The Ambassador Nobody Knows," in 1928. He wanted to see Morrow in 1930 as soon as his campaign ended to "talk about the national situation." But Morrow's death in 1931 left that chapter unwritten.[44]

In 1936 Barton's party again recruited his talents. The Republican National Committee (RNC) needed urgent help: the party's early salvos that election year had backfired. One such fiasco played out when Iowa Senator Lester Dickinson charged that New Deal scarcity economics, especially in its agriculture programs, had so miscarried that many of the elderly were being driven to eat dog food. Since neither the proliferation of dogs nor a change in their appetites explained the rise in dog food sales, it was an "inescapable conclusion" that humans were consuming it, thus accounting for the industry's "unprecedented prosperity." This made for amusement all around. One Democratic colleague, noting

Dickinson's presidential aspirations, demanded to know where two other possible candidates then in the Senate chamber stood on the dog food issue. The debate soon collapsed into raillery; Dickinson, accused of concealing a stash of dog food in his office, left the Senate red-faced. The usually sober pundit Arthur Krock even joined the levity, asserting that "not even the historians of pre-revolutionary France have presented such a picture." Dog food makers offered a blander explanation: human consumption of the product had actually declined, so its increased sales stemmed from its wider popularity among pet owners.[45]

Grand predictions that he would remake the face of the GOP met Barton's appointment to the RNC. He would "humanize" Alf Landon, the Republican candidate in 1936, as he had Coolidge, and "put Landon over," assured one column. He would enter the lists as the Republican champion to counter the Democratic National Committee's Charles Michelson, whose publicity barbs had so lacerated Hoover in 1932. But he was only to survey RNC publicity and advise on improving production, not to run it or the campaign. He made a number of suggestions and helped arrange the material in one of the RNC's pamphlets, but his role was minor compared to his exertions in earlier campaigns.[46] His chief advice seems to have been predicated on the need to entertain the radio audience listening to the convention: he suggested frequent breaks during which a broad assortment of ethnically varied choruses would offer music. He reviewed suggestions for the party platform and helped "a little in the arrangement of the material," but not in overall content. After the convention he excused himself from the project.[47]

Barton had some contact with Landon as the campaign drew near, offering suggestions for his acceptance speech.[48] He had far less to do with Landon than he had had with Coolidge or Hoover. There was much speculation and talk about his role—more than there was action on his part. A Democratic party wit quipped that Barton was working to sell "The Nomination Nobody Wants." One newsman reported that "Landon strategists," Barton prominent among them, were going for broke in an effort aimed at "throwing the fear of terrific taxes into the hearts of the voters." Eschewing the usual handshaking and "bally-hoo," the plan envisioned having butchers display signs showing how taxes raised meat prices, while industrialists and retailers would put similar stickers on products.[49] The campaign did not live up to these expectations, and Landon, carrying only Maine and Vermont, was routed. Barton had little to do with the campaign, and thus he avoided being immersed in the Roosevelt tidal wave.

While aspirants to the White House continued to seek Barton's help, and he would continue to provide it, years would pass before another Republican became president. BBDO would again play a role in Dwight D. Eisenhower's campaign, but Barton's involvement would be far less important than under Coolidge and Hoover. In the nearer term, neither Hoover's retirement nor the Democratic party's dominance in national politics would end Barton's active presence in political affairs. Far from it. For his clients, the business benefits of the work he and his agency did for them meshed closely with the political dividends, and the latter grew to be a more important element of institutional advertising for corporations. Then too, Barton would soon take a more direct role in American political life.

6

Worn Pants and Optimism

DURING THE Great Depression, Bruce Barton rode somewhat above the crowd as he carried on with his usual patterns of activity. He remained busy practicing and advocating advertising, though this occupation continued to compete with his other endeavors. He maintained his crowded schedule of writing for newspapers and magazines, but no significant books issued from his typewriter. He continued to participate in politics. For Barton, though, as for the nation, the decade brought trials—literally so in one instance. These years put strains on his marriage, his reputation as a moral pundit, the health of his advertising agency, and his political thinking about the role of the federal government in economic life and of the United States in world affairs.

On the United States the depression inflicted what one writer has termed an "angry scar." Barton himself weathered it far better than most other Americans, but he could observe its inroads. Some family members encountered financial hardship, and he gave them help. Graduates of Amherst in New York experienced want so commonly that Barton and fellow alumni improvised a sort of cooperative employment service for them. Business friends and acquaintances importuned him for help as jobs vanished. His partners and he felt the pressure of keeping the BBDO family together without massive dismissals. In the ten years after BBDO's 1928 merger, billings steadily declined from $32.6 to $17.3 billion. Reflecting the nature of the times,

BBDO produced an "Unemployment Concert" for the 1933 presidential inauguration.[1]

The public Barton braved the depression with optimism. A few months after the stock market crash he told a Pittsburgh audience that "any one who looks gloomily at the business prospects of this country in 1930 is going broke." This depression was "fast disappearing"; that of 1920 had been much grimmer; business should recover "by April." In a September 1930 article meant to cheer up recent college grads, he recalled that his own "class of 1907 walked into a panic that *was* a panic." In late 1930 he was finding comfort in the patterns of earlier depressions, which he gauged to be of six months' duration, and predicted a turnaround when "the robins return" (but he hedged that this depression might be "different"). "We are pretty close to the bottom of our bureau drawers; when Spring comes we shall have to outfit ourselves all over again," thus reigniting business. In December 1930 he expressed hope that, together with the normal penchant for depressions to last an average of thirteen months, "Christmas shopping" would spark recovery.[2] He found special reassurance in the axiom that the natural history of depressions was that they ended once people wore out the pants to their suits. He quoted the "wag" who said depressions were governed by the "life cycle of the pants of a man who typically has two suits—when they wear out." Three months later he declared that business was picking up, that "most of the people have worn out their extra trousers and are buying new ones." He asserted that fighting economic hardship was an individual task. Or that it was a challenge calling for tuned-up morality. Noting that farmers were feeding wheat to hogs in Kansas while men in New York starved for bread, and that U.S. warehouses groaned with cotton while "thinly clad Chinese freeze to death," he suggested that the problem "needs to be attacked 'in the spirit of Jesus.'"[3]

At times his professed optimism wore thinner than pants. Home from a trip to Europe in 1930, he praised "the sense of national obligation which Mussolini has re-created in the soul of Italy." "Must we abolish the Senate and have a dictatorship to do it?" he wondered. "I sometimes think it would be almost worth the cost." He was not the only business spokesman to see something in the fascist experiment as contrasted to American political gridlock. Later, when Barton ran for office, foes frequently threw this ill-considered remark in his face. Within a decade it had become writ in deep-left circles that he was a "Fascist." George Seldes called him "a native Fascist," citing the Mussolini reference as proof.[4] More characteristic was Barton's comment disembarking after a later trip: "Personally, I do not like dictators, but if we have to have one I prefer Mr. Roosevelt to the top sergeants who are running some of the countries of Europe."[5]

Perhaps the robins' failure to bring prosperity north in their beaks, or the absence of stampedes on pants departments, persuaded Barton to be less jaunty and glib. By mid-1931 he conceded that "economics is not a science; it is a hokum." He realized that the status quo could not be maintained. An article stating bravely that communism would not succeed in the United States took heart in the country's "universal education" and the fact that "our wealth, though very inequitably distributed, is enjoyed by a far larger proportion of people than has ever been true in any nation before. Millions own homes and land and stocks." No one "imagines the present social structure ideal, but very few care to risk losing what they have on the vague promise of acquiring more." And finally, "we can't alter the fundamentals of human nature," as communism sought.[6] In April 1932 he recognized that the depression was "serious and world-wide" but hoped its very gravity would convince statesmen to throw out "old-fashioned" policies of economic "isolation"; that plus America's "marvelous recuperative powers" would end it. He took solace from the growth he perceived in "human values"—greater "brotherliness and sympathy and simpler, more genuine living." Amid the desperate conditions of 1932, he offered the hope that "we are re-laying the foundations of faith," and on those material well-being would be built.[7] But by 1931–1932, Barton, whose own business put him in touch with the nation's blue-chip corporate hierarchy, found little in their predictions and pronouncements to encourage much optimism.[8]

Barton's efforts to ameliorate conditions relied on uplifting rhetoric and voluntary assistance programs. In writing his friend Roy Howard in late 1929 soliciting support for the YWCA, "a big force in the prevention of distress," he declaimed that "we publishers and advertising men" had a heavy responsibility in the deepening crisis. "It is preeminently our duty to preach faith in America, to insist upon the tremendous recuperative power of America, and to do everything possible to prevent distress and build up purchasing power." In 1930 BBDO put its weight behind the "Buy Now" campaign that newspapers and their advertisers were pushing to stimulate the economy. Although he supported this drive, privately he labeled it "merely sound and fury." He served in Hoover's President's Organization on Unemployment Relief (POUR), which sought through voluntaristic means to maximize relief work, chiefly by promoting publicity for various local efforts. Barton embraced such approaches. He drafted a message to be issued by POUR entitled "Morale": "It wins wars. It beats depressions." He urged readers to support a month-long appeal in their locality to raise funds for "welfare and relief agencies everywhere to provide for local needs." "Feel the thrill that comes with victory." He was the principal speaker when Minneapolis launched its Community Fund drive.[9]

Barton often expressed the view that the capitalist system had proven faulty and that changes must come. He agreed that the skewed distribution of wealth in America needed redress. While much in the early New Deal troubled him, mostly he guarded his tongue. He even suggested privately in October 1933 that Roosevelt's election, which "all of us smart people opposed and mistrusted," bore out Jefferson's faith in the wisdom of the people as against Hamilton's bleaker view. His valedictory *Herald Tribune* column, announcing his 1934 trip around the world, confessed that he remained tentative on all topics and his own judgment, hoping the trip would bring perspective. "We believe in the chief actor, Mr. Roosevelt. We believe we are headed for a happy ending. But we should like to confirm the impression by a longer view." He returned from his travels convinced that "we are in a revolution" which would bring "personal inconvenience, trouble and financial loss," but he philosophically discounted that if he emerged "with half of what I think I have today," it would be "a very successful and fortunate passage."[10]

In 1931 Leonard Hatch published *The Book of Dilemmas*, a compendium of moral predicaments on which, along with three other widely read men of letters, Barton dispensed his moral advice. The book's first quandary envisioned a family man on a transcontinental rail trip meeting an attractive unmarried woman who frankly and flatteringly proposes a liaison. How to respond? Barton answered briskly: "I should show her the pictures of my three children, raise my hat, and be on my way."[11]

Would that in real life he had done so. Minus the romance of a cross-country train junket, a grittier version of this episode had befallen him. Details remain murky, but this, the ugliest moment in Barton's life, came to public attention in 1933. He was implicated in a sexual affair with a woman who had worked at BBDO. It apparently began in 1928 when a man Barton knew, Hugh Rogers King, urged him to hire Frances Wagner, described as "smart, pretty, and down on her luck." Given temporary clerical work, she bumped into Barton, flattered him, told him she aspired to become a writer, and asked for help on her "script." This led to dinner, a dalliance at her apartment (she said she was unmarried), and several more such meetings over the next month. Then her husband—Hugh King!—appeared. He threatened to sue Barton for alienation of affections. On legal advice, Barton "bought them off" for $25,000.

This, alas, did not end the problem. Next, Frances King listed Barton as a reference on a job application. He warned the employer off, saying she had blackmailed him. In 1932, in an arranged meeting at a lawyer's office (presumably in contemplation of further legal steps), she informed Barton that she had written a novel about one "Roos Martin," an ad executive with a roving eye. With its numerous personal touches drawn from life, surely he didn't want to see it in print. He called her a "blackmailer" and dared her to go ahead. (He claimed she later sent galley proofs to his house.) She next sued for slander, seeking $250,000 in damages, but later wrote to say that for $50,000 she would bury the suit and the book. All this went public when newspapers reported Barton's arrest under a civil order growing out of her slander suit. He now pressed blackmail charges against her, and she was indicted on April 17, 1933. Her suit against him was dismissed.[12]

Lasting from July 18 to August 2, 1933, the trial of Frances King went badly for the defendant and often reached exalted levels of absurdity. Barton testified and was accompanied every day by his wife Esther. Incredibly, Mrs. King's attorney on cross asked Barton to amplify what he had meant months before in saying that with her reputation she would never convince people to believe her book. This permitted Barton to detail findings of sleuthwork done at the time of the alienation suit. Mrs. King's checkered past included name changes, dismissal from nursing school (for "misconduct with a male patient"), a divorce, an "illegal operation" in an Ohio hospital, a firing "for cause" as a hotel hostess, and lies on her latest marriage license. Her "book" was read to the jury: while the assistant D.A. droned on, the judge began paging through reading of his own, and six spectators dozed off. A witness testified that the blackmail letter was in Mrs. King's hand; another (a police detective), that he had heard her make a harassing phone call to Barton.

Mrs. King buried herself with her own testimony. She asserted that her affair with Barton had lasted three years, ending only when Barton, anticipating a seat in President Hoover's cabinet, sought to marry her off (hence Mr. King); and her novel was not about Barton. There was also a baby in 1928 (which conveniently died after one day). And, she said, the Bartons were secretly obtaining a divorce. Then she broke down, and next she balked at testifying further. Her ex-husband came in to refute her claim that Barton arranged their marriage. She responded with a tirade against the court. The summations were anticlimactic but revealing. The prosecuting attorney praised Barton's courage in coming to court, adding that Mrs. Barton, "his wife for the past twenty years, listened and by her presence forgave." Lamely the defense termed the trial a "persecution" behind which stood Barton's

"millions." On August 2 the jury found Mrs. King guilty (though, presumably in view of her condition, it recommended mercy). The judge
lauded it for having returned the first blackmail verdict in the county
in a decade.[13]

The judge sentenced Mrs. King to five to ten years in prison, hoping the penalty would serve as a "deterrent" to further blackmail. (The
maximum sentence for that crime was seven-and-a-half to fifteen
years.) She vowed to take her case up the line, all the way to President
Roosevelt if need be. After she was two years into her sentence, an appeals court cut it to three to six years. In 1936 her attorney was dis-
barred. He had handled the slander suit, paid to typeset King's novel,
arranged Barton's arrest, and offered to rescind it in exchange for a settlement.[14]

In all, Barton had won a somewhat pyrrhic victory, but it might
have been worse. He was lucky, by one account, that only two New
York papers reported the entire trial, the "ultrarespectable" *Times* and
the *Sun*. The other dailies provided either skimpy or no coverage.
Cynics wondered if they had forgone this story of "stellar tabloidal
magnitude" in deference to the heft of advertising, "from cheese to
steel," that BBDO swung their way. An anonymous BBDO employee used
the back of a Barton newspaper column to suggest that the trial had revealed his hypocrisy, adding that most of his co-workers had known
about the affair and efforts of his senior colleagues to get the woman
out of the agency.[15] Barton emerged less mangled in reputation than
he might have. There were cheers in the courtroom when the verdict
came in. He received praise for his courage, albeit belatedly. *The Commentator* termed his ordeal "one of the vilest blackmail plots to en-
mesh a decent citizen" and said Barton "showed guts."[16]

The affair had to have jolted Barton's marriage, but it survived.[17]
There had been earlier rumors, of whose credibility there is no evidence. A Walter Winchell gossip column of August 1929 stated flatly
that "The Bruce Bartons are this and that way." His friend Gertrude
Lane called it to Barton's attention; he replied that Esther and he
would "still be happily married when there won't be two people left on

Broadway who can answer the question, 'Who was Walter Winchell?'"
If Barton ever strayed from his marriage vows on other occasions, it is
not clear. Louise MacLeod, his fiercely protective secretary, conceded
that "being a male, he occasionally fell by the wayside." But she bri-
dled at a graduate student's phrase that he was "weak where women are
concerned," lest it connote "promiscuity or frequent affairs—wholly
untrue in Mr. Barton's case. Many women," she added, "made a big
play for him," and she "always felt he was afraid of women."[18]

FOR ANY NUMBER of reasons, Barton might have chosen to take a
trip around the world with his wife and daughter in 1934: a desire to
get away from New York's wagging tongues may have been one of
them, and reknitting a raveled marriage, another. Barton claimed that
his motive was simply to "give my mind a real rest" after a long period
of work. He had initially committed himself to advertising for only an
intermediate term, whose length was now about up. On the trip he did
some thinking about whether to stay in the business. To a friend and
associate he declared that what he would do on his return was "in the
lap of the gods." He speculated whether his partners "really want me
to come back?" He was not, he confessed to W. H. Johns, "at all happy
about my own performance" and hoped an absence would clarify
"where and how I can be most useful." References en route to his improving health suggest some problems in that quarter, perhaps including a return of insomnia. In early February he filed his last newspaper
column. The announcement of his plans was enough to prompt a
poem in the New Yorker, in which Phyllis McGinley rhymed that Barton, "who sponsored God, has given Shakespeare a friendly nod. . . ."[19]
    Barton headed west with Esther and Betsey, making a stop in
Phoenix, his favorite winter location, moving on to Palo Alto to visit ex-
President Hoover, and then taking ship in San Francisco. He kept a diary of his trip, which included stops in Hawaii, Japan, Shanghai
(where he interviewed T. V. Soong, Marshal Jiang Ji-shei's brother in
law), Hong Kong, Canton, Singapore, Rangoon, across India, Port

Said, Cairo, and back through Europe. It was a leisurely, luxurious trip. In many ports, agents of BBDO clients took him and his needs in hand.[20]

While in Asia he mused that the Western powers had little business and less leverage in this part of the world, whose problems would prove intractable. Besides his diary, he also wrote a few articles which he sent home. One that he wired from Shanghai predicted war between the USSR and Japan. He detailed the problems facing the Japanese, suspected they were underprepared for any military challenge, and saw China, tethered to four thousand years of tradition, as owning chiefly the weapon of impermeable patience. In later years he often returned to his diary epiphany that "the White man is on his way out of the Orient"—usually to reinforce his view of the unwisdom of American interventions in Asian affairs.[21]

His European sojourn confirmed to him the scant appeal of Italian and German fascism. He now judged glib and ill-thought the oft-heard claim that "What we need in the United States is a dictator." He conceded Mussolini's "efficiency and progress" and Hitler's grasp on "psychology," but the price, "the most ruthless disregard of human rights and human life," was far too high. He delivered that message when he was interviewed at the gangplank on his return to New York in June 1934.

Sometimes, though, Barton philosophized more neutrally about global political trends than later tastes would find appropriate. An August 1934 speech emphasized that Mussolini understood Italian aspirations and thus would win any free election, that Hitler had a like "understanding of popular psychology" and "embodie[d] the hope of a people who until he came were almost hopeless. . . ." In a tangled argument, Barton avowed he had no "sympathy with a government or any policy, whether you call it Ku Klux in our own country or anything else, that has done some of the things that have been done under all those dictatorships"; but, judging from his own recent visit to Germany, he suggested that "sometimes our papers present crises which are much more serious than they actually turn out to be." While not "defending" it "in any way," he reported on the propaganda show he viewed in Berlin which documented the heavy Jewish representation in positions of skill and influence in Germany and thus why Hitler's "plan . . . was not an unnatural thing to have happen." He had met no one who had seen Jews beaten up and witnessed a large crowd attending one synagogue.[22]

Barton plunged back into the affairs of his advertising agency, for which the 1930s proved a stiff challenge. As its clients suffered, they naturally sliced expenses, and so ad agencies suffered too. It was difficult to stay afloat and preserve jobs, but the agency rode out the Great Depression fairly successfully. BBDO managed to endure the bottom of the depression with only one losing year, 1932. Although massive layoffs may have been avoided, one veteran remembered: "People were disappearing from every aisle," and salaries were cut. After 1929, billings declined dramatically, reaching their low point of $14.8 million in 1933. Finally and slowly they began to climb, reaching $20.6 million in 1937. They fell sharply the next year before inching back up. Not until 1944 would billings exceed those of 1929. Most of the employees' jobs were preserved. Barton returned to his agency after his trip—apparently his doubts as to whether his colleagues wanted him back were ill-founded—as the depression ground through its fifth year. He credited Osborn with bringing in new business in this period, which "did much to help us come through as we did."[23]

Ironically, the intensified hostility toward business in general during the economic crisis proved a boon to the advertising industry—and to Barton. Given both New Deal attacks on business and their resonance among the public, the times called for more institutional advertising. A 1937 brochure put out by the American Newspaper Publishers Association defined (and touted) institutional advertising as a means to answer "popular discontent with our social and economic position" fanned by both "sincere rabble-rousers" and "plain demagogues." The N. W. Ayer agency predicted that industry's "most serious problem" in the next ten years would not be sales, production, capital, or credit but "the problem of public goodwill and friendship." Industry must recognize that it was engaged in a "war" against an enemy with the goal of "the complete destruction and dissolution of our entire industrial system."[24]

Barton preached a similar message. In December 1935 he told members of the Congress of American Industry that they must advertise themselves, for "industry and politics . . . are competitors for the confidence and favor of . . . the public." Industry "must persuade them that we are more reliable than the politicians. . . ." The battle for the public's allegiance must be joined. "No major industry has any moral right to allow itself to be unexplained, misunderstood, or publicly distrusted, for by its unpopularity it poisons the pond in which we all must fish." This task required spending less "time with our lawyers trying to circumvent the politicians, and twice as much time with our sales managers and our advertising agents seeking to make ourselves popular with the Boss of the politicians, the public."[25]

Barton's talents in the field of institutional advertising served his agency well in such times. In a major coup in 1935, BBDO won the account of United States Steel. Barton and Durstine worked together to obtain it. On hearing that Big Steel had decided to drop its national advertising, Barton plied its chieftains with a version of his "Knew Not Joseph" argument. They were merely canceling "the limited fraction of your advertising you originate and place." The part which others, "politicians" and "demagogs," circulated would continue—to their detriment. With the New Deal at high tide, the steel men reversed themselves. Barton, who one colleague said "hit a high spot in his career" with his presentation, also received credit for another famous contribution to institutional advertising, his encomium to the company's founder, Andrew Carnegie: "He came to a land of wooden towns and left a nation of steel." BBDO's advertising for U.S. Steel targeted chiefly the boardrooms of large industrial corporations that were its main customers. Billings on the U.S. Steel account climbed to $712,000 in 1936, and Barton paid close attention to such an important client.[26]

BBDO acquired another jumbo client in the DuPont Corporation. DuPont had been weathering gales of adverse public relations in the

1930s. Its name as a leading producer of explosives had speckled the "merchants of death literature" which sprouted in the mid-thirties; the munitions investigation led by the isolationist Senator Gerald Nye had given further velocity to charges that the interests of major U.S. corporations in war-dependent profits had dragged the country into the bloodshed of 1917. The DuPonts had also played a key role in creating the American Liberty League, which spearheaded opposition to FDR and the New Deal, only to see its viewpoint humiliatingly crushed in the 1936 election.[27]

DuPont had, however, been actively diversifying its product line, moving into paints and dyes, adhesives, Cellophane, plastics, and artificial fibers (nylon was unveiled in 1938). BBDO helped retool the company's image from that of "the gun powder people, the people who start wars," as Barton subsequently reminisced, to the people who brought "Better Things for Better Living Through Chemistry," the slogan the company adopted in 1935. The products were DuPont's, but much of the favorable publicity was engineered by BBDO. After numerous stops and starts and resistance from one of the DuPonts, BBDO persuaded the company to sponsor the radio series *Cavalcade of America*, which offered dramatizations of American progress exemplified in the stories of its "plain" people. The series played to the agency's (and Roy Durstine's) strengths in radio. Ever a hard sell, DuPont canceled, then reinstated its sponsorship of *Cavalcade* several times and also discarded BBDO's "Better Things for Better Living" slogan after three years.[28]

Despite triumphs such as these, the agency was experiencing a certain friction and discontent. Barton would later remark that in flush times the creative people in advertising (in other words, in BBDO) "can flame with enthusiasm," but "they can wilt and become useless in an atmosphere of friction and frustration. This latter was our situation in the middle thirties."[29]

Mid-decade brought changes in management. In 1936 the elderly William Johns retired as president and Roy Durstine, already charged with most of the administrative burden (and president of BDO before the merger), replaced him, a succession that would have near-term consequences. Barton continued the kinds of activities that had engaged him in the twenties—calling on actual and potential clients, writing copy, proselytizing businessmen on the need for continued PR, and writing for himself. In 1934 he wrote a booklet, "What I Have Learned About Life Insurance," of which an industry committee distributed over two million copies and for which he was paid $2,500. BBDO managed to weather the hard times of the early 1930s, and in 1936 Barton was able to draw a salary of $50,000.[30]

Yet for advertising it was still a shaky time. The political culture of the depression years had scant room for the Businessman Hero of the 1920s—or for the sort of lavish praise Barton had heaped on business leaders. Advertising and public relations came in for mounting criticism as one more instance of wasteful and sometimes deceitful behavior by business. The strenuous efforts of the PR firm founded by Ivy Lee to fight New Deal efforts to impose a "death sentence" on utilities holding companies in 1935 prompted a counterattack in the form of a Senate investigation into these activities. The probe exposed practices lavishly funded by the utilities, such as a campaign of telegrams from fake senders. It was just as well that Barton no longer had a prominent connection with the utility industry. In these hard times the American consumers' movement also grew robustly. Books critical of useless or harmful products (such as patent remedies) and those who shilled for them found publishers and markets. Consumer's Research, an organization that tested and rated products, grew fourfold from 1930 to 1936.[31]

Advertising was losing credibility among the public—and especially among New Dealers. Critics said it was still deceptive, that it still added cost but not value to products. The emerging consumers' movement found nothing kind to say about it. James Rorty, a radical who had worked at BBDO, wrote His Master's Voice, which assailed the advertising industry and sought to skewer his ex-boss Barton. He offered a typical advertising scenario in which the hypothetical Primrose Cheese account is won by a hypothetical agency commanded by "Calvin Kidd, author, editor and advertising man," who worshiped aphorisms that could only be Bartonian. (And yet in outlining how he himself would approach advertisers, Rorty declared that he would counsel less advertising and more "Service"—using the very incantation of a key argument in Barton's *The Man Nobody Knows*.)[32] In titling his first chapter "The Business Nobody Knows," Rorty claimed he did not mean to "parody" Barton. But he devoted an entire chapter to lampooning *The Man* and other of Barton's writings. Mass advertising in general he defined as "reader-exploitation, cultural malnutrition and stultification." He likened it to "a grotesque, smirking gargoyle set at the very top of America's sky-scraping adventure in acquisition *ad infinitum*. The tower is tottering," but meanwhile its gargoyle "corrupts everything she touches—art, letters, science, workmanship, love, honor, manhood. . . ." Advertising created a "pseudoculture" which smothered any "organic culture." It made people "twitch with little fears and itch with little greeds."[33] The tower, it would turn out, had greater staying power than Rorty suspected.

Barton made no public reply to Rorty, but his partner Roy Durstine did, with a brief dismissal of the book in *Advertising & Selling*: "some of it is pretty cheap. . . ." He compared Rorty, "pretty red" but discreet while at BBDO, to other "bright young men who have passed through our door both ways. They can write parodies of [Barton], they can kid his style. . . . The only thing they can't do is to write like him."[34]

Critical authors constituted only one flank of a deeper menace to advertising: the possibility of government discipline. The New Dealers, Rex Tugwell of the Agriculture Department in particular, loomed as a more dangerous enemy to Madison Avenue. In 1933 Tugwell had proposed adding teeth to the 1906 Pure Food and Drug Act, bringing cosmetics under its purview and reining in false advertising.[35] The ad industry's rhetoric—and Barton's—escalated against Tugwell, who absorbed so many jolts as a political lightning rod for the New Deal that he resigned from the administration in 1936. Admen warned that the New Deal was embarked on a crusade to destroy their livelihood. Barton would serve as an important defender of his business against threatened inroads by New Deal criticisms.

As usual, Barton did not close his eyes to the imperfections of his line of business. In a 1933 speech on the excesses attributable to "ballyhoo" (a term often applied to episodes of noisy publicity common in the 1920s), Barton himself conceded that "we advertising men have been far from guiltless. We have told men that if they would change their breakfast food they would become vice presidents, and women that if they would use a different soap they would become social leaders." He could see how these and worse transgressions had led to threats of federal regulation.[36]

The threat from the New Deal remained largely speculative, however. For BBDO the more immediate danger lay deeper and closer to home. Its original three-man partnership was unraveling. In 1938 the agency lost $121,000 for the year as a result, Osborn later recalled, of "internal dissension." BBDO was facing a crisis, and some thought Roy Durstine was at its core. He had long held the lead role in management, and his insistence that every BBDOer could write copy, handle art, and treat with clients was proving faulty and costly. One veteran described the agency, its members with such specialized skills dispersed among "contact groups," as "thirty little agencies with nothing in common but the toilets." Moreover, as Barton later acknowledged, in the mid-thirties, Durstine and he had "drifted further apart in our ideas of management. As his personal difficulties intensified, Durstine withdrew into himself, was unapproachable, shunned contact even with our own personnel." In-house talk suggested that Durstine's distractions included drink, an imminent personal bankruptcy, and a new wife. Barton was "unhappy"; so were "our creative people," and "good people left us." There was a sense on the street that BBDO was in decline. Early in 1939, while Barton was in Washington serving in Congress, Osborn notified him of an emergency directors meeting, triggered by threats by a dozen key men to leave the agency unless drastic actions were taken. Several directors insisted that Osborn must leave Buffalo and come to New York to "manage the entire business"; Osborn would not accede unless Barton agreed to be "active as president." Barton gave his assent.

BBDO's lawyer was dispatched to Phoenix to inform the honeymooning Durstine that he was out.[37]

Even after the shakeup, uncertainty stalked the agency's corridors. There was talk on the street that Durstine would be raiding BBDO accounts.[38] The emergency required hands-on efforts by the firm's senior members. Barton drafted a cheering memo for the internal newsletter, laying out the nature of the reorganization. He reassuringly described how all the top managers—senior, but not too senior—were scrambling to pick up the agency's abdicated responsibilities. Barton himself planned "to do more, both in New York and in the outside offices" once Congress adjourned. He was "beginning to get the same kick out of working for BBDO" as he had when Osborn and he "toiled shoulder to shoulder for 12 hours a day in volunteer war work." He also sent a letter to clients pledging to spend at least two days a week in the office.

Osborn assumed the helm. He refocused the agency's emphasis from institutional advertising to packaged goods; strengthened BBDO's talents in research and marketing; and guided the move to broaden ownership of the agency by making stock available to the more talented employees whose loyalty needed anchoring to the firm. In 1940 a client cost-accounting system enabled BBDO to get a better handle on expenses. Osborn's analysis of what was wrong in New York concluded that the chief problem was "inadequacy of creative effort." He gathered BBDOers together of an evening and, acting as a "creative coach," got them to think up solutions to current problems. Thus originated the "brainstorming" that became Osborn's most widely recognized legacy to advertising. The situation improved. The agency managed to hang on to its clients. By June 1939 salary cuts imposed in 1938 were rescinded. By 1940, with business generally on the upswing, the heeling ship seemed righted. BBDO had survived, with perhaps most of the credit due Osborn.[39]

BARTON CONTINUED writing during the 1930s, though his succession of books ended in 1932 with his life of Paul and *A Parade of the*

States, a compilation of the brief tributes he had written to all the states and recited on a radio show sponsored by his client General Motors.[40] In the late twenties, his father and he had plotted out a book to be called *The Story of Business*. They had both worked on it, and a preliminary draft was well begun. Various forces, which may have included his father's declining health and then death, and his own preoccupations after the Crash, raised obstacles to the project. He told his publisher it was "on the shelf for an indefinite period and perhaps . . . forever." By 1935 he said himself that his days of book writing had probably passed.[41] He continued to publish in magazines and wrote for newspapers through much of the early 1930s. He published a Sunday column, distributed first by the McClure's syndicate, starting in 1926, and later by the *New York Herald Tribune*, until early 1934, when his trip around the world brought it to an end. From early 1935 until October 1936 he contributed a thrice-weekly column for the *New York American*.[42]

It was not an easy time for ambitious new writing projects. The depression proved wearing on Barton, who found himself occupied by family problems. His father died in December 1930. Reverend Barton had maintained a busy life and good health until near his death. He kept busy in religious affairs, occupied a pulpit ad interim, held a chair in "practical theology" at Vanderbilt University (and preached at a church there), and wrote profusely on historical subjects, particularly Lincoln. His studies of the Rail Splitter, built on elaborate travels on Lincoln's home turf and new findings from fresh research, met high standards of scholarship.[43] The senior Barton's death deeply affected his son; Bruce recalled that in his father's last decade or so, and especially after Bruce's mother died, "he and I were like brothers." Letters crossed three to four times a week; Bruce "took over the management of his literary affairs" and got his father generous payments from leading magazines.[44]

Members of Bruce's family suffered from the economic downturn, and he tried to find them jobs. He helped two of his brothers with their finances and their health. He also aided the family of the now-grown lad whom his parents had rescued from want during their stay in Tennessee.[45]

In August 1934 Barton was awakened in the middle of the night and summoned to a hospital in Connecticut. His daughter Betsey had been in a car crash that left her seriously injured with a broken vertebra and her legs paralyzed. She required operations, long hospitalization, and rehabilitation. Slowly she struggled to regain her ability to walk. A doctor in California got her "up on her feet," with braces and crutches; with great labor she could move but still suffered paralysis.[46] Then tragedy struck a second time. Sent to Arizona for health reasons, in February 1937 she was riding in a car driven by her nurse/companion which was broadsided by another car. She was seriously injured again, with multiple broken bones.[47] She was able later to walk with the aid of crutches, but for extended mobility she remained dependent on a wheelchair.

Betsey adjusted to her condition. "Now, this is what I have to live with," she told an interviewer. "Now, what can I make of it." She had a wide circle of friends in New York, Washington (when her father went to Congress), and Arizona, where the Bartons wintered. She would go on to take up painting and writing; she published four books, including one about dealing with her handicap, plus magazine articles.[48]

BARTON (as well as his clients) also faced various challenges from Franklin D. Roosevelt's New Deal. Barton had held a low opinion of Roosevelt as governor of New York and as a presidential candidate. He had tried several routes to circumvent FDR's election in 1932. One device was an ad Barton drafted on behalf of fellow New Yorkers urging the Democratic convention to find someone other than this candidate without ideas or convictions: "Don't nominate your weakest man."[49] He had maneuvered in vain to get the Democrats to select Newton Baker instead, and then he worked for the futile Hoover campaign.

Once FDR took office, he seemed a more impressive leader than Barton had anticipated. He came to see Roosevelt as "preeminent

The Barton family ca. 1893 in Wellington, Ohio. Webster Barton Beatty, the lad taken in by the Bartons in Tennessee, stands behind Reverend and Mrs. Barton. In front (left to right) are Charles, Helen, Fred, and Bruce. (Robert Shawmut Barton was not born until 1894.) [*Congregational Library*]

Bruce Barton (left) with his next-eldest brother Charles, at roughly ages eight and six. The photograph was presumably taken in Boston, when Reverend William E. Barton was minister at Shawmut Church. [*Congregational Library*]

Bruce, in what appears to be a portrait taken in high school in Oak Park, Illinois. Into his prime and beyond, Barton would sport some variation of a curly wave in the hair over his forehead. [*Congregational Library*]

(Left to right) L. Dudley Field, Bruce Barton, Clarence Davis, Alex Osborn, and J. C. Lamorotte at the Amco office in Rochester, New York, ca. 1920. [*Wisconsin Historical Society*]

Reverend William E. Barton and Bruce in the early to mid-1920s. The two were always close, and Bruce relied on his father for advice in many areas, including the theology that distinguished his writings. [*Congregational Library*]

The party *after* the party

THE strains of the music still sing in her ears; her
pulses beat to its rhythm, her cheeks are aglow—
So, flushed and happy, she slips into her mother's
room, to live through the evening again.

They are very rich, those *after* hours—when the
hearts of mothers and daughters draw close, and sons
discover that fathers are pals. A friendly lamp invites confidences. In every such family party it plays
its silent part.

YOU have noticed how, on the stage, a
gloomy room is changed into a cheerful
room by merely rearranging the lights.

Your Edison MAZDA Lamp dealer knows
something of the application of the stage
manager's art to the home. He will tell you
which Edison MAZDA Lamp will light each
room of your home to make your comfort
greater and your work easier.

EDISON MAZDA LAMPS

EDISON LAMP WORKS OF GENERAL ELECTRIC COMPANY

In 1920 Barton teamed his
prose with Norman
Rockwell's art in a series of
ads for Edison Mazda Lamps,
a division of General
Electric. As "a friendly lamp
invites confidence," so GE
could enrich family life.
[*Roland Marchand*, Creating
the Corporate Soul,
University of California Press]

This ad, one of Barton's particularly
renowned efforts, formed part of a 1926
GE institutional campaign for which
BDO received a Harvard Advertising
Award, one of several it won. [*Roland
Marchand*, Creating the Corporate Soul,
University of California Press]

Any woman who
does anything which
a little electric motor
can do is working for
3¢ an hour !

There are few hard tasks left
in the home which electricity
cannot do at trifling cost. You
will find the G-E monogram
on many electrical household
conveniences. It is a guarantee
of excellence as well as a
mark of service.

Ask your electric company or dealer to help
you select the labor-saving electrical appliances best suited for your home.

GENERAL ELECTRIC

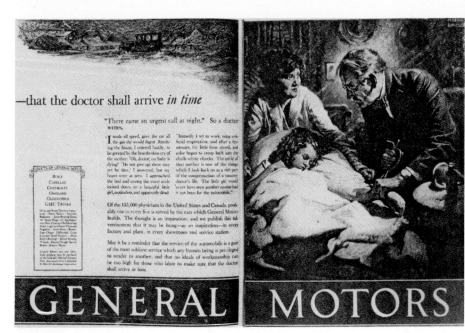

As in this GM ad, Barton wove stories more than he recited selling points. Thus he humanized a vast, sprawling corporation, showing it to be a reliable deliverer of service to the public. [*Roland Marchand*, Creating the Corporate Soul, *University of California Press*]

The initials of a friend

You will find these letters on many tools by which electricity works. They are on great generators used by electric light and power companies; and on lamps that light millions of homes.

They are on big motors that pull railway trains; and on tiny motors that make hard housework easy.

By such tools electricity dispels the dark and lifts heavy burdens from human shoulders. Hence the letters G-E are more than a trademark. They are an emblem of service—the initials of a friend.

GENERAL ELECTRIC

Barton strove to reframe giant enterprises on a human scale, as in this rendering of General Electric's logo as "the initials of a friend." Agency lore suggests that he may have gotten the idea for this design from a streetcar, manhole cover, or some such everyday item. [*Roland Marchand*, Creating the Corporate Soul, *University of California Press*]

Roy S. Durstine, co-founder of BDO (the other "B" came after the 1928 merger with the George Batten Agency). A jack-of-all-trades, as chief administrative officer Durstine pushed BDOers to take on a variety of account responsibilities rather than specialize. He helped position BDO as a leader in the new medium of radio. [BBDO]

Barton with film mogul Cecil B. De Mille, who holds a copy of *The Man Nobody Knows*. In 1926 Bruce and his father went to Hollywood to advise De Mille on his biblical epic *King of Kings*. As with all new media, the movies fascinated Barton. [*Wisconsin Historical Society*]

Bruce and Esther Randall Barton disembarking from the *Ile de France* in April 1930 after a trip to Europe. To reporters, who often sought interviews on such occasions, he held forth on topics ranging from tipping and cheating on customs duties to Prohibition. [*Wisconsin Historical Society*]

Barton (left) with two pals, famed sportswriter Grantland Rice (next to him) and John Wheeler of the North American Newspaper Alliance. Gesturing is Frank E. Gannett, founder of the New York State–based newspaper chain. The photo was probably taken in Rochester in 1937. [*Wisconsin Historical Society*]

Bruce Barton (second from right) at the reception center of the Time-Life Building in New York, 1949, with former GE executive Owen D. Young (center) and Time-Life publisher Henry Luce (right). [*Wisconsin Historical Society*]

Both in his work at BBDO, which was actively involved in producing radio and television shows, and as a public figure in his own right, Barton hobnobbed with celebrities. Here he concludes a deal with Lassie, a mainstay on TV in the 1950s. [*Wisconsin Historical Society*]

One of many depicting Barton the politician, this cartoon highlights his 1937 pledge, if elected to the House of Representatives, to repeal one "useless" law a week (not per day as suggested by the artist C. K. Berryman). [*Wisconsin Historical Society*]

Barton on the hustings at Cooperstown, New York, October 5, 1940, opening his Senate campaign. He devoted much of his oratory to championing Wendell Willkie's GOP presidential candidacy. [*Wisconsin Historical Society*]

Barton smiling his way through the crowd at a rally during his 1940 Senate campaign. [*Wisconsin Historical Society*]

Barton in front of his famous office mural of Coney Island's boardwalk, meant to remind him of the target audience for his ads. With him (left to right) are longtime partner and friend Alex F. Osborn and other BBDO executives Ed Cashin, Fred Manchee, Dave Danforth, and then-president Charles H. Brower. [*Wisconsin Historical Society*]

Barton captured in a pensive mood, probably in the late 1950s. He had relinquished most of his executive responsibilities at BBDO, but he retained a legendary star quality among many of the agency's clients. [*Wisconsin Historical Society*]

among all men in public life in his ability to think in selling terms and
to speak in advertising language."[50] The economy was in flux in 1933
and so, with his involvement in the blackmail trial, was Barton's world.
He was reticent to comment on the early New Deal. In the fall of 1933,
while he much preferred the certainties of Coolidge's era, Barton
praised FDR for knowing "that in a time of crisis almost any courageous action is preferable to vacillation and inaction." He applauded
the bank closure, the "group thinking" under the National Recovery
Act, which was ending child labor and raising wages, and public
works. Adjustments would be needed; but human nature had not
changed, and previous "New Deals" had promised much and delivered little. While this one would not "give us a bridge to the moon," it
might "stop some of the leaks in the roof of our national wood-shed."[51]

Barton conceded that congressional inquiries of the early 1930s
had shown some American business leaders to be "so shamefully false
to their trust that they dealt a staggering blow to the faith of Americans
in their institutions." (Yet he also resented the New Deal implication
that everything in "the Old Order" was wrong.) He did express qualms
about the readiness of federal muckamucks to hire press agents. He
had other criticisms, but the New Deal merited a chance to prove itself and might have "a happy ending." So he announced in the final
column before his world trip, which he hoped would give him some
perspective on the New Deal experiment.[52] Fresh down the gangplank
on his return, he reported the worldwide interest in the question, "'will
Roosevelt succeed?' They ask it with great and almost tragic earnest-
ness. . . ." At a time radicals were likely to rail against FDR, Barton
thought conservatives "ought to be slow to criticize and generous in
our support whenever we can be." He still hoped (as did others) in late
1934 that support and close attendance upon FDR by business might
keep the New Deal on an acceptable track.[53]

Barton accepted the need for government to ease swings in the business cycle and to reform a business system he had never thought perfect. He had come to admire the Spanish political philosopher Jose
Ortega y Gasset, whose insights in *The Revolt of the Masses* frequently

underpinned Barton's analysis of sociopolitical trends. Thus when he suggested that corporations might well place on their boards of directors "one or more representatives of the public," he seasoned this concession with a dose of Ortega-inspired perspective about the ongoing "revolt of the masses," whose lives had been made less precarious by advances in industry and health, and whose demands were correspondingly more insistent. Governing classes could no longer ignore their clamor. He told a 1936 baking industry audience that "the most important fact in business today is that the mass of the people are in power, both politically and financially." He advised a manufacturers association to focus less on the upcoming 1936 election as the answer to their prayers and more on the long-term goal of making business competitive with politicians by being and showing itself more honest and otherwise deserving of public confidence. Businessmen needed to compete on this higher plane, wasting less energy fighting the New Deal and devoting more to convincing the public that they delivered on more promises than did politicians. A 1939 speech cited Ortega's teachings that the people, now literate and aware of their rights, were in control of most governments. Leaders held power at the will of the masses, and Barton found hope in the possibility that business might once again win their allegiance. Talleyrand was a favorite historical model drawn from his extensive readings in Napoleon, who understood that whatever the gyrations of political fortune, the people ruled.[54]

A related theme recurred in writings and speeches: America was plunged into a revolution, but revolutions are survivable. As he put it to a business group in early 1935, businessmen must accept this condition philosophically. If they did, they could "attain a certain degree of mental poise and serenity." Loss there would be, but it could be anticipated and endured. He relished Ralph Waldo Emerson's tale of a friend who, on trips to Europe, always budgeted funds "to be robbed of" and then ceased to worry. Similarly, while history was filled with New Deals, recuperation was equally frequent. (Barton had a penchant for cyclical views of history.) Similarly for the depression: "we shall recover partly because of the government, partly in spite of it."[55]

Barton found his voice after his return from abroad. By 1935 he was decrying what he deemed the excesses of New Deal "Social Planners." "A fundamental fault with so many brain trust schemes is that they start with *projects* and not with *people*." He lauded FDR's courage and cheer but wondered whether the times now called for less of them and more of "moral fear." He rummaged through history for relevant cautionary parallels. King John's public works program had resulted in oppressive taxes which led to the barons' revolt; rising taxes under the New Deal raised the "possibility of another Magna Charta." By 1936 his tone sharpened. Businessmen, a column generalized, played the game; intellectuals like New Dealer Rex Tugwell and his group "are natural born side-liners." Another potshot described the "liberal" as "against" rather than "for" anything, and wondered whether this negativism might not stem from "torpid livers and unfortunate financial experience."[56] He also criticized the New Deal's tendency to let the "emergencies" under which it had first legislated last forever. Asked to review a pamphlet of the Federal Housing Administration, he thought it good enough but caviled at how "'emergency' institutions, like yours, are digging themselves in deeper all the time and reenforcing their defenses by propaganda." The FHA's answer noted that Congress had meant most of the housing program it created to be permanent, and even the emergency provisions had been extended at the behest of "business men." Twitting Barton (who had once cautioned that succeeding generations "Knew Not Joseph"), an FHA functionary reminded the PR advocate: "You too know what happens to even the best article when mention of it is not kept constantly before the public. Remember Pear's soap?"[57]

Barton balanced sharp criticism with the philosophical understanding of a onetime would-be historian that many changes required acceptance and adjustment rather than mere opposition. Yet however praiseworthy the New Deal's "avowed purposes," it seemed unaware that "History teaches us three things, plainly": that ongoing deficits cause inflation and thus "disaster"; that a suffering people "eventually will revolt"; and that "a despotism of labor is even worse than a despotism of capital." Government must meet human needs but preserve freedom, and "for such a program I am willing to be well taxed in time, effort, and income. . . ." Later that year he spoke of the "great changes . . . going on" and leading, however murkily, "toward some goal that we must believe represents social betterment." He did not wish to "be maneuvered by my natural conservatism or by tradition or prejudice onto the wrong side of this war," nor for his grandchildren to say, "'A great social revolution went on in the old man's life time, and he contributed nothing.'" He denigrated devil-take-the-hindmost social policy by citing the parallel of golf, labeling its handicap system "an instrument of social justice." Any member of a handicap committee knew how very few could shoot in the 70s and how many "pound around from trap to trap and never crack a hundred." Like such panels, and just as reasonably, "all over the world Government is setting itself up as a huge handicap committee," aiming to "smooth out the inequalities so that even the poorest player can have some chance to enjoy the game and participate in the prizes."[58]

Barton also dabbled in the foreign policy debates of the era. A full-blown critic of war, he invested some of his energies in the peace issue. He applauded the wisecrack of the late Socialist party leader Eugene V. Debs, not otherwise a likely talisman for this defender of capitalism, that all the belligerents got out of the Great War was "influenza and the income tax." He proposed to Printers' Ink's editor that the 1928 Kellogg-Briand Pact, which aimed to outlaw war, would be improved by a clause mandating that each signatory cancel one battleship and use the savings for a "continuous advertising campaign" to keep the treaty before the public.[59] He revisited this notion in 1932 in a piece titled "Let's Advertise this Hell!" It urged that nations spend a pittance of their defense budgets on promoting peace. Anti-war ads might emphasize how trivial were the issues that led to wars—"the shooting of an obscure prince in the Balkans." They might warn that "war machinery" such as mobilization tables made war "practically start itself." Or publicize that war had ceased to be an "outdoor sport" involving small groups, with room for heroism. Modern war should be renamed "Slaughter," with "as much chance for heroism as cattle in the Chicago stockyards." The United States, he suggested, should use 5 percent of its defense spending for publicity for peace. A small new organization, World Peaceways, reprinted the column and sought through various media to make people "peace conscious." It also used the sample ads Barton had included with the article and later persuaded other agencies to contribute new ones. One, for example, showed distraught parents at their child's bedside and was captioned, "A hospital would save his life . . . but he will have to die." The text described the nation's underfunded hospitals and concluded: "You see, we spent our money in the war," for which the collective cost of four days' fighting was the entire U.S. hospital budget.[60]

Barton also continued to work in Republican politics. He belonged to local Republican organizations and campaign committees. In 1936, as noted earlier, he was asked to counsel the Republican National Committee on how to construct a "publicity machine" comparable to what functioned for the Democratic National Committee under the guidance of the legendary Charles Michelson, the "ghost" who had so effectively soured public opinion against Hoover and promoted FDR's first election. The GOP tried to harness the emerging techniques of polling and mass marketing to its campaign, but FDR's forty-six-state juggernaut seemed to discredit their utility. To such insinuations Barton retorted that the election actually showed the efficacy of advertising techniques. Despite the overwhelming hostility of the newspapers and a costly radio campaign against him, FDR had won reelection "because for three years every word and act of his had been an advertisement in a tremendously powerful and effective campaign." He had succeeded, Barton said with grudging admiration, in making "the man in the street feel 'He is trying to do something for me.'" In fact Barton had earlier tried to advise business groups intent upon using the 1936 election to oust the New Deal to stick instead to their knitting, to do what business did best, to take a longer view, and to recognize that FDR had an unexcelled ability "to speak in advertising language."[61]

Although 1936 was not an auspicious political sally against the popular New Deal, it was not Barton's last. The next would be more successful, would define his career for the rest of the 1930s, and would embed Barton's name in one of the most famous tag lines in the history of American elections.

7

Mr. Barton Goes to Washington

THEODORE A. PEYSER had represented New York's Seventeenth District in Congress since 1932, when he defeated Ruth Baker Pratt. Pratt had occupied the seat once held by fellow Republican Ogden L. Mills until he became undersecretary and then secretary of the Treasury from 1927 to 1933. The Seventeenth was a classic "silk stocking" district. Notoriously gerrymandered, it ran up the center of Manhattan, stretching north from Fourteenth Street between Fourth and Eighth Avenues, extending one appendage through the high-rent corridor between Lexington and Fifth Avenues to Ninety-third Street on the East Side, while another arm jutted across Central Park to the Hudson River and elbowed north up to Eighty-third Street on the West Side. Containing much of Gotham's glitz, it was normally a Republican islet in a sea of Democratic voters, the charges of New York's infamous Tammany Hall. In 1932 the depression proved too strong even for the Seventeenth District's silken dikes. Proposing to gut the Volstead Act to "tax the thirsty and feed the hungry," Teddy Peyser charged that Hoover had so impoverished the Seventeenth that it was now only a "cotton stocking" district, and he won it for the Democrats. A son of Tammany and ally of Senator Robert Wagner, Peyser gave his constituents low-profile representation that was described as pro–New Deal with occasional flashes of independence. Well enough liked, he won reelection twice, the last time by seven thousand votes. Then, suddenly on August 8, 1937, he died. Bruce Barton's life was about to change.[1]

In youthful reveries Barton had imagined himself a Western editor whose crusading zeal elevated him to the United States Senate. Eventually Hollywood director Frank Capra gave that role to Jimmy Stewart in *Mr. Smith Goes to Washington*, the screen version of this fantasy. A region of Barton's brain had always been reserved for dreams of statesmanship, and these may have helped prompt the caveat he had insisted upon in 1918 that left him free to opt out of BDO after ten or fifteen years. His assistance to Coolidge, Hoover, and other notables had kept him politically focused, as did the passing interest he took in local GOP affairs in New York. There was chatter in 1936 that he might seek office. In June that year he reported that "some of the local leaders are trying to put the heat on me to run for Congress." He did not wholly dismiss the prospect. Nothing resulted, but Peyser's unanticipated death altered the political landscape.[2]

Seeking to reclaim the Seventeenth for the GOP, New York County party chairman Kenneth Simpson prevailed on Barton to run. His phone call, which dragged Barton off a golf course in Canada, came "out of a clear sky." Barton first insisted on having the support of New York's fiery mayor, Fiorello H. La Guardia, who was also running in 1937, as well as a spot on La Guardia's Fusion party ticket. La Guardia agreed (and would endorse Barton during the campaign). The Democrats put up Stanley Osserman, a Tammany loyalist who ran as a staunch New Dealer. The American Labor party candidate, George Backer, engaged in a family real estate business, was a wealthy civic activist and "philanthropist" who claimed to be the most loyal Rooseveltian in the race. He termed Republicans "just a few nostalgic persons who think everything was swell in 1926."[3]

Barton set forth his theme as soon as he announced. "Any nickel-in-the-slot district in the South or West gets more consideration in Washington" than the Seventeenth, he lamented. His district needed more than "an errand boy for Tammany or a rubber stamp for the White House." He aspired to return the Seventeenth to its former sta-

tus as an influential congressional district, as its heavily taxed constituents deserved. A trade journal reported that Barton "visualized his
constituency more realistically as 60% middle-class" rather than silk-
stocking. Hence he planned to target his electioneering on the issue of
the high cost of living.[4]

He mounted an unusual campaign. He delayed its start, saying,
"an advertising man knows something about human nature. People get
tired and bored very quickly." He conducted a campaign more performative than oratorical. In La Guardia's New York it was hard to compete with the Little Flower's theatrics, but Barton—after all, only a
candidate for the House in an off-year election—managed to get generous newspaper coverage. He did so more by being seen in kinetic
roles in various locations in his district than by bloviating. Speak he
did, but more often in contexts that were as visual as aural. Innovating,
he took "a photographer and a man from our publicity department,
and had myself photographed talking to voters all over the district."
His partner Roy Durstine claimed to have thought up the idea. The
newspapers ate it up, as did several picture magazines. He may not
have invented but he clearly understood the virtues of what today we
term the "photo-op," and as an adman he realized that while individual *beaux gestes* could get him into the papers, his product needed frequent exposure. This it received from an energetic campaign of
billboards, car cards, and newspaper endorsements coming from his
business competitors—ads, essentially. He formally opened his campaign by claiming to have drafted a "stream-lined, twelve-cylinder, air-
conditioned plan" for his campaign—but then thrown it out. "I'm just
going to run."[5]

Barton managed to preempt most newspaper coverage from his rivals Osserman and Backer. The dailies covered his electioneering
more as a ramble than a campaign. A picture showed him wading
waist-deep into a gaggle of smiling street urchins, part of his "personal
survey" of the district.[6] He claimed to discover through this experience
that his silk-stocking district, if not relieved of the New Deal's "plow-
ing under cotton, . . . won't even be a cotton stocking district. It will be

a barefoot district." He cited a housewife he met who, shepherding her husband's modest pay and four children, hadn't served meat in ages because of its cost. He hoped to give this "nearly frantic" family a "break" as congressman. He allowed that FDR had achieved much, "but his brain trusters have gone too far." Two weeks later his picture garnished newspapers covering another of his forays into the district to spy out his constituents' hardships with the high cost of living: he was pictured with a butcher inspecting a slab of beef.

Barton pointed out how hard it was for small businesses to survive in the current economic climate: "the little man is getting squeezed littler and littler." He closed his appeal with a gimmick that came out of the ad world: he offered a reward of $25 to the first small entrepreneur in his district who wrote a letter documenting that he or she was "completely happy." He also invited letters expressing contrary sentiments. Later in the campaign, he toured, and condemned, slum housing in his district, and was pictured peering into one such building. His sally into Union Square, "a no-man's land" for GOP candidates and a stage for radical soapbox oratory, elicited a photograph of him engaged in democratic give-and-take with a group of unemployed men.[7]

Well-wishers and critics both noticed Barton's advantageous press coverage and pictorial campaign. The latter grumbled that the $40 million of advertising his agency ladled out annually accounted for the favorable treatment his campaign received. The left-wing gadfly journalist George Seldes concurred, suggesting that this advertising clout also explained the thin coverage of Barton's court run-in with Frances King. Columnist Heywood Broun joked that the Democrat Osserman "almost lives up to" the title of Barton's book, *The Man Nobody Knows*.[8]

Barton began with an unusual edge: heavy support from fellow advertising men. A number of prominent Madison Avenue competitors mobilized behind his candidacy. At a campaign lunch their leader boasted that Barton "will be the first real advertising man ever to occupy a position of importance and prominence in Congress." The Advertising Women of New York also sponsored a lunch. Barton made his profession practically part of his platform. "The trouble with Congress," he argued, was "that there are too many lawyers there" and "not enough salesmen." Salesmen "know people."[9]

HE PARADED HIMSELF as an independent, beholden to no one. He claimed that many "first-class experts are trying to develop me into a third-class politician," sending advice to speak this way on wealthy Park Avenue, that way in Union Square; or offering nuggets to be used before one or another ethnic group. "The appeal to class and race and special groups is the curse of American politics." He would make "no promise to any class or group" but would offer simply his independent judgment on all measures. He boasted that he answered no questionnaires sent him by organizations. Reflecting anti-modernist sentiments against emerging political trends, he warned against "bloc government" (having the American Labor candidate particularly in mind), citing as a chilling example France, "where the government has changed seventy-two times since the war."[10] He was very much a Republican but positioned himself within the party's liberal wing. He said the GOP needed to be "re-packaged"—an advertising term, as some newspapers noted. It needed new candidates, "young men" unsaddled with defeat who were "fresh and enthusiastic." Postmaster General James A. Farley singled out this proposal by "a well known advertising man" for derision. Citing a recent meeting of ex-President Hoover and ex-candidate Landon, the New Deal's political marshal doubted that a party so led would win public support "no matter what kind of pretty package" it was wrapped in.[11]

Barton subscribed to affirmative government. The GOP had sponsored "splendid social and humanitarian reforms," such as the first antitrust act, regulation of the commodities exchanges, and the Railway Labor Act, and bore the tradition of Teddy Roosevelt. It was ill-suited to be "a party of mere negation."[12] He warned an audience of fellow admen that grumbling was futile. "We must realize that people are determined to have a better life and that they will continue to expect government to play an important part in giving it to them. We must bring about rapprochement between government and business." That called for businessmen to contribute their talents to government. Barton offered few specifics, but he did say he would support any measure that enabled "the poor people of this great city to be decently housed." In his tramps through his district he had found some dwellings appalling. He knew of apartments where the stove provided the only heat and tenants scavenged wood from wrecked buildings and chopped it up in the street. Noting that England's housing program had pulled it out of depression, he thought a sound housing program a better idea than "putting billions into leaf-raking and irrigation dams."[13]

But Barton's main constituency lay elsewhere. He told the Business and Professional Women's Club that he would represent "the small business man," who was "the Forgotten Man of 1937." He repeatedly offered himself as the tribune of the middle class. He inveighed against the high cost of living, charging that New Deal "waste and extravagance" had propelled it "through the roof." "They killed little pigs in the South and the price of pork and ham in Manhattan skyrocketed," so that butcher shops threatened to become "museum pieces." Similarly, plowed-under cotton in Alabama meant that his district, silk-stocking or not, "can't afford decent clothes." His most dramatic campaign pledge was "to introduce a resolution every week to repeal one useless law." He invited lawyers, businessmen, and others to nominate statutes meriting this fate. The pace of legislation, he claimed, had sped up beyond control in recent years—nine hundred bills in the last session alone. While his colleagues might aspire to become great lawmakers, he wanted to be known as "the great repealer." A news photo showed him behind a bunker of statute books poring through superfluous enactments.[14]

Barely visible in the campaign, Barton's bewildered foes resorted to desperate attacks. Resurrecting Barton's favorable, if tentative, remarks about Mussolini's Italy in a 1930 magazine article, the Democrat Osserman warned: "Don't send a Fascist to Congress." Calling himself the only "liberal," he added that a vote for the "rich man" Backer on the American Labor ticket only aided "the Fascist!" Backer said the choice lay between progress (with him) or "Big Business" and "the road that leads to 'Fascism'" with the Republican. The noted attorney, reformer, and Democratic loyalist Samuel Untermyer (general counsel in the congressional investigation two decades earlier which had exposed the foibles of the U.S. banking system) wrote a blunt "Open Letter": "The knowledge that Bruce Barton is a Fascist should force every New Yorker into the realization of the grave danger we face if we send a man of such views of government to Congress."[15]

Barton brushed off such charges. At a party dinner he "ridiculed 'a very good whispering campaign . . . that I am anti-Semitic'" and "laughed at a similar campaign that 'I am a friend of Hitler and Mussolini and therefore a Fascist.'" Steering clear of alarmism, he suggested that "neither Fascism nor Communism will ever make much progress against the independent character of the American people."[16] His pro-Mussolini remarks seem not to have damaged him. A rough poll by his adherents found that only 4 of 784 constituents queried had even heard the charges. Barton won the election easily with 34,618 votes—more than the combined total of his opponents Osserman (21,845) and Backer (9,697).[17]

Barton's was a campaign unique or at least unusual in American political annals. He was hardly the first candidate to "package" himself, nor the last. But the combined leverage of his own skills as a publicist plus those of fellow admen who rallied to him produced a singular contest. Even Mayor La Guardia, who set the standard for colorful politics, granted that "Bruce Barton is waging an interesting campaign." *Advertising Age* (an outlet admittedly likely to tout the brilliance of a Madison Avenue venture) said Barton "struck a new note in political campaigns." It marked "the presence of a new, colorful, intangible something in the political arena." It was not always clear what that was. Barton himself tried to convey it at a victory celebration at his agency the morning after. He thought the election proved "that we in the advertising business know more about people than the politicians do." His supporters and he "got close to a lot of folks in this campaign. We didn't hold mass meetings in Carnegie Hall, or luncheons at the Waldorf. We went from door to door and store to store and talked with people about what we were thinking. We didn't talk about Constitutional rights. We talked about steak and pork chops." He attributed the outcome to the voters' "intelligence." They discounted charges "that I was a Fascist, a prohibitionist, anti-Semitic, even that I was a member of the Ku Klux Klan." His assistant, Louise MacLeod, asserted that he never once mentioned his opponents by name or made compromising pledges to anyone.[18]

Beyond this, no one was quite clear on *what* was novel or original about Barton's campaign. Surely he was not the first politician to merchandise his own personality. Although he was running for office, he did so by promising less "politics." He was not the first to claim the government required "business methods"—that cliché had festooned the oratory of Sinclair Lewis's satirical treatment of business ideology fifteen years earlier in *Babbitt*. And yet he also managed, by his infantry sweeps through the district and the newspaper coverage they drew, to avoid being caricatured as so many Republican office-seekers of that era were. He managed to escape portrayal with the tuxedoed, top-hatted graphics applied to the rich in the best-selling game of Monopoly (whose rights were purchased by Parker Brothers in that same year). He did not look or sound like the bejeweled couples in the famous *New Yorker* cartoon, who called at a mansion to invite its occupants to go with them to the Bijou to hiss Roosevelt.

Fully aware of his party's reputation for moneyed callousness, Barton set out to change it. Using media congruent with a single congressional district (yet managing to spill over into more national media), he managed to individuate himself, to stand out from the crowd.[19] He was a personality (in an age when "personality" was becoming a dominant commodity), not a mere spokesman or representative for a group; and when he did call himself a spokesman, he claimed to be the tribune for a vast group of individuals, whom he called "the forgotten man" in the middle.[20] He managed to project the same "sincerity" that enabled him to sell advertising campaigns, and he conveyed a sense that he cared about the problems of the broad sweep of his constituents. Much like some of the institutional ads he wrote (the little girl spared by the doctor's timely arrival in his GM car, the housewife saved hours of numbing labor by her GE appliance), Barton campaigned by spinning stories of individuals. His oratory outlined general concerns, but he illustrated them with individual tales—the "nearly frantic" mother nursing sick children and trying to feed a family amid high prices, the butcher squeezed by high costs. As he sold products (or companies), so he sold himself as a figure promising to be cognizant of, and sympathetic toward, the problems of the isolated citizen in a sprawling, demanding society. All politicians so endeavor. Barton succeeded.

At the same time he insisted he was a representative but not a rubber stamp. His individuation involved, he claimed, a commitment to independent judgment. He deplored a politics operated by "blocs." He was troubled by the emergence of New York's American Labor party. If it got its members into Congress, "that is the beginning of the bloc system." He equally opposed a "Rockefeller-Morgan" or anyone else's bloc, the end result of which would be the weak arrangement that was France's current government. Barton prided himself in having "made no pledges, answered no questionnaires, and committed myself to no minority pressure groups." Congress already had enough "promisers and yes-men."[21]

People noticed Barton's victory. Some celebrated with high jinks. On his arrival at BBDO the day after the election, the radio department, its members tootling red-white-and-blue horns and banging the studio drum, led a procession of revelers. Barton's pal Rube Goldberg, the cartoonist, greeted his election with a list of demands: "make people pull in their knees at the movies, stop fruit men from putting the best berries on top . . . and prohibit the indiscriminate photographing of pheasants." Barton's profession also plucked pridefully at its lapels. *Advertising Age* reported that Manhattanites "were aware of the presence of a new, colorful, intangible something in the political arena," citing large portraits of Barton gazing down over Times Square and Columbus Circle, and peering out from bus and trolley car cards and subway platforms. These and other devices, including the many photo-driven news stories, prompted the trade magazine to declare that "a professional advertising job, a professional publicity job and a colorful personality" determined the outcome. Although it was elbowed aside by the mayoral rumble, Barton's campaign achieved a "tremendous fancy" among New Yorkers—to a point that "at numerous polling places outside the Seventeenth district voters were heard to ask why Bruce Barton's name wasn't on the voting machine." "Even seasoned politicians" marveled at the "remarkable 'play' given Barton in the daily press," both pictures and stories.[22]

The Barton race was viewed by Republicans as a "repudiation of the New Deal," a "dress rehearsal" for the upcoming congressional elections of 1938 (which would see strong Republican gains in both houses and signal an end to the New Deal's legislative reign) and a current "barometer of Roosevelt prestige." Barton himself was told that all eyes were on his effort, one of only two congressional campaigns that year, which might serve Republicans as "a favorable omen" for the 1938 elections.[23] This partisan dimension to his victory also carries the reminder that, while his flamboyant campaign certainly helped him, his district was Republican by tradition. Recent events—the 1937 economic recession that seemed to mock the boasts of the Democratic New Deal and other political errors by FDR—made it easier for the Seventeenth Congressional District to return to its roots.

SERVICE IN the House brought several benefits to Barton. It partially slaked his political ambitions. The best medical care for his daughter Betsey was located in Washington. There were new friendships to be made (he found Congress "an exceedingly friendly body") and a dazzling new society to be conquered. One columnist reported that the new arrival had replaced John L. Lewis as the capital's "social lion": "the ladies are all agog over his wit and curly hair." His luncheon date with Mary Pickford, "America's Sweetheart" just in from Hollywood, caused a sensation in the House dining room. Train service was good and the congressional schedule such that Barton could commute back and forth to New York and keep a hand in his business. For his congressional staff he retained Teddy Peyser's secretary, Rose Hornstein, who had years of Washington experience. He also hired two extra secretaries with his own money.[24]

BBDO took pride in Barton's enhanced prominence in Congress, even if it added nothing immediate to the bottom line. Not every client shared the glow, however. One feared the agency was now placing its advertising so as to benefit Barton politically; Osborn had to reassure him that nothing of the sort had occurred. Osborn shared Barton's political views and was happy to make the corporate sacrifice to the general weal. When Barton proved a success as a candidate and an officeholder, his senior colleague William H. Johns exulted that he "shed lustre on the advertising profession." Still, Barton recalled that a number of BBDO clients who had dealt primarily with him took their accounts to other agencies. Barton cut his salary from the agency from $50,000 to $16,000 to reflect his divided energies.[25]

Barton quickly achieved celebrity unusual for a freshman congressman. He intended not to speak at the special session that met that November, knowing Capitol Hill protocol. "The people hired me to work," he declared, "not to talk." He planned to play the role of "a business man who never speaks just to get his name in the papers. . . ." But soon oratory got the better of him. Two weeks after taking the oath of office, he inserted "extended" remarks into the *Congressional Record* to offer testimony on behalf of small entrepreneurs "whose businesses are being murdered"—mostly by the New Deal's undistributed profits tax but also by excessive union demands. His contribution to debate on a farm subsidy bill was a lament for the long-suffering middle class in his constituency who would now face higher prices. Although "unorganized," they were "beginning now to stir," and his Democratic colleagues from New York "will hear a murmuring when they go back" to their distinctly nonagricultural districts.[26]

He did not go to Washington intending merely to blast the Roosevelt administration. Even in the fifth year of Republican chafing under the New Deal yoke, there was greater civility in partisan politics than sixty years later, and Barton himself was cordial and polyglot in his good-fellowship. He had cultivated contacts with some New Dealers before going to Congress. On his arrival in Washington he hoped that FDR might be persuaded to cooperate with business to alleviate the current recession. Aspiring to be an "off-the-record messenger boy" between the two, he made an appointment at the White House. Barely had he entered the Oval Office before FDR was calling him "Bruce" (they had never met), regaling him with stories and jokes, all part of "an oil shampoo." This was standard Roosevelt procedure. Barton came away critical of FDR's "charm." He spent evenings with some economists whom he labeled "inside insiders," who were influencing FDR toward a program of spending and a crusade against monopoly in 1938 (which Barton opposed).[27]

He looked for ways to carry out his mandate as a liberal Republican but found the options meager. Three weeks after taking office he told the Republican House minority leader, "I wish to God the Democrats would bring in something that I could vote for. I hate to spend my whole first term simply saying 'no.'" The current farm bill and wages-and-hours proposals had too many flaws. "To a man who likes to think of himself as social minded, the difficulty down here is that so many things which are good in principle, are put up to him in a form which is vicious in method and administration." He saw "a clear-cut place for myself in the House, as the protagonist of the little business man and the white collar worker. They are the forgotten men. . . . They are not organized, and they have no spokesman." He managed to convince Minority Leader Bert Snell to appoint him to the House Labor Committee so that he could pursue his goal of achieving some reconciliation between the GOP and labor.[28]

For Barton, however, the sugar coatings on most New Deal bonbons concealed centers that were indigestible. He wanted a minimum wage/maximum hours bill (the Fair Labor Standards Act would be enacted in 1938, pretty much the New Deal's last legislative hurrah), but labor would "rue the day if it ever permitted hours and wages to be fixed by bureaucrats at Washington," as the current proposal mandated. Similarly, while "business must recognize" that "there is a farm problem," and Barton "wish[ed] to heaven there was a bill . . . I could vote for," the Administration's bill was a "hodge-podge."[29]

Barton made good on his promised effort to repeal a useless New Deal law each week—but only on the effort. Soon after arriving, he began putting such proposals in the hopper. Often he tried to cancel legislation, such as the 1933 Emergency Banking Act that was premised on an "emergency" now past. He saw more current measures in this same category, including a major portion of the New Deal's housing activities. He even proposed creating a special joint committee to seek out "bad, obsolete, and useless laws" to repeal. He soon understood what every aspiring freshman congressman learned: Congress had tried-and-true ways to block such obstreperousness. All sixteen of his repealers were sent to committee for burial. At the end of his first full session he confessed, "my score was No Hits, No Runs, No Errors. Not a single one of my repeal resolutions had been allowed to find its way out of Committee."[30]

Barton also worked to establish his credentials as a spokesman for small business. Within three weeks of his election he had circularized two thousand merchants in his district, asking them to itemize their "business problems" and propose remedies. Later he would enter some of these replies into the *Congressional Record* to support such causes as simplification of the tax code and repeal of the undistributed profits tax. He favored action to curb monopolies, a direction in which the New Deal was currently veering, but argued against "a long investigation or political shadow boxing." He opposed congressional efforts to launch a major anti-monopoly inquiry as redundant and political, a way for New Dealers to scapegoat business for their own failures, to drag "prominent businessmen . . . before a drumhead court" to win headlines.[31]

Barton participated peripherally in debate on legislation pertinent to his other career, a bill to punish "false advertising" and to tighten regulations on drugs and cosmetics. He asserted that the "95 percent of American business and American advertising [which] is honest" favored the bill, which Barton hoped would pass (though his "limiting" amendment to it was defeated). Eventually, later in the session, the weakened Copeland Bill would pass, adding cosmetics to the substances to be regulated under the Food and Drug Act and otherwise tightening regulation, though far less stringently than some desired. That the law gave the Federal Trade Commission rather than the Department of Agriculture responsibility for overseeing advertising was considered a victory for those who favored a lukewarm measure.[32]

Settling into his duties, Barton set about to service the needs of his constituents. Some of these were depression related—they needed jobs. Barton's office kept a "file of hundreds of names of men and women," their skills, their resumés. "Now and then we are able to get one or more of them placed." In one particularly fruitful week in September 1938 his office sent three people on the list off to jobs as stenotypers, got a laborer fixed up with a digging job, and helped a ship's officer get hired onto a boat. This experience encouraged Barton to ask businessmen to make an effort to "provide jobs for the neighbors across the street." If they could "provide 5,000 extra jobs in each Congressional District in the next two months," that would swing the 1938 House elections.[33]

Barton had to provide another kind of constituent service more specific to his district—helping Jews escape Hitler's Europe. In the late 1930s, with aggressors on the march, foreign policy ceased to be the remote issue it had been early in the decade. Hard times seldom stimulate brotherhood; these plus the world crisis sharpened racial, ethnic, and religious tensions in the United States. With many Jewish voters in his district, Barton often confronted their concerns about rising anti-Semitism. He no longer suggested that the horror stories from abroad were exaggerated. No congressman, he asserted, "has had a more intimate contact with the human tragedies of central Europe than I. . . . Every week a score of my constituents have come to the office with stories of the suffering and desperate struggle of relatives abroad." One could not hear them "without having his heart rung and his sense of justice outraged," and Barton worked to expedite the entry of those whose cases he took up. He criticized the "anti-alien" bills enjoying a vogue among some of his colleagues. But he had no hope that Congress would raise the currently stringent immigration quotas to accommodate refugees from fascism.[34]

In the United States, anti-Semitism was growing apace. Increasingly Barton found himself trying to reassure audiences such as the Council Against Intolerance in America. He could note that outbreaks of intolerance were cyclical. Ultimately they confronted Americans' "innate sense of fairness; never have they been fooled very long." In Congress he "severely reprimanded" his colleague Jacob Thorkelson for comments that "might be construed as anti-Semitic." The Montana congressman had noted critically that "several Jews head House committees and subcommittees." The remark was "in inexcusably bad taste," and, said Barton, conveyed "a shockingly untrue and cruel inference." The rebuke met "a roar of applause" from colleagues.[35]

Representative Barton consistently identified himself as a liberal Republican. He accepted an enlarged role in economic life for the federal government and, as he had before, encouraged other businessmen to make the same philosophical adjustment. He endorsed the New Deal's questions, based on the line in FDR's Second Inaugural about "one-third of a nation" still ill-fed, ill-clad, ill-housed; he faulted its answers. As one newsletter parsed his argument, "In practice this means: At least 70% to 80% of the institutions and laws that have been created" under the New Deal "will have to be continued even under a Republican administration." To an audience of Bay State Republicans he said: "I might as well blurt it out and get it over with. I am a liberal. I am in sympathy" with most of FDR's objectives, including "the ideal of social security," "full and free collective bargaining," and a "house cleaning of Wall Street." With radicals threatening to shove "the chariot of progress" into the ditch and reactionaries likely to have it run over them, only liberals could "guide the chariot into the middle of the road again."[36]

Barton evangelized fellow Republicans with his political views. In January 1938 he told New York Young Republicans that their party must do a better job. "Are we humbled enough by our long defeat to be truly and sincerely willing to serve?" At GOP Lincoln Day observances he warned that his party too often spoke "in selfish-sounding phrases—the undistributed profits tax, the capital gains tax, balanced budgets, economic laws." These did not appeal to "the common man," to whom Republicans needed to talk about jobs, living conditions, health, "and the removal of the fear of old age." "These things he wants and he feels he has a right to have them." Republicans must heed the fact that such folks were "in the majority." They must remember their origins as a "party of freedom," once considered "almost radical."[37] They needed "a constructive, not merely a negative, labor policy. We must realize that great new forces are astir in the land" and that the New Deal had aroused people's "aspirations." He saw more promise in working to improve the proposed wages-and-hours bill than in the temptation to cry "Communist." Nor was "I hate Roosevelt" an effective cry. He cited the model of England's Conservative party, which had survived "by making itself a liberal party," taking the opposition's good ideas and making them work. In his keynote speech to the state Republican convention in September 1938, he invoked the party's "liberal" past—and future.[38]

Yet for a liberal he found much to criticize in the New Deal. If FDR was listening, he heard a speaker with a talent for clever gibes. In early 1939 Barton, recalling Wilson's 1916 campaign slogan, "He kept us out of war," suggested that 1940's election would be contested with: "They kept us out of work." (Less cleverly, he predicted that the issue in 1940 "will not be foreign affairs.") Occasionally he reverted to the sort of plutocratic lamentation he urged his party to shun, as when in depicting the harm that high taxes inflicted upon the middle class, he asserted that these had also done damage to the poor: "Families that kept two maids are getting along with one; those that had one are getting their own breakfasts. . . ."[39]

Barton quickly acquired a voice in his party's official chorus. By late 1938 he was getting fifty to a hundred speech invitations a month from around the country and was in high demand for GOP conclaves.

His first major road tryout led him to Indiana for a much-publicized keynote speech to the state's Republican convention, urging his party to put forward liberal candidates. This won him notice and suggestions that he might be a presidential dark horse. On the other hand, his counsel that the Hoosier GOP choose candidates who were not "100 per centers"—either pro– or anti–New Deal—fell on deaf ears: the convention promptly slated one of the latter.[40] Barton persisted in nudging his party toward a less instinctively anti–New Deal stance. In 1938 he urged the nomination of congressional candidates who evolved with the times and were "prepared to cling to whatever is good in the new order and discard only that which is bad." His call for his party to foster more youthful leadership became familiar enough to warrant a reference in one of the comic skits at Washington's 1939 Gridiron Club dinner. New York gossip columnist Leonard Lyons went so far as to quip that Barton "is trying to adapt the New Deal methods to the Republican Party."[41]

Yet he also was quick to voice objections to New Deal measures and viewpoints. He inveighed with particular feeling against the New Deal's design to "destroy national advertising" and thus undermine the independence of the press and radio. He cited names (Donald E. Montgomery, consumers' counsel for the Agricultural Adjustment Administration) and agencies (the Federal Trade Commission) in his charges. While some New Dealers expressed disdain for advertising, Barton's charges may have exaggerated the aims of the New Deal— and certainly the political potential of any such offensive.[42] Barton was not alone among admen, however, in sensing a hostility toward advertising in some New Deal precincts. He argued, as always, that some members of his profession had exceeded the bounds of propriety, but admen "have been much more conscious even than our critics that false, unwholesome, or exaggerated advertising is a menace to our whole business structure." He took pride that admen—or at least his sort—unlike members of the Stock Exchange, had not offered blanket opposition to all regulatory efforts. "We did not oppose, but rather welcomed, the Wheeler-Lea Bill" which armed the Federal

Trade Commission with powers to punish false advertising, and helped make it "sound, workable, and fair."[43]

While any increased federal control over its activities made the advertising industry nervous, most of its spokesmen claimed they welcomed the law. The president of the AAAA predicted it would have a "beneficial effect." Its definition of false advertising, he said, constituted "a masterpiece of protection" for both customers and upright advertisers. They could only sigh in relief that the FTC rather than the Agriculture Department, a source of voluble anti-advertising agitation, had jurisdiction. The measure, as once trade association chief put it, ended the immediate "danger of drastic national legislation." Ad industry spokesmen even deployed the new law as a shield against the New Deal's inclusion of advertising among the targets of its renewed interest in trust-busting.[44]

HOWEVER LIBERAL Barton claimed to be, he often espoused conservative values to appreciative fellow Republicans. At a party picnic in Rochester in 1939, he lamented that a people "noted for their Yankee shrewdness" had let themselves "buy a second-hand idea" of the British economist John Maynard Keynes, who had failed to sell even his own country "the fantastic notion that debt and investment are the same thing." This generation was "the first in America to reverse the traditional process of self-denial" for its children's good "and independent effort," instead "laying their future on the altar of our own convenience and comfort."[45] He put a reverse twist on his conservatism by asserting for the GOP the claim of being the party of youth and optimism: it had renewed itself with younger standard-bearers while the Democrats had become tired and flabby and now took the debilitated and defeatist position that "'There are no more frontiers.'"[46]

His party seemed to appreciate Barton as a source of fresh ideas. He received credit for the Republican National Committee's 1939 promotion, National Debt Week, though one journalist likened this effort to raise public consciousness of the national debt to Prohibition—a "noble" but futile experiment. An anonymous staffer at the *Philadelphia Evening Bulletin* reported to his publisher that Barton, a "novelty in politics," had "focused more attention on himself" than most junior congressman; his project of repealing a law a week drew "the fancy of the correspondents," and his speeches had allure. But he was not especially "exerting an influence" in Congress; that would take more than engaging speeches.[47]

Clever and voluble, Barton was an agile picador working against a distracted New Deal bull. He found it easy to make the newspapers with quickly mounted jousts against the latest enactments. He won coverage with his criticism of Postmaster General Farley's 1938 reconfiguring of the nation's stamps, which gave prime positions to Jefferson (three cents) and Jackson (six) while burying Lincoln (relocated in Jefferson's favor), McKinley, and TR and placing Coolidge, "prophet and symbol of thrift and economy" on the extravagant two-dollar stamp. This looked like a plot to make sure "that all Republicans are forgotten." A Gallup Poll recorded resounding public support of jail sentences for those who used federal work relief funds to influence elections and attributed the idea to Barton.[48] He made the papers by urging FDR to stay away longer from Washington on his vacations, for when he was out of the city the stock market usually gained. (Critics noted that the market also rose when FDR was back in town.)[49] Quick-witted, savvy in matters of publicity, Barton proved adept in the repartee of floor debate, often evoking laughter from his colleagues.

Barely arrived on Capitol Hill, Barton faced a race for reelection in 1938. His first year in office left him unscathed and in fact the beneficiary of publicity as flattering as if he had written it himself. His pal Roy Howard, of the Scripps-Howard newspaper chain, had newsmen from the *New York World-Telegram* and the United Press alerted to publish news, presumably favorable, about the rookie congressman. The best year in a decade to be a Republican candidate was 1938, as Roosevelt and the New Deal stumbled under the political weight of the defeat of FDR's court-packing plan, the economic recession that began in 1937, middle-class unhappiness with the recent wave of sit-down strikes, and

raveled feelings in the Democratic party under the lash of FDR's effort
to "purge" it.[50] Barton even picked up some labor support. William F.
Green, president of the American Federation of Labor, gave him that
group's endorsement. Barton had been careful to tend his relations with
the labor movement. In April he had chided a GOP spokesman for
"careless use of names" in referring to Green or other labor leaders as
"communistic." He agreed with wage and hour guarantees if they did
not require "another bureaucracy," and he did support such a measure
reported out of his committee. He also echoed the AFL position that
the Wagner Labor Relations Act was biased in the favor "of only one
type" (CIO) of union organizers.[51]

Nonetheless, Democrats wanted their seat back. Barton learned
from political reporters that FDR's postmaster general and party factotum Jim Farley made "a special trip" to New York in July "to urge the
Democratic leaders in my District to do everything possible to purge
me," including cooperation with the American Labor party. The
Democrats chose a prominent young attorney, Walter H. Liebman, to
oppose Barton. The hope that he might also obtain the American Labor nomination, to prevent the split in forces that had occurred in
1937, proved vain: the American Labor party again nominated George
Backer. Liebman charged Barton with trying to "blackjack" the New
Deal (and, somewhat inconsistently, of failing on his promise to repeal
a New Deal law a day). When Barton flippantly suggested shrinking
the size of the House and raising members' salaries, Liebman called it
"step No. 1 on the road to dictatorship," which would benefit only "the
enormously rich corporations who are Barton's clients." The Democrat called the roll of BBDO's "reactionary" and monopolistic clients,
complained that the agency's lavish advertising made the newspapers
into Barton's cheerleaders, and termed it tragic that anyone might be
swayed by his opponent's claims to be a liberal.[52]

And to the left, Barton *had* become anathema. The New York
County Committee of the Communist party targeted him and two
other candidates who "represent the pro-fascist elements of the nation." The Young Communist League picketed BBDO's Madison Av-

enue office. One demonstrator wore a barrel and carried a sign saying: "If Barton and His Anti-New Deal Gang Are Elected We'll All Be Going Around This Way."[53] When a group of Communists picketed his house too, to protest his congressional voting record, Barton invited them in for a beer. They refused but asked that the beer be sent outside. He complied.[54]

Barton's reelection campaign proved easy. He continued to get lavish newspaper coverage. Noting this, an exasperated critic challenged: "Try to find out what [Barton's two rivals are] doing by reading the papers! The only newspapers in New York that have so far resisted the spell are the *News* and the *Post*."[55] There was room for humor. Some of Barton's ad-business well-wishers confronted him as pickets with posters (a spoof perhaps of the episode when Communists picketed his home). One sign was a reworking of his own campaign poster, with his photograph touched up to cast him as Honest Abe. Another urged, "Keep Barton Incongruous. He's unfair to ghost writers."[56]

On Election Day Barton received more than 40,000 votes—55 percent of the three-party vote—to Liebman's fewer than 27,000 and Backer's 6,000. It was a Republican year, but not necessarily in Democratic Gotham. Barton did better than the district attorney, Thomas E. Dewey, drawing nearly 20,000 more votes in the Seventeenth District than did the racket-buster in his gubernatorial race. The morning after the election, Barton was greeted at his agency with "horns blowing, a band blaring, and somebody beating on the studio drum."[57] Like the pundits, Barton interpreted the results as a sign that many voters had tired of the New Deal. "America has been treated like a debutante who is kept so busy changing her clothes that she has no time to work or sleep." It was time, he said, to legislate less and instead to improve administration.[58]

FOR A JUNIOR CONGRESSMAN, Barton enjoyed remarkable publicity. Given his calling, that should come as no surprise. To an easily jaded Washington press corps, he offered a fresh face and voice. Joseph

Alsop and Robert Kintner, authors of an important Washington-based political column, called him "one of the first thoroughly presentable, really able new figures to appear in the ranks of the Republican party in the last five years." According to a 1939 *Life* poll of Washington newspaper correspondents, Barton ranked in the top ten House members. He achieved this status not through having any impact on the legislative process—not that a fledgling congressman could be expected to—but via his skills with words and people. He made friends easily in Congress. A Washington columnist described him, in early 1939, as "the most popular member" of the House. He was always good for a pointed, clever quote. He brought wit into the windswept precincts of the House chamber. His earliest oratorical sally attacked a New Deal agriculture bill and gibed at his Democratic colleagues from New York City for supinely supporting a measure that would offer their distinctly urban constituents only increased taxes and higher food bills. He warned—to applause—that they would hear "murmuring when they go back to the cotton fields of Brooklyn, the rolling wheat fields of Manhattan, the warm tobacco fields of Harlem, and the sunny rice fields of the Bronx."[59]

From the day of Barton's first election, people mentioned him as a 1940 presidential prospect. As victory materialized on election night in 1937, his campaign manager George Frankenthaler told Barton to pose for photographs "like a Senator, Bruce. Like a Governor. Like a—like a President!" In four years, Frankenthaler noted, Barton would be the same age as FDR was currently. Some of this talk was playful and random. Some, a product of local ties. Akron, where his brother Fred lived, was an early "hotbed" of Barton support. A Barton for President Club established itself there before Barton even alighted in Washington.[60] Some of the momentum came from off-the-cuff comments; some was gossip-column rebound.

Organizationally there was nothing to the Barton boom—or almost nothing. One man, Roy Howard, took it seriously. As early as mid-1938 he was talking up Barton. To hear Howard tell it, some of Barton's virtues operated as shortcomings—or did they? "He isn't as energeti-

cally ambitious as he might be, and he's cursed with a simple honesty"
that barred "demagogy and flap-doodle." Howard liked Barton's independence and his "liberal ideas" and acceptance of many New Deal
premises. His partners Osborn and especially Durstine also supported
the boom, working with Howard.[61] Betsey Barton faithfully logged
dark-horse clippings into her scrapbooks. Barton himself seems to
have taken the idea with no seriousness at all. His correspondence
yields no hint of activism on his own behalf. The only evidence of any
interest on his part was the absence of a Shermanesque denial.[62]

Yet mentions of Barton's prospects dotted newspaper columns in
1938–1940. One even popped up in *Air Conditioning & Refrigeration
News*.[63] Along with well-wishers, his foes also assumed he was available. An acid-laced article in the Communist *New Masses* saw a candidacy as likely for the man who talked as a liberal while "cutting
sheepskins to fit for America's biggest and fiercest [corporate]
wolves."[64] Barton's easy reelection confirmed his dark equine status.[65]
This notion was sufficiently in play that one column recorded FDR
being asked about Barton's "campaign": the president gave a light-
hearted reply. When the pollster George Gallup offered his periodic
handicappings of GOP presidential hopefuls, Barton always made the
list—though never among the leaders, whose percentages were indicated. Even the absence of a Barton boom was news. An "inside dope"
column reported that the question on Midwestern Republican lips was
what had happened to it. If Barton needed a issue for his noncandi-
dacy, he got a lot of mileage, in speeches to varied audiences, by
dwelling on the threat to the middle class posed by the uncaring New
Deal and the perils of an age of pressure-group politics.[66]

Soon Barton's dark-horse status became a virtual axiom. Rube
Goldberg sketched a cartoon showing the door of the "GOP Casting
Office" with a sign, "Now Casting 'Gone with the New Deal.'" Shown
in drag were "Carole Vandenberg, Paulette Dewey, Miriam Barton,
Myrna Taft." Barton was thus linked with Senators Arthur Vandenberg
and Robert A. Taft and District Attorney Tom Dewey as presidential
timber. Even Britain's *Economist* saw him as a contender.[67] Looking

backward, one might surmise from the Coolidge and even the Harding efforts of 1920 that a modest nucleus of supporters plus the right political circumstances at convention time could make lightning strike for Barton. Looking forward to 1940, one would have to foresee that the amateurs supporting Wendell Willkie had the larger legions, that his media artillery had longer range, and that "circumstances," which clearly upset every other candidate's preparations for the nominating convention, thundered on the Hoosier utility man's behalf.

AS THE 1930s—called by the poet W. H. Auden that "low dishonest decade"—labored to an end, foreign crises steadily crowded economic ills aside. On foreign policy, as against domestic questions, Barton was less likely to find anything positive to applaud in Roosevelt's position. While in Congress, Barton figured prominently in the "isolationist" camp. That imprecise label was soon serving as a rhetorical cudgel. Interventionists applied it to Roosevelt-haters, especially reactionaries who loathed all his works; foot-dragging critics of activist government; exponents, whether from ideological or ethnic promptings, of pro-Hitler, pro-fascist, pro-German, anti-British views; head-in-the-sand foes of foreign involvement (or things foreign in general); or mere noninterventionists of all stripes. Pearl Harbor, Hitlerian *blitzkrieg*, and the horrors of Auschwitz helped make "isolationist" for many years a slur word in American political jargon. Sobered by later events, however, particularly the Vietnam War, historians began to offer less damning and more nuanced analysis of isolationism.

Barton too thought the label "isolationism" inexact. Although he accepted many of its tenets, he was not 100 percent isolationist. He supported reciprocal trade agreements—the first House Republican to endorse the program in 1940. His foreign policy thinking was shaded and complex. His disillusionment with the Great War had deepened over time. He echoed the line that all that conflict had given the country was prohibition, influenza, and the income tax. He befriended anti-war activists (including some leftists) and their cause, and they were receptive to his ideas about how to "advertise" it. Yet he always thought himself more a realist than a pacifist. He decried how defense spending sapped money from worthier causes, but he did not oppose such appropriations. He detested emotional appeals against the "enemy." The year 1939, he feared, was coming to resemble 1914–1915 in the one-sidedness of anti-German propaganda. He doubted that "aid short of war" to the Allies could stop short of war. He rooted for the British over the Germans but shied from renewed involvement in Europe. He loathed "dictatorship" but warned Americans that their own system, under current trends, was endangered.

Barton spoke often and diversely about foreign policy. Although he enjoyed travel there, he dismissed Europe as "an anachronism. . . . It is just as if the Bronx were one country, speaking one language, and Brooklyn another country, speaking another language, both with strong armies and fighting for two thousand years over who would control Staten Island." For America to take sides in every such dispute seemed reckless. "The whole course of events seems to me a repetition of the pattern of 1914–1918." At bottom he loathed war—any war—and feared for what he liked to call "the republic," already battered by the New Deal. FDR's quest for a third term was the last straw, in his view, and the campaign would be the last stand for republican government.[68]

These were difficult years to keep America home centered. The president of the Gridiron Club said at the 1939 annual banquet of that Washington journalistic institution that it was "an unstatic world. Rand McNally has to publish its maps now in five-star daily editions like a tabloid." But Barton favored neutrality. He supported the neutrality legislation that Congress had been elaborating since 1935 to wall the country off from foreign conflicts. His fluency in the foreign policy debate won him membership among the leading spokesmen for that position. It also brought him criticism from interventionist pundits like Walter Lippmann, who named him with other GOP isolationists as obstructing speedy assistance to the Finns, who were battling a Soviet invasion in the winter of 1939. Consistently, Barton opposed FDR's foreign policies. He did not, however, join America First, the most important noninterventionist organization, believing it more effective to take his stand as an individual. He underestimated the length and destructiveness of the war, suggesting in late 1939, wrongly (but not uniquely), "it is entirely possible that the present war will be over by next summer," because each government involved "was afraid of its own people" and shied away from sustaining large casualties.[69]

When new House committee assignments were announced in January 1939, Barton won a seat on the Foreign Affairs Committee. The first critical test for him in foreign policy was the issue of revising the Neutrality Act to end its ban on shipment of arms to all belligerents. Barton considered himself a realist. He understood that "no neutrality law is realistic. It will neither put us in nor keep us out of war" and was largely a matter of "psychology." In June 1939 he supported repeal of the arms embargo, because it was in the nation's interest that England and France prevail (or at least hold on to a manageable "stalemate") in the ever more likely war. It was better to take that step, perhaps deterring action by Hitler, before war began than to take it after the fact and so act unneutrally. To maintain the arms embargo would make the United States "a silent partner of nations that have prearmed" and would give Americans "a false sense of security." The repeal effort failed.[70]

In the fall, however, after war had begun and Congress was again urged to act, Barton opposed repeal of the arms embargo, despite his sense that a majority of his constituents favored it. Now, he said, it would be "an act of war" from Germany's perspective, an "empty gesture" to the unready French and British (much like those two countries' vain guarantees to Poland), and a reprise of the errors that had pulled the United States into the last war. The Nazi-Soviet Pact made a change even more futile, he thought.[71] The nation was embarked on a rancorous two-year debate between isolationism and interventionism. The isolationists were no mere corporal's guard, but on issue after issue the interventionist position acquired the support of more Americans. A compilation of polls on the issue of repealing parts of the Neutrality Act confirmed that by October 1939 a majority of citizens—often upward of 60 percent—favored repeal of the arms embargo.[72] Although he had switched, Barton was still on the losing side.

For Barton, the issues of the New Deal, the approaching threat of war, FDR's quest for a third term, and the global menace to democracy converged to prompt him to express his views in more apocalyptic terms. In March 1939 he warned that FDR had declared thirty-nine "emergencies" since he took office—a rate of "one new emergency every six weeks." In an only partly facetious tone, he warned one correspondent to vote Republican in 1940 if she wanted to retain a republic. Another four years of Roosevelt "will be the beginning of Fa[s]cism, and you know what that means for you girls—Kirch [sic], Kuchen und Kinder."[73]

BEING A SENATOR had been a boyhood dream, but Barton trod cautiously through the minefield of Empire State politics in approaching that goal. There was talk of slating him for the Senate in 1938, but he discouraged suggestions that he run for the office (or for governor), though as late as early September he was calculating his senatorial prospects. Newspaper columns bantered of a possible Senate candidacy in 1940, and he too gave it thought—which may have motivated his active speaking schedule outside his district in 1939. But in February 1940 Barton had sat with local party leader Ken Simpson and his partner Osborn and decided to run for reelection, not for the Senate. As late as September 11, 1940, he treated his campaign for reelection to the House as a certainty. But events were accelerating.[74]

First there was the presidential candidacy of Wendell Willkie, the transplanted Hoosier, now New Yorker, who as head of the Commonwealth and Southern utility empire had become a leading opponent of the New Deal's programs in the Tennessee Valley and its attack on utility holding companies. Other GOP aspirants in 1940 failed to measure up, and as the German army hurtled through Belgium into France and Republican delegates packed for Philadelphia, the Draft Willkie campaign, ably assisted by many prominent, internationalist East

Coast Republicans and a powerful alliance of newspapers, gained momentum as the Germans framed surrender terms. Still listed as a dark horse himself, Barton decided three weeks before the convention to cast his delegate vote for Willkie. (Previously he had backed Dewey.) He was promptly asked to second the nomination. Although there were rumors that Barton masterminded the Willkie draft, he claimed he had "absolutely no connection with the pre-convention Willkie movement."[75]

He put it too strongly. Willkie was no stranger to Barton, so long a cheerleader for the electric power industry. In fact, in telling Tom Dewey that he was switching to Willkie, Barton said, "Wendell . . . is one of my old friends and a constituent." Barton's political sponsor Kenneth Simpson was one of the sparkplugs of the Willkie machine. In April, Barton had sent Willkie the name of a possible speech writer. He also apparently supplied the Willkie group with a list of advertising and public relations contacts, many of whom were recruited to the cause. He decided, he told Dewey, that "the war situation has introduced a wholly new and overwhelming factor into the Republican picture." The present crisis prompted "many people" to find Dewey's youth a handicap. "I share this view." (A joke then current called Tom Dewey "the first American casualty" of World War II.) When Congressman Charles Halleck suggested that Barton be one of Willkie's seconders, Barton consented.[76]

The Willkie campaign leaders succeeded in stampeding the convention with a deftly orchestrated campaign of press publicity (many of the press "lords" backed the Hoosier), a flood of telegrams to delegates, and galleries packed with Willkie partisans. Years later Fred Smith, a BBDO employee who had worked on Barton's congressional campaigns, confessed to a veteran reporter of New York politics that he had been detailed to assist the Draft Willkie effort and that the "cadres" of the Willkie Clubs, so important to the draft movement, had typically been drawn from the staffs of local power companies in far-flung cities. Barton's ally Simpson, a leader of the Willkie movement, had a bitter rupture with Dewey, who considered this a betrayal of his own presidential hopes. Dewey spitefully purged Simpson as the state's Republican national committeeman. Barton (who nominated Simpson) had previously tried "to answer the doubts of colleagues" who feared Dewey was "arrogant and dictatorial, and now he insists on coming out and proving it to them."[77]

Barton became prominent in the Willkie circle. At the time, he re-called, "it seemed to me that the Almighty, who had neglected the Re-publican party for too long a time, had at last given us a new face, a new voice and a new hope." When Willkie's train chugged into Philadelphia, Barton was among a small group drawn up to greet him. Willkie then determined not to drive but to walk to his convention headquarters, inviting reporters along to quiz him as they ambled, meanwhile greeting and answering queries from people he met en route, from the bootblack who shined his shoes to random passersby. This seemingly unrehearsed but inspired improvisation stirred a sen-sation. It bore the earmarks of a Barton idea, recalling the sort of ca-sual, democratic, personable street rambles of his own 1937 campaign. During the presidential roll call, boisterous cheering from the galleries packed with Willkie adherents and boos from rivals' delegates made both the nominating speech and Barton's own an acoustical challenge. Barton called the drama of the Willkie selection unprecedented since the days of TR; "barbers, waiters and everybody" came up to Barton to share their enthusiasm for the tousle-haired ex-Democrat. On the sixth ballot, Willkie was nominated. Meeting with the nominee to decide on a vice-presidential candidate, Barton suggested Senator Charles McNary of Oregon, the eventual choice.[78]

Willkie knew he must carry New York State, and he needed help. As early as June he had urged Barton for the Senate in order to boost party prospects. Willing enough, Barton thought he had the inside track unless Dewey insisted on the nomination (as he did not), but he withdrew his name from consideration. New York Republicans held their convention late, on September 27. Barton was not the first choice of the Dewey-controlled conclave to run against Democratic incum-bent Senator James Mead, but pressures mounted to name him. Barton himself received phone calls from "non-political people" arguing that "the public-interest obligated him to run for Senator." A convention-eve call from Willkie, who labeled Barton his "first, second, and third choice," dispelled any remaining doubts. Word of Willkie's insistence swayed party leaders, and the delegates dutifully chose Barton.[79] His acceptance speech previewed themes he would accent in the bare six weeks before Election Day. The "only issue" was whether Americans would "gamble with their liberties" by giving FDR a third term. This, of course, became a national theme. It appeared in dramatic orations about the dangers to the republic entailed by breaking the sacred tradition laid down by Washington. It showed up on lapel buttons saying, "No Man Is Good Three Times." (Democrats rebutted: "Better a Third Termer than a Third Rater.") Barton campaigned not against the New Deal but "the third term" and "the end of freedom."[80]

Barton's 1940 rhetoric emphasized the presidential race. Perhaps he thought this would improve his chances in the senatorial campaign, but his rhetoric had a ring of belief more than of tactic. Almost every speech mentioned, and few failed to emphasize, the third-term menace. He had pressed this same theme in pro-Willkie speeches before his own nomination. He suggested, for example, that FDR's rhetorical treatment of Hitler was "rough" given that the Nazi leader had "saved" his third-term nomination by moving on Paris. He had speculated about the third-term possibility for some time, and it had long bothered him. In February he had declared that the president was maneuvering to be drafted as the nominee, and presciently predicted that Chicago's Mayor Ed Kelly would carefully pack the galleries and stage the convention.[81]

Barton opened his Senate campaign in Cooperstown on October 5 with a speech that foreshadowed the rest of his campaign. The core question was, "Can our democratic form of government survive a Third Term?" The key to the outcome was the middle class, often apathetic, having "neither an organization nor a champion." Barton warned that "when the middle class is gone, democracy is gone," vanished as in Russia, Germany, and Italy. The New Deal held, he claimed, "that you and I—the middle classes of this country—are incurably dumb."[82]

Barton did touch on other issues. He accused Mead of having no program but the tired old New Deal, which siphoned tax money from New York to other states. His opponent would thus "make a good senator for Florida, Alabama, Georgia or Mississippi, but not for New York." Neither had Mead paid attention to the nation's "shockingly defenseless condition." He wagered that ex-Postmaster General Jim Farley's "Irish heart" would not permit him to back the third term; the Irish had several reasons for such a stand, including their detestation of the "communism" that had seeped into New Deal bureaus. He rallied the middle class, so "systematically neglected" by the New Deal. When FDR's running mate Henry A. Wallace charged that Hitler preferred a Willkie victory, Barton challenged him to phone the Nazi dictator and ask whom he preferred. "I will bet $1,000 in cash that Mr. Hitler will say Roosevelt." He insinuated that "rumors of our going to war with Japan a few days after a Roosevelt victory, current in many naval circles, could be true for all I know." But mostly he assailed the threat that FDR, "a power-hungry president," posed to the constitutional order.[83]

There was an element of self-sacrifice in Barton's emphasis on the presidential race. His opinion of Willkie had plummeted after the infatuation of spring. He discovered that Willkie was loath to take advice from anyone, "that his thinking was shallow, that his techniques were totally wrong, and that under no circumstances could he possibly be elected." Soon after the convention, *Collier's* asked Barton to write an article about the candidate. Sitting with several of Willkie's fellow executives at Commonwealth and Southern utility company, he could not elicit "a single kind word" from them. Later, one of them apologized for the appearance of rudeness, confirming that they had nothing positive to say.[84] Still, he plugged away at the third-term issue.

According to a confidant, Roosevelt was working on his campaign speeches and looking to "take a crack" at opponents of repeal of the arms embargo, a list that included Congressmen Barton, Joe Martin,

and Hamilton Fish. One group of FDR's speech writers, federal of-
ficeholders holed up in the Commerce Department, probed for ways
to counter Republican charges that the nation had been left under-
armed. Running down the list of Republicans who had voted against
defense appropriations, G. Griffith Johnson found, in fellow economist John Kenneth Galbraith's phrase, "three wonderfully euphonious
Republican names."[85] Roosevelt too liked the sequence. He used the
litany in his October 28 Madison Square Garden speech to top off a
list of Republicans who in 1939 had voted against repealing the arms
embargo. Ticking off four Senators' names, he then dwelt on "a perfectly beautiful alliteration, Congressmen Martin, Barton and Fish." It
went over so well that FDR planned to use it again in Boston, but his
audience was ahead of him: some listeners shouted the phrase before
he could. Thus the main tag line of the 1940 campaign came to life in
the week before the election. Not for years an obscure figure, Barton
now had another association in the public mind. He replied to the
Garden speech by attacking FDR's inaction on defense earlier in the
thirties, "when I was not in public life."[86]

The 1940 Senate campaign did not work as well for Barton as had
his 1937 race, even though again he began it with a "pulse-taking tour."
He continued to benefit from positive press coverage. A two-page spread
in *Life* depicted him in his office, at home with Mrs. Barton, speaking,
exercising in a gym, and reading a newspaper, while a brief article
puffed him as seeking "to sell the stodgy, defeatist Republican Party a
new, dynamic philosophy." Perhaps conditions were too different—the
presence this time of a presidential race, the need to address a broader
constituency. Perhaps the late start in 1940 hurt him. It is not clear why,
but Barton's Senate campaign was more oratorical, less performative,
than his run of 1937. It was more ideological as well. In 1937 he had a
general orientation and some winning gimmicks. In 1940 he had deep
concerns. He expressed them eloquently—the third term, the threat of
war, the dangers of encroaching government—but they obviously did
not move the electorate as much as they moved him. He also suffered a
certain decline in political innocence. He forbore to make promises or

cater to specific groups in 1937; in 1940 he made appeals to the various fears of the Irish, the Italians, and others. He also promised that his and Willkie's first job, if elected, would be to "purge" Communists and fascists from the federal government.[87]

Probably there was little danger of Barton's or Willkie's winning election. The pollster Rogers C. Dunn predicted Barton would win— and that Willkie would be elected, carrying New York by a quarter-million votes. But the wheels were coming off Willkie's campaign by October, just as Barton's was getting started. (Indeed, in an October 5 speech, Barton felt compelled to discount a Gallup poll pointing to a pro-FDR trend.) Barton himself was discouraged by Willkie's barn-storming techniques, which seemed disorganized and outmoded in an age of movies and radio. Willkie lost the state by more than 200,000 votes while Barton drew 434,000 fewer votes than the popular incumbent Mead. Barton did not bring the strength to the GOP ticket on which Willkie had counted, running 100,000 behind the presidential ticket even in his own Manhattan.[88] It was a nasty campaign, with candidates on every side labeled as Hitler's darlings; both parties contributed to the demagoguery.[89]

Barton was of several minds in accounting for his defeat. To one Republican he recalled his efforts since 1937 to improve his party's standing with labor; not enough progress had been made in this direction. He also concluded that, as the nation's defense industries geared up, "the flood of war orders licked us." "Every town that had a little factory in it [in upstate New York] sent us down a disappointing report" in its vote; thousands of men "all think the President gave them their jobs." He also suspected that the Martin, Barton, and Fish "gag" cost him "many thousands of Jewish votes" because his dissent from FDR's foreign and defense policies was viewed as weakness in the face of Hitler. He was "enough of an adman to appreciate a terrific gag line when I hear one." He compared it to "Rum, Romanism and Rebellion." Yet a phrase is unlikely to turn an election, and Barton did not fixate on FDR's. He noted that unlike Fish (whose district included FDR's Hyde Park home), neither Martin of Massachusetts nor he had incurred FDR's "wrath." His sallies against the New Deal and FDR's foreign policy might have been piquant enough to get under Roosevelt's skin, but there is no evidence of any special animosity on the president's part.[90]

In any case, Barton's boyhood dream of crusading his way to the Senate went unrealized. Perhaps his most enduring political fame came when FDR, adopting the Martin, Barton and Fish litany, helped end it. Of the three congressmen so singled out, Barton was the only one defeated in 1940. The arch-isolationist Fish lost his seat in 1944. Martin would go on to serve many more years and would twice become speaker of the House. Barton's political activity after 1940 would play out on Madison Avenue, not on Capitol Hill.

8

The Later Years

AFTER HIS congressional term ended, Barton returned to New York. Briefly his name remained in play in connection with office. Some Willkie loyalists wanted him to head the Republican National Committee, but he bluntly took himself out of the running. When Kenneth Simpson, who won Barton's House seat in 1940, died suddenly twenty days into his term, there was talk of Barton's reoccupying it, but again he declined. That summer some Republicans who had come to repent their support of the volatile Mayor LaGuardia weighed Barton as an alternative to the Little Flower in the 1941 election, but he discouraged the idea. BBDO was short of top management at that point, and so he found "the whole show back in my lap." He also resisted urgings that he run for City Council on a Willkie-ite reform slate. The 1940 campaign would prove to be his last hurrah.[1]

In these years BBDO had great need of his talents. It had weathered the depression and the tempest of Roy Durstine's departure in 1939. Alex Osborn, as executive vice president and general manager, took the lead in reorienting the firm. He reestablished and then expanded functional departments like marketing and research. The new leadership "changed BBDO from essentially an institutional agency," according to a commemorative history, "to one based broadly on packaged goods." (The biggest signal of this new orientation came in 1948 when, in a startling coup, Ben Duffy, who had become president of BBDO, captured the Lucky Strike account.) Ownership also was reconfigured. BBDO was mutualized, with a widened group of employees offered the opportunity to buy stock and thus a stake in control.[2]

Yet more rapids lay ahead. The depression had eased. BBDO picked up new accounts after Barton's return, but the coming of war brought novel challenges. For vast stretches of the economy, there was nothing to advertise: people at last had money, but many civilian products simply disappeared as assembly lines, their managers aching to produce cars and refrigerators for a reviving economy, converted to make planes and tanks. A fabricator of guns or parachutes faced a command economy with virtually a single buyer. Manufacturing was being concentrated in fewer plants; brand names were fading.[3] Who now needed advertising? Rosser Reeves of the Ted Bates agency lamented in March 1942 that "the advertising business looks pretty bad. Priorities and material shortages have played havoc with many of the big agencies." Many top admen were jobless. The gallows joke along the street was: "Do you think the advertising business is here to stay?" The reply was, "Well, until Friday anyway."[4]

Challenged in the 1930s by hostile New Dealers, admen had come to fear for their profession's survival. Barton shared such concerns— and expressed them. In 1940, still in Congress, he warned of "men in the Federal Trade Commission and the Department of Agriculture who hate national advertising, who want to destroy national advertising." That in turn would enable them to "end the independence of the press and radio." "A lot of us . . . are going to be pushed out by an Administration that has never had any appreciation of the part that selling and advertising play in the national economy," he confided in 1941. The chorus of criticism prompted the two major trade groups, the Association of American Advertising Agencies and the Association of National Advertisers to convene in late 1941 a special joint meeting charged with "Meeting the Attacks on Advertising."[5]

The advent of war unnerved many advertising professionals. Barton reported that leaders of the Advertising Federation of America had decided it was vital not to cancel its 1942 convention or only go through the motions, lest that "be interpreted in Washington and else-where as a tacit confession that advertising is merely a peace-time luxury." Barton agreed to head the AFA program committee. The president of the AAAA wrote Barton that "there is much speculation, as you know, as to what kind of an economy we are going to have—how far regimented and how far free," and what role advertising would retain in it.[6]

The profession moved to fortify its position by establishing the War Advertising Council (restyled the Advertising Council after the war), which eagerly offered its services to the government to design war-related public relations campaigns. The government thus received skilled assistance in propagating its message, and the profession earned legitimacy via patriotic service. The WAC saw a basis for optimism. Its labors were "beginning to lay the groundwork for greater believability in advertising, which will be so much needed after the war." In 1942 FDR sent a message to the Advertising Federation of America's convention (which Barton keynoted), citing advertising's role in strengthening "the desire for liberty and freedom" and suggesting that such efforts assigned it "a worthwhile and patriotic place in the nation's total war effort."[7]

The onset of war made people at BBDO jumpy. Privately Barton thought prospects for 1942 looked "dubious," but to buck up co-workers after Pearl Harbor he underscored that the agency had won business recently from Lever Brothers and B. F. Goodrich and a contract to promote the navy's recruitment program. Given all the uncertainty, 1942 looked good; no client had canceled. BBDO stood relatively secure because it was diversified. Those who once carped about all its lesser accounts and looked longingly at agencies with fewer but bigger clients were now reconsidering, because those agencies were at greater risk. By mid-1943 Barton found his firm's business holding up "surprisingly well." During the war BBDO managed to gain as clients Standard Oil of California, the Dodge division of Chrysler, the 3M Company, and others. Volume was high but profits were slim, yet Barton professed to a colleague now in uniform that the executives hoped to "keep the organization together and have jobs for the hundred and fifteen boys who have gone into the service." One of his co-workers described 1944 as "the biggest year in our history."[8]

The agencies found ways to survive. Given how recently admen had fretted at New Deal schemes to destroy their industry, wartime tax policies proved remarkably benign. They made advertising a fully deductible expense, thus encouraging businesses to maintain it with money that otherwise would simply flow into federal coffers. (As a consequence, for example, institutional advertising soared from $1 billion in 1939 to $17 billion in 1943.) Filling depleted agency ranks grew difficult as men departed for military service. Another challenge was to drum up business when civilian products were either rationed or simply unavailable. BBDO, considering Barton's earlier success with institutional advertising, stood as good a chance as any agency to withstand the war. In fact his senior colleague William H. Johns predicted confidently and evangelistically three weeks before Pearl Harbor that "nearly every business executive believes not only in what advertising will do to help carry his business through the difficult transition that must follow this war, but he also believes in advertising as an indispensable factor for the maintenance of American standards of living and the American systems of government and sociology." No one, he believed, had done more than Barton "to convince American business of the merits of advertising."[9]

Advertising would endure amid the fighting, as companies either boasted about the new military products they were churning out, or touted their sacrifices ("Lucky Strike Green Has Gone to War"), or limned a radiant future replete with familiar products to be available in plenty or new gimmicks (personal airplanes) that would brighten postwar life. Not every ad dressed in khaki or red-white-and-blue struck the response desired. One BBDO client, Hormel, produced SPAM, and advertised the filling but unloved meat product as a weapon of victory. A BBDO employee in the army begged Barton to remove soldiers' pictures from the ads. "If you lived 'somewhere in New Guinea' you would never again wish to see, hear, or smell SPAM. For every new customer you make in the states, there are ten future anti-SPAMers being created over here."[10]

The war and its approach made for busy days for Barton. In June 1941 he found himself "working harder than ever." He traveled steadily that fall. BBDO clients faced "many difficult problems incident to the defense program," which required "a good deal of hand-holding" by him. After Pearl Harbor the heavily male ranks of agency employees were quickly winnowed of draftees and volunteers. By April 1943 BBDO had lost 110 out of 650 employees. To one such serviceman, Barton wrote that "almost every day another boy comes in to shake hands with me and tell me he hopes we'll keep the business going so he will have a place to come back to." To his son "Pete" (Bruce Jr.), serving in the Pacific, Barton observed that by late 1944 New York City had "become a ladies' town," so few young men were left.[11]

BBDO engaged heavily in war-related projects. Its campaign to spur navy recruiting proved so effective that the other service branches could not compete and forced the navy to resort to the draft, thus ending the link with BBDO. Barton also served as chairman of the part of the Third War Bond Drive that covered advertising and the graphic arts in New York City, an effort that exceeded its quota. A Treasury Department official first recommended him to head the entire crusade in the city. Secretary Henry Morgenthau demurred, wondering if Barton was "too political," but an aide termed him a man who "can get people to do things." Morgenthau relented, Barton was contacted, but for reasons not disclosed he ended up heading only his own profession's portion of the drive. He also chaired the publicity committee of New York's National War Fund campaign in the fall of 1945.[12]

Barton, who had once expected to be retired at his current age, was able, after the war, to relax his pace. He claimed (not entirely accurately) that once he left Congress he had "quit making speeches," and he chiefly charged himself with "the very pleasant task of helping my younger associates to take over this business, which . . . they are doing with increasing success and satisfaction every day."[13]

The old BBDO order was passing. William H. Johns, a source of flinty reassurance in the crisis of Durstine's departure, died in 1944. In 1946 Ben Duffy succeeded Barton as president of the agency, Barton becoming chairman of the board. Duffy, Barton recalled, "was our first office boy." As a high school student, he had been hired out of Hell's Kitchen because the firm had liked the work of his brother, a messenger, and needed another. Duffy so enjoyed the job that he left school, but his college-grad colleagues all thought him the right choice as the agency's new president. Once in BDO's early days, after quitting time Duffy had wandered into Barton's office and enthroned himself in the swivel chair, only to be caught in the act when the boss suddenly returned. Duffy said he was "trying it on for size." (He also painted Barton's door green on St. Patrick's Day.) Barton had a sense of humor and helped Duffy move up in the firm. By 1925 he headed the space and media department, running "space buying." He was a vice president, director, general manager, and then in 1946 head of the agency. Among his triumphs had been snaring the Lucky Strike cigarette account, a feat in which the original partners Barton and Osborn played no part.[14]

As BBDO grew up and around its two remaining founders, Barton eased back on his activities. He now came into the office each morning and worked hard until noon. "But if the sun is shining, and somebody calls up and puts temptation in my way, I am very easy to lure out into the sunshine, in the afternoon." He felt not guilt but "tremendous satisfaction in seeing young people do things better than I ever could do them." He claimed to be "having just about the happiest period of my whole business life," working actively but getting much joy from the success of "my business sons and daughters." By 1950 he reported himself "pretty much out of active management."[15] Yet clients wanted to see him—his name still resonated. He toured BBDO branches regularly, bracing the troops and jollying clients. He made it his duty "to get into every one of our offices two or three times a year," He enjoyed it, and Duffy and more engaged management lacked the time for it. The BBDO newsletter trumpeted Barton's busy troubleshooting in May

1949: "Two hours with top officials of one of our large New York clients to help solve a difficult public relations problem, three hours with another New York client on an important production matter; a meeting with the president and advertising manager of still another New York client; and participation in the presentation that brought us our newest account, Schick Shaver." He also gave speeches at the behest of clients General Mills and DuPont and at an annual dinner of local auto dealers. A man in the Minneapolis BBDO office remarked that Barton had "a beautiful knack for meeting a lot of people easily and for saying just the right thing at the right time."[16]

If he no longer wielded BBDO's crucial pen, his work still lured customers. A New York Stock Exchange official commented that his committee had selected BBDO over twenty other agencies, and that if Barton could write "as appealing a message" for NYSE as he had in one of his recent philanthropic fund-raising letters, "our industry will be on the crest of the wave before we know it." Barton kept a close watch over BBDO's output and was quick to criticize. He deplored the repetition of cigarette ads on TV, which treated the listener "as a moron." This technique may once have worked, he conceded, but ever since the turbulent 1920s, "all life is speeded up." Indeed, life had so accelerated that Barton thought the best theme for selling Luckies was as a remedy for "tension."[17]

BBDO enjoyed a number of successes in the postwar period. In 1945 it produced the famous "Chiquita Banana" song for United Fruit—a ditty that could be heard whistled or warbled on the streets. The jingle was first presented to the company (with Barton present) in a BBDO control room, sung by a BBDO secretary. "Paper clips in paper cups" stood in for the missing maracas that would accompany the fully finished jingle. The first visual performance of the song occurred in a ninety-second ad screened in movie theaters in 1948. An animated banana lip-synched the song. Sour about some innovations, Barton thought this Latin-rhythmed jingle "a masterpiece."[18]

While BBDO maintained its leadership on Madison Avenue, not every client remained happy. Barton himself thought BBDO was producing "bad advertisements" for the Polaroid Company and expected to lose the account. Murine decamped in 1955 because that company's management objected after BBDO had created the sales pitch that Murine would relieve "tired eyes," then put the same phrase on the package of a competing product. The Ethyl Corporation, to which Barton had provided public relations counsel since the early 1920s, dropped BBDO for another agency in 1956. The 1957–1958 recession hit home on Madison Avenue, and BBDO responded by pruning its payroll by 5 to 10 percent.[19]

Yet the agency continued to flourish. In 1954, according to a brochure it prepared in order to resell a shaky client, it stood third among all agencies in total advertising produced; first in TV advertising and second in combined radio-TV; second in newspapers and third in magazines; and had total billings of $148 million. Since the war, BBDO claimed to have been "chosen by more important new advertisers than any other agency, and ha[d] the fastest rate of growth of any large agency." Six of the twelve "best-managed companies in the U.S." were clients. The agency continued to stress, Barton claimed, hiring young, imaginative talent and retaining them through competitive salaries and a wide distribution of ownership. Since women did most consumer buying, BBDO strove to "use the brains and intuition of our women to the utmost." Barton made much of the agency's use of Alex Osborn's "brain storm sessions."[20]

By 1959 the company had offices in sixteen cities and employed nearly 2,100 people. It opened branches in Montreal, Toronto, London, Milan, Paris, and Frankfurt. It retained clients an average of fourteen years. (The industry figure was five years.) At its 1957 annual convention, management crowed about having enjoyed "the best year we ever had," with billings of nearly $195 million from 153 clients. As chairman of the board, Barton offered upbeat remarks about the even better business prospects to come. While younger, smaller firms sometimes proved themselves more maneuverable and responsive to changes in society than BBDO, that agency retained its appeal in important boardrooms. One publisher told Barton that his firm had the reputation that its people "have some consideration of the other fellow's time"—they did not enjoy "keeping you waiting in the reception room" as at other agencies. To most of its insiders, BBDO was a pleasant place to work—more relaxed and casual than the "grey flannel suit" standard of the 1950s. Charlie Brower called BBDO "about the least hucksterish in the business," with few grey flannel suits visible and no "floss and gloss." In surveying Madison Avenue, Martin Mayer described BBDO's home office as spartan, housing "senior employees like junior employees in a rabbit warren of cream-colored corridors and closets," not exactly radiating "elegance and power." More positively, employees saw it as a place where people with chronic problems were told to seek help but not fired. Some BBDOers gave Barton part of the credit for this atmosphere.[21]

Batten, Barton, Durstine & Osborn was more than holding its own in middle age. Although Madison Avenue had preserved its WASP male clubbiness for a long time, and BBDO remained a largely "whitebread agency" (according to an anonymous BBDO lifer), rivulets of change bubbled up. In 1952 BBDO proposed to market a sauce as one that would "give spaghetti that real Italian goodness." In the same year BBDO "gave Madison avenue something to talk about when they hired a Negro executive." This, said the *Chicago Defender*, marked "a pioneering step" amid the "gilded cages" of the advertising district.[22]

AS A POLITICAL FIGURE, Barton continued his critique of FDR's foreign policies, but, no longer in Congress, his pulpit had shrunk. In early 1941 he confided his view that while "an amateur in foreign affairs, even a Republican President, might have succeeded in gaining the enmity of either Japan or Russia . . . to line up both of them [plus Germany and Italy] requires the touch of a master."[23] His "close friendship" with Willkie ended after the campaign when he tried to convince the defeated candidate to "take the leadership of a diligent, critical minority" on foreign policy. But Willkie "had already made up his mind to help Roosevelt get us into the war." He later surmised that Willkie had "no real sense of history."[24] On his part, Willkie recounted a bitter meeting with publisher Roy Howard and Barton, asserting extravagantly that ex-President Hoover was "the brains of this isolationist movement today," Howard its "field marshal," and Barton its "advertising manager and contact man."[25]

Amid war and public debate over America's postwar global role, Barton grew fretful. He took counsel with other critics of FDR's foreign policy, like the historian Charles A. Beard and the sociologist and polemicist Harry Elmer Barnes. He launched a correspondence and friendship with Lawrence Dennis, publisher of a quirky dissenting newsletter, who did research and writing for him and served as a sounding board.[26] Dreading the internationalist trend in both U.S. foreign policy and the public mood, he chided Henry Luce for thinking, in his noted *Life* essay "The American Century," that "the Kingdom of Heaven can come all at once," and he blanched at the notion that Britain and the United States could be "a sort of combination of Queen Victoria and Eleanor Roosevelt ruling and brightening the world."[27]

Barton soon embarked on a "Post War Book" that aimed to tutor Americans in the unhappy fates of overambitious great powers of the past. Writing "under great heat," he had a first draft by early 1943.[28] He included worried speculations about the nation's character. He hoped war might erase those blemishes, but, in a vein seldom seen in his opinionizing in the 1920s, he noted the "decay" visible in England and France and lamented that Americans had started to imitate "the long English week-end, shortened our working hours, and gone in for luxury and amusement in a big way." Our enemies had more discipline. Citing Flinders Petrie's *Revolutions of Civilization*, he wondered whether our "surrealism, our mad pursuit of nervous excitement, our boogie-woogie music, and the unblushing obscenity of the stage" did not foreshadow American decline. He waved away the dated labels "isolationist" and "interventionist," conceding that the former had erred in thinking we "could never be attacked," the latter in claiming aid to England would deter Hitler and so shield America from war. Instead he espoused a "nationalist" view against that of the "world savers or do-gooders or evangelists." His postwar vision saw a United States militarily prepared (especially in air power), focused on the Pacific, engaged in the United Nations, but avoiding excessive promises of economic aid—no "international WPA."[29]

This book, tentatively titled "Shall Not Have Died in Vain," proved frustrating. Barton was unhappy with his first draft, though friends praised it. A *Reader's Digest* editor labeled it "a highly charged and very hard-headed appraisal of some of the romantic hog-wash that's being slopped over the people about post-war problems." Barton had begun it when "the air was full of the talk of [Henry A.] Wallace and the other dreamers," but now he detected a more realistic tone in debate. Yet he feared first that it might be premature to publish it in 1943, then that other "postwar" tomes that were piling up in bookstores would blanket it. Willkie had returned from his global journey and written *One World*, a paean to internationalism. Walter Lippmann offered *U.S. Foreign Policy: Shield of the Republic.* Other foreign policy manuals poured forth, elections came and went, mind-sets developed, competition multiplied. Simon and Schuster declined the book because it was publishing Willkie's tract and "exploring . . . projects" with Wallace and others. Barton would ponder taking the manuscript to market, but then recoil with every "change in the news that cools my ardor." In early 1944, heartened that "many things which I said with fear and trembling are now being said quite openly and in highly respectable quarters," he partly revised the work.[30] Ultimately, however, there was no book. Barton would continue to write about foreign policy, but in magazines.

Barton deplored most elements of postwar foreign policy. It was costly, overweening, and windy. It militarized and regimented the economy. Behind the scenes in 1947 he worked to muster witnesses to give congressional testimony against the Marshall Plan. He lamented "'our ideological war with totalitarianism.' I find nothing in the Constitution which gives our government the right to engage in ideological wars. . . ." He thought the nation "engaged in an attempted imperialism which so far has proved a failure." He was particularly

taken with the ideas of Major Alexander de Seversky in such books as
Air Power: Key to Survival. He cheered ex-president Hoover's speech of
late 1950, which opposed sending troops to Europe under NATO and instead urged building invincible air and sea power to defend North
America. He feared that America's interventionist policies were achieving the Soviets' goal—of bankrupting us. He proposed for the nation a
"solemn day for soul-searching and prayer, on which [the U.S.] would
confess that everything it has done in foreign policy, beginning with
the Spanish-American War, was based on the false premise that when
any people anywhere in the world are doing something we don't like,
it is our moral duty to shoot them."[31]

The outbreak of war in Korea in 1950 particularly depressed him.
He even queried Norman Thomas, the perennial Socialist party leader,
with whom he was on friendly terms (as with other pacifists or isolationists of the left): "Could I get myself nominated for Congress on the
Socialist ticket this fall?"[32] As the war darkened and the nation hun-
kered down for a long struggle, Barton inveighed against the ominous
trend to "Stalin-like controls over every activity and department of our
daily lives." He warned that Americans were being "'conditioned'" to
accept such measures and that they faced a war against "totalitarianism
abroad and the creeping—now leaping—growth of totalitarianism at
home."[33]

In the 1930s Barton had treated the Communist threat lightly. "You
aren't going to have Communism," he reassured, "in a country that
owns twenty-five million automobiles." Perhaps the events of 1937–1940
chipped away at his equanimity. The Red Menace was entering American politics, nowhere more stridently than in New York City. The
Democrat who ran against La Guardia during Barton's first congressional race gave the topic an airing. In 1938 it resounded in the neigh-
boring congressional campaign of John J. O'Connor, the Democrat
whom FDR successfully purged. One might speculate too that the frequent picketing carried on against Barton by Communists and left-wing
WPA unions in this period might have tested his patience. He dabbled
with the Communist issue in his 1940 campaign.[34]

After 1940 Barton felt increasingly free to add the topic to his political discourse. He encouraged Governor Dewey's "blasts at the
Communists" in the 1946 campaign. He drafted a manifesto for congressional Republicans in 1945 that pledged "to ventilate the State
Department from top to bottom" and to staff it with those "who know
. . . the difference between American Communists and real Americans." He also apparently helped organize a group of writers to contest with leftists for control of their profession. Eugene Lyons, whose
The Red Decade sounded an early tocsin against Communist influences in the United States, invited him to join a group to be named,
half in jest, "Redbaiters, Inc.," thus aiming to "convert a term of
abuse into a title of pride."[35]

Although long critical of Democratic tenderness toward communism, he steered clear of Joe McCarthy's crusade. In May 1950, as the
Wisconsin senator collected headlines, Barton privately observed that
foreign policy errors would not be cured with "little changes in the personnel of our State Department." Yet neither did he rebuke McCarthy,
though he conceded the senator's "manners are bad." At times he in-
dulged in McCarthyite metaphor: he disliked a TV kinescope that
showed "dancing boys" frolicking in the background. "They gave me
a little of the feeling of a garden party at the State Dept." He also cited
approvingly the senator's frequent rejoinder to critics: "'Name one innocent person that McCarthy has hurt,' and there has never been any
answer."[36] Barton thought intellectuals had grown hysterical about
McCarthy—they always seemed to fear "mass movements." But he
commented about television coverage of the 1954 Army–McCarthy
hearings that the senator's "antics . . . his constant 'point of order'
when he had no point, and even less sense of order—this bored the
viewers and cost him friends." By getting "all worked up over communism," he thought, "good people get mad about the wrong things."[37]

BBDO was heavily implicated in "the blacklist," the device by which
Communists and leftists were purged from jobs in the field of entertainment. As an agent for radio and TV sponsors and a producer of
many shows, BBDO found itself enmeshed in the problem of clearing

entertainers for work in these media and denying jobs to those whose names appeared on various "lists" of Communists or pro-Communists. Barton voiced no misgivings about this nasty feature of the era. He even boasted to a leader of the emerging blacklisting industry (perhaps to deflect his interest) that "we here at BBDO were among the first to recognize the Communist menace and have had a full-time expert . . . on the job for several years."[38] The president of Armstrong Cork Company recommended to his peer at Borden's that he hire BBDO for TV advertising and talent vetting: "BBDO does a fine job in keeping Armstrong out of trouble on this score." On the other hand, Barton wrote to urge early release for Ring Lardner, Jr. (an old acquaintance) from prison, where he was serving, as one of the "Hollywood Ten," a sentence for contempt of Congress.[39]

Often Barton's observations of the American polity and society had a gloomy cast. The mood of his end-of-the-republic rhetoric in the 1940 campaign lingered. In 1945 he confessed he had begun but then discarded efforts to write short newspaper pieces: his past essays drew readers with "their optimistic tone and self-help quality," but "I don't feel very optimistic these days." Although he had always claimed to be a liberal Republican, he did not accept the new synthesis adopted by more liberal business spokesmen which held that government should play a key role in guiding the economy and that federal expenditures could stabilize it. When *Fortune* issued a pamphlet to this effect, Barton sent the magazine a set of queries. Given society's current makeup, with powerful, ravenous interest groups and no sector in government to resist them, how would the state ever muster the discipline to halt its spending? The headline for an account of a 1949 speech to a business association blared Barton's view that "Our Enterprise System Is Dead." He renewed his lament that FDR's third term had ended the republic; we were now governed by selfish "pressure groups."[40] He took counsel with pessimistic books arguing that permanent structural changes had befallen the United States and other industrial societies. In 1942 he listed James Burnham's *The Managerial Revolution*, Ortega y Gasset's *The Revolt of the Masses*, Lawrence

Dennis's *Dynamics of War and Revolution*, Lothrop Stoddard's *The Rising Tide of Color*, and Pitirim Sorokin's *The Crisis of Our Age* among the key books of the time. Ortega especially impressed him. He thought his book one of "the three most important books in our lifetime" and signed a memorial to mark Ortega's death. Other works that swayed him were Oswald Spengler's *Decline of the West*, Herbert Spencer's *Man Versus the State*, Havelock Ellis's *Essays in War Time*, Fairfield Osborn's *Our Plundered Planet*, and Alexander de Seversky's *Air Power: Key to Survival*.[41] All these studies shared a penchant for seeing the dark side of present trends.

Nothing convinced Barton that American government had the self-discipline or capacity to resolve any of these problems. He again cited Flinders Petrie's *Revolutions of Civilization*, in which the archaeologist described "the cycle of governmental evolution, from autocracy to oligarchy, and from oligarchy to democracy, and his gloomy note that 'when democracy has attained full power, the majority without capital necessarily eat up the capital of the minority, and the civilization steadily decays'" along with democracy. An address to the Grocery Manufacturers of America typified Barton's doomsday rhetoric: both the "American republic and the private enterprise system are dead and gone," leaving "a democracy which is ruled by pressure groups."[42]

Barton persisted in labeling himself a member of the downtrodden middle class. He lamented that "all of us in the middle class belong to a past era," and returned often to this theme. A notice for a 1953 speech in Denver advertised his self-identification as "a typical specimen of America's vanishing middle class." This self-positioning appears preposterous, yet Barton did have that sense of middleness so often ascribed to Progressive era reformers. Sometimes he worried about the unslakable demands of the great unwashed, the revolt of the masses. But the selfishness or unconcern of the wealthy also alarmed him. In his appeals on behalf of the Community Chest, he warned that "if our democracy is ever destroyed," neither "a foreign foe" nor "primarily the poor and underprivileged" would bear responsibility. Rather, it would result from a leadership failure, "when the sense of obligation perishes at the top, and when those to whom so much has been given cease to realize that from them much is required."[43]

Some of Barton's gloom had a racial basis. Always something of an Anglo-Saxonist, he admired Lothrop Stoddard's 1920 book, *The Rising Tide of Color*, and suggested to his old friend and editor at Bobbs-Merrill that the out-of-print volume should be reprinted. He thought some group differences were innate. Many "colored people have decided . . . that they will sit in the sun, not worry, and live out their days with a minimum of responsibility, work and strain." "We white people are differently constituted. . . . The Jews, of course, are at the extreme end of the spectrum."[44] But he avoided public references to concerns such as these and maintained good relationships with groups working for racial and religious tolerance. He was one of three admen to win awards from the National Conference of Christians and Jews in 1950 for "promoting good-will and understanding between Protestants, Catholics and Jews."[45]

Barton's concerns about rising tides partly underpinned his dissent from American globalism. He often harked back to the perception gained on his 1934 world tour that the day of the white man in Asia was passing. Such attitudes may also have influenced his thinking about population growth. Fear of an exploding world population increasingly troubled him. He believed that "what causes wars is babies, too many babies in too little room and with too little to eat." "I have been a nut on this subject of population for a long time," he wrote in 1951. (Havelock Ellis's *Essays in War-Time*, among other readings, had a strong impact on him.)[46]

But Barton could not stay permanently gloomy. A speech amid World War II's dark days contended that progress persisted through and despite wars and politicians. A 1949 speech also offered a sunny view. He held—one of his pet notions—that if the Russians "had a choice between the promises of Stalin and the promises of the Sears Roebuck catalog, capitalism would win out a thousand to one." Rather than socialism or communism, it "is the great dynamic force of the

modern world." His notion of "dropping a few thousand Sears Roebuck catalogs on Russia" earned the sort of press notice at which he
was adept.[47] Similarly, while Malthusian worry darkened his foreign
policy views, rising population cheered him when he surveyed the
home market. A 1948 speech asked his listeners to visualize the postwar birthrate "in terms of more baby carriages, diapers, medicines, and
all the things that babies need." A 1950 column recalled his suspicion
that his agency would never equal its 1929 billings; they were now
more than triple the earlier figure. In 1956 he said that, barring a war,
the nation had embarked on "the greatest and most exciting period in
the history of the human race," what with the baby boom and the wonders of automation and atomic power pointing to the certainty of the
four-day week. In 1959 he prepared speech material for the tire magnate Harvey Firestone, which claimed that, whatever challenges faced
America, "over the years it is the optimists who have proved to have
been right, and the pessimists who have consistently been wrong. Barton balanced his misgivings with his belief in "hope and hustle."[48]

His own business activities prompted a positive outlook. Barton saw
that television would do for advertising what radio had in the 1920s.
When TV took off, its trajectory was near vertical. One BBDO report es-
timated that in early 1950 the television audience was "growing at a
rate of over 40,000 viewers per day." TV penetration of most major
markets increased by 6 to 9 percent in the first half of 1951. Barton kept
up with it, was conversant with the latest shows of sponsors, and had
plenty to say about the quality of programs. Yet he was quick to reassure newspapermen that their medium still had a role. He offered the
mot that "the more I see on television, the more I want to read about
it in newspapers." He noted that when New York newspapers went on
strike in 1953, a BBDO survey found that what people missed most was
advertising.[49]

BBDO grew with the new medium. It won Campbell's Soup as a
client in 1954 and soon pushed the elfin, red-cheeked "Campbell Kids"
onto television (accompanied by the persistent if not artistically inspired ditty "Mmm-mmm Good . . ."). It flooded TV with "L.S./M.F.T."

ads for Lucky Strike. "Which Twin has the Toni?" was another BBDO product. In 1959 the agency hired the cartoon character Mr. Magoo to shill nearsightedly for GE light bulbs. It helped telecast a number of high-profile shows: Jack Benny, "GE Theater" (for which it hired actor Ronald Reagan as host), "The U.S. Steel Hour," and the "DuPont Show of the Month." Pepsi-Cola came on board in 1960, and BBDO sold it as the product "for those who think young." One of its clients, Revlon, was a sponsor of the popular quiz show *The $64,000 Question.* By 1957 nearly 40 percent of BBDO's billings came from television.[50]

BBDO remained a flagship agency. Of course it had its reversals. When one client, *Reader's Digest,* published an article critical of Hit Parade cigarettes, a product of another client, American Tobacco, BBDO felt the need to resign the *Digest* account. It lost Revlon too. Yet for the year billings rose. In several years of the 1950s, more clients left than arrived. Still, BBDO won *Advertising Age's* "Year's Best" agency title three times of four in the early 1960s.[51]

As advertising continued to grow in the 1950s and to occupy a role central to the national culture, the profession again attracted the attention of critics. Frederic Wakeman's novel *The Hucksters* became a best-seller in 1946, as did Sloan Wilson's *The Man in the Gray Flannel Suit* in 1955. Vance Packard wrote *The Hidden Persuaders,* a nonfiction best-seller in 1957. Again Barton came to Madison Avenue's defense. He discounted talk of admen as "hidden and irresponsible persuaders" and asserted he had never even taken note of a "grey flannel suit." His partner Osborn declared of Barton: "nobody—*nobody*—has done as much to put advertising in its right light."[52]

After World War II Barton continued writing for magazines and newspapers. His most widely remarked effort, "Are We Biting Off More than We Can Chew?," published in *Reader's Digest* in 1948, offered the "isolationist" case against the Truman administration's foreign policies. He fretted about what later historians would label imperial overstretch. Pointing to the fates of forerunners like Greece, Rome, Spain, England, and Germany, he asked, "And where are they now?" (Most, he said sardonically, were seeking an American "dole.")

The United States was making too many "sweeping," unsustainable promises and was losing popularity abroad despite its giveaways. While the Soviets did seek "world conquest," like all other such aspirants they were doomed to failure. He urged a less adventurous, less ruinous, "realistic" foreign policy backed by an air force that would deter any attack. The *Digest's* publisher told Barton that his article drew more correspondence than any other in the *Digest* that year.[53] Another piece, "The Fallacy of the Atlantic Pact," appeared in *Look* in September 1949. Barton warned that what looked "defensive" to us appeared threatening to the Soviets. Thus the fears and miscalculations engendered by rearmament programs might lead to an "incident" of the kind that had sparked earlier wars. Barton argued that alliances like NATO created the inertial guidance that propelled sequences of events toward disaster, as when Austria-Hungary's mobilization in 1914 triggered Russia's, then Germany's and England's. Arming meant arms races and war, not deterrence and peace. He also feared that lucrative arms contracts would addict businessmen and other "pressure groups" to a defense-driven economy and tie them to the temporal needs of politicians. Barton was echoing critical themes of U.S. foreign policy that traversed the political spectrum, from Henry A. Wallace to Robert A. Taft.[54]

Beginning in 1949 Barton also wrote a syndicated column for King Features, the Hearst syndication company. He hoped to resume the "inspirational articles" he had produced twenty years earlier. He put his younger son, Bruce Jr., to work in an editorial function, sharing proceeds from the column, which appeared in the Hearst dailies and a number of noncompeting papers. The Barton in these columns was more upbeat than the private Barton. He upheld American capitalism as "the system of hustle and hope." He hoped this coinage made a better label for American capitalism than "profit system" or "private enterprise system," which smacked of "a big fat man, with a cigar in his mouth. . . ." Themes from earlier writings returned for encores: Barton even drafted a critique of liberals which insinuated, as he had forty years before, that they neglected to feed their cats.[55]

The weekly column continued until 1955 when King Features, reviewing its thin returns, asked for a change in terms. This would yield
Barton so little that it did not seem worth the "time and effort"; hence
the column expired in October.[56] Barton had undertaken it with trep-
idation. His earlier "inspirational articles" succeeded because "they
were addressed mostly to young people by a man who was himself
young." A keen sense that youth had passed often occupied his
thoughts and made him cautious about writing for younger readers.
He dreaded being an old man ranting to a younger generation. He
placed himself among those who "are moved by a very real fear . . . of
being old-minded and behind the parade."[57]

Demand for his earlier religious writings, particularly *The Man
Nobody Knows*, persisted. In the 1950s Bobbs-Merrill published new
editions. Barton had always been sensitive to criticisms leveled at the
book. He had tried to convince D. L. Chambers to drop the chapter
on advertising when a cheap reprint was afoot in the 1930s, but the
publisher talked him out of it. Barton thought about rewriting the
whole book; then, feeling the absence of his father's counsel, backed
away from the scheme. He never followed through on this or other notions for book-length projects he broached.[58]

With Barton's approval, editors at Bobbs-Merrill heavily amended
the text for a 1956 edition. They cut "references to business and advertising" that Gertrude Lane had once thought likely to offend readers.
They changed the chapter titles "The Executive" and "The Founder
of Modern Business" to "The Leader" and "His Way in Our World."
The chapter "His Advertisements" had drawn the most complaints.
Restyled "His Work and Words," it was fuzzied up, and most references
to advertising vanished. Heeding the suggestions of a wide array of
consultants, the editors removed or changed passages that might offend. Zacchaeus, depicted by Jesus' followers in the original edition as
a "dishonest little Jew," became a "dishonest little man" in the updated
version.[59] Barton's doubts that younger readers could relate to the 1920s
celebrities who had peopled his book prompted removal of references
to Henry Ford, George Perkins, and Jim Jeffries. This cleanup thus

buffed out most connections between Jesus and the world of business and advertising as well as virtually every reference that anchored the book to its original time and place, leaving it a kind of prematurely New Age religious tract. Of these changes in the text, readers were told nothing.[60]

The book nonetheless continued to charm readers. A combined edition of *The Man* and *The Book*, published in 1956, surprised Barton by selling in "considerable quantities." By early 1959 Bobbs-Merrill calculated that in twelve different versions, including such combined editions, *The Man* had sold 755,000 copies. *Reader's Digest* serialized an abridgement of it in 1965.[61] On and off, the book stayed in print for most of the twentieth century, and it remains so in the twenty-first.

For a time in the 1950s Barton considered writing yet another religiously themed book, to be titled *He*. It would, like his previous works, strip away the myths with which formalized religion had encrusted Jesus, pointing out, for instance, that there was little biblical basis for the doctrine of the virgin birth. Barton wanted to write an "honest book" but feared that by arguments like this one "all our Catholic friends will be hurt," and where would be the benefit? The book did not come to fruition.[62]

THE END OF his congressional service had afforded Barton more leisure time. Esther and he had fallen in love with Arizona, a frequent winter destination. In 1941 they bought a house in Phoenix. Barton also briefly owned a one-third interest in a ranch in Arizona, where he "rode in the round-ups several times."[63] Betsey was a frequent visitor in Phoenix; increasingly independent despite her paralysis, she would eventually settle in California. She began to display talent as a writer, publishing four books plus a number of magazine articles. Her 1944 book *And Now to Live Again* addressed her rehabilitation and adjustment to her accident. It received "pleasant reception by the reviewers and the customers," according to her proud father. The *Washington Post* praised it as timely, given the many wounded returning from the war, and inspiring for showing people "they possess within themselves the power to transcend . . . disaster" and to live worthwhile lives. Betsey often visited army hospitals during and after the war to buck up men who had suffered similar injuries; in turn they encouraged her to walk with greater confidence and balance. The army was so grateful for her work that they taught her to drive one of the new cars "equipped especially for handicapped veterans" and put her on the priority list to buy one. She also wrote a novel about the rehabilitation experience, *The Long Walk*, on which movie producer David O. Selznick took an option. The death of her mother, to whom she was very close, was a blow; her memoir, *As Love Is Deep*, helped Betsey to cope with it. She edited an aviation magazine and showed talent as an artist in pastels.[64]

The Bartons' two sons found their niches after the war. Randall, who had bounced around in his pursuit of an education, finally settled on engineering. During the war he worked as superintendent in an aircraft plant in California. Later he worked for two Phoenix newspapers controlled by Eugene Pulliam and became assistant publisher and (with Bruce) a part-owner; he lived in Phoenix with his second, then third wife. Graduating *magna cum laude* from Harvard in 1943, Bruce Jr. joined the navy and served in the Pacific as a deck officer on a destroyer escort. In 1945 he survived the sinking of his torpedoed ship. He went to work at *Time*, where, a skilled writer, he soon was made an editor. He presided over *Time*'s religion and education departments, moved to foreign news, and later took over the art section.[65]

Although his children were well launched, Barton would confront a series of losses in the postwar years. After a two-and-a-half-year illness from cancer and a lengthy period of being bedridden, his wife Esther died on November 20, 1951.[66] Their marriage had lasted since 1913. She had been busy in good works (especially for Wellesley College). She had kept their homes functioning and cared for the children during Barton's many travels. She had stood by Bruce through the ugly 1933 blackmail trial and all it entailed. Of their thirty-eight-year marriage he said: "If we had it to live all over again, I don't know how we could ask for anything better." Bruce alluded to the illness in an article he wrote, whose moral was that regular medical checkups might catch such diseases in an early stage. The piece elicited hundreds of letters.[67]

After Esther's death, Barton soldiered on. He tore down his house in Foxboro soon after she died: the family used it little, and it harbored too many memories. He continued to travel, spending parts of the winter in Arizona, though he sold the house he and Esther had bought. Betsey and he became friendly with the renowned architect Frank Lloyd Wright.[68] He maintained an active social life. Friends threw eligible women in his way. He told one such matchmaker: "from now on my principal activity is going to be to dodge women, except you and a few other happily married, virtuous wives." But not always. His frequent companion at ball games, Broadway shows, and dinner parties was Ann Honeycutt, whose company he enjoyed and who offered him "great protection from the widows."[69] At various junctures she had run a catering service, worked as a radio producer, and co-authored a "classic" guide to raising dogs. She belonged to the New Yorker set in the 1930s (at one point married to another of its members), and some described her as having been the great love of James Thurber's life. (Thurber provided the drawings that graced her dog manual.)[70] Sometimes when Barton entertained at home, Louise MacLeod, his longtime assistant, filled out the company. In April 1959 he dined at Herbert Hoover's, in September 1960 with Hoover and General Douglas MacArthur. In September 1959 he attended the mayor of New York's luncheon for Nikita Khrushchev during the Soviet premier's whirlwind American tour. He maintained ties with his three best friends from Congress, Republicans Robert Rich, Robert Smith, and Leslie Arends (who became GOP whip in the 1950s). They tried to rendezvous every year, often over Easter, for fellowship and golf. They spent a weekend at Barton's townhouse in 1961, when Bruce's health had turned frail, and managed to get in a round on the links.[71]

These years were also filled with more family deaths. A favorite nephew's suicide in 1947 pained Bruce. His sister Helen and brothers Bob and Charles had all died by 1956, as had Webster Barton Beatty, the African-American child his parents had taken into their home in Tennessee and raised as part of the family.[72] Fred was his only surviving sibling. Betsey had bought a house in Los Angeles. She died there in December 1962 when she apparently toppled into her swimming pool in her wheelchair. In September 1963 Bruce Jr. was discovered in his apartment dead of a heart attack at the age of forty-one. By this point the only one of Bruce and Esther's children still living was Randall, who in the 1960s came increasingly to handle his father's business decisions.[73]

The anchor of Barton's spiritual life also slipped a link or two in his later years. Locating an enduring spiritual home proved difficult. He never quite found in New York the sort of institutional nest he had enjoyed in his youth at Oak Park First Congregational. (He kept his membership there long after moving away.) His wife and he began attending services at Madison Avenue Presbyterian Church. Later, when they moved south to Fifty-fifth Street, they worshiped at Central Presbyterian, at Sixty-fourth Street and Park Avenue. But he never joined that congregation, and over time his developing "anti-gregarious spirit" caused him to avoid church. Still, he liked the preaching of Reverend Theodore Speers and applauded Speers's efforts to assist soldiers and sailors during the war (cots for Saturday night stays, Sunday breakfasts, and other spiritual and physical amenities). In 1943 he joined the church's board—on which he would serve for six years—but still not the congregation. He divulged to Dr. Speers in 1948 that he sometimes attended Quaker meetings and in 1952 told one friend, "Spiritually I am a Quaker." In the 1950s, after Esther's death, his attendance slipped further; he confessed to having "become a kind of hermit," but by early 1956 said he had begun going more frequently "and fe[lt] good about it." [74]

Barton maintained his interest in Republican politics after 1940. He backed Tom Dewey for governor in 1942 and in his 1944 presidential race. He suggested personnel to direct publicity for Dewey in 1944. He escorted Dewey adviser Herbert Brownell to a conference with former congressional colleagues to brief them on that campaign. He sent advice and encouragement and explored possible angles to exploit the issue of FDR's health. He roundly supported unlimbering the Communist issue, which was a popular one among Republicans in 1944.[75]

In late 1945, at the request of Congressman Charles Halleck, Barton took a stab at drafting a "report" for the party's congressional leaders to use in postwar politics. In 1948 he advised Dewey again, urging him not to commit to an extensive campaign by train. "This is horse-and-buggy campaigning—pre-newspaper, pre-radio, and pre-television." Better ten good speeches by a rested candidate "than a thousand back platform chats any one of which could produce an embarrassing slip." He encouraged Dewey to have his "boys" travel beyond the reach of the New York City media to get a clearer sense of what the nation was thinking. But Dewey remained insulated within his "Albany circle" and from guidance outside his entourage, and thus cut himself off from broader public opinion. Barton himself witnessed some of the complacency of Dewey's staff when one of the governor's top advisers told him, "we may be entering an era of 'good feeling' as it occurred in the days of Monroe."[76]

Barton was eclectic in his GOP tastes. He liked both Senator Robert A. Taft, the strong voice of conservatism and "isolationism," and General Dwight D. Eisenhower, favorite of the party's internationalist wing. He chummed with Ike during the latter's stint as president of Columbia University and was much impressed. In 1952 he had a hard time choosing. Although he stated privately in April that he was inclined to back Ike, he maintained public neutrality before the convention, after which he supported Eisenhower with gusto.[77]

The 1952 election was the first contest in which television played a critical role. BBDO was "pulled into the Eisenhower campaign" as a result of its contribution to Governor Dewey's 1950 reelection. Barton said he "did all I could to have our organization excused" from the Eisenhower campaign, fearing that costs would outrun benefits. But "Eisenhower had fallen in love" with BBDO president Ben Duffy, who assumed the major role for BBDO in designing Ike's grand media strategy, though his was not the only agency involved. Barton passed along several suggestions to Duffy, but he was not in command.[78]

In 1952 the famous short "spot" advertisements featuring representative Americans asking a question, followed by Ike's spliced-in
replies, exemplified for many observers the intrusion of admen and
hucksterism into the selling of political candidates. George Ball, adviser to the Democratic candidate Adlai E. Stevenson, tried preemp-
tively to belittle these plugs as more appropriate to "the sale of soap
and toothpastes." (The Democrats, be it said, also ran some spots.)
Ball doubted that BBDO would succeed by these methods in making
Ike "look like Hercules." In truth it was not BBDO but Rosser Reeves
of the Ted Bates agency who designed the spots. Later Reeves would
argue that the choice between candidates in the voting booth did resemble the "choice between competing tubes of tooth paste in a drug-
store."[79] The use of "Madison Avenue" techniques appalled some
observers. BBDO became *the* agency identified with the new politics of
appearances and fabricated candidates. Before long (perhaps as early
as 1956), the ad-word "image" entered the political lexicon.[80] To
crusty former president Harry Truman, BBDO stood for the decline of
American politics. He dismissed a 1957 Eisenhower administration
TV presentation as "Bunko, Bull, Deceit & Obfuscation"—even
though the agency had nothing to do with the program.[81]

Exaggerations aside, BBDO did retain a conspicuous role in Republican politics. Ben Duffy orchestrated the nationally televised pro-
Eisenhower program that aired on election eve in 1952. Rosser Reeves
termed it "an absolutely superb production" with considerable "psychological effect on the undecided voters." BBDO's involvement continued. It gave technical advice on Eisenhower's televised report to the
nation in June 1953. The Republican National Committee chose the
agency to handle the party's national radio and TV appeal for the 1954
off-year elections. BBDO consented, even though its board had determined to reduce political involvement "that would bring us close to
the local level." BBDO had come, said its president, to be "looked upon
as the agency o[f] record for the Republican National Committee." It
retained that status until 1964, when the Committee shifted its business to the Leo Burnett agency.[82]

Barton maintained his ties to prominent Republicans. He ranked as an Eisenhower friend (however Ike's foreign policies clashed with his views). He sought no position but did tell Herbert Brownell, Eisenhower's future attorney general and his "screener of applications for jobs," that he would be interested in serving on a commission to do the essential task of examining "the whole public relations and propaganda machinery" of the government, at home and abroad. He came to think highly of Richard M. Nixon, attending off-the-record dinner and briefing sessions when the vice president came to New York. He also liked Nelson Rockefeller, the liberal Republican elected New York's governor in 1958, but that did not deter him from supporting the conservative senator Barry Goldwater for reelection in Arizona.[83]

As chairman of the board at BBDO, he had surrendered managerial responsibilities to younger colleagues. He liked to say that the chairman of the board filled the same function as "parsley on fish." He now had "a good deal of free time." He still showed up a lot, as a "star" in the advertising firmament, a circuit rider among the company's many branch offices, a figure who yet could help attract new clients. He had collected memberships on the boards of several business entities over the years, including the East River Savings Bank and the State Street Investment Corporation (to which, having in the twenties achieved indifferent results in his own efforts to cash in on the stock market, he increasingly entrusted his funds for investment).[84]

He applied his energies to various causes. He joined an advisory committee to the city's Welfare Department. He contributed financially to Amherst and gave both money and talent (in composing appeals) to Berea College, on whose board of trustees he had served since 1931 (taking his father's seat).[85] Other educational causes took his fancy as well. He was a trustee and benefactor of Deerfield Academy, which his sons had attended. He crafted winning pleas for funds for the prep school (though in later years Louise MacLeod took over much of this work). A dorm named after him was dedicated in 1963. He took a shine to Macalester College (encouraged by his friend De Witt Wallace); he gave it money, and the college awarded him an honorary degree.[86] He

served as a trustee of the Columbia-Presbyterian Medical Center, the
Herald-Tribune Fresh Air Fund, and as president of the board of the Institute for the Crippled and Disabled (on whose board his daughter also
served), which was affiliated with Columbia University and its hospital.
The work of this organization was of natural interest to both Bartons.
For many years Bruce enjoyed taking part in cruises up the Hudson
which it laid on for its clients, and he twanged heartstrings with his
fund-raising letters.[87] He also became national chairman of the American Heart Association and chairman of the United Negro College
Fund.[88]

    Barton was a member of the National Conference of Christians
and Jews, which worked to build mutual acceptance, though the subject sometimes made him testy. He counseled against inordinate complaining about discrimination and prejudice, citing the advice of a
client never to advertise that his company's radiators did not leak. That
and the Jews' "constantly reminding people that they are abused and
disliked" were "very bad advertising." He suggested that prejudice rose
less from theological differences than from "bad manners" among
both Christians and Jews. He had a strong reputation, however, as a
supporter of intergroup tolerance and a long record of opposing anti-
Semitism. He won one of its Brotherhood Awards and received other
tributes from the organization.[89]

    Barton harvested a number of honors in his later years. He won
one of the Benjamin Franklin Awards conferred as part of that worthy's 250th anniversary celebration. In 1961 he received the *Printers' Ink*
advertising gold medal. *Printers' Ink* titled the article about his award
"Everything Ad Men Should Be, He Is." Amherst, his alma mater, conferred an honorary doctorate on him in 1957 (fifty years after his graduation).[90]

    Barton's business, social, and philanthropic schedule, already cur-
tailed, suffered a jolt in July 1957 during a trip to visit several BBDO re-
gional offices. In Cleveland he felt tired; his dinner speech "didn't
make much sense." But he and Charles H. Brower flew to Minneapolis, where he insisted on introducing the firm's new president to

clients. The junket was wearing. On a long hot boat ride, he showed signs of exhaustion. That night, in his hotel room, while drawing a bath, he flipped off the edge of a stool and knocked himself out; water flooding into the hallway tipped off the hotel staff to his distress. Brower packed him on a plane back to New York, where he was sent to a hospital for a rest. There he suffered a stroke. Although labeled "minor," it affected movement on his left side. After a long home stay and considerable physiotherapy, he enjoyed a robust recovery, though he remembered none of the details of the trip home from Minneapolis, would walk more hesitantly, and seemed to associates to have aged rapidly. Photographs from the time confirm this assessment. He also found that occasionally statements he intended to make scrambled themselves by the time they left his mouth. Yet he convalesced successfully enough by late October to be able to walk to BBDO and preside over the monthly board of directors meeting. It would not be his last bout with unwellness. Later in the year he contracted phlebitis, which disqualified him for a time from flying.[91] The stroke marked a definitive turn in Barton's health, which would deteriorate over the next decade, decisively after 1961.

But soon he was coming back to the office, if only for an hour or so. His life slowed down by several gears. He had two Finnish maids and, as increasingly needed, nursing care. He spent leisurely mornings in bed, where he ate breakfast and perused the paper. In a variant of a very old joke, he said he checked the front page, then the advertising column, then the obituaries, "and—if my name isn't there—I get up and go to work." He came to accept that "most of the things I used to do I can't do any more. I come to the office almost every day, though I haven't much to do here, and I read and take long walks." Health and age were having an effect. Having passed seventy-five, he decided late in 1961 that it was time to step down as BBDO's chairman of the board, effective at the end of the year.[92]

In the next few years he required a great deal of rest. His public appearances increasingly were devoted to receiving honors. He still attended social events and, at least in the early sixties, kept up a busy correspondence, one so full of reminiscences that it was clear he had kept his memory. He remained an avid, engaged reader. He continued to see Ann Honeycutt and other friends.[93]

He also remained connected with various good works. He headed the annual drive of the United Negro College Fund in 1959 and 1960. He continued, on a reduced scale, to comment publicly on issues that concerned him, though his offerings were letters to the editor rather than articles, and dealt with more peripheral matters. Thus a 1959 letter in the *New York Times* condemned the insistence of news photographers that their subjects offer "a great big smile," leaving an impression on foreign visitors that "we are ruled by a phalanx of slaphappy morons."[94] Public relations had boundaries of propriety beyond which he would not stray.

One of his later causes was not so peripheral. The issue of population growth continued to vex him. He helped fund-raise for the World Population Emergency Campaign, sponsored by the Planned Parenthood Federation, to aid family planning in "underdeveloped areas" around the world. He had a role in distributing *The Population Bomb*, a pamphlet orchestrated and subsidized by Hugh Moore, a wealthy Pennsylvania industrialist, which reached a circulation of nearly a million copies. (In 1961 the organization behind the booklet merged with Planned Parenthood.) One of the last instances in which he took a public stand came in 1960, when he joined a number of prominent Americans, ranging from Martin Luther King, Jr., to Eleanor Roosevelt to General Omar Bradley and a glittering international group of Nobel Prize–winners in petitioning the UN to press for a global policy on birth control. He attended an "emergency meeting of leading citizens" at Princeton University which devoted its attention to the problem.[95]

Such engagements thinned out as his health continued to decline. He managed to make it to his office some mornings in 1961, go out for lunch, spend time on his causes, but he was failing. He complained about having "so many women" in his house and kept inquiring, "what's the matter with me?" The matter was cerebral arteriosclerosis.

In 1962 he skipped the annual BBDO stockholders meeting but attended the ensuing cocktail party at his own home. In August a servant found him fallen on the floor of his home elevator. A year later, out on a walk, he collapsed on the street. His correspondence tailed off in 1963 and soon ceased. Louise MacLeod, who had managed his daily obligations since 1925, took responsibility for answering his mail and, with Randall, for paying bills and supervising domestic arrangements. By 1964 "Miss Mac" reported that he was "unable to take care of his affairs." "It grieves me to tell you," she wrote to a friend of his, "that Mr. Barton's memory is almost non-existent."[96] He was often confused, frequently irascible. By 1966 she told one correspondent that he "is quite unable to converse with any one." He had loved the agency's Christmas party, where he handed out bonus checks, accessorizing those he gave to women with a kiss. He managed this Christmas duty in 1964, for the last time, at least the part about "kissing the girls." By 1966 he continued "to fail, slowly but surely." He took a walk every day but avoided the office.[97]

He died on July 5, 1967, of bronchial pneumonia. In a eulogy distributed in the agency, Charles Brower called him "The Man Everybody Knew." This embattled tribune of the "middle class" left a $2.8 million estate. He made numerous bequests to various people and causes, gave a considerable sum to his "good friend" Ann Honeycutt, a larger trust for his secretary Louise McLeod, whom he described as "a real business partner for many years," and the balance to his only surviving child, Randall.[98]

Barton's passing was national news, marked by widespread obituaries. These summed up the highpoints of his polychromatic career—the founding of the successful ad agency, well-recalled ads and slogans, the best-seller *The Man Nobody Knows* and the companionability between business and religion it described, the political career culminating in and cut short by FDR's "Martin, Barton and Fish" line. The *New York Times* began its obituary on page one, with three columns on an inside page. The president of a competing agency credited Barton with helping "bring advertising away from its quackery days . . . to values that came from the creative process." Another competitor lauded him for improving "the level of advertising" and conveying "the notion that advertising is a force for economic good."

In some quarters, however, he seemed to have become what he always dreaded, a survivor who had outlived his era and entered an age which "knew not Joseph." The *Washington Post* editorialized at his death that "contemporary readers" would find *The Man Nobody Knows*, with its chapters on "The Executive" and "His Advertisements," "somewhat vulgar, but so were many aspects of life in the bygone era when Mr. Barton's formidable talents flourished." *The Times* of London astringently described him as a man "whose influence on the common culture of his time was pervasive, if hardly profound." On the other hand, *Newsweek* found combined in his copy a "gift for the compelling phrase . . . coupled with an early appreciation of America's instinct for self-betterment." The British journalist Alistair Cooke, noted for his observations of the American scene, referred to Barton as the "Moses of advertising."[99]

9

Legacy of an Adman

BARTON'S LIFE played out in several arenas—business and advertising, politics, and religion and morality. Added together, these roles gave him a signal presence in American culture at a time of important transitions. It must be said that he rarely warranted the label of pioneer, except sometimes in his ability to join these edges and facets of life. In an age of growing specialization, he remained, if not a generalist, someone with an ability to hopscotch among the various avenues of his life, importing the terms and metaphors of one into another, as with Jesus the Advertising Man.

In all these fields he showed obvious talent. Perhaps his varied interests account for his failure to attain acknowledged supremacy in any one, save perhaps advertising, and it was about that one that he remained often ambivalent. He was never as smug as he may sometimes have sounded. As a writer, he often considered himself "second-rate," according to his secretary. He wondered whether his partners would want him back after his round-the-world trip.

Barton managed to juggle various roles, several careers, and the past with the present. These seemed more often to provide integration than dissonance in his life. Religion and advertising usually meshed with ease—despite the distaste for this blend declared by critics of his religious writings. The sacred and the profane increasingly intermingled. Advertising, as one historian has noted, "literally grew up telling

Americans what to do: how to behave, where to live, what to wear, whom to associate with. . . ." Indeed, Barton once wrote that advertising's task was to tell the public "what they should eat and wear; how they should invest their savings; by what courses they can improve their minds; and even . . . what laws they should make, and by what faith they may be saved."[1] Certainly that had once been primarily the preacher's job. Others now contended for that role. Nor was Barton the first to connect materialism with godliness and uplift. The Protestant divine Josiah Strong, a firm nineteenth-century advocate of America's missionary destiny, by which the world was to be converted and civilized, exhorted: "A savage, having nothing, is perfectly contented so long as he wants nothing. The first step toward civilizing him is to create a want. Men rise in the scale of civilization only as their wants rise. . . ."[2] Even leaving aside the Protestant Ethic (which Barton enlarged to make room for the righteousness of consumption), religion had found space for the marketplace. Admen themselves also claimed to perform an educational function. "Education" was a benefaction Barton frequently cited in defense of his profession. Many contemporaries marveled at his "sincerity" in pursuing and justifying his calling. It seems to have been a sincere sincerity.[3]

In some instances the Barton of one role jostled against the Barton of another. In judging foreign policy, he criticized America's penchant for imperialism. Yet he never got beyond his delight in BBDO's invention of the Chiquita Banana song to the company behind it (United Fruit) or to that firm's surely "imperialistic" domain over its vast properties and even the polities of poor Central American nations. As a critic of the New Deal, he issued dicta that no "planning" could effectively cover American society as a whole, yet he never made so limiting a claim for any advertising campaign. Helen Woodward, a judgmental observer of (and toiler on) Madison Avenue, noted: "as an advertising man of nearly thirty years' experience, Mr. Barton knows perfectly well that this country is not too big or too complex to be trained swiftly into using a new food, or a new car, trying a new icebox or a new vacuum cleaner. He knows that through advertising it is possible to turn this country into complete uniformity in daily habits."[4]

Perhaps the most consistent ingredient of his views was the priority he cherished for the individual. Although he made his living dealing with people in groups, in bulk, he prized individual autonomy. In his religious writings, his God spoke—often kindly—to the individual (and Jesus despised bureaucrats and number crunchers). Churches were fine (though they must adapt to modern times), but the single soul needed no intermediary. In politics he defended individual prerogative in an age characterized, in his favorite book's title, by "the revolt of the masses." These masses had a sense of their just due, and Barton thought it reasonable they be served, but he distrusted the large institutions created to service their demands and the "interest groups" that enforced them. He seemed not to mind giant corporations as clients, and he excelled at creating advertising to humanize these vast bodies, to make them a "family" or "friend" who provided "service." He worked in a smaller, less formal organization himself. As BBDO approached a payroll of one thousand, he stressed the importance of maintaining "the wonderful family spirit that has meant so much to us all through the years." The old regime managed to convey that atmosphere to new hires. BBDOers who greeted him as "Mr. Barton" were told, "Call me Bruce."[5]

He managed to mix play and work, keeping his options open (working at home, continuing his outside writings). He thought meaningful work required its quota of play, remarking that "the radicals and the critics of business have no idea what fun business is" and noting the critical importance of (male) friendships made in business.[6] He evangelized on behalf of and hobnobbed with those who succeeded in "big business" and lived the corporate life, writing about them as heroes, but he managed after 1918 to avoid entanglement in any such structured existence.

From his experience in advertising he concluded that "personal selfishness" was one of the "human impulses that are elemental and perpetual."[7] Advertising could tap that reality, and without guilt. Political programs that failed to allow for this fact of human life were doomed to fail. Religion was another matter. Viewed through this lens, humans were capable of losing themselves in their work, in the single-minded focus on "service" that so colored *The Man Nobody Knows* and other of his writings. In professing his faith, Barton declared his fellow beings basically good. It may be revealing that after 1930 the number of such declarations fell off—and, similarly, that his comfort level with the religious institutions available to him wavered. He never repudiated the religious tenets of his youth or the writings of his prime; he periodically found renewed inspiration in churchgoing; and God continued to make appearances in the writings of his later years, but the Barton of his last four decades was less outwardly religious than he had been.

As he strove to find goodness in humans, so he endeavored to discern progress in their affairs and their future. In this quest he succeeded, though here too he found disturbing signs. The New Deal's impress made him question the political virtue of the average citizen, who seemed to rank his demands above his contributions. Barton's reading (especially of Ortega) compelled him to accept this fact of life, but not always easily. The rise of the New Deal Leviathan and the nation's venture into internationalism in and after World War II made Barton pessimistic. Often he mourned, "it was a good republic while it lasted."

These events boded ill to him, but he could then turn around and give a talk that thrilled to the economic vistas to which America's baby boom was leading. Similarly, as an adman he was alert to the new media crowding into his field and into the lives of Americans—movies, radio, eventually television. He understood (with some mild contempt) that the new generation preferred moving or at least graphic images to the printed word. He was a child of an oral and written culture who prospered amid different, speeded-up communication modes. He could live and thrive in the new world but was nostalgic for the old. That sentiment may have lurked beneath his comment in the 1950s that he preferred reading about television to watching it.

He generally upheld a cheery theology. (He liked to say that no religion that frightened a child was worthwhile.) Yet he was drawn to gloomy history and social commentary. For all his buoyancy about the progress the future promised, in 1944 he told a BBDO colleague (who thought to record it): "I have no desire to live in the future. I have had such a good time in the past, I am going to keep on living in the past."[8]

HE KEPT at advertising for a long time. Yet he was also active, though more sporadically, in politics from 1920 into the 1950s, and he wrote in various publications from 1908 on. Which of these roles was central to his being was not always clear. Despite his numerous and vigorous defenses of the advertising profession, it seldom received his undivided attention. It served the public good by stimulating wants, thus stirring ambition and energy, creating demand that in turn caused business to expand supply and thereby hire workers and invest in productive capacity. But Barton was not fully wedded to all the implications of this picture. One obituary said he "approached ad writing with a curious detachment. He was more interested in the fashioning of words that their ultimate impact on selling the product." He might have disputed this: he claimed to be fully engaged in the pragmatic side of the business. In his younger days, as he watched a crowd of women doing their Easter shopping on Fifth Avenue, he ventured: "Isn't it dreadful that each of those women typifies the soul-blasting toil of some man?"[9] Some scholars have seen an ambivalence in this facet of his life.

He served in several important respects as a "transitional figure." For him the transition was not always smooth, but he steered through history's tides and society's changes well enough to offer assistance to others in coping with change, in preserving parts of the old and accepting parts of the new. His columns and other preachments offered hints on navigating the changes of the early twentieth century. They were a paradoxical mix: cities were vibrant places which gave the ambitious a stage on which to thrive, but one could renew one's nerves and being by digging in the (nonurban) earth; hard work was rewarded, but one should occasionally eliminate a "necessity" so as to afford a luxury.

Both his successes and his failures in welding the various fragments of his experience and his thinking into a coherent whole make him a representative, and thus instructive, figure in the nation's own transition to what we recognize as "modern." He was often conflicted. Most Barton scholars so conclude. As Jackson Lears put it, he was "confused and ambivalent—a doubting high priest of prosperity, whose work both celebrated and protested the emerging consumer culture." Indeed, conflict has frequently been the Rosetta Stone for deciphering the broader meaning of Barton's life.[10] Louise MacLeod, who knew him as well as anyone did, summed him up as "a man of great contradictions."[11]

Barton himself would have agreed with such findings. For an article he was drafting in 1931, he read books on psychology by the likes of Dr. Karl Menninger. His conclusion: "Life is a fight. No personality is simple. We are all battle grounds in which many selves, many instincts are constantly battling. Every moment involves adjustment." Some succeeded in adjusting and were "normal and contented. Most of us set up defenses, or escapes"—like ill health, drink, hysteria, or seclusion.[12] Barton made his living and his mark at the nexus of such concerns. While he has been identified as a exemplar of business-as-religion (or vice versa) and of "Madison Avenue," and an exponent of the American Gospel of Success and Horatio Alger business triumphs,[13] he was also a long-distance therapist, trying through his writings to help other Americans resolve some of the conflicts that came with modern living. Thus he has earned investigation as a representative of the nation's "positive thinkers," of mental self-help.[14] As an adman, it was incumbent upon him to know the workings of the human mind. On this subject both Barton and his partner Alex Osborn (the father of brainstorming) read widely.[15]

Barton was also "transitional" in the context of America's move from rural to urban life. One of the rough seams in his thought involved the role of the city. Despite the pleasures of his life in Gotham, he often dwelled on the joys of small-town living and expressed nostalgia for that bygone existence. He enjoyed referring to his younger self as "a gawky kid from the country," and in his first years in New York he "traded considerably on the fact [sic] that he was a boy from a country parsonage."[16] This theme appeared in *The Making of George Groton* and *The Man Nobody Knows*, in shorter writings, and in his paeans to successful business leaders—who generally moved, he claimed, from confining hamlets to the opportunity-rich city. In 1944, in a piece in Metropolitan Life's annual report, he noted reassuringly that "like most of America's biggest enterprises, it is run by 'small-town boys.'" After a brief try at living in suburban Long Island, he cast his lot permanently with Manhattan, which became home for over half his life. Barton once praised a friend's book on farm living: "Through him I live on a farm vicariously, which—in my humble notion—is the only way to live on one."[17] Perhaps he partly bridged the gap between his life and his idealization by having the ability to summer in Foxboro (where golf and the cocktail hour tempered the rusticity).

Barton had fewer second thoughts in providing a rhetorical bridge between older producerist attitudes—work, accumulate, save, live within one's means—and the new consumerism of the modern age. It was all right to buy and enjoy: that made for a fuller life. He rationalized the covetousness that advertising induced by arguing that it made people work harder and so added to society's cornucopia. In the twenties he cheered the closing of an age when Americans cared about "petty economies. They want convenience; they want action; they want style and comfort, and they are willing to pay." He termed it "idle to call Americans back to petty thrift, and I personally am glad of it." He likewise eulogized his friend the sportswriter Grantland Rice for having "made us want to play." That was "his gift to his country; few men have made a greater."[18]

Yet from the 1930s on, a number of social and moral trends, including the devaluing of hard work and individual responsibility, chagrined him. He feared Americans were moving toward the Continental model of the long weekend when no one remained to mind the store. He continued to cherish the values of work and self-restraint associated with the middle class. He often called himself the last representative of that declining sector—he with his stabled horse, clubs, vacations, and what we would call "corporate lifestyle."

Barton also commented on class relations. His homilies argued that there was a way up from the bottom. He sometimes voiced distrust of the masses; he disliked the prospect of a society ruled by organized interest groups swayed by the politics of the New Deal. Yet he also feared the insouciance of the topmost. Like Andrew Carnegie, he thought it almost sinful to die rich; he implied that people would snicker if they know how little income he took from his agency. Yet he left an estate of $2.8 million. In all these contradictory attitudes, Barton was one more individual agitated by the challenges of adjusting to a life moving from "community" to "society."

Change was a frequent thread in Barton's speaking and writing. It was inevitable, he preached. One must adjust. A famous Barton aphorism held: "When you're through changing, you're through."[19] Usually he was philosophical. In 1938 he pointed to the frequent upheavals of the past and declared that these "changes have been harmless." He lectured Republicans that when an "organization ceases to change it has begun to die."[20] But soon, however, he came to fear—in the mutations accelerated by the New Deal, the rise of pressure-group politics, America's global reach, and FDR's third term—that change could be irreversible, and bad. From 1940 on he suggested repeatedly that the republic had expired. Then too, a speech knelling the end of the republic might be followed by a pep talk arguing that business was good and getting better.

Barton often wrote to praise successful leaders of business. He termed "service" their ultimate goal, with material success a mere by-product, and while some saw such talk as eyewash, he believed it. He recalled a conversation between Charles Mitchell of National City Bank and Walter Gifford of AT&T, in which Mitchell had argued that "big cash prizes" out of a company's profits must be spread among its officers lest it "cease to attract first-grade men." Gifford countered that his company "had developed an esprit de corps like that of the army" or the British civil service. Barton sided with Gifford, urging (in 1932) the need to "develop in American business an emphasis and an incentive which are quite apart from mere money reward."[21] His writings, especially *The Man Nobody Knows*, have been taken as apologetics for wealthy businessmen, yet the book itself argues that the truly successful think not of profits or advancement but of "service."

While Barton eagerly chronicled the success of others, celebrating the traits that enabled them to prosper, he sometimes entertained doubt about his own achievements. He frequently contended that success was a matter of luck. His ambivalence about the ad game emerges in Harford Powel's thinly disguised rendering in *The Virgin Queene* and in his own crack that he might be remembered as "the father of 'Clean Rest Rooms'" (in a Socony Oil campaign).[22]

He was also conflicted about the relative virtues of progress and inertia. In the thirties he suggested that America was "past the period when we need to be concerned about 'progress' (our god for so many generations. Progress is bound to be rapid enough. What we need is security, conservation, less speed, and a respect for something besides mere money." Yet he spent his life touting bringers of progress—Ford with his devotion to building an affordable, serviceable car for the masses; Skid Row preachers who provided meals and beds for the down-and-out; Christianity at the street level which had some successes in reforming individuals; Carnegie leaving America a "nation of steel." In one of his religious works he praised Jesus for having "forgot the past." What he liked about the advertising business was than an adman "cannot afford to look backward—his eyes should be pointing to the future. . . ."[23] An yet in other contexts the past was Eden.

He recognized the acceleration of American life and, while advertising had augmented that trend, he only partially endorsed it. A letter to the radio editor of the *New York Times* noted that "the thrilling thing about the universe is that everything has to change." This upbeat sermon was triggered by an inquiry about television's future—in 1931.[24] He realized that aging warred with such elasticity and took a keen interest in making BBDO a place where younger employees could take up

the reins. He exalted youth (even if he didn't like its music). He hoped
as he aged "that I shall not become a grumbler, nor entertain the foolish notion that a generation bred of the automobile and the motion
picture can be slowed down to the pace of the horse and buggy." But
he did hope that high school and college curricula would include "a
good, strong dose of Thoreau."[25]

Barton sometimes expressed doubts about advertising—not so
much for the social and economic functions it filled, which he could
laud on demand. But the minutiae of advertising and the tedium it
could induce struck him on occasion. As television was widening its
reach, he announced to his partners, "I get so terribly bored with the
long Lucky Strike and Schaefer [beer] commercials," which became
repetitive and numbing. Why not, he asked, dispense with "LSMFT,"
the famed Lucky Strike slogan, and say instead, "Lucky Strike is paying for this half of the ball game in the hope of pleasing you, not an-
noying you. If you haven't tried Luckies lately we hope you will. . . . If
you are a Lucky smoker already, please give us credit for not boring
you by telling you a lot of things you already know." Barton suspected
that the public was getting as tired as he was of "long, repetitious commercials, put forth by voices that have such polished [e]nunciation and
no sense of conviction whatever."[26] Third-party observers saw strains in
Barton's role on Madison Avenue too. *Space & Time* thought his heyday had passed in the 1920s, when "Preacher's-Son Barton was in great
demand" to beatify business. As BBDO shifted toward becoming "a merchandising agency," Barton came to look, as a rival on Madison Avenue put it, "like a preacher in a whore house."[27]

Whatever his inner doubts, Barton stood up publicly for advertising, and history went his way. BBDO grew from its initial fourteen employees to more than two thousand during Barton's time with the
agency. It branched into other cities and went international. By 1958,
advertising expenditures in the United States amounted to $62 per
capita (as against $18 in Great Britain and $6 in France).[28] His own
firm continued to flourish. (In 1986, in what was described as advertising's "big bang," it merged with Doyle Dane Bernbach and Needham

Harper, and today remains a constituent part of Omnicon, a London-based, global advertising conglomerate.)

If Barton displayed a divided self, that would hardly make him unique. Many other humans live thus, picking and choosing between what worked in the past and what looks better in the future. Barton in this sense was merely representative, but he was unique in his talent for drafting prose dramas that accommodated the comforting past with the onrushing present.

Notes

1. A SON OF THE MANSE

1. William Eleazar Barton (hereafter WEB), *Lieutenant William Barton of Morris County, New Jersey, and His Descendants* (Oak Park, Ill.: privately printed [The Vaile Press], 1900), 100, 115, 120.

2. WEB, "Thus Far: The Life Story of a Lincoln Biographer," unpublished autobiography, 29–30, Box 143, Bruce Barton MSS, Wisconsin Historical Society (hereafter BB MSS); WEB, *The Autobiography of William E. Barton* (Indianapolis: Bobbs-Merrill, 1932), 160; Bruce Barton (hereafter BB), "Our Country," *Redbook* (June 1937), 5. Although Rev. Barton's published biography hews close to the unpublished version cited above, some elements of the latter, including this description of William Barton's Revolutionary War exploits, are omitted from the published version. It was also family lore that Gen. George Washington personally wrote out a pass for Barton after the latter noted that his father (whom Washington remembered) had served with him in the French and Indian War. WEB, *Lieutenant William Barton*, 30.

3. Bruce Barton's father had a pastorate in Wellington, Ohio, where Willard lived; the two were friends. Willard F. Gordon, *"The Spirit of '76" . . . an American Portrait: America's Best Known Painting, Least Known Artist* (Fallbrook, Calif.: Quail Hill Associates, 1976), 23, 34, 65.

4. WEB, *Autobiography*, 32–33, 39–44, 47, 50–51, 57–59, 74–75, 77–78, 81–83; WEB, "Thus Far," 31, 51; death notice, "Jacob B. Barton," n.d. (ca. 1912), Box 6, BB MSS; WEB, *Lieutenant William Barton*, 56–59; BB speech, University of Buffalo, Oct. 17, 1929, Box 145, BB MSS; clipping, Alistair Cooke, "Moses of Advertising," *Manchester Guardian*, (ca. July 6, 1967), Shelf A8/5, BBDO Archive (hereafter shelf number and "BBDO.")

5. BB to Will Durant, June 18, 1931, Box 18, BB MSS; WEB, *Autobiography*, 52, 84–85, 97, 100, 104, 107–108, 116, 124–125, 139, 142, 154, 156–159.

6. WEB, *Autobiography*, viii–ix (BB Introduction), 160–163, 174–176, 185, chaps. 13–14; BB editorial, "The Capital City of Faith," *Hartford Times*, June 21, 1951, Box 25,

BB MSS. The motley procession to their new home became a staple of family lore. See BB, "I Remember," *Christian Herald*, Sept. 1931, 8.

7. WEB, *Autobiography*, xiii, 214–218, 228, 236–239, chap. XVII; WEB, "Thus Far," 306; BB, "This Is *My* Home Town—Where Is Yours?" *American Magazine*, June 1918, 42–45; "Address by Rev. William E. Barton," *Harding. Lincoln. Two Memorial Addresses Delivered on Foxboro Common* (Foxboro: The Print Shop Incorporated, 1923), Chicago Historical Society (hereafter CHS); Fred B. Barton (FBB), "Robert S. Barton Memorial" (mimeo, The Lincoln Group of Boston, 1954), ibid.

8. WEB, *Autobiography*, 263, 265; WEB to "My dear children," Oct. 27, 1907, Folder 4, William E. Barton Papers, Congregational Library, Boston (hereafter WEB Papers). On Oak Park's history, see Arthur Evans Le Gacy, "Improvers and Preservers: A History of Oak Park, Illinois, 1833–1940" (Ph.D. dissertation, University of Chicago, 1967); and Kathryn Elizabeth Ratcliff, "The Making of a New Middle-Class Culture: Family and Community in a Midwest Suburb, 1890–1920" (Ph.D. dissertation, University of Minnesota, 1990).

9. Still, Oak Park's *Oak Leaves* reported that Barton, two years after graduating from college, presented a plan for a "Christian non-denominational 'fraternity'" for the town's young people. Ratcliff, "New Middle-Class Culture," 163. Yet while in high school Barton, invited to join both the school's fraternities, declined membership because "the feeling against fraternities ran so high in my father's church. . . ." BB to Dolph Jansen, Jr., Feb. 15, 1944, Box 33, BB MSS.

10. BB to Jansen, Feb. 15, 1944, ibid. On the culture of Oak Park, see Ratcliff, "New Middle-Class Culture," 2–3, 26, 91, 102, and passim.

11. Ratcliff, "New Middle-Class Culture," 34, 128, 143, 144–145, 166; BB to William Hard, July 10, 1945, Box 25, BB MSS.

12. Ratcliff, "New Middle-Class Culture," 146–147; FBB, "Robert S. Barton Memorial"; Rev. Charles E. Burton to WEB, Oct. 4, 1926, Folder 27; "Unity of Church Urged by Former Oak Park Pastor," clipping, *Chicago Tribune*, July 6, 1930, Folder 24, both in WEB Papers; Charles Ward Seabury to BB, July 9, 1956, Box 103, BB MSS.

13. WEB, *Autobiography*, 249–250, 255–256; *Oak Leaves*, Sept. 9, 1916, 1; Mar. 30, 1918, 1, clippings at CHS.

14. WEB, "Jesus in the Twentieth Century," Dec. 25, 1898, Box 143, BB MSS; WEB, "The Secret of the Charm of Oak Park," in Frank H. June and Geo. R. Hemingway, publishers, *Glimpses of Oak Park* (Oak Park, 1912), 1, 3, Historical Society of Oak Park; Ratcliff, "New Middle-Class Culture," 136.

15. Otto McFeely to BB, Feb. 6, 1956, Box 42, BB MSS; FBB, "Bruce Barton as a Brother," Box 4, ibid. Leo Ribuffo clearly itemized Bruce's debt to his father in the realm of religious ideas in "Jesus Christ as Business Statesman: Bruce Barton and the Selling of Corporate Capitalism," *American Quarterly* 33 (Summer 1981), 208–209, 217.

16. BB to Wesley Hartzell, Oct. 1, 1952, Box 50, BB MSS; Frank Hatch to BB, n.d. (ca. 1955), Box 26, ibid. In 1933 Barton recalled seeing little of the Hemingway children. "Thus, I can claim no boyhood acquaintance with . . . Ernest. . . ." BB, "Glory," *New York Herald Tribune*, Mar. 19, 1933, Box 131, ibid.

17. J. Shiffman to BB, Feb. 21, 1949, Box 50, ibid.

18. FBB, "Bruce Barton as a Brother" (dated 1927), Box 4, BB MSS; BB, "A Shepherd of the Sheep," *Collier's*, Oct. 18, 1924, 7.

19. Ben N. Braun to BB, Dec. 12, 1938, Box 50, BB MSS; WEB to BB, n.d. (1920s), Box 143. ibid.; "Mrs. William E. Barton Dies at Sunset Lake," *Journal of the Illinois State Historical Society*, XVII, No. 4, 1086; BB, "My Mother's Check Book," *American Magazine*, Mar. 1930, 18, 96, 98.

20. FBB, "BB as a Brother," (1927), Box 4; "April 1940," Box 4; BB to Charles H. Brower, May 11, 1953, Box 8; BB, "Ministers' Sons," *New York American*, May 12, 1936, Box 130, all in BB MSS.

21. Robert Barton, "William E. Barton—Biographer," *Abraham Lincoln Quarterly*, June 1946, 80–93; FBB, "Robert S. Barton—in Memoriam," (1954), CHS; WEB, *The Wit and Wisdom of Safed the Sage* (Boston and Chicago: The Pilgrim Press, 1919), 123–125 and passim; WEB to Gov. Calvin Coolidge, Coolidge Gubernatorial Papers, Forbes Library, Northampton, Mass.; "The Fifteen Biggest Men in America," *New Yorker*, Jan. 25, 1930, 17.

22. BB, "My Thirty-two Years at School," *American Magazine*, Apr. 1919, 32; biographical sketch, "Bruce Barton," n.d. (1937), Box 4, BB MSS; BB to Joseph B. Forsee, Jan. 3, 1950, Box 21; —— to "McCary," Sept. 29 (1937), Box 4; unsigned, undated biographical sketch, ibid.; FBB, "Bruce Barton as a Brother," ibid.; BB to T. A. DeWeese, Feb. 2, 1925, Box 25, all BB MSS; *Advertising Age*, July 10, 1967, 80.

23. Biographical sketch "B," n.d., Box 4; biographical sketch, Apr. 1940, ibid.; BB to W. C. Mattox, Dec. 10, 1954, Box 43, ibid.

24. Reprint, Charles W. Barton review of BB, *On the Up and Up*, n.d. (1929), Box 110, BB MSS; FBB, "Bruce Barton as a Brother," Box 4, ibid.; clipping, *Oak Leaves*, June 19, 1903, Folder 88, WEB Papers; FBB, "Robert S. Barton—in Memoriam" (1954), CHS; Alma E. Henderson, "Bruce Barton," *The American Author*, June 1932, 12.

25. BB to De Witt Wallace, Apr. 2, 1941, Box 70; BB to W. C. Mattox, Dec. 10, 1954, Box 43, ibid.; BB speech over WMCA, Nov. 3, 1940, A8/5, BBDO.

26. It may have been after his sophomore year that Barton worked on a farm to recuperate from his health problems. In a rural community this halfway college man was asked to preach. He did well enough until a delegation of his auditors asked him to stop—having learned he smoked a pipe! He told the story nearly thirty years later, leaving unidentified the locale. He had relatives in farming in Illinois (where his grandfather still lived) and in Ohio. BB, *He Upset the World* (London: Constable, 1932), 75–76.

27. BB, "I Remember," *Christian Herald*, Sept. 1931, 10; BB, "A Shepherd of the Sheep," 7; BB to Gertrude Lane, Feb. 24, 1925, Box 104, BB MSS.

28. BB to Mrs. Henry W. Austin, July 28, 1959, Box 2; to T. A. DeWeese, Feb. 2, 1925, Box 25; to "Pete" (Bruce Barton, Jr.), Mar. 20, 1941, Box 6; FBB, "BB as a Brother," Box 4; Louise MacLeod to Ray Gravett, Feb. 7, 1949, Box 117; undated biographical sketch, "B," Box 4; BB draft article for *Reader's Digest*, "A Three Year Post Graduate Course," Box 100, all BB MSS; BB, "A Student Canvasser," clipping, unknown newspaper, Oct. 31, 1906, Folder 87, WEB Papers; clippings, *Chicago Record Herald*, July 2, 1907, Folder 88, ibid.; BB to Claude M. Fuess, June 10, 1955, Box 22, BB MSS. Whatever his recalled anxieties, Barton remained his class's most generous donor to Amherst.

29. FBB, "BB as a Brother," Box 4; BB to De Witt Wallace, Apr. 2, 1941, Box 70, BB MSS. In 1932 Barton avowed the episode as a "nervous breakdown." *Printers' Ink*, Jan. 28, 1932, 40. Insomnia would continue to afflict him, at least into the late 1920s.

30. BB, "My Father's Business: A Preacher's Life as Seen by a Preacher's Son," *Outlook*, June 27, 1914, 494–497; Richard F. Warner, "It Pays to Preach," *New Yorker*, Nov. 1, 1930, 21. Authors who suggest Barton's self-reproach for not having a calling are Ribuffo, "Jesus Christ as Business Statesman," 209; and Edrene Stephens Montgomery, "Bruce Barton and the Twentieth-Century Menace of Unreality," (Ph.D. dissertation, University of Arkansas, 1984), 39.

31. BB to Louis W. Koenig, Feb. 29, 1960, Box 49, BB MSS; handwritten letter, Frederick Jackson Turner to BB, Apr. 20, 1907, Folder 1, WEB Papers.

32. Biographical sketch, n.d. (1937?), "B," Box 4, BB MSS; BB to Mrs. John J. Starr, May 23, 1952, Box 102, ibid.; clipping, *Advertisers' Weekly*, Mar. 24, 1928, 33, A8/5, BBDO; clipping, "Barton, (R) N.Y.," n.d. [1937], A11/3, ibid.

33. BB, *On the Up and Up* (Indianapolis: Bobbs-Merrill, 1929), 140; BB to De Witt Wallace, June 2, 1959, Box 70; BB to Charles E. Denney, Feb. 18, 1948, Box 78; BB article draft, "A Three-Year Post Graduate Course," Box 100; BB to Mrs. R. T. Morris, July 15, 1925, Box 89, all BB MSS.

34. BB, "A Three-Year Post Graduate Course"; BB, "All Dressed Up . . . and No Place to Go," *Reader's Digest*, Jan. 1956, 23; BB to De Witt Wallace, Apr. 2, 1941, Box 70, BB MSS; clipping, BB, "The Resurrection of a Soul as Described by an Eye Witness," *Christian World* (1913), 7–8, Box 126, ibid.; BB, "Are You Happy in Your Work?" *Good Housekeeping*, Sept. 1930, 251.

35. BB speech, 1931 (ca. June 16), Box 135; BB to Wallace, Apr. 2, 1941, and Dec. 30, 1940, Box 70; BB ms, "Why Boys Leave Home," n.d., Box 1; BB to William L. Chenery, Jan. 3, 1940, Box 12, all BB MSS.

36. BB to R. E. Currie, Dec. 19, 1929, Box 115, BB MSS; Richard F. Warner, "It Pays to Preach," *New Yorker*, Nov. 1, 1930, 21; Montgomery, "Bruce Barton," 61.

2. WORDSMITH

1. BB to De Witt Wallace, Apr. 2, 1941, Box 70, BB MSS; "From Bruce Barton," n.d. (ca. May 11, 1932), Box 87, ibid.

2. Harold U. Faulkner, *The Decline of Laissez-Faire, 1897–1917* (New York: Harper and Row, 1968 [1951]), 28–30; George E. Mowry, *The Era of Theodore Roosevelt and the Birth of Modern America, 1900–1912* (New York: Harper, 1958), 206–211, 216–219.

3. John Caples, *Advertising for Immediate Sales* (New York: Harper and Brothers, 1936), 100–101. See *Home Herald*, Apr. 8–June 10, 1908. Copies of the articles are in Box 152, BB MSS.

4. Philip N. Schuyler, "Bruce Barton Offers Pointers for Success," *Editor & Publisher*, Dec. 3, 1960, 17; "Bruce Barton Obit," n.d. (ca. 1966), and obituary by Ed Roberts, June 18, 1965, both Shelf 8/5, BBDO; BB to De Witt Wallace, Apr. 2, 1941, Box 70; untitled biographical sketch, "April, 1940," Box 4; BB draft article, "A Three-Year Post Graduate Course," Box 100, all BB MSS; biographical sheet on BB, Dec. 9, 1935, shelf A8/5, BBDO; BB, "I Believe," *Advertising & Selling* (Oct. 29, 1936), 20; "Bruce Barton" (obituary), Sept. 18, 1967, Box 145, BB MSS; Montgomery, "Bruce Barton," 40;

"Bruce Barton: Everything Ad Men Should Be, He Is," *Printers' Ink*, Feb. 10, 1961, 55; BB, "The One-Hoss Typewriter," *New York American*, May 10, 1935, Box 135, BB MSS. The amount of Barton's back salary and Passion-play profit also varied over time.

5. BB to Belmore Gold, Feb. 10, 1936, Box 116, BB MSS; "Bruce Barton Biographical sketch," Oct. 24, 1924, Box 4, ibid.; "Bruce Barton: Everything Ad Men Should Be, He Is," 55; Caples, *Advertising for Immediate Sales*, 101; Montgomery, "Bruce Barton," 42; "Bruce Barton" obituary, Sept. 18, 1957, Box 145, BB MSS; Harford Powel, Jr., pamphlet, *The Man Every One Knows* (Bobbs-Merrill, n.d., reprint from *New York Herald Tribune*, Dec. 11, 1927, Box 4, ibid.; Powel, "As You Were—III," *Advertising & Selling* (Aug. 29, 1935), 36. Barton's dates with *Housekeeper* were 1910–1911.

6. Arthur S. Link, "What Happened to the Progressive Movement in the 1920s?" *American Historical Review* 64 (July 1959), 843.

7. BB, "Wanted: A Bull Fighter," *Theatre Magazine*, June 1928, 5, in Box 130, BB MSS; BB, "Concerning Reformers," *Collier's* (Mar. 20, 1926), 21; BB, "Little Old New York," *New York Herald Tribune*, July 9, 1933, Box 131, BB MSS; Stephen Fox, *The Mirror Makers: A History of American Advertising and Its Creators* (Urbana: University of Illinois Press, 1997), 102. Barton had a thing for "the West," but a few months in a railroad construction camp seemed to assuage it—until in middle age he took a liking to wintering in Arizona.

8. List of articles by BB in *The Continent*, n.d., Box 126, BB MSS; BB, "In a Modern Manger," *Continent*, Dec. 14, 1911, 1836–1837.

9. *Continent*, Feb. 11, 1915, 173–174; BB, "Tending His Flock by Night," ibid., Dec. 11, 1913, 1740–1741; BB, "What Sort of Chaps Are They?" ibid., Apr. 1, 1915, 399.

10. Clipping, BB, "The Pro and Con of Billy Sunday," *Congregationalist* (1913), 564–565. Barton would later claim that the experience of writing this article and finding that Sunday was not a "charlatan" helped dampen his muckraker's zeal. BB, "But They Don't Go to Church," *Christian Herald* 54 (Feb. 1931), 7.

11. Clippings, BB, "With the I.W.W. in New Bedford," *Congregationalist*, n.d., 142–143; BB, "Where the Little Leaven Comes From," *Advance*, Sept. 25, 1913, 80–81, Box 130, BB MSS. Barton also wrote a generally positive story about Sunday in the *National Weekly*, July 16, 1913 (clipping, ibid.) Also see "Billy Sunday," *Collier's* (July 26, 1913, 7ff. The *Congregationalist* later operated under the title *Congregationalist and Christian World*.

12. BB to E. B. H. James, Sept. 1, 1938, Box 4; Louise MacLeod to Ray Gravett, Feb. 7, 1949, Box 117; J. P. Mathews to BB, Sept. 3, 1958, Box 43, all in BB MSS; Ed Roberts, Barton obituary, June 18, 1964, A8/5, BBDO; BB, "Handling 1,000 Men Working on Commission," *Printers' Ink*, Feb. 4, 1915, 3–8.

13. Barton letter (anon.) to stockholders of State Street Investment Trust, n.d. (ca. Oct. 11, 1927), Box 10, BB MSS.

14. One of their addresses, probably this one, the Bartons shared with the famed socialist Max Eastman. BB to Edna Austin, July 28, 1949, Box 2; obituary, n.d. (1951), "Esther Randall Barton," Box 6; BB to Charles Lucey, Jan. 15, 1940, Box 144, all BB MSS; "Randall-Barton," *Oak Park Oak Leaves*, Oct. 4, 1913; BB, "It Just Won't Work," draft of King Features article, June 19, 1955, Box 127, BB MSS.

15. "We Pay Our Respects to—Bruce Barton," *Broadcasting*, Nov. 15, 1937, 41; ad, "This is Marie Antoinette . . . ," A8/5; William H. Johns to F. C. Kendall, Nov. 14, 1941,

A11/3, both BBDO; Kenneth M. Goode and Harford Powel, Jr., *What About Advertising?* (New York: Harper and Brothers, 1927), 255–256; Julian Lewis Watkins, *The 100 Greatest Advertisements: Who Wrote Them and What They Did*, 2nd rev. ed. (New York: Dover, 1959), 29.

16. Roland Marchand, *Advertising the American Dream: Making Way for Modernity, 1920–1940* (Berkeley: University of California Press, 1985), chap. 1; Ed Roberts, Barton obituary, A8/5, BBDO. Barton did not, however, invent the "fifteen minutes a day" line.

17. BB to David A. Balch, Sept. 17, 1956, Box 3, BB MSS; clipping, *Evening Sun*, Apr. 24, 1919, Box 153, ibid.; BB to Gertrude B. Lane, June 23, 1915, Lane MSS, Library of Congress (hereafter LC); Powel pamphlet, *The Man Every One Knows*; [BB], "John M. Siddall," *American Magazine*, October 1923, 7; Webster Harwood, "The Crowell-Collier House of Ideals," *Popular Finance*, Oct. 1923, 39–41. The *American Magazine* had been published as *Frank Leslie's Monthly* until 1905.

18. BB, "H. G. Wells Picks Out the Six Greatest Men in History," *American Magazine*, July 1922, 13–14ff.; ibid., May 1918, 23ff.; ibid., Mar. 1919, 43ff.; "Michael Randall," "How Well Do You Know Your Job?" ibid., Apr. 1919, 24–25; ibid., Apr. 1921, 50ff.; ibid., Apr. 1919, 32ff.

19. Frederick Lewis Allen, *The Lords of Creation* (New York: Harper and Brothers, 1935), 304–305. Like other high-flying heroes of the 1920s, Mitchell came a cropper in the depression, when the 1933 Pecora investigation uncovered his liberality with the money of his bank's depositors. He was indicted but later acquitted. Ibid., 311ff.; Robert S. McElvaine, *The Great Depression: America, 1929–1941* (New York: Times Books/ Random House, 1984), 136.

20. BB, *A Young Man's Jesus* (Boston, New York, Chicago: The Pilgrim Press, 1914), ix–x, 80, 107, 115, and passim. For reviews, see Box 112, BB MSS. This was the heyday of the Protestant movement toward "muscular Christianity"; Barton was in full agreement. Clifford Putney, *Muscular Christianity: Manhood and Sports in Protestant America, 1880–1920* (Cambridge: Harvard University Press, 2001). On Barton's book, see Ribuffo, "Jesus Christ as Business Statesman," *American Quarterly* 83 (Summer 1981), 211–212.

21. Millersville's God much resembles the Jesus of *The Man Nobody Knows*. Anon. [BB], *Finding God in Millersville* (Chicago: Reilly & Britton, 1917), 28, 36–37, 40–42. Barton never wanted his authorship of the story revealed. BB to Jean Siddall, Jan. 22, 1924, Box 64; BB to F. K. Reilly, July 5, 1928, Box 106, both BB MSS.

22. *The Making of George Groton* (Garden City, N.Y.: Doubleday, Page & Co., 1918), 24, 37, 323, 329, and passim.

23. Clipping, *Boston Sunday Post*, June 19, 1921 (J. R. Milne), Folder 87, WEB MSS; John Anson Ford to BB, Apr. 23, 1918, Box 82, BB MSS; clipping, undated review, Box 107, ibid.

24. In 1919, after Barton had moved on, Crowell would acquire P. F. Collier & Son. Fred B. Barton, "Bruce Barton as a Brother," n.d. (1927), Box 4; BB to E. E. Calkins, Oct. 26, 1959, Box 10; clipping, *Evening Sun*, Apr. 24, 1915, Box 153, all BB MSS; Harwood, "The Crowell-Collier House of Ideals," 38ff.

25. BB quoted in Ed Roberts, "Beggars, Peddlers and Advertising Men" (1964 rewrite), p. 229, A7/3, BBDO; Fred Barton, "Bruce Barton as a Brother," n.d. (1927), Box

4, BB MSS; BB to Harrison Smith, Aug. 27, 1951, Box 62, ibid.; William H. Johns to F. C. Kendall, Nov. 14, 1941, A11/3, BBDO; BB to Charles H. Brower, May 11, 1953, Box 9, BB MSS; Montgomery, "Bruce Barton," 53–55.

26. For the popularity of Barton's editorials, see reader correspondence in Box 88, BB MSS.

27. Clipping, *Every Week*, Jan. 31, 1918, Box 126; "Are You a Good Ad for Yourself?" column reprinted in *Fruit Dispatch*, n.d., Box 153; clipping, BB, "Do You Live in a Home or Only in a House?" *Every Week*, Feb. 14, 1918, Box 126; cf. BB column, "Is Your House a HOME?" *New York Herald Tribune*, Nov. 4, 1928, clipping, Box 131, all in BB MSS.

28. Reprinted in BB, *More Power to You: Fifty Editorials from Every Week* (New York: The Century Co., 1917), 16.

29. See Box 153, BB MSS, for examples of reprints.

30. BB to Brower, May 11, 1953, Box 9; three readers' letters, May–June 1918; W. Albert Thompson to BB, June 12, 1918; clippings, *Chicago Herald and Examiner*, June 6, 1918; *Chicago Daily News*, May 19, 1918, all Box 88, BB MSS.

31. BB to Charles M. Richter, Apr. 19, 1926, Box 103, BB MSS; Louise MacLeod to Earl Nightingale, Dec. 27, 1954, Box 89, ibid.

32. MacLeod to Ray Gravett, Feb. 7, 1949, Box 117, BB MSS; Richard Warner, "It Pays to Preach," *New Yorker*, Nov. 1, 1930, 22; cf. reprint, "The New York Herald Tribune's Estimate of Bruce Barton," July 5, 1925, Box 141, BB MSS; BB to "Dear folks," n.d. (summer 1918), Folder 11, WEB Papers.

33. "Bruce Barton's radio talk in behalf of The Salvation Army," Mar. 20 (1933), Box 62, BB MSS. Barton coined other slogans, including *Vogue* magazine's pitch that a year's subscription cost a pittance compared to the price of an ill-chosen dress. Fred Barton, "Bruce Barton as a Brother," Box 4, ibid.

34. See, e.g., BB, "Out of the 'Y' and in Again," *Outlook*, Oct. 16, 1918, 257–258.

35. Copy, Woodrow Wilson to Raymond B. Fosdick, Sept. 3, 1918; Minutes, United War Work Campaign Publicity Committee, Sept. 5, 1918, both Box 144, BB MSS; BB to Charles H. Brower, May 11, 1953, Box 9, ibid.; Ed Roberts, BB obituary (June 18, 1965), Drawer A8/5, BBDO; George Creel, *How We Advertised America* (New York: Harper, 1920), 4, 159ff., 247, 266; Robert H. Ferrell, *Woodrow Wilson and World War I, 1917–1921* (New York: Harper and Row, 1985), 62–63.

36. BB to Brower, May 11, 1953, Box 9, BB MSS; BB speech, University of Buffalo, Oct. 17, 1929, Box 145, ibid.; Creel, *How We Advertised America* 87, 137; "Bruce Barton: Everything Ad Men Should Be, He Is," *Printer's Ink*, Feb. 10, 1961, 55; Elizabeth McKeown, *War and Welfare: American Catholics and World War I* (New York: Garland, 1988), 149–152.

37. Louise MacLeod to Hugh H. Gray, June 20, 1934, Box 3; BB to Edward Julian Nally, Aug. 9, 1943; BB to W. Arthur Cole, Mar. 16, 1955, Box 12, all BB MSS.

38. BB, "They Who Tarry by the Stuff," in *It's a Good Old World: Being a Collection of Little Essays on Various Subjects of Human Interest* (New York: The Century Co., 1920), 162–165.

39. BB, ". . . And they shall beat their swords into—Electrotypes: Being some thoughts on the place of advertising in a cleansed and chastened world," reprint (New York: Barton & Durstine Co., n.d. [1919]).

40. BB, "For Your America," *Collier's*, May 28, 1921, 14; BB, *It's a Good Old World*, 26; BB to Editor, *Evening Post*, Aug. 15, 1933, Box 64, BB MSS.

41. BB, "A Personal Letter to the Kaiser," reprinted from *Every Week*, Aug. 7, 1916, Box 153, BB MSS. Several pro-German replies sought to refute his claims of Prussian savagery with Allied counterexamples. One critic wondered if he had not been "fool-hardy" to challenge the coachmen. "The Kaiser's Reply to Bruce Barton by Proxy," *Fatherland* (George Sylvester Viereck, ed.), Aug. 30, 1916, ibid.

42. BB to Thomas L. Lamont, Nov. 16, 1929, A11/3, BBDO; BB comment in *The World Tomorrow* (June 1931), 196, Box 130, BB MSS.

43. BB, "What We Could Do with What We Waste," *Home Herald*, Mar. 31, 1909, 3–4; BB, "'Unknown,'" *Good Housekeeping*, June 1922, 48; clipping, BB, "Other Unknown Soldiers Recall 'Last Battles,'" *New York Journal-American*, June 4, 1950, Box 128, BB MSS.

44. *New York Herald Tribune*, Oct. 10, 1937, 8.

45. BB speech, University of Buffalo, Oct. 17, 1929, Box 145, BB MSS; Barrett Andrews to BB, n.d. (1910), Folder 6, WEB Papers; Earnest Elmo Calkins to BB, Feb. 18, 1959, Box 10, BB MSS.

46. On the Oyster Bar story, see BBDO *Newsletter* (February 1966), 3; "Biographical Information" and draft obituary for Alex F. Osborn, n.d. (ca. 1960), A5/1, BBDO; "Bruce Barton: Everything Ad Men Should Be, He Is," *Printer's Ink*, Feb. 10, 1961, 55; BB speech, University of Buffalo, Oct. 17, 1929, Box 145, BB MSS; etc.

47. Harford Powel, "As You Were—XI," *Advertising & Selling*, Dec. 19, 1935, 28.

48. BB to "Dear folks," n.d. (summer 1918), Folder 11, WEB Papers.

49. BB memorandum, Nov. 1, 1944. This memo has the appearance of a draft affidavit and is similar to one executed in April 1946 for an unidentified legal proceeding that deals with the BDO partnership, which had unraveled in the late 1930s. Both are in Box 144, BB MSS.

50. [McLeod?] to "McCarty," Sept. 19 (1937), Box 4, BB MSS; *New York Times*, Nov. 19, 1918, 13.

3. A NEW NAME ON MADISON AVENUE

1. Daniel Pope, *The Making of Modern Advertising* (New York: Basic Books, 1983), 30–31, 51, 60, 113; Laird, *Advertising Progress: American Business and the Rise of Consumer Marketing* (Baltimore and London: Johns Hopkins University, 1988), 18, 22, 26–29, 34–37, 77, 83, 167, 184, 250, 272, 284, 288, 328; photograph in *The Advertising Age Encyclopedia of Advertising* (New York: Fitzroy Dearborn, 2003), 700; Fox, *The Mirror Makers*, 13.

2. Pope, 17, 139–144, 176; T. J. Jackson Lears, "From Salvation to Self-Realization: Advertising and the Therapeutic Roots of the Consumer Culture, 1880–1930," in Richard Wightman Fox and Lears, eds., *The Culture of Consumption: Critical Essays in American History, 1880–1960* (New York: Pantheon, 1983), 20.

3. Batten remarks, "Dinner at Twenty-fifth Anniversary, George Batten Company," Mar. 1916, A8/5, BBDO; Pope, *Making of Modern Advertising*, 202ff.; William H. Johns to F. C. Kendall, Nov. 14, 1941, A11/3, BBDO.

4. BB speech, "Changes and Trends in Advertising," Boston Chamber of Commerce, Mar. 17, 1928, A8/5, BBDO; BB remarks before the C.N.A.M.A., San Francisco, June 7, 1957, ibid.; Helen Woodward, *It's an Art* (New York: Harcourt, Brace, 1938), 32.

5. Osborn, "Advertising, the Life of a Nation—Used Wisely, It Leads to the Pot of Gold," *Newspaperdom*, Sept. 9, 1915, clipping in A5/1, BBDO.

6. Marchand, *Advertising the American Dream*, 9–11, 13. There are many brilliant interpretations of the history of American advertising, but probably none better than Marchand's.

7. Pope, *Making of Modern Advertising*, 175, 180–181; agency chronology, n.d. (ca. 1965), A7/3, BBDO; BBDO *Newsletter*, February 1966, 14; Charles Brower, *Me, and Other Advertising Geniuses* (Garden City, N.Y.: Doubleday, 1974), 211–212; Fox, *Mirror Makers*, 85–86, 95; Stuart Ewen, *PR! A Social History of Spin* (New York: Basic Books, 1996), passim.

8. "The Reminiscences of Roy S. Durstine," Columbia Oral History Project, 2, 23, 29, 33; BBDO *Newsletter*, Feb. 1966, 3, 5, 8; Harford Powel, "Tiger Man," *Advertising & Selling*, Jan. 19, 1933, 54; extract from *Space & Time*, Apr. 12, 1939, Box 18, BB MSS.

9. "Biographical Information" and draft obituary, Alex F. Osborn, n.d. (ca. 1964), A5/1; Ed Roberts biographical sketch, "Alex F. Osborn," n.d. (ca. 1964), ibid.; BBDO News Letter, Sept. 10, 1937, ibid.; undated chronology (ca. 1965), A7/3, memo, Osborn (AFO) to Ed Cashin, Aug. 9, 1956, A5/1, all in BBDO.

10. BBDO commemorative history, "The First 100 Years" (1991), 15; BB to Mrs. R.T. Morris, July 15, 1926, Box 89, BB MSS; BBDO News Letter, Dec. 24, 1952, A8/5, BBDO; "Bruce Barton: Everything Ad Men Should Be, He Is," *Printers' Ink*, Feb. 10, 1961, 55; Minutes, Board of Directors, Dec. 29, 1919; July 16, 1920; Mar. 26, 1920; Aug. 17, 1921, A2/4, BBDO; BB to William Feather, Mar. 27, 1958, Box 20, BB MSS; "Remarks by Alex Osborn" at stockholder's annual meeting, Feb. 25, 1956, A3/5, BBDO.

11. Untitled memo, Dec. 15, 1925 (BDO ranking and acquisition of clients), A7/3, BBDO; (*Good Housekeeping*) pamphlet, n.d. (1923), "Where Are You on This List?" Box 7, Series I, Dwight Morrow MSS, Robert Frost Library, Amherst College, Amherst, Mass.; BB to Roy S. Durstine, Aug. 3, 1923, Box 18; BB to G. Ray Schaeffer, Nov. 5 and Dec. 13, 1926, Box 77; BB to C. W. Barron, Dec. 31, 1926, Box 3, all BB MSS.

12. Untitled memo, Dec. 15, 1925; undated chronology, n.d. (ca. 1965), both A7/3; *Sparks*, June 11, 1923, A3/3; Ed Roberts, "Beggars, Peddlers and Advertising Men" (1964 rewrite), p. 231, A7/3, all BBDO; memo, Louise MacLeod to Ben Duffy et al., Dec. 14, 1954, Box 18, BB MSS.

13. "BBDO, Close to Top of Heap, Is Still Growing," *Advertising Age*, June 19, 1950, 60; Arthur H. Deute, "An Outsider Looks In: An Impression of Barton, Durstine & Osborn," reprint, n.d. (ca. 1927), A7/3; BDO "Experience Book. Unusual Services Rendered to Clients," n.d. (1926), A4/4; memo, "New Product," Oct. 7, 1926, ibid.; undated chronology (ca. 1965), A7/3; memo, Roy S. Durstine to account representatives, n.d. (June 1931), A4/4; clip, *The Gasoline Retailer*, Oct. 1, 1932, ibid.; BBDO News Letter, Sept. 15, 1933, ibid.; memo from Management Committee, July 28, 1926, all BBDO; *Advertising & Selling*, Sept. 30, 1931, 31. Soon after Deute's complimentary article, he showed up on a list of BDO account executives.

14. Undated chronology (ca. 1965), A7/3, BBDO; clip, *Boston Sunday Post*, June 19, 1921 (J. R. Milne), folder 86, WEB Papers; Charles Brower eulogy, "The Man Everybody Knew," BBDO Newsletter, July, 1967; Brower, *Me, and Other Advertising Geniuses*, 74; Julian Lewis Watkins, *The 100 Greatest Advertisements: Who Wrote Them and What They Did* (New York: Dover, 1959, 2nd rev. ed.), 70–71; excerpt from BB speech to Associated Business Papers, New York City, Oct. 1922, A5/3, BBDO; BB to Ray Long, Mar. 29, 1927, Box 90, BB MSS.

15. Barton is thus well documented from 1925 on. His papers are in many ways the MacLeod papers; if historians of advertising had a cathedral, "Miss MacLeod" or "Miss Mac" would surely warrant a shrine in it. Memo, MacLeod to O. Jay Blake, Apr. 24, 1944, Box 122, BB MSS.

16. Unsigned biographical treatment (Ed Roberts?), "Bruce Barton," n.d. (1960), Box 24, BB MSS; BB to F. G. Hubbard, Apr. 15, 1929, Box 26, ibid.; Ed Roberts, "BBDO Short History," n.d. (ca. 1965), A7/3, BBDO, undated list (ca. 1926), "Accounts," ibid.; Alex Osborn to George S. Anderson, Sept. 27, 1926, Box 79, BB MSS; John Allen Murphy, "When a Board of Directors Balks," *Sales Management*, Jan. 30, 1932, 1511.

17. Memo, BB to C. H. Ferguson, Apr. 6, 1949, Box 80, BB MSS.

18. The ad is in "The First 100 Years," 16. See Watkins, *100 Greatest Advertisements*, 58.

19. Ad copy, "The Years That the Locust Hath Eaten" (1921), Box 75, BB MSS; biographical treatment, "Bruce Barton," n.d. (1960), Box 24, ibid.; Watkins, *100 Greatest Advertisements*, 58–59.

20. "The Big Idea," *The Wire* (Alexander Hamilton Institute), Aug. 1967, A8/5, BBDO.

21. BB memoranda to J. D. Danforth et al., June 29, 1951; to J. S. Smith and D. W. Burke, Jan. 16, 1957, both Box 76; BB to Gerard Swope, Dec. 1, 1952, Box 66, all BB MSS.

22. Memo, Jan Paladino, "General Electric — Circa 1920," July 7, 1957, A8/5, BBDO; interview with Alphonse Normandia, July 13, 2001; untitled memo, marked "Roberts"; copy of ad in "The First 100 Years," 23; *Newsweek*, July 17, 1967, 79.

23. Roland Marchand, *Creating the Corporate Soul: The Rise of Public Relations and Corporate Imagery in American Big Business* (Berkeley: University of California Press, 1998), 149, 156–157.

24. William H. Johns to F. C. Kendall, Nov. 14, 1941, A11/3, BBDO; " — That the Doctor Shall Arrive *in Time*," "The First 100 Years," 20–21; Marchand, *Corporate Soul*, 142–143

25. Marchand, *Corporate Soul*, 137–138, 140–141; David Farber, *Sloan Rules: Alfred P. Sloan and the Triumph of General Motors* (Chicago: University of Chicago Press, 2002), 69–70; BB to Truman A. DeWeese, Feb. 5, 1928, Box 25, BB MSS.

26. See William Leach's illuminating *Land of Desire: Merchants, Power, and the Rise of a New American Culture* (New York: Vintage, 1994) for this theme.

27. Barton and Tom Cronyn wrote the copy for this series. G. R. Schaeffer to BB, Sept. 13, 1927; ad copy, "WOMEN," Sept. 17, 1927; Schaeffer to BB, Nov. 23, 1927; Tom Cronyn to Schaeffer, Feb. 7, 1928, all Box 77, BB MSS; Marchand, *Corporate Soul*, 172–174.

28. Crocker was the name of the popular, late secretary of the company; "Betty" sounded "familiar" and "companionable." Cf. Otis Pease, "Barton, Bruce," in John A.

Garraty and Jerome L. Sternstein, eds., *Encyclopedia of American Biography*, 2nd ed. (New York: HarperCollins, 1996), 65; and James Gray, *Business Without Boundary: The Story of General Mills* (Minneapolis: University of Minnesota Press, 1954), 172–173. BBDO designed some of General Mills' advertising, so they helped define Ms. Crocker. Memorandum, BB to Ben Duffy et al., May 24, 1954, Box 77, BB MSS.

29. BB to J. Norton Brennan, Apr. 12, 1957, Box 50, BB MSS.

30. A. D. Chiquoine speech, "From the Other Side of the Counter," Mar. 14, 1932, A4/4, BBDO; memo, AFO to BB, Nov. 14, 1946, Box 50, BB MSS; Marchand, *Corporate Soul*, 133–134.

31. BB, "A Charity Solicitation That Returned 100 Per Cent Plus," *Advertising and Selling*, Feb. 10, 1926, 36–37.

32. BB to Ann Sprayregen, May 25, 1959, Box 97, BB MSS; to B. C. Forbes, Oct. 15, 1946, Box 101; to Earl G. Sanem, May 20, 1959, Box 97; 1951 Christmas card, Box 65; Len Lesourd to BB, July 13, 1954, Box 97; Henry Weber to BB, Sept. 18, 1953, Box 12, all in BB MSS.

33. Louise MacLeod to Norbert Schlaff, June 7, 1950, Box 122; biog. material on BB, n.d. (ca. 1960), Box 24, both ibid. A version appears in Barton's collection of editorials and short pieces, *It's a Good Old World* (New York: The Century Co., 1920), and also in *The Advertiser's Digest*, Oct. 1942, Box 82, ibid.

34. Sen. Hugo Black in *Congressional Record* 72 (Feb. 28, 1930), 4468–4470.

35. Pamphlets, "What About 'Service at Cost'" and "What Is a Holding Company?" n.d.; leaflets "Service at Cost!" and "Orator & Business," n.d. (1925), all Box 78, BB MSS. Texts of all these messages are in U.S. Senate, 70th Cong, 1st Sess., *Utility Corporations. Letter from the Chairman of the Federal Trade Commission transmitting in Response to Senate Resolutions Nos. 83 and 112* (Feb. 14, 1930), 199–204.

36. U.S. Senate, 70th Cong., 1st Sess., *Utility Corporations. Letter from the Chairman of the Federal Trade Commission Transmitting in Response to Senate Resolution No. 83, a Monthly Report on the Electric Power and Gas Utilities Inquiry*, No. 3 (May 15, 1928), 201; clipping, *Cleveland Plain Dealer*, Mar. 18, 1928, "Fund Exposed by Trade Body," Box 146, BB MSS.

37. *New York Times*, Sept. 22, 1928, 22.

38. BB, "Excerpt from remarks at Bok Award dinner," Feb. 27, 1931, Box 25, BB MSS.

39. *Printers' Ink Monthly*, Apr., 1929, 97; BB to F. T. Bedford, Mar. 7, 1925; BB to Roy Durstine, Dec. 20, 1924; BB to T. A. DeWeese, Feb. 2, 5, 1925, all Box 25, BB MSS; *Baltimore and Ohio Magazine*, Apr. 1931, 10–11, Box 78, BB MSS; Fox, *Mirror Makers*, 106.

40. BB to James W. Young, Sept. 19, 1946, Box 1, Thomas D'Arcy Brophy MSS, Wisconsin Historical Society. Barton did allow that "I have quieted my conscience about this sort of advertising with the thought that, after all, it's relatively harmless, and certainly not worth crusading against in a world where there are so many more important evils."

41. BB to George Burton Hotchkiss, May 17, 1926, Box 30, BB MSS; BB speech to Boston Chamber of Commerce, Mar. 17, 1928, A8/5, BBDO; clipping, "Calls Advertising Power to Keep Business Striving for High Ideals," *New York Evening Post*, Jan. 3, 1928, Box 82, BB MSS; BB, "The Great American Yen—Its Place in Keeping Business in High," *Chicago Commerce*, Nov. 9, 1929. Thanks to Prof. Perry Duis for providing me with the latter item.

42. Fox, *Mirror Makers*, 101.

43. *Your Money's Worth: A Study in the Waste of the Consumer's Dollar* (New York: Macmillan, 1927).

44. BB, "Of Course Distribution Is Costly," *Printers' Ink*, Oct. 29, 1925, 101–102.

45. BB, "The Creed of an Advertising Man," *Printers' Ink*, Nov. 3, 1927, 3ff.

46. *Washington Post*, Dec. 1, 1928, M7; clipping, BB, "A Kind Word for Business," *New York Herald Tribune*, Jan. 6, 1929, Box 131, BB MSS.

47. BB, "I Believe," *Advertising & Selling*, Oct. 29, 1930, 21.

48. BB, "Advertising: Its Contribution to the American Way of Life," *Reader's Digest*, Apr. 1955, 1–5. This article led the issue, which saw that magazine's first resort to advertising.

49. BB, clipping, *New York Herald Tribune*, Oct. 14, 1928, Box 131, BB MSS.

50. Lynd in President's Research Committee on Social Trends, *Recent Social Trends in the United States* (New York: McGraw-Hill, 1933), 867; John Dewey, *Individualism Old and New* (New York: Minton, Balch, 1930), 43–44. Lynd received advice and space in BBDO's library while he wrote this essay. Memorandum, M. L. Alexander to Tom Crabbe, Aug. 18, 1931, A7/1, BBDO.

51. Warren I. Susman, "Culture Heroes: Ford, Barton, Ruth," in Susman, *Culture as History: The Transformation of American Society in the Twentieth Century* (New York: Pantheon, 1984), 123.

52. Chase and Schlink, *Your Money's Worth*, 166–167.

53. Arthur H. Deute, "An Outsider Looks In," article reprint (ca. 1927), A7/3, BBDO. For a critique, see Brower, *Me, and Other Advertising Geniuses*, 46, 73.

54. Roberts, "Beggars, Peddlers and Advertising Men" (1964 rewrite), A7/3; Batten's Wedge, Mar. 1905, A5/4; *George Batten's Directory of the Religious and Agricultural Press of the United States, 1895* (New York: George Batten Newspaper Advertising Agent, 1895), A8/5, BBDO; Ed Roberts biographical material, "George Batten," n.d., A5/3; historical summary, "As It Was in the Beginning," n.d. (ca. 1930), A3/5, all BBDO.

55. With Chester Bowles, who left BBDO in 1929, Benton founded Benton & Bowles, an agile, inventive agency that flourished through the depression. Notes, "News letters 1925," n.d. A7/3, BBDO; Sidney Hyman, *The Lives of William Benton* (Chicago: University of Chicago Press, 1969), 115–116, 129, and passim; Benton, "Be Glad You Were Fired," *Printers' Ink*, Sept. 20, 1957, 106.

56. Barton had been unknowingly in the Batten orbit earlier, when Joseph Knapp, at the time the war was imperiling the future of *Every Week*, recommended him to Johns. Brower, *Me, and Other Advertising Geniuses*, 46, 82; Roberts, "Beggars," 162, 182, A7/3, BBDO.

57. Actually, there was a conflict: Continental Baking was Batten's client, and General Baking was BDO's, and each side had a smoking tobacco account. *Time*, Oct. 1, 1928, 34; *Advertising Age*, Sept. 30, 1991, S-40; undated chronology (ca. 1965), A7/3; "Announcing the organization of Batten, Barton, Durstine & Osborn, Inc.," n.d. (1928), A3/3; "As It Was in the Beginning," n.d. (ca. 1930), A5/4; undated history of the merger (1930s), A7/3, all BBDO; Brower, *Me, and Other Advertising Geniuses*, 81.

58. "BBDO Chronology," n.d., A7/3; "Durstine Becomes Head of BBDO," *Sales Management*, Feb. 15, 1936, 264; Roberts, "Beggars, Peddlers and Advertising Men"

(1964 rewrite), 174, 185, A7/3; William H. Johns to "The Organization," Sept. 21, 1928, A7/4, all BBDO; John Allen Murphy, *Merchandising Through Mergers* (New York: Harper and Brothers, 1930), 11–12; Brower, *Me, and Other Advertising Geniuses*, 87; BB to Frank E. Gannett, Sept. 26, 1939, Box 23, BB MSS.

59. Stuart Peabody apparently coined the "trunk" line. BDO, *Sparks*, June 1922; Woodward, *It's an Art*, 178(n); *Ad-Letics*, Bowling-Basketball Number, 1928, A7/4; "BBDO, Close to Top of Heap, Is Still Growing," *Advertising Age*, June 19, 1950, 60; clip, *Minneapolis Star*, March 2, 1966, A4/4, all BBDO; Brower, *Me, and Other Advertising Geniuses*, 80–81.

60. BBDO was also cited in the 1970 film *Prisoner of Second Avenue*, starring Jack Lemmon. BB obituary by Ed Roberts, June 18, 1965, A8/5; BBDO News Letter, Sept. 15, 1933, A4/4; News release, "BBDO Marks 100th Birthday," Sept. 30, 1991, A7/3; memo, "BBDO Thirty-Two Years Ago," n.d. (1966?), ibid.; clipping, "New Blues Is Born at Ad Man's Jazz Concert," *New York Herald Tribune*, Oct. 22, 1957, ibid., all BBDO.

61. BB, "This Magic Called Radio," *American Magazine*, June 1922, 11–13, 72; "We Pay Our Respects to Roy Sarles Durstine," *Broadcasting*, Feb. 15, 1936, 27, A9/4, BBDO; Harford Powel, "Tiger Man," *Advertising & Selling*, Jan. 19, 1933, 22, 54; Durstine speech, "Spoken Advertising with a Musical Background," May 28, 1929, in *The Wedge*, XXIX, No. 3, Box 35, Roy W. Howard Papers, LC; Durstine, "Talk Before ANPA," Apr. 27, 1938, A9/4; Ed Roberts, "Radio TV Spread Text," n.d., A7/1; Durstine memo, Nov. 4, 1929, "Radio in General," A7/2; memo, "BBDO Thirty-Two Years Ago," n.d. (1966?), A7/3; undated typescript (Roberts?), "Radio Decade," A7/3, all in BBDO; Fox, *Mirror Makers*, 162.

62. Harford Powel, Jr., "As You Were—VIII," *Advertising & Selling*, Nov. 7, 1935, 30–31, 50.

63. Irwin Barbour to BB, July 9, 1926; Barbour to Charles M. Richter, May 21, 1928; BB to Richard Waldo, Mar. 15, 1929; newspaper ad, "Bruce Barton—Every Week," (1929); Waldo to Louise MacLeod, Feb. 14, 1930, with list of papers dropping BB's column; Waldo to BB, Apr. 6 and 21, 1932, all in Box 97, BB MSS.

64. Robert Cresswell to BB, July 7, 1932, Box 97, BB MSS; BB, "A Vacation," *New York Herald Tribune*, Feb. 4, 1934, magazine section, 2.

65. The precise date Osborn cited is unclear—probably the early 1920s. AFO to Louis J. Kolb, Sept. 20, 1938, A11/3, BBDO; *Sparks*, June 1922, BBDO; BB to John W. Lewis, Jr., Oct. 8, 1928, Box 114, BB MSS; *New York Times*, July 6, 1967, 35.

66. BB, "I Believe," for *Advertising & Selling*, Oct. 29, 1930, 20.

67. Harford Powel, Jr., to Dean D. W. Malott, Dec. 10, 1927, Box 104, BB MSS; Hitchcock Publications newsletter, n.d., quoted in BB biographical resume, n.d. (ca. 1947), Box 141, ibid.

68. BB, "Foreword" to John Caples, *Advertising for Immediate Sales* (New York: Harper and Brothers, 1936), ix–xi. Barton's historical judgment parallels some of the findings of Marchand's *Advertising the American Dream*.

69. Clipping, *Christian Science Monitor*, Dec. 15, 1937, 3, Box 155, BB MSS.

70. See BB's anonymous letter to fellow stockholders (ca. Oct. 11, 1927), Box 10, BB MSS. Barton later served on the board of directors of State Street.

71. BB to D. L. Chambers, Sept. 8, 1926; *New York Daily News*, Aug. 27, 1927; Louise MacLeod to Thomson and Thomson, Oct. 18, 1928; BB to R. E. Seiler, June 4, 1932, all Box 5; MacLeod to John Anson Ford, Aug. 5, 1931, Box 9, BB MSS.

72. Previously, Aylesworth had been managing director of NELA, for which Barton had written propaganda. H. S. Raushenbush, *High Power Propaganda* (New York: New Republic, 1928), 2, 77–78.

73. George H. Allen, "'He Munches on Chiclets,'" *Advertising & Selling*, Sept. 30, 1931, 64; BB to Henry Luce, Mar. 19, 1936, Box 40, BB MSS; BB to John N. Wheeler, Aug. 5, 1925, Box 97, ibid.; clipping, *Philadelphia Public Ledger*, Oct. 16, 1921, Folder 86, WEB MSS; BB to Col. Frank Knox, Apr. 29, 1929, Box 36, BB MSS; F. O. Billings to BB, Jan. 24, 1930, Box 21, ibid.; *Washington Post*, Jan. 13, 1933, 9; W. M. Walker, "J.P. the Younger," *American Mercury*, XI (June 1927), 129. On BB's clubs, see Box 12, BB MSS.

74. Allen, "'He Munches on Chiclets,'" 64; BB to J. Harvey Howells, Feb. 25, 1953, Box 78, BB MSS; BB, "Introduction to: 'All the King's Horses' (Osborn Fort)," n.d., Box 21, BB MSS; BB to Conde Nast, Sept. 29, 1923, Box 87, BB MSS; BB to John Robert Brook, Sept. 27, 1960, Box 58, BB MSS; BB to Charles Lucey, Jan. 15, 1940, Box 144, BB MSS; "Defrosting the Town House," *Town and Country*, Oct. 1936, 79.

75. BB, "I Remember," *Christian Herald*, September 1931, 10; "Mrs. William E. Barton Dies at Sunset Lake," *Journal of the Illinois State Historical Society*, XVIII, No. 4, 1084–1086; BB speech, Community Chest, n.d. (1953), Box 120, BB MSS; BB, "My Mother's Check Book," *American Magazine*, Mar. 1930, 18.

76. MacLeod to Col. Joseph R. Meacham, Apr. 1, 1964, Box 144, BB MSS.

77. WEB to BB, Aug. 20, 21, 1924, Folder 7, WEB Papers; BB, various published items, 1927–1931, Box 9; BB to W. F. Bigelow, Aug. 18, 1924, Box 89; BB to D. L. Chambers, Apr. 15, 1927, Box 105; Louise MacLeod to Chambers, Apr. 11, 1927, ibid.; BB to Merle Thorpe, June 2, 1928, Box 28; BB to O. O. McIntire, July 30, 1928, Box 41, all BB MSS.

78. Brower, *Me, and Other Advertising Geniuses*, 16; *New York Times*, July 6, 1967, 35. Possibly the second comment also came from Brower.

79. Harford Powel, Jr., "As You Were—III," *Advertising & Selling*, Aug. 29, 1935, 36; clipping, *Mademoiselle*, June 1943, Box 142, BB MSS.

4. THE GOSPEL ACCORDING TO BRUCE

1. The allure of journalism persisted: he later had a yen to buy a newspaper in Boston; and he had a small equity position in the two Phoenix papers owned by Eugene Pulliam. BB to Francis W. Hatch, Feb. 15, 1929, Box 26; BB to Earl Warren, Aug. 10, 1948, Box 2; BB to Henry P. Kendall, Feb. 20, 1933, Box 35, all BB MSS.

2. BB, "The Story of a Book," for *Woman's Home Companion* (1931), Box 104, BB MSS; BB, "The Tumult in the Churches," *Collier's* (Mar. 24, 1923), 9–10.

3. Jackson Lears, *Fables of Abundance: A Cultural History of Advertising in America* (New York: Basic Books, 1994), 24–25, 34–36, 139, 160–161 and passim.

4. He also saved, without comment, a clipping quoting Republican editor William Allen White's opposition to Al Smith's presidential candidacy, on grounds that included the threat Smith and his Tammany links posed to "the whole Puritan civilization, which has built a sturdy, orderly nation." White, "Warns Nation Against Smith," n.p., July 12, 1928, Box 19, BB MSS.

5. Barton's joining of Madison Avenue consumerism and Thoreauvian simplicity was not always smooth, as Daniel Horowitz suggests in *The Morality of Spending: Attitudes Toward the Consumer Society in America, 1875–1940* (Baltimore: Johns Hopkins University Press, 1985), 118.

6. William E. Leuchtenburg, *The Perils of Prosperity, 1914–1932* (Chicago: University of Chicago Press, 1958), 7, 144.

7. *New York Times*, May 3, 1927, 24; BB remarks, "Grantland Rice," July 16, 1954, Box 59, BB MSS.

8. Robert T. Handy, "The American Religious Depression, 1925–1935," *Church History* 29 (Mar. 1960), 3–16; George M. Marsden, *Fundamentalism and American Culture: The Shaping of Twentieth-Century Evangelicalism, 1870–1925* (New York: Oxford University Press, 1980), 118–122 and passim; Martin E. Marty, *Modern American Religion*, vol. 2: *The Noise of Conflict, 1919–1941* (Chicago: University of Chicago Press, 1991), chap. 5 and passim.

9. Quoted in Handy, "American Religious Depression," 6.

10. Lippmann, *A Preface to Morals* (New York: Macmillan, 1929), 9. A valuable perspective on Lippmann's thinking is Barry D. Riccio, *Walter Lippmann—Odyssey of a Liberal* (New Brunswick, N.J.: Transaction Publishers, 1994).

11. Stephen Prothero, *American Jesus: How the Son of God Became a National Icon* (New York: Farrar, Straus and Giroux, 2003), 10, 51, 56–56; Leo Ribuffo, "Jesus Christ as Business Statesman: Bruce Barton and the Selling of Corporate Capitalism," *American Quarterly* 33 (Summer 1981), 211. Also see Clifford Putney, *Muscular Christianity: Manhood and Sports in Protestant America, 1880–1920* (Cambridge: Harvard University Press, 2001).

12. Ribuffo, "Jesus Christ as Business Statesman," 208–209; BB, *The Book Nobody Knows* (Indianapolis: Bobbs-Merrill, 1926), 103.

13. BB, "Grantland Rice," July 16, 1954, Box 59, BB MSS; McClure's ad, "Such Popularity Must be Deserved," June 1929, Box 97, BB MSS.

14. BB, "The Tyranny of the Text," *Outlook*, Dec. 30, 1914, 1014; BB to Rev. Harry Emerson Fosdick, Mar. 3, 1923, Folder 89, WEB MSS. See the religious messages in many articles in Barton's 1920 collection *It's a Good World* (New York: The Century Co., 1920).

15. Ribuffo, "Jesus Christ as Business Statesman," 217.

16. BB preface for new edition, n.d. (1959), Box 105; BB to Louis Ludlow, Aug. 10, 1938, Box 109; BB to Gertrude B. Lane, Aug. 12, 1929, Dec. 28, 1923, Mar. 29, 1924, Box 104; BB to William Hard, Nov. 18, 1959, Box 25; Lane to BB, Nov. 19, 1923, Box 104; George B. Hotchkiss to BB, Apr. 25, 1924, Box 30; Harford [Powel] to BB, Jan. 2, 1923, Box 108, all in BB MSS. On Lane, see Helen Woodward, *The Lady Persuaders* (New York: Ivan Obolensky, 1960), 106–107 and passim.

17. In 1926 Scribner forgetfully asked Perkins why he had not acquired the book. Perkins recalled past discussions. "But you didn't tell me," Scribner riposted, "that it would sell four hundred thousand copies." A. Scott Berg, *Maxwell Perkins, Editor of Genius* (New York: E. P. Dutton, 1978), 107–108; Perkins to BB, Nov. 30, 1923, and Apr. 8, 1924, Box 107, BB MSS.

18. BB to D. L. Chambers, Jan. 19, 1924; Chambers to BB, Sept. 20, 1923; Hewitt H. Howland to BB, Jan. 18 and Apr. 7, 1924; BB to Howland, Apr. 9, 1924, all Box 105, BB MSS.

19. Myron S. Allen to BB, Jan. 14, 1958, Box 1, BB MSS. More skeptical of Barton's version of Sundays at his father's church is Ribuffo, "Jesus Christ as Business States-man," 217.

20. The leader quoted was Ford. BB, "He Wanted to Clean Up," *Red Book*, December 1922; BB to William Feather, Aug. 5, 1952, Box 20, BB MSS.

21. BB to Pvt. W. D. Brown, May 29, 1944, Box 114; First Congregational Church, Detroit, calendar, Oct. 23–29, 1927, Box 111; clipping, "Bruce Barton Scans Great and Near-Great in Pittsfield Lecture," *Berkshire County Eagle*, Jan. 11, 1928, Box 118, all BB MSS.

22. Putney, *Muscular Christianity*, 172 and passim. Barton's next book depicted ten strong women, but he sometimes stretched to find strength.

23. Clipping, *Boston Herald*, Jan. 2, 1926, Box 104, BB MSS; *New York Times Book Review*, May 10, 1925, III, 11; quoted in McClure ad, "Such Popularity Must be Deserved," June 1929, Box 97, BB MSS.

24. BB to D. L. Chambers, Jan. 16, 1926, Box 105; clipping, n.p., n.d., Box 107; Olga Sorkin to BB, Mar. 12, 1926, Box 108, all BB MSS.

25. James A. Angell to BB, Sept. 20, 1925, Box 107; Frank N. D. Buchman to BB, Feb. 27, 1927, Box 108; Dr. Frank Crane to BB, Jan. 4, 1926, Box 109; G. Bromley Oxnam to BB, July 12, 1954, Box 96, all ibid.

26. Brochures in Box 107; "Alex" to BB, July 3, 1925, ibid.; "Some Sidelights on Making a Best Seller out of Bruce Barton's Story of Jesus . . . ," n.d. (1925), ibid.; BB to Herbert S. Baker, Oct. 3, 1925, Box 105; D. L. Chambers to BB, Oct. 26, 1925, ibid., all BB MSS.

27. Chambers to BB, Oct. 15, 1925, Aug. 17, 1926, Box 105; Herbert S. Baker to BB, Nov. 7, 1925, ibid.; Bobbs-Merrill brochure, "The Discovery of Jesus" (1926), Box 107, all BB MSS.

28. Undated publicity materials, n.d. (1926?), Box 106; ad copy with BB to Herbert S. Baker, Oct. 23, 1925, Box 107; William H. Duff, II, to BB, July 15, 1925, ibid.; William J. Montgomery to Louis J. Kolb, Dec. 19, 1925, ibid.; BB to D. L. Chambers, Sept. 29, 1925, Box 105; brochure, "The Discovery of Jesus," n.p., n.d. (ca. 1926), Box 107, all BB MSS.

29. Lane to BB, Dec. 30, 1924, Box 107, ibid.; Edrene S. Montgomery, "Bruce Barton's *The Man Nobody Knows*: A Popular Advertising Illusion," *Journal of Popular Culture* 19 (Winter 1985), 22; "The Reminiscences of Roy S. Durstine," Columbia Oral History Project, 42.

30. Clipping, n.d., "Popularizing Error," Box 107, BB MSS.

31. Gaebelein, *The Christ We Know: Meditations on the Person and Glory of Our Lord Jesus Christ* (Chicago: The Bible Institute Colportage Ass'n, 1927), iii–iv. Although the book was sub-subtitled "The Best Answer to the Book *The Man Nobody Knows*," it contained mostly spiritual meditations. Gaebelein was the premillennialist editor of *Our Hope*. See Marsden, *Fundamentalism and American Culture*, 93, 125ff., 148; Gaebelein, *Half a Century: The Autobiography of a Servant* (New York: "Our Hope," 1930).

32. Gottschall, "The Book Entitled 'The Man Nobody Knows' Under the Dissecting Knife" (Harrisburg, Pa.: Amos H. Gottschall, [ca. 1928]), Box 107, BB MSS; BB to Herbert S. Baker, Box 105, ibid.

33. Rev. C. Everett Wagner, "Religion Rings the Cash Register," *Plain Talk*, April 1928, 455–459; *New York Times*, Apr. 23, 1928, 30, Dec. 17, 1928, 28; Hubert C. Herring, "The Rotarian Nobody Knows," *World Tomorrow*, Dec. 1925, 382; Richard Wightman Fox, *Jesus in America: Personal Savior, Cultural Hero, National Obsession* (San Francisco: HarperSanFranciso, 2004), 321–322.

34. Clippings, *New York Sun*, May 2, 1925, Box 97, BB MSS; Mencken column, n.p., n.d. (1926), Box 107, ibid.

35. *Washington Post*, Apr. 3, 1927, 5; *New Republic* 18 (June 24, 1935), 127.

36. William Henry Chamberlin, *The Confessions of an Individualist* (New York: Macmillan, 1941), 114, 134. Barton liked the memoir despite "what you say about me and my book," conceding he "would write it very differently" a second time. Chamberlin regretted his "frivolous and perhaps hypercritical comments." BB to Chamberlin, Mar. 11, 1941; Chamberlin to BB, Mar. 14, 1941, both Box 109, BB MSS.

37. BB to Chambers, July 12, 1935, Box 105. It had already been made to vanish from the excerpts of the book published in *Reader's Digest* (Mar., Apr., June, July 1925).

38. Houston Boyles to Louise MacLeod, Aug. 25, 1948, Box 56; BB to Victor O. Schwab, Sept. 14, 1944, Box 63; Janet Goldman to BB, Sept. 1, 1950, Box 9; Edward D. Gates to BB, Mar. 29, 1957, Box 41, all BB MSS.

39. *Washington Post*, May 1, 1927, F5.

40. The year 1925 was an authorial triumph for the family: Reverend Barton's *Life of Abraham Lincoln* (also from Bobbs-Merrill) became a best-seller. Alice Payne Hackett and James Henry Burke, *80 Years of Best Sellers, 1845–1975* (New York: R. R. Bowker, 1977), 91, 93, 95, 97, 99, 101, 103; Keith L. Justice, *Bestseller Index* (Jefferson, N.C.: McFarland, 1992), 34, 198, 238.

41. Harford Powel, Jr., "The Man Every One Knows," pamphlet in Box 54; Chambers to BB, July 20, 1943, and July 21, 1938; "Copies sold to 3–31–59, in D. L. Chambers to BB, n.d. (Apr. 1959), all Box 105, ibid.

42. BB to D. L. Chambers, Dec. 11, 1926, Box 105, BB MSS.

43. Lippmann, *A Preface to Morals*, 3, 6, 48.

44. BB to D. L. Chambers, Apr. 5, 1926, Box 105; BB to Walter Wanger, June 5, 1925; [?] to Jesse Lasky, Nov. 29, 1926; George Palmer Putnam to BB, Feb. 3, 1927, all Box 112, ibid.

45. Telegram, BB to Jesse L. Lasky, July 17 and 19, 1926; Gladys Rosson to BB, Sept. 1, 1926; BB to Carl Gazley, Dec. 26, 1926; C. B. DeMille to BB, June 17, 1927, all ibid. An insightful treatment of *King of Kings* is in Fox, *Jesus in America*, 313–318.

46. T. Arnold Rau to H. E. Bischoff, Oct. 3, 1932; Schuyler E. Gray to Durstine, Nov. 20, 1924; Rau to BB, Feb. 3, 1932; W. R. Kelley to BB, Aug. 3, 1925; Pictorial Clubs, brochure, "The Man Nobody Knows," n.d., all Box 112, BB MSS. There are film scenarios by BB in Box 135.

47. *New York Herald Tribune*, Dec. 27, 1925, 1, 12.

48. *What Can a Man Believe?* won out. *Washington Post*, Apr. 3, 1927, SM7; Chambers to BB, Feb. 21 and Nov. 21, 1927, Box 105; draft ad copy with BB to Irwin Barbour, Mar. 27, 1927, Box 97; clipping, *New Yorker*, Oct. 9, 1926, Box 141; Anne Johnston to BB, Nov. 16, 1926, Box 105; Powel reprint (Bobbs-Merrill), Box 54, all BB MSS.

49. *Washington Post*, Dec. 27, 1930, 6; Apr. 22, 1931, 6; May 11, 1930, JP5; clipping, BB review, *Atlantic Monthly*, April 1927, Box 130, BB MSS.

50. Harford Powel, Jr., *The Virgin Queene* (Boston: Little, Brown, 1928), 3, 9–10, and passim. Powel came to BDO after serving as editor of *Collier's* until 1922; he left for another magazine in 1925. Barton said he was "lonesome without him, for he and I have many tastes in common and have been associated in one way or another for more then ten years." Frank Luther Mott, *A History of American Magazines, 1885–1905* (Cambridge: Belknap Press, 1957), 468–469; BB to C. E. Kelsey, Oct. 1, 1925, Box 104, BB MSS. A 1935 series of Powel's reminiscences in *Advertising & Selling* provides numerous details about Barton's early career.

51. Frederick Lewis Allen, *Only Yesterday: An Informal History of the 1920s* (New York: Harper and Brothers, 1931 [Perennial Library, 1964]), 146, 147, 149.

52. On how influential (and skewed) was Allen's analysis of Barton: James M. Ferreira, "*Only Yesterday* and the Two Christs of the Twenties," *South Atlantic Quarterly*, Winter 1981, 77–83.

53. James W. Prothro, *Dollar Decade: Business Ideas in the 1920s* (Baton Rouge: Louisiana State University Press, 1954), 229–230.

54. Leuchtenburg, *Perils of Prosperity, 1914–1932*, 188–189.

55. For a sampling: Mary Beth Norton et al., *A People and a Nation*, 5th ed, II (Boston: Houghton Mifflin, 1998), 697; John M. Murrin et al., *Liberty, Equality, Power*, 4th ed. (Belmont, Calif.: Wadsworth, 2005), 737; James West Davidson et al., *Nation of Nations*, 3rd ed., II (Boston: McGraw-Hill, 1998), 835; James L. Roark et al., *The American Promise* [compact ed.] (Boston: Bedford/St. Martin's, 2000), 622; Steven M. Gillon and Cathy D. Matson, *The American Experiment*, II (Boston: Houghton Mifflin, 2002), 933; Alan Brinkley et al., *American History: A Survey*, II (New York: McGraw-Hill, 1991), 706; Eric Foner, *Give Me Liberty!*, II (New York: W. W. Norton, 2005), 777. The "twelve men from the bottom ranks" quote is found in all but Roark.

56. Ribuffo, "Jesus Christ as Business Statesman"; "Barton, Ford, Ruth," in Susman, *Culture as History*, 131; Lynn Dumenil, *The Modern Temper: American Culture and Society in the 1920s* (New York: Hill and Wang, 1995), 195–196; Pease, "Barton, Bruce," in Garraty and Sternstein, eds., *Encyclopedia of American Biography*, 66.

57. Chambers to BB, Mar. 4, 1926, Box 105; *Collier's*, Aug. 22, 1925, 9.

58. BB to Gertrude B. Lane, Feb. 24, 1925, Box 104, BB MSS; BB to William H. Watts, Oct. 19, 1931, Box 106, ibid.

59. BB, *The Book Nobody Knows*, 22, 25, 55, 86, 102–103, and passim. The *Collier's* serialization began in November 1925. On Barton's aversion to "doctrinal particularity," see James A. Nuechterlein, "Bruce Barton and the Business Ethos of the 1920s," *South Atlantic Quarterly* 76 (Summer 1977), 298–299—yet another perceptive interpretation of Barton.

60. As of 1955, sales for *The Book* totaled nearly 306,000 in various formats. Photo, Box 106, BB MSS; Justice, *Bestseller Index*, 34; *Saturday Review*, Aug. 14, 1926, 39; "Memorandum for Herman" [Ziegner], Aug. 19, 1955, Box 105, BB MSS. For reviews, see, e.g., *Saturday Review*, Aug. 14, 1926, 39.

61. BB to D. L. Chambers, Jan. 25, 1927, Box 105, BB MSS; Chambers to BB, July 8, 1927, ibid.; BB to WEB, Nov. 4, 1925, Folder 11, WEB MSS; BB to WEB, Feb. 21, 1928, ibid.

62. WEB to BB, Sept. 7, 1926, Folder 89, WEB MSS; BB to WEB, Oct. 13, 1927 (and drafts of parts of the book), Folder 85, ibid.

63. Robert Barton, "William E. Barton—Biographer," *Abraham Lincoln Quarterly*, June 1946, 80–93. Fred Barton's appreciation of his brother notes that Robert too was a Lincoln scholar. "Robert S. Barton—In Memoriam" (1954), CHS.

64. WEB, "What Can a Modern Man Believe" (1930), sermons, Collegeside Church, Nashville, Tenn., Folder 11, WEB MSS; D. L. Chambers to BB, July 8, 1927, Box 105, BB MSS.

65. The letter used as his preface came from M. H. Aylesworth, a golfing buddy and president of NBC. BB, *What Can a Man Believe?* (Indianapolis: Bobbs-Merrill, 1927), 25 and passim; D. L. Chambers to BB, Nov. 11, 1926; BB to Chambers, Aug. 17, 1927, both Box 105, BB MSS.

66. Justice, *Bestseller Index*, 34; clippings, *New York Herald Tribune*, Nov. 9, 1928; *Times Literary Supplement*, May 24, 1928; *Portland Journal*, Jan. 15, 1928, all Box 111, BB MSS.

67. *New York Times Book Review*, Oct. 9, 1927, 20; "Editorial Comment," *Catholic World*, Dec. 1927, 399–408; clipping, *Church Militant*, Apr. 1928, both Box 111, BB MSS.

68. *New York Herald Tribune Books*, Sept. 25, 1927, 29; clipping, *Yale Divinity Review*, Nov. 1927, Box 111, BB MSS; *Saturday Review of Literature*, Sept. 3, 1927, 81–82.

69. BB, *He Upset the World: A Book About St. Paul* (London: Constable, 1932), vii, 59, 60, 83, 106, 125–126, 127, 133.

70. Chambers to BB, Sept. 30, 1931, Box 105, BB MSS; BB, *He Upset the World*, 137–139.

71. *Forbes*, Mar. 15, 1932, 11; clipping, *Christian Leader*, XXV, no. 15 (Apr. 9, 1932), Box 106, BB MSS.

72. A forty-nine-cent edition of *What Can a Man Believe?* was available in the 1940s. Louise MacLeod to D. L. Chambers, Nov. 9, 1944, Box 105, BB MSS.

73. *Washington Post*, Dec. 1, 1928, M7; clipping, *Atlanta Journal*, Feb. 21, 1931, Box 119, BB MSS.

5. THE TENTS OF THE MIGHTY

1. BB, "Mr. Candidate, Please Don't!" *Collier's*, May 29, 1920, 8–9; BB, "Wanted: A Bull Fighter," *Theatre Magazine*, June 1928, 5; BB to Roy Howard, Apr. 9, 1932, Box 30, BB MSS; "First Feed Your Cat," in BB, *Better Days* (New York: The Century Co., 1924), 144–146; BB, "Reform," *On the Up and Up* (Indianapolis: Bobbs-Merrill, 1929), 101. Evidence hints that the noted radical Max Eastman may have been the cat-deserting neighbor.

2. BB, "Just What Would Bolshevism Do to Me? An Interview with John Spargo," *American Magazine*, Dec. 1920, 110, 113.

3. BB to George Barr Baker, July 7 and Aug. 6, 1924, Box 13; BB to Herbert Hoover, July 11, 1932, Box 29, all BB MSS. For these themes in advertising, see Marchand, *Advertising the American Dream*, 1–4, 10–12, 66–69, 84, and passim. For useful coverage of Barton's political labors, see Terry Hynes, "Media Manipulation and

Political Campaigns: Bruce Barton and the Presidential Elections of the Jazz Age," *Journalism History* 4 (Autumn 1977), 93–98.

4. Irving Stone, "Calvin Coolidge: A Study in Inertia," in Isabel Leighton, ed., *The Aspirin Age, 1919–1941* (New York: Simon and Schuster, 1949 [1963]), 141; for a less colorful version, see Claude M. Fuess, *Calvin Coolidge: The Man from Vermont* (Boston: Little, Brown, 1939), 129–130; and BB, "Calvin Coolidge as Seen through the Eyes of his Friends," *American Review of Reviews*, Sept. 1923, 275.

5. Robert K. Murray, *Red Scare* (New York: McGraw-Hill, 1964 [1955]), 132–133; poem, n.d., "Get up and get out," Calvin Coolidge Papers, Forbes Library, Northampton, Mass. (hereafter CC Papers).

6. Harold Nicholson, *Dwight Morrow* (New York: Harcourt, Brace and Co., 1935); Frank W. Stearns to Coolidge, Apr. 2, 1920, CC Papers; BB to Morrow, Nov. 6, 1919, Series I, Box 13, Morrow MSS, Robert Frost Library, Amherst College, Amherst, Mass.

7. Nicholson, 232; Donald R. McCoy, *Calvin Coolidge: The Quiet President* (New York: Macmillan, 1967), 111; [Stearns] to Morrow, n.d. (1920), Series I, Box 14, Morrow MSS.

8. BB, "A Governor Who Stays on the Job," *Outlook*, Apr. 28, 1920, 756–757; BB, "Concerning Coolidge," *Collier's*, Nov. 22, 1919, 8; Fuess, *Calvin Coolidge*, 196. An astute analysis of Barton's role in promoting Coolidge is Kerry W. Buckley, "A President for the 'Great Silent Majority': Bruce Barton's Construction of Calvin Coolidge," *New England Quarterly* LXXVI (Dec. 2003), 600 and passim.

9. BB to Coolidge, Dec. 10, 1919; BB to Stearns, Nov. 12, 1919, Mar. 24, 1920; BB to Henry F. Long, Nov. 21, 1919, July 14 and Oct. 9, 1920; Stearns to Coolidge, Mar. 19, 1920, all CC Papers; Buckley, "President for the 'Great Silent Majority,'" 607; BB to Gertrude B. Lane, July 15, 1930, Box 104, BB MSS; BB to Morrow (Nov. 1919), Series I, Box 13, Morrow MSS; BB, memo to Ben Duffy, Aug. 17, 1948, Box 58, BB MSS.

10. Clipping, *Omaha Sunday Bee*, June 17, 1920, CC Papers; BB pamphlet, "Calvin Coolidge: A Close-Up of a Real American," n.d. (1920), Box 13, BB MSS.

11. William Allen White, *A Puritan in Babylon: The Story of Calvin Coolidge* (New York: Macmillan, 1938), 213; clipping, *Boston Herald*, May 21, 1920, Series I, Box 14, Morrow MSS; BB to Claude M. Fuess, June 19, 1937, Box 13, BB MSS; copy, Samuel W. Reyburn to Joseph W. Martin, July 31, 1961, ibid.

12. BB to Coolidge, Aug. 19, 1920, CC Papers.

13. Roberts, "Beggars, Peddlers and Advertising Men" (1964), 57, 61; Brower, *Me, and Other Advertising Geniuses*, 129.

14. John A. Morello, *Selling the President, 1920: Albert D. Lasker, Advertising, and the Election of Warren G. Harding* (Westport, Conn.: Praeger, 2001), 54–58, 81, 84, and passim. On the shift in campaign styles, see Richard Jensen, "Armies, Admen and Crusaders: Types of Presidential Election Campaigns," *History Teacher* 2 (1969), 33–50.

15. Morello, *Selling the President*, 9–11; Buckley, "President for the 'Great Silent Majority,'" 599.

16. BB, "The Faith of Frank Stearns," *Outlook*, Sept. 8, 1920, 60; David Riesman with Reuel Denney and Nathan Glazer, *The Lonely Crowd: A Study of the Changing American Character* (New Haven, Conn.: Yale University Press, 1950).

17. Fuess, *Calvin Coolidge*, 300; McCoy, *Calvin Coolidge*, 145; BB diary entry of Sept. 18, 1930, Box 145, BB MSS. Barton kept his diary for only a week.

18. BB to Coolidge, Aug. 19, Nov. 16 and 28, 1920, CC Papers; Stearns to BB, Mar. 9, 1922, Box 65, BB MSS; BB to Dwight Morrow, Jan. 31, Apr. 3, 1922, Series I, Box 7, Morrow MSS.

19. BB to Durstine, Aug. 3, 1923, Box 18, BB MSS.

20. BB to Wheeler Sammons, Jan. 8, 1924, Box 63, BB MSS; BB, "Calvin Coolidge Through the Eyes of his Friends," *American Review of Reviews*, Sept. 1923, 273–278; BB to Ray Long, Dec. 28, 1923, Box 107, BB MSS; two letters, BB to Frank Stearns, Dec. 31, 1923, Box 2, Edward T. Clark MSS, LC.

21. He also had a hand in a 1925 compilation of Coolidge's statements. BB to E. T. Clark, Feb. 29, and Dec. 19, 1924, Jan. 20, 1925; Maxwell E. Perkins to Clark, Mar. 14, 1924, all in CC Papers; French Strother to BB, Apr. 2, 1925, Box 104; BB pamphlet, "The Farmer Boy . . ." (1924), Box 13, both in BB MSS.

22. BB to George Barr Baker, July 7 and Aug. 6, 1924, Box 13; BB to Frank W. Stearns, Mar. 20, 1924, Box 65, all BB MSS. For the emergence of "personality" in this era, see Warren I. Susman, "'Personality' and the Making of Twentieth-Century Culture," in *Culture as History*, 271–285.

23. Coolidge to BB, n.d. (1920), CC Papers; BB to Frank W. Stearns, Apr. 21, 1924, Box 65; BB to John Hays Hammond, Dec. 11, 1926, Box 24; BB to WEB, Dec. 3, 1926, Box 143, all BB MSS.

24. BB to Roy Howard, Jan. 20, 1926, Box 30; D. L. Chambers to BB, Oct. 26, 1925, Box 105; French Strother to BB, Sept. 26, 1926, Box 104, all BB MSS; *Washington Post*, June 22, 1926, 3.

25. BB to Ernest M. Hopkins, n.d. (ca. Sept. 7, 1926), Box 82, BB MSS; BB to Coolidge, n.d. (Sept. 1926), Box 2, Clark MSS; Clark to BB, Oct. 2, 1926, ibid.

26. "Government by Publicity," *New Republic* 48 (Sept. 22, 1926), 110–111; *Washington Post*, Sept. 18, 1926, 4.

27. BB to Coolidge, n.d. (Sept. 1926), Box 2, Clark MSS; "A Conversation with the President" (Sept. 1926), Box 13, BB MSS; Kent Cooper to Coolidge, Sept. 14, 1926, ibid.; *New York Times*, Sept. 23, 1926, 1; Coolidge to Clark, Oct. 28, 1932, Box 3, Clark MSS.

28. Clipping, *New York Evening Sun*, Sept. 23, 1926, Box 13, BB MSS; *Washington Post*, Sept. 26, 1926, M5; James C. White to BB, Sept. 27, 1926, Box 85, BB MSS.

29. *Editor & Publisher*, Oct. 2, 1926, 10; Carl D. Groat to Coolidge, n.d. (1926), Box 13, BB MSS; *Washington Post*, Sept. 23, 1926, 1; Dec. 12, 1926, M1; clippings, "Coolidge Unrevealed," *Baltimore Evening Sun*, Sept. 23, 1926, Box 86; "Moulton Tells Secrets of President's Private Life," *Boston Daily Advertiser*, Sept.[??] 1926, Box 13, all BB MSS.

30. Clipping, *New York Evening Post*, Sept. 23, 1926, Box 13; "American Letter No. 421," Whaley-Eaton Service, Sept. 26, 1926, Box 3, both ibid.; *New York Times*, Sept. 28, 1926, 27.

31. BB to Coolidge, Oct. 7, 1926, and attachment, and Oct. 29, 1926, Box 13, BB MSS; *New York Times*, Oct. 28, 1926, 20.

32. BB to E. T. Clark, Oct. 17, 1928, Box 13; BB to Herbert Hoover, June 19, 1934, Box 29; BB to Roy Howard, May 14, 1932, Box 30; James Derieux to BB, Nov. 27, 1930, Box 13; BB, "Back in Ward Four," McClure Newspaper Syndicate, Apr. 18–19, 1931, Box 97; ad text, May 26, 1932, "For Vice President: Calvin Coolidge," Box 13; Republican

National Committee press release, Jan. 22, 1940, BB remarks to United States Potters Association, Box 137, all BB MSS.

33. BB to Herbert Hoover, Dec. 12, 1927; Memo, William H. Johns to BB, Oct. 4, 1928; BB to Merle Thorpe, Mar. 30, 1928; Louise MacLeod to Merle Thorpe, June 18, 1928; BB to William C. Donovan, Oct. 10, 1928; memo, Alex Osborn, Mar. 26, 1931; Barton speech draft, all in Box 28, BB MSS; *New York Times*, Aug. 12, 1928, 2.

34. Hoover to BB, May 25, Aug. 31, Sept. 7, Nov. 14, 1928, all Box 28, BB MSS.

35. Telegram, Louise MacLeod to BB, Sept. 14, 1928; clippings, *New York Telegram*, Aug. 11, 17, 18, 1928; Ted Thackrey to BB, n.d. (ca. Aug. 23, 1928), all in Box 28, BB MSS.

36. Clipping, "TRB," "Washington Notes," *New Republic* (ca. Dec. 8, 1928); various invitations; BB to Hoover, Sept. 28, 1931; BB to "Larry" [Richey], Dec. 31, 1931; BB to Hoover, Sept. 28, 1931; BB to Richey, Jan. 21, 1932, all in Herbert Hoover Presidential Papers—Secretary's File, Herbert Hoover Library; *Washington Post*, May 29, 1929, 9; June 28, 1931, M2; Hoover to BB, Sept. 12, 1931, Box 29, BB MSS.

37. BB to Hoover, June 6, 1932, Hoover Presidential Papers—Secretary's File, Hoover Library; BB to Mrs. William Brown Meloney, Sept. 16, 1932, Box 99, BB MSS; BB to W. J. Cameron, Mar. 18, 1933, Box 20, ibid.

38. Hoover to BB, Aug. 23, 1932; extract from BB to Mrs. Ogden Reid, Aug. 17, 1932, sent to Hoover, Aug. 18, 1932, both Box 29, BB MSS.

39. Barton did not much exert himself for Baker. Clipping, *New York Evening Post*, Apr. 22, 1932, Box 29, BB MSS; Roy Howard to BB, Apr. 13, 1932; BB to Howard, Apr. 9, 14, 1932, all in Box 65, Roy W. Howard MSS, LC.

40. BB to Paul C. Cabot, Oct. 5, 1932, Box 10, BB MSS; BB to E. M. Hopkins, Apr. 16, 1945, Box 30, ibid.

41. David A. Balch to BB, Sept. 4, 1956, Box 3, BB MSS; *Washington Post*, May 8, 1938, TT6.

42. BB to Hoover, Oct. 3, 1933, June 15, 1936; BB to "Dear Friends," Friday (Feb. 22, 1934), all in Post-Presidential Papers, Individuals File Series, Box 13, Hoover Library; BB to Hoover, June 19, 1934; Hoover to BB, June 23, 1934; phone message, Edgar Rickard to BB, June 8, 1934; BB to Russell Doubleday, July 30, 1934; Whitney Darrow to BB, Aug. 17, 1934, all Box 29, BB MSS.

43. BB diary, "Around the World," 3–4, Box 148; BB to Hoover, May 29, 1941, Box 29; Hoover to BB, Oct. 26, 1949, ibid.; BB to Hoover, Dec. 27, 1961, ibid., all BB MSS; BB to "Dear Chief," Nov. 26, 1951, Hoover Post-Presidential Papers, Individuals File Series, Box 13.

44. BB, "The Ambassador Everybody Knows," *Collier's*, Aug. 4, 1928, 9ff.; BB to Dwight Morrow, Oct. 31, 1930, Series I, Box 7, Morrow MSS.

45. *New York Times*, Oct. 15, 1934, 10; Apr. 28, 1936, 1, 15, 20; Aug. 18, 1937, 9; *Newsweek* (May 23, 1936), 16.

46. Clipping, John O'Donnell and Doris Fleeson, *New York Daily News*, May 6, 1936, Box 57, BB MSS; BB to Claude D. Kimball, July 22, 1936, ibid.; *New York Times*, May 5, 1936, 22 (Krock); "G.O.P. Publicizer Bruce Barton Picked to Offset Democratic Michelson," *Literary Digest*, May 16, 1936, 6–7; BB to Paul Bellamy, May 16, 1936, Box 90, BB MSS. On Michelson, see his *The Ghost Talks* (New York: G. P. Putnam's Sons, 1944).

47. *New York Times*, May 13, 1936, 1; BB to Claude D. Kimball, July 22, 1936, Box 57, BB MSS; BB to J. Caden Jenkins, Aug. 21, 1936, Box 34, ibid.

48. BB to Alfred M. Landon, Nov. 4, 1935; Jan. 30, 1936; May 22, 1936, all Box 37, BB MSS.

49. Clippings, *Minnesota Union Advocate*, May 21, 1936; "GOP Puts All Political Eggs in One Large Basket," Aug. 24, 1936, both Box 146, ibid.

6. WORN PANTS AND OPTIMISM

1. Caroline Bird, *The Angry Scar* (New York: David McKay, 1966); memo, BB for Amherst Alumni Association of New York Placement Bureau, "Eighty Amherst Men," n.d., Box 1, BB MSS; *Advertising Age*, Sept. 30, 1991, S-8; Roberts, "Beggars, Peddlers and Advertising Men" (1964), A7/3, BBDO.

2. Clipping, Jan. 21, 1930, Box 120, BB MSS; BB, "Are You Happy in Your Work?," 251; clipping, "Trade Revival Due in Spring If History Repeats Itself . . . ," *The Talking Machine and Radio Weekly*, Dec. 17, 1930, Box 97, BB MSS; BB, "OFR," *American Magazine*, Dec. 1930, 166.

3. Clippings, BB, "Advertising and the Business Depression," *Ad-vents*, December 1930, Box 130; *Atlanta Georgian*, Feb. 21, 1931, Box 119; BB, "Stop Long Distance Worrying," *Bridgeport Sunday Post*, Feb. 28, 1932, Box 98; *Atlanta Constitution*, n.d. (ca. Feb. 21, 1931), Box 119, all BB MSS.

4. *American Magazine*, June 1930; John P. Diggins, *Mussolini and Fascism* (Princeton, N.J.: Princeton University Press, 1972); Seldes, *Facts and Fascism* (New York: In Fact, 1943), 77. For further examples of the left's focus on Barton's remark, see Seldes, *One Thousand Americans* (New York: Boni & Gaer, 1947), 122–123; Ruth McKenney, "Bruce Barton's Clients," *New Masses*, Oct. 11, 1938, 15.

5. Earlier Barton wrote in his diary of this trip: "You get results with a dictator. But still I prefer to keep my lot with democracy, and all its troubles. (So, I imagine, would thousands of Italians. . . ." The line about FDR as against "top sergeants" echoed the diary too. *Washington Post*, June 10, 1934, B7; BB, "Around the World," 65, 68–69, Box 148, BB MSS.

6. BB, "How to Fix Everything," *Vanity Fair*, Aug. 1931, 31; clipping, BB, "Communism Will Fail," n.d. (ca. Aug. 1931), Box 99, BB MSS.

7. *New York Times*, Apr. 13, 1932, 33; BB, "Are We Getting a New Idea About 'Values'?" *American Magazine*, July 1932, 128; clipping, *Chicago Merchant*, February 1932, Box 142, BB MSS. Cf. *Washington Post*, Apr. 1, 1932, 20. As hard times lingered, some observers wryly noted Barton's undue optimism, but he escaped inclusion in Edward Angly's sardonic collection of Pollyanna-ish dismissals of the depression. H. I. Phillips, "Once Overs," *Washington Post*, Mar. 23, 1935, 9; Angly, *Oh Yeah?* (New York: Viking Press, 1931).

8. See his correspondence with Paul C. Cabot (Box 10, BB MSS) of the State Street Investment Trust. Barton invested his funds with State Street beginning in the late 1920s.

9. BB to Roy W. Howard, Nov. 29, 1929, Box 35, Howard MSS, LC; clipping, "'Buy Now' Campaign Spreading Rapidly," *Editor & Publisher*, Nov. 1, 1930, Box 141; BB to Lee Maxwell, Dec. 9, 1930, Box 82; BB draft, "Morale," n.d. (1931), Box 54; clipping, *Minneapolis Journal*, Oct. 30, 1931, Box 141, all BB MSS.

10. BB to Edwin Balmer, Oct. 6, 1935, Dec. 28, 1934, Box 103; clippings, BB, "Communism Will Fail," n.d. (ca. Aug. 1931), Box 99; and "A Vacation," *New York Herald Tribune*, Feb. 4, 1934, Box 99, all BB MSS.

11. The other contributors were Heywood Broun, Franklin P. Adams ("FPA"), and Christopher Morley. Leonard Hatch, *The Book of Dilemmas* (New York: Simon and Schuster, 1931), 18–20.

12. Mrs. King claimed in a bizarre affidavit that her husband had sued for alienation of affections without her knowledge or approval; that Barton and he jointly inveigled information from her and "tricked" her; and that she told her husband to divorce her so she might marry Barton! *New York Times*, Nov. 3, 1932, 29; Apr. 20, 1933, 10; Apr. 21, 1933, 15; May 2, 1933, 15; July 19, 1933, 15; July 21, 1933, 15; clipping, *New York Sunday News*, Jan. 1, 1939, Box 141, BB MSS.

13. *New York Times*, July 19, 1933, 15; July 21, 1933, 15; July 22, 1933, 9; July 25, 1933, 22; July 27, 1933, 2; July 28, 1933, 34; July 29, 1933, 26; Aug. 2, 1933, 34; Aug. 3, 1933, 36; clipping, *New York Sunday News*, Jan. 1, 1939.

14. The lawyer testified that the book was initially titled "The Man Who Knew Presidents"! *New York Times*, July 25, 1933, 22; Aug. 5, 1933, 26; Oct. 19, 1935, 5; Feb. 8, 1936, 32. Mrs. King apparently vanished, but her attorney returned as a nuisance years later. In 1961 he sued for $1 million in damages, alleging that Barton, then in ill health, and his attorney had "fraudulently conspired" to have him disbarred through false and malicious misrepresentations; and that Barton had reneged on a promise to help him win reinstatement. Barton's lawyer had died, removing one of two witnesses to the conduct leading to disbarment. The case was thrown out. Ibid., Jan. 13, 1961, 37; *Herman C. Pollack, Appellant, v. Bruce Barton, Respondent*, Court of Appeals of New York, 13 N.Y. 2d 658 (May 9, 1963), consulted on LexisNexis.

15. George Seldes, "Barton, Barton, Barton and Barton," *New Republic*, Oct. 26, 1938, 327–328; typed comment on clipping, BB, "A Double Life," *New York Herald Tribune*, Dec. 31, 1933, Box 131, BB MSS.

16. "The Man of the Month," *Commentator*, Apr. 1938, 25, Box 130, BB MSS; cf. clipping *New York Sunday News*, Jan. 1, 1939.

17. In 1930 Esther Barton went for an extended stay in France, putting the children in schools there. Edrene S. Montgomery describes this as a year in which the couple were "separated." "Bruce Barton and the Twentieth Century Menace of Unreality" (Ph.D. dissertation, University of Arkansas, 1984), 84.

18. Perhaps Winchell got wind of the threatened alienation suit. Clipping, Walter Winchell, "On Broadway," *New York Daily Mirror*, n.d.; Lane to BB, Aug. 14, 1929; BB to Lane, Aug. 15, 1929, all Box 104; MacLeod to Col. Joseph R. Meacham, May 18, 1964, Box 144, all BB MSS.

19. Fox, *Mirror Makers*, 112; BB to Paul C. Cabot, Jan. 12, 1934, Box 10; BB to MacLeod, Feb. 27, Apr. 16, 1934, Box 6; BB to W. H. Johns, Feb. 6, 1934, Box 34, all BB MSS; Phyllis McGinley, "O.K., Parnassus," *New Yorker*, March 10, 1934, 20.

20. "A Round the World Itinerary," n.d. [1934]; BB to Durstine et al., Mar. 23, 1934; BB to MacLeod, Mar. 28, 1934, all Box 6, BB MSS.

21. *New York Times*, Apr. 22, 1934, IV, 2; BB to Barry Goldwater, Apr. 27, 1954, Box 23, BB MSS.

22. As a candidate Barton would face attacks based on his 1930 comment about Mussolini. He was lucky no one tracked down this 1934 utterance—or his gangplank interview after his trip: "Every new deal has to have some one to blame when all its promises do not come true. We blame the reactionaries; Hitler blames the Jews." BB diary, "Around the World," 65, 68–69, 86; BB speech to Hammermill Agents, Aug. 21–22, 1934, Box 136, BB MSS; *Washington Post*, June 10, 1934, B7.

23. Fred Manchee, *The Huckster's Revenge: The Truth About Life on Madison Avenue* (New York: Thomas Nelson & Sons, 1959), 173 (quoting Jean Rindlaub); BB to Rep. Leslie C. Arends, Apr. 15, 1958, Box 2, BB MSS; remarks by Alex F. Osborn, Annual Stockholders Meeting, Feb. 25, 1956, A3/5, BBDO; *BBDO Newsletter*, 75th Anniversary, February 1966, 31; BB memo, "For BBDO News Letter of May 19, 1939," A11/3, BBDO.

24. Quoted in Helen Woodward, *It's an Art* (New York: Harcourt, Brace, 1938), 288–290.

25. BB, "The Public," speech to Congress of American Industry, Dec. 4, 1935, *Vital Speeches of the Day*, Dec. 16, 1935, 174–177.

26. *New York Times*, Nov. 29, 1962, 37; BBDO News Letter, Oct. 26, 1935, A8/5, BBDO; *Public Relations Journal* 34 (September 1978), 3; copy of ad in BBDO Newsletter, Feb. 1966, 34; "Bruce Barton Obit," n.d., A8/5, BBDO; BB to Samuel Crowther, Aug. 3, Nov. 28, 1936, Box 14, BB MSS; Woodward, *It's an Art*, 294. This ad also appears in Watkins, *100 Greatest Advertisements*, 192–193.

27. William L. Bird, Jr., *"Better Living": Advertising, Media, and the New Vocabulary of Business Leadership, 1935–1955* (Evanston: Northwestern University Press, 1999), 66–68. BBDO had won some DuPont business in 1929. *BBDO Newsletter*, Feb. 1956, 32.

28. BB to Paul Markman, Mar. 12, 1956, Box 76, BB MSS; Alfred D. Chandler, *Strategy and Structure: Chapters in the History of the Industrial Enterprise* (Cambridge: MIT Press, 1969), 78ff.; Bird, *"Better Living,"* 65–82, 97ff.

29. Affidavit, State of New York, County of New York, Apr. 1946, Box 144, BB MSS.

30. Clipping, *New York Herald Tribune*, Feb. 4, 1936, A9/4, BBDO; Henry E. North to BB, Apr. 9, 1934, Box 112, BB MSS; *Washington Post*, Jan. 7, 1937, 2. The 1936 figure was included in a Treasury Department report to Congress pursuant to a New Deal tax law.

31. Richard S. Tedlow, *Keeping the Corporate Image: Public Relations and Business, 1900–1950* (Greenwich, Conn.: JAI Press, 1979), 89–91; Joseph J. Seldin, *The Golden Fleece: Selling the Good Life to Americans* (New York: Macmillan, 1963), 32–33.

32. James Rorty, *Our Master's Voice, Advertising* (New York: John Day, 1934 [Arno Press reprint, 1976]), 10, 61, and passim.

33. Ibid., 13, 32–33, 66–67, 69, 312–331. Rorty's argument was confected of large dollops of Marx and especially Thorstein Veblen.

34. "Roy Durstine on Reading Jim Rorty," *Advertising & Selling*, May 10, 1934, 26, 69.

35. Bernard Sternsher, *Rexford Tugwell and the New Deal* (New Brunswick, N.J.: Rutgers University Press, 1964), 224–227, 244–249. A diluted measure was enacted in 1938.

36. BB speech, "The Deflation of Ballyhoo," Nov. 24, 1933, Box 145, BB MSS. Frederick Lewis Allen illustrated, but barely defined, "ballyhoo" in chap. 8 of *Only Yesterday*.

37. Osborn, "BBDO's Business Problem," March 1939, A5/1; Remarks by Osborn, Annual Stockholders Meeting, Feb. 25, 1956, A3/5, both BBDO; BB affidavit, Apr. 1946, Box 144, BB MSS; Brower, *Me, and Other Advertising Geniuses*, 46, 84. BBDO retained its "D," and the juicier speculations about the breakup did not leak into the press. Durstine went on to found his own agency.

38. Excerpts from *Space & Time*, Apr. 12 and 17, 1939, Box 18, BB MSS. The first of these articles attributed most of BBDO's success to Durstine and described Barton as still living in the twenties. Barton dismissed *Space & Time* as a "scandal sheet. Total[l]y unreliable."

39. (Ed Roberts?), "Radio Decade," n.d., 1, A7/3; BB, "For BBDO News Letter of May 19, 1939," A11/3; memo, n.d. (1970s?), "How the BBDO Cost System Works," A3/3, all BBDO; BBDO *Newsletter*, 75th anniversary issue (1966), 6; BB affidavit, Box 144, BB MSS; Donald E. Parente and John R. Osborn, "Alex F. Osborn," in Edd Applegate, ed., *The Ad Men and Women: A Biographical Dictionary of Advertising* (Westport, Conn.: Greenwood, 1994), 242–243.

40. BB, *A Parade of the States* (Garden City, N.Y.: Doubleday, Doran, 1932); Bird, "Better Living," 29–30, 32–35.

41. (WEB) to BB, Oct. 14, 1927; BB to Prof. Abbott Payson Usher, Oct. 25, 1927, both Box 111, BB MSS; ms drafts, Folder 86, WEB Papers; D. L. Chambers to BB, Dec. 31, 1929; BB to Chambers, July 26, 1935, both Box 105, BB MSS.

42. Irwin Barbour to BB, July 9, 1926, Box 97; Robert Cresswell to BB, July 7, 1932, Box 99; BB to Sumner Blossom, July 27, 1936, Box 82, all BB MSS.

43. See, e.g., Carl Becker's review in *New Republic*, Oct. 14, 1925, 207.

44. *Washington Post*, Dec. 8, 1930, 3; BB to Otto McFeely, Oct. 20, 1955. Box 41, BB MSS.

45. BB to Clinton Woods, Mar. 25, 1936, Box 73; BB to D. L. Chambers, Nov. 9, 1926, Box 105, both BB MSS; Alex Osborn, "Memo re Howard Letter," July 7, 1938, A11/3, BBDO; BB to Rev. C. Levi Shelby, Jan. 24, 1936, Box 63; BB to George M. Reynolds, Jan. 6, 1941, Box 9, both BB MSS.

46. BB to Donaldson Brown, June 11, 1951, Box 31, BB MSS; *New York Times*, Aug. 29, 1934, 36; Aug. 30, 1934, 40; BB to Roy Howard, Dec. 3, 1935, Box 100, Roy Howard MSS; Louise MacLeod to Zilpha Lloyd, Dec. 18, 1936. Box 39, BB MSS.

47. BB to Roy (Howard?), Feb. 22, (1937), Box 5, BB MSS; clipping, "Betsy Barton Injured Again," *New York World-Telegram*, Feb. 23, 1937, Box 124, Roy Howard MSS.

48. *New York Times*, Dec. 13, 1962, 5. The book dealing with her adjustment to disability was *And Now to Live Again* (New York: D. Appleton-Century, 1944).

49. Draft ad, "Don't Nominate the Weakest Candidate" (1932), Box 60, BB MSS; BB to R. L. Hurst, June 22, 1932, ibid.

50. "Strive for Goodwill Bruce Barton Urges," *Editor & Publisher*, May 16, 1936, 48.

51. Clipping, *Bakers' Helper*, Oct. 21, 1933, Box 119, BB MSS; cf. clipping, "Bruce Barton Says NRA Helps," *Minneapolis Tribune*, Oct. 12, 1933, Box 141, ibid. Barton was also friendly with FDR's secretary, Col. Louis McHenry Howe. BB to Howe, July 20, 1933, President's Personal File 7550, Franklin D. Roosevelt Library, Hyde Park, N.Y. (hereafter FDRL).

52. Clipping, BB column, "Fourteen Questionnaires," *New York Herald Tribune*, Dec. 10, 1933, Box 131; BB speech, "The Deflation of Ballyhoo," Nov. 24, 1933, Box 145; clipping, BB, "A Vacation," *New York Herald Tribune*, Feb. 4, 1934, Box 131, all BB MSS.

53. *Washington Post*, June 10, 1934, B7; BB to Paul C. Cabot, Nov. 15, 1934, Box 10, BB MSS. Barton organized several informal dinners to bring together Raymond Moley, one of FDR's brain trusters (but soon disaffected), and a group of "leading men in various industries." Louise MacLeod to J. S. Crutchfield, Sept. 4, 1934, Box 44, BB MSS; BB to T. K. Quinn, Sept. 19, 1934, ibid.

54. *Washington Post*, July 2, 1936, X9; clippings, *Baker's Helper*, Oct. 17, 1936, Box 119; *New York Evening Post*, May 12, 1936, Box 121, both BB MSS; BB, "The Public," *Vital Speeches of the Day*, Dec. 16, 1935, 174–175; BB speech, Outdoor Advertising Association of America, June 15, 1939, Box 136, BB MSS.

55. BB speech, Minneapolis Civic and Commerce Association, Feb. 27, 1935, Box 122, BB MSS; extracts from speech to the Congress of American Industry, Dec. 4, 1935, both Box 122, BB MSS.

56. Clippings, BB columns, *New York American*, Aug. 19, Sept. 11 and Sept. 30, Oct. 9, 1935; Jan. 11 and Jan. 22, 1936, all in Box 130, BB MSS.

57. BB to Stewart MacDonald, July 2, 1936; J. P. Yoder to BB, July 7, 1936, both PPF 7550, FDRL.

58. BB, "Address to Special Libraries Association Banquet," June 20, 1934; BB speech to Emergency Campaign of 1935, Boston, Dec. 19, 1934; BB Speech to Illinois Manufacturers' Association, May 12, 1936, all Box 136, ibid.

59. BB, "Who Won the War?" article reprint (McClure's Syndicate), n.d. (1929–1930), Box 97, BB MSS; "Bruce Barton Would Add a Clause to the Kellogg Peace Treaty," *Printers' Ink*, Jan. 31, 1929, 57.

60. The group included Reinhold Niebuhr and Norman Thomas; Barton was on its organizing committee. World Peaceways, Inc., reprint of BB, "Let's Advertise This Hell!" *American Magazine*, May 1932, Box 125, BB MSS; H. J. Barrett to BB, May 10, 1933, Box 73, ibid.; memorandum, Louise MacLeod to Ed Roberts, June 10, 1965, A8/5, BBDO; *Washington Post*, Jan. 27, 1938, 13; clipping, BB ad, in *Merchandise Manager* Feb. 1934, A8/5, BBDO.

61. BB to Thomas R. Shipp, Apr. 22, 1937, Box 63, BB MSS; *Chicago Tribune*, May 13, 1936, 35. Cf. Bird, "Better Living," 94–95.

7. MR. BARTON GOES TO WASHINGTON

1. *New York Times*, Aug. 17, 1932, 2; Oct. 25, 1932, 10; Oct. 29, 1932, 7; Aug. 10, 1937, 4; *New York Post*, Oct. 13, 1927, 35; BB to Robert H. Jackson, Sept. 22, 1937, Box 33, BB MSS.

2. BB to Sen. Mike Mansfield, Nov. 13, 1959, Box 42, BB MSS; BB to Paul Bellamy, June 18, 1936, Box 90, ibid.; clipping, *New York World-Telegram*, Sept. 22, 1936, Box 141, ibid.; memo, NL to RWH [Roy Howard], Oct. 26, 1934, Box 89, Roy Howard MSS.

3. Barton also checked with Durstine, who approved and "may even have been somewhat relieved to have me transferred to a different field of activity." BB to Hubert Eaton, Apr. 1, 1940, Box 19; BB to Ben Duffy, May 6, 1952, Box 18; BB to Roy Howard,

Oct. 21, 1937, Box 30, all BB MSS; *New York Times*, Aug. 10, 1937, 4; *New York Post*, Sept. 21, 1937, 30; Oct. 15, 1937, 7; Oct. 20, 1937, 17.

4. "Campaigner," *Tide*, Nov. 1, 1937, 16, A8/5, BBDO; *New York Times*, Aug. 18, 1937, 9; Oct. 2, 1937, 4.

5. "The Reminiscences of Roy S. Durstine," Columbia Oral History Project, 37–39; BB to George S. Jones, Jr., Feb. 13, 1952, Box 34, BB MSS; *New York Times*, Sept. 10, 1937, 12; *New York Daily News*, Oct. 1, 1937, Manhattan Section, 1. Durstine thought that the coverage in *Life* and *Look* (just before Election Day) helped make Barton a national political figure.

6. "Fact-finding" tours are now a time-honored campaign device. New York's Governor Nelson Rockefeller was later renowned for his blintz-gnoshing street strolls, punctuated with his "Hiya, fella" greetings. Hillary Rodham Clinton embarked on a "fact-finding" journey through the same state to launch her senatorial campaign in 2000.

7. *New York Herald Tribune*, Oct. 3, 1937, 2; Oct. 24, 1937, 27; *New York Daily News*, Oct. 8, 1937, 7.

8. Helen Woodward, "Republican in Sheep's Clothing," *Nation*, Nov. 5, 1938, 476; Seldes, "Barton, Barton, Barton and Barton," 327–329; clipping, *New York World-Telegram*, Oct. 26, 1937, Box 154, BB MSS.

9. Fred Smith, press releases, Oct. 22, 25, 1937, Box 136, BB MSS.

10. BB, Remarks, Republican Committee of 100, Oct. 15, 1937, Box 136, BB MSS; *New York Herald Tribune*, Oct. 17, 1937, 27; *New York Post*, Oct. 14, 1937, 9.

11. *New York Herald Tribune*, Oct. 21, 1937, 13; Oct. 24, 1937, 17.

12. BB Remarks as Temporary Chairman of Meeting of Republican County Committee, Sept. 27, 1937, Box 136; *New York Post*, Oct. 14, 1937, 9.

13. *New York Herald Tribune*, Oct. 22, 1937, 15; Fred Smith, press releases, Oct. 20, 22, 1937, Box 136, BB MSS.

14. Fred Smith, press release, Oct. 8, 1937, Box 136, BB MSS; *New York Post*, Sept. 30, 1937, 8; *New York Herald Tribune*, Oct. 15, 1937, 5; *New York Times*, Oct. 15, 1937, 25.

15. *New York Times*, Oct. 12, 1937, 14; *New York Daily News*, Oct. 25, 1937, 22; newspaper clipping, n.d. (1937), "An Open Letter by Samuel Untermyer," Box 154, BB MSS.

16. *New York Herald Tribune*, Oct. 26, 1937, 9, 11; Oct. 27, 1937, 4. It was Democratic mayoral candidate Jeremiah Mahoney who test-marketed red-baiting in 1937, charging that La Guardia's New York was "a haven for Red agitators destroying property and violating the laws." Ibid., Oct. 1, 1937, 18; Oct. 24, 1937, 1; *New York Post*, Oct. 25, 1937, 19.

17. Clipping, Heywood Broun, *New York Daily News*, July 7, 1939, Box 154, BB MSS; BB to Roy Howard, Oct. 29, 1937, Box 124, Howard MSS; *New York Times*, Nov. 3, 1937, 1.

18. *New York Herald Tribune*, Oct. 20, 1937, 4; "Congress Gets an Advertiser; Barton Elected," *Advertising Age*, Nov. 3, 1937, 4; BBDO News Letter, Nov. 6, 1937, A11/3, BBDO; Louise MacLeod to Anne Herendeen, Nov. 26, 1937, Box 27, BB MSS.

19. I owe the notion of "individuation" to Prof. David Farber's comment on my paper delivered at the Organization of American Historians meeting, Mar. 25, 2004.

20. *Tide* (Nov. 1, 1937), 16, reported that Barton played up his "personality," de-emphasizing "issues." On this general topic, see Susman, "'Personality' and the Making of Twentieth-Century Culture," 271–285.

21. BB to Roy W. Howard, Oct. 21, 1937, Box 30, BB MSS; BB, memorandum to Howard, Oct. 28, 1938, ibid.; *New York Times*, Oct. 17, 1937, 9.

22. BBDO News Letter, Nov. 6, 1937, A11/3, BBDO; clipping, *New York World-Telegram*, Nov. 3, 1937, ibid.; "Congress Gets an Advertiser," 4.

23. *New York Post*, Oct. 13, 1937, 35; *New York Herald Tribune*, Oct. 21, 1937, 13; Oct. 23, 1937, 18; Nov. 3, 1937, 11; BB to Frank L. Boyden, Sept. 3, 1937, Box 15, BB MSS.

24. BB to Hubert Eaton, Apr. 1, 1940, Box 19, BB MSS; BB, "What Surprised Me About Congress," *Redbook*, August 1938, 11; clipping, *Washington Daily News*, Dec. 5, 1937, Box 146; *Washington Post*, May 8, 1938, R15; BB to Sidney R. Rosenau, Dec. 20, 1939, Box 122; BB, Memorandum to Roy Howard, Oct. 29, 1938, Box 30, all BB MSS.

25. Some clients departed when Barton went to Congress. Osborn to Louis J. Kolb, Sept. 20, 1938, A11/3, BBDO; Johns to F. C. Kendall, Nov. 14, 1941, ibid.; BB to Stewart J. Alsop, July 9, 1958, Box 1, BB MSS.

26. *New York Times*, Nov. 14, 1937, 2; BB to James H. Perkins, Nov. 25, 1937, copy in Box 124, Roy Howard MSS; *Congressional Record* 82 (Nov. 29, 1937), A212–213; ibid. (Dec. 3, 1937), 840.

27. BB to Harry L. Hopkins, Oct. 17, 1936, Box 30; BB, "The Too High Price of 'Charm,'" article draft, Dec. 16, 1951, Box 127; BB to Paul Cabot, June 4, 1938, Box 10; BB to Henry R. Luce, Dec. 11, 1942, Box 89, all BB MSS.

28. BB to Roy Howard, Nov. 25 and 20, 1937, Box 124, Howard MSS. Barton's other committees were Census and Indian Affairs. *New York Times*, Nov. 25, 1937, 27.

29. *New York Times*, Dec. 5, 1937, 6. In 1940 an effort to amend the wage-hour law stirred conflict between House members from urban and rural districts; Barton supported the compromise amendments offered by New Deal Congresswoman Mary Norton. Ibid., Apr. 27, 1940, 7.

30. *Congressional Record* 83 (Jan. 4, 1938), 30; (Jan. 12, 1938), 360; (Jan. 31, 1938); 1323, (Mar. 24, 1938), 4066; *New York Sun*, Jan. 4, 1938, Box 155; BB, "Foreword to Dick Hyman's book," n.d. (Aug. 1938), Box 90; BB to Robertina Bruce, Nov. 9, 1938, Box 50, all BB MSS.

31. *New York Times*, Nov. 23, 1937, 6; *Congressional Record* 83 (June 13, 1938), A2609.

32. *Congressional Record* 83 (Jan. 12, 1938), 413; Sternsher, *Rexford Tugwell and the New Deal*, 249; Charles O. Jackson, *Food and Drug Legislation in the New Deal* (Princeton, N.J.: Princeton University Press, 1970), 174.

33. Press release, Sept. 21, 1938, Box 136, BB MSS. This speech was very much a part of his campaign for reelection. *New York Times*, Sept. 22, 1938, 14.

34. Remarks at Temple Emanuel, Oct. 13, 1938, Box 136, BB MSS; *New York Times*, Mar. 18, 1940, 12.

35. Remarks, Council Against Intolerance in America, Mar. 3, 1939, Box 136; clipping, *New York Herald Tribune*, June 29, 1939, Box 154, both BB MSS; *Congressional Record* 84 (June 28, 1939), 8155.

36. Newsletter, "Periscope Service," Oct. 1938, Box 120, BB MSS; Remarks before Massachusetts Republican Finance Committee, Sept. 22, 1938, Box 136, ibid.

37. Remarks, Jan. 28, 1938, Box 136, BB MSS; *New York Times*, Feb. 12, 1938, 32; Feb. 13, 1938, 39, 40.

38. Remarks, 15th Assembly District Republican Club, Apr. 21, 1938; remarks, Federation of Republican Women of Nassau County, Aug. 31, 1938, both Box 136, BB MSS; *New York Times*, Sept. 29, 1938, 18.

39. Remarks, Republican County Committee of Kings County, Mar. 24, 1939, Box 136, BB MSS; *New York Times*, Apr. 23, 1940, 12.

40. BB to W. Colston Leigh, Dec. 14, 1938, Box 28, BB MSS; clipping, *Commerce and Finance*, July 1938, A8/5, BBDO; *Washington Post*, June 30, 1938, X6.

41. Clipping, n.p., n.d. (1938), "Barton Advises Liberal Labor Policy in Party," Box 146, BB MSS; *Washington Post*, Apr. 16, 1939, 15; Sept. 24, 1938, X10.

42. *New York Times*, Feb. 16, 1940, 14; Ernest K. Lindley, "The New Conspiracy," *Washington Post*, Feb. 23, 1940, 11. On this episode, see Kathy M. Newman, *Radio Active: Advertising and Consumer Activism, 1935–1947* (Berkeley: University of California Press, 2004), 156–157.

43. Remarks, American Association of Advertising Agencies and Association of National Advertisers, May 12, 1939, Box 136, BB MSS.

44. *New York Times*, Mar. 15, 1938, 37; May 27, 1938, 33; Sept. 21, 1938, 35.

45. Remarks, 18th Ward Republican Picnic, Rochester, N.Y., Aug. 19, 1939, A8/5, BBDO. Contrast this statement to some of Barton's defenses of consumption in the previous decade.

46. BB speech, Convention of New York State Young Republican Clubs, May 27, 1939; remarks, Niagara County Pioneers Association, Aug. 16, 1939, both ibid.

47. *Washington Post*, May 29, 1939, 9; memo, n.d., enclosed in Robert McLean to Roy Durstine, July 7, 1938, Box 137, Roy Howard MSS. Durstine had asked for a progress report on his partner.

48. *New York Times*, Mar. 9, 1938, 2; *Washington Post*, May 13, 1938, 2.

49. *New York Times*, Mar. 29, 1940, 2; clipping, *Chicago American*, Mar. 30, 1939, Box 154, BB MSS.

50. BB to Roy Howard, Nov. 25, 1937, Box 124, Howard MSS; William E. Leuchtenburg, *Franklin D. Roosevelt and the New Deal, 1932–1940* (New York: Harper and Row, 1963), chaps. 10–11.

51. *New York Times*, Mar. 4, 1938, 2; Apr. 22, 1938, 7; Sept. 1, 1938, 3; Sept. 13, 1938, 3. The CIO did not endorse him. In 1940 Barton sponsored a proposal, favored by the AFL, to amend the Wagner Act. *Congressional Record*, 86 (June 7, 1940), 7776.

52. BB to Paul S. Clapp, July 12, 1938, Box 11, BB MSS; BB to Roy Howard, July 13, 1938, Box 30, ibid.; *New York Times*, July 15, 1938, 10; July 16, 1938, 2; Sept. 13, 1938, 9; Sept. 25, 1938, 4; Oct. 3, 1938, 16; Nov. 4, 1938, 17; Nov. 5, 1938, 12.

53. *New York Times*, Oct. 4, 1938, 26.

54. Ibid., Sept. 23, 1938, 27; BB obit by Ed Roberts, June 1965, 11, A8/5, BBDO.

55. Woodward, "Republican in Sheep's Clothing," 477. In fact the *Times* printed a number of stories about Liebman.

56. Photo, n.p., n.d. (1938), Betsey Barton scrapbook, Box 146, BB MSS.

57. *New York Times*, Nov. 10, 1938, 24; BB to Hubert Eaton, Apr. 1, 1940, Box 19, BB MSS; clipping, *New York Daily News*, Mar. 28, 1939, Box 146, ibid.; BBDO News Letter, Nov. 11, 1938, A11/3, BBDO.

58. Remarks before School of Politics of Women's National Republican Club, Dec. 6, 1938, Box 136, BB MSS.

59. Clipping, "John Roosevelt Seeks a Job with Bruce Barton Agency," n.d. (1938), Box 146, BB MSS; BBDO News Letter, Mar. 27, 1939; *Washington Post*, Jan. 29, 1938, 2; *Congressional Record* 82 (Dec. 3, 1937), 840.

60. *New York Post*, Nov. 3, 1937, 12; clipping, Akron dateline, Nov. 4, 1937, "Bruce Barton Boomed for Presidential Post," A11/3, BBDO.

61. Copy, Roy Howard to Wallace Alexander, June 30, 1938, A11/3, BBDO; Durstine to BB, July 5, 1938, Box 30, BB MSS; Durstine to Howard, July 7 and 12, 1938, Box 137, Howard MSS. His friend Harford Powel also boomed his candidacy. BBDO News Letter, Nov. 1938, A11/3, BBDO.

62. BB to William L. Chenery, Jan. 3, 1940, Box 12, BB MSS.

63. Clipping, *Air Conditioning & Refrigeration News*, Apr. 26, 1939, A8/5, BBDO. For a small sample of presidential blurbs: *New York Times*, July 2, 1939, IV, 2; clipping, n.p., n.d., "GOP Booms Advertising Man for Presidency in 1940" (Walter O'Keefe); Thomas L. Stokes, unknown Scripps-Howard paper, n.d., "Bruce Barton Listed in GOP 'Winter Book'"; clipping, Charles T. Lucey, *New York World-Telegram*, n.d. (May 1939), all Box 146, BB MSS; Mark Sullivan in *Washington Post*, July 30, 1939, B6; Robert C. Albright, ibid., Dec. 17, 1939, B3.

64. Ruth McKenney, "Bruce Barton's Clients," *New Masses*, Oct. 11, 1938, 14.

65. Clipping Fred Pasley, *New York Daily News*, Mar. 28, 1939, 8, Box 146. See also clippings in A11/3, BBDO.

66. Clipping, Drew Pearson and Robert S. Allen, "Washington Merry-Go-Round," *New York Daily Mirror*, July 22, 1938, Box 155, BB MSS; *Washington Post*, July 14, 1939, 2; July 17, 1939, 2; *New York Times*, Mar. 10, 1940, 4.

67. The search for an actress to portray Scarlett O'Hara in the movie *Gone with the Wind* and its premiere were hot news in 1939. The first names were those of film stars Carole Lombard, Paulette Goddard, Marion Davies, and Myrna Loy. Goldberg cartoon, n.d. (1939), Box 146, BB MSS; clipping, "Overseas Correspondence," *Economist*, July 30, 1938, ibid.

68. *Washington Post*, Feb. 23, 1940, 10; BB, remarks before U.S. Brewers Association, Oct. 3, 1938, Box 136, BB MSS; BB to Thomas W. Lamont, Nov. 16, 1939, A11/3, BBDO.

69. *Washington Post*, Apr. 16, 1939, 15; Dec. 16, 1939, 11; BB to Walter Winchell, Dec. 19, 1940, Box 73, BB MSS; clipping, Lancaster, Pa., ca. Dec. 19, 1939, Box 3, Series 10, Thomas E. Dewey Papers, Rush Rhees Library, University of Rochester.

70. BB to Roy Howard, June 21, 1939, Box 150, Howard MSS; *Congressional Record* 84 (June 28, 1939) 8155–8156; (June 29, 1939), 8307.

71. *Congressional Record* 85 (Oct. 30, 1939), A592–594; (Nov. 1, 1939), 1162–1163; BB to Raymond Clapper, Sept. 14, 1939; Apr. 25, 1941, Box 11, BB MSS; BB to Sen. Wallace H. White, Jr., Nov. 3, 1941, Box 72, ibid.

72. Undated compilation of polls on Neutrality repeal (Oct. 1939), Folder HR76A-F17.3, Committee Papers, Committee on Foreign Affairs, Neutrality Legislation, RG 233, Records of the U.S. House of Representatives, National Archives.

73. *New York Times*, Mar. 17, 1939, 14; BB to Catherine A. Sheridan, Dec. 14, 1939, Box 3, BB MSS.

74. *New York Times*, Aug. 30, 1938, 1; Sept. 4, 1938, IV, 6; Feb. 11, 1940, 47; Alex Osborn to Louis J. Kolb, Sept. 30, 1938; BB to T. P. Littlepage, Sept. 1, 1938; Osborn

memo, "About Barton for Senator," Oct. 2, 1940, all A11/3, BBDO; BB to F. W. Hatch, Oct. 6, 1939, Box 43, BB MSS; BB to Dean P. Taylor, Sept. 11, 1940, Box 123, ibid.

75. BB to Account Executives, Apr. 7, 1941, Box 5, BB MSS; *Washington Post*, June 16, 1940, 2; memorandum, BB to Thomas E. Dewey, Sept. 15, 1939, Box 17, BB MSS.

76. BB to Dewey, June 13, 1940, Box 3, Series 10, Dewey Papers; Steve Neal, *Dark Horse: A Biography of Wendell Willkie* (Garden City, N.Y.: Doubleday, 1984), 91; BB to Willkie, Apr. 16, 1940, Box 43, BB MSS; BB to Donald Bruce Johnson, May 10, 1960, Box 72, ibid.

77. Warren Moscow, *Roosevelt and Willkie* (Englewood Cliffs, N.J.: Prentice-Hall, 1968), 40, 52, 55; *New York Times*, June 13, 1940, 1, 9; Herbert S. Parmet and Marie B. Hecht, *Never Again: A President Runs for a Third Term* (New York: Macmillan, 1968), 113; BB to James H. Perkins, Apr. 15, 1940, Box 51, BB MSS.

78. BB to Donald Bruce Johnson, May 10, 1960, Box 72, BB MSS; Moscow, *Roosevelt and Willkie*, 68–69; *New York Times*, June 23, 1940, 2; *Washington Post*, June 16, 1940, 2; June 27, 1940, 5; BB to Osborn, June 30, 1940, A11/3, BBDO.

79. Part of Barton's reluctance may have been a desire to stay out of bruising New York political rivalries. BB to AFO, June 30, 1940, A11/3, BBDO; Osborn memo, Oct. 2, 1940, ibid.; transcript, phone message, Roy Howard to BB, Sept. 26, 1940, Box 162, Howard MSS; *New York Times*, Sept. 2, 1940, 13; *Washington Post*, Sept. 27, 1940, 3; Sept. 30, 1940, 3; *Time*, Oct. 7, 1940, 16.

80. *New York Times*, Sept. 25, 1940, 18; Sept. 26, 1940, 13; Sept. 27, 1940, 1, 14; Sept. 28, 1940, 1, 8; *Washington Post*, Sept. 30, 1940, 3.

81. *Washington Post*, Aug. 21, 1940, 17; clipping, *Chicago Herald-American*, Feb. 15, 1940, Box 3, Series 10, Dewey Papers.

82. BB speech, Cooperstown, Oct. 5, 1940, Box 145, BB MSS. A *Washington Post* editorial (Oct. 8, 1940, 6) queried several of his premises: the middle class was not unorganized; nor had it a unified interest for the New Deal to ignore. And anyway, Barton should cease his divisive practice of "stressing class differences."

83. *New York Times*, Oct. 22, 1940, 18; Oct. 4, 1940, 17; Oct. 6, 1940, 43; Oct. 11, 1940, 15; Oct. 27, 1940, 41; press release, BB speech, Jamestown, N.Y., Oct. 16, 1940, A8/5, BBDO.

84. BB to Donald Bruce Johnson, May 10, 1960, Box 72, BB MSS. The article was "Inside Willkie's Head," *Collier's*, Sept. 21, 1940, 15ff.

85. Galbraith, *Name-Dropping: From F.D.R. On* (Boston: Houghton Mifflin, 1999), 26. Barton's source on the moment was apparently manpower expert Anna Rosenberg. BB to Mark Blank, June 9, 1960, Box 9, BB MSS.

86. The line was said to resemble "Wynken, Blynken and Nod." *New York Times*, Oct. 29, 1940, 17; Oct. 30, 1940, 20; Parmet and Hecht, *Never Again*, 260, 263.

87. Clipping, *New York World-Telegram*, Oct. 17, 1940, A11/3, BBDO; *Life*, Oct. 21, 1940, 100–101; *New York Times*, Oct. 4, 1940, 17; Nov. 3, 1940, 55; Nov. 5, 1940, 20.

88. *New York Times*, Nov. 3, 1940, 53; Nov. 7, 1940, 20; BB speech excerpts, Oct. 5, 1940, Box 167, Howard MSS; Roy Howard to Willkie, Sept. 21, 1940, ibid; BB telegram to Howard, ca. Sept. 21, 1940, Box 167, ibid.; "The Dunn Survey Forecast of the Presidential Election 1940," n.d. (ca. Oct. 10, 1940), Box 163, ibid.; Parmet and Hecht, *Never Again*, 244, 278.

89. Richard M. Fried, "Voting Against the Hammer and Sickle: Communism as an Issue in American Politics," in William H. Chafe, ed., *The Achievement of American Liberalism: The New Deal and Its Legacies* (New York: Columbia University Press, 2003), 104–105.

90. BB to Joe R. Hanley, Nov. 9, 1940, Box 3, Series 10, Dewey Papers; BB to Roy Hoffman, Nov. 7, 1940, Box 27; BB to Raymond E. Baldwin, Nov. 20, 1940, Box 3; Louise MacLeod to Robert Bedner, Nov. 30, 1948, Box 7; BB to Mark Blank, June 9, 1960, Box 9, all BB MSS.

8. THE LATER YEARS

1. *Washington Post*, Nov. 10, 1940, B8; Nov. 22, 1940, 1; *New York Times*, Jan. 27, 1941, 1; Jan. 28, 1941, 9; July 18, 1941, 21; Donald R. McCoy, *Landon of Kansas* (Lincoln: University of Nebraska Press, 1966), 463; BB to Alfred M. Landon, Feb. 5, 1941, Box 37, BB MSS; BB to John Ellis, July 24, 1941, Box 19, ibid.

2. Future agency president Charlie Brower suggested that this "was not exactly a generous gesture." The owners "simply wanted to unload." "The Duffy Story: A Tap on His Shoulder," *Printers' Ink*, Nov. 1, 1957, 22; BBDO Newsletter, 75th Anniversary, 1966, 5–6; Brower, *Me, and Other Advertising Geniuses* 83, 142–143.

3. BBDO News Letter, Aug. 29, 1941, A8/5, BBDO; BB to Egbert White, Nov. 27, 1942, Box 72, BB MSS.

4. The gloom was premature. Bates quickly acquired accounts of some enduring food, soap, and liquor products and by fall was enjoying good times. Reeves to "Dad and Mother," Mar. 3 and Sept. 19, 1942, Box 1, Rosser Reeves MSS, Wisconsin Historical Society.

5. Clipping, *Wichita Beacon*, Feb. 15, 1940, Box 120, BB MSS; BB to Joe Hollister, Aug. 25, 1941, Box 116, ibid.; AAAA Bulletin 1240, Sept. 27, 1941, Box 6, Thomas D'Arcy Brophy MSS, Wisconsin Historical Society.

6. Barton served as AFA's chairman of the board in 1943. BB to Paul W. Kesten, Aug. 12, 1942; John Benson to BB, Apr. 22, 1942, both Box 118; clipping, *Chicago Tribune*, June 30, 1943, Box 142, all BB MSS.

7. Draft letter to AAAA nonmembers, July 1943, Box 4, Brophy MSS; *Chicago Tribune*, June 23, 1942, 25. See Robert Griffith, "The Selling of America: The Advertising Council and American Politics, 1942–1960," *Business History Review* 57 (Autumn 1983), 388–412.

8. Marchand, *Creating the Corporate Soul*, 320; BB to Lucious Boomer, Apr. 20, 1942, Box 29; BB "To the Men and Women of BBDO," Dec. 23, 1941, Box 144; BB to George Bushfield, July 16, 1943, Box 9; BB to Maj. Harry A. Berk, July 28, 1943, Box 7; copy, George Gouge to Rear Adm. F. E. M. Whiting, Aug. 30, 1944, Box 72, all BB MSS; BBDO International, *Annual Report 1975* (Mar. 1976), 21.

9. Mark H. Leff, "The Politics of Sacrifice on the American Home Front in World War II," *Journal of American History* 77 (Mar. 1991), 1312; William H. Johns to F. C. Kendall, Nov. 14, 1941, A11/3, BBDO.

10. V-mail, Maj. Harry A. Berk to BB, n.d. (1943), Box 7, BB MSS. Also see Frank W. Fox, *Madison Avenue Goes to War: The Strange Military Career of American Advertising, 1941–1945* (Provo: Brigham Young University Press, 1975).

11. BB to Gertrude Lane, June 10, 1941, Box 104; Louise MacLeod to A. W. Holman, Oct. 22, 1941, Box 114; BB to Pvt. Nicholas Mauro, Apr. 14, 1943, Box 43; BB to D. M. Bressler, June 21, 1946, Box 9; BB to BB, Jr., Nov. 28, 1944, Box 6, all BB MSS.

12. BBDO News Letter, Aug. 29, 1941, A8/4, BBDO; Roberts, "Beggars, Peddlers and Advertising Men" (1964), 399, A7/3, BBDO; BB to John Ellis, July 24, 1941, Box 19; BB to Jack Denove, Sept. 29, 1943, Box 17; BB to William Robinson, ca. June 11, 1945, Box 47, all BB MSS; entries of July 26 and 27, 1943, vol. 180, 19–21, 180, 194, Henry Morgenthau, Jr., Diaries, FDRL. My thanks to Eric Smith for his prospecting at the FDR Library.

13. BB to Ernest R. Breach, Jan. 16, 1947, Box 120, BB MSS.

14. BB to E. C. Lechner, Feb. 1, 1955, Box 95; BB to William C. D'Arcy, Apr. 12, 1948, Box 75, both BB MSS; BBDO Newsletter Extra, Sept. 1, 1972, A9/4, BBDO; "The Duffy Story: A Tap on His Shoulder," 16, 18; BB, Foreword to Ben Duffy, *Advertising Media and Markets* (New York: Prentice-Hall, 1939), v, copy in A9/4, BBDO.

15. BB to Frank G. Hall, Nov. 18, 1948, Box 78; BB to D'Arcy, Apr. 12, 1948, Box 75; BB to James Davidson, Nov. 7, 1949, Box 91, all BB MSS.

16. BB to Bob Anderson, Aug. 19, 1955, Box 118, BB MSS; BBDO News Letter, May 18, 1949, A8/5, BBDO; Bobb Chaney to Ben Duffy, May 21, 1954, Box 7, BB MSS.

17. Homer Vilas to Frank Boyden, Nov. 22, 1950, Box 78, BB MSS; memos, BB to Ben Duffy, Apr. 4, 1950, Apr. 21, 1953, Box 75, ibid. Barton cited the conclusions of specialists at a recent American Heart Association convention, who argued that avoiding tension was the key to avoiding heart disease.

18. BBDO, "The First 100 Years," 36, 46; memo, BB to Bob Foreman, Mar. 14, 1951, Box 81, BB MSS.

19. Memo, BB to Duffy et al., June 15, 1954; James B. Braun to BB, July 20, 1955; memo, H. H. Haupt to BB, July 18, 1955, all Box 78; BB to Duffy, Sept. 6, 1956, Box 76; Bayard Pope to Charlie Brower et al., June 15, 1957, ibid.; BB to Rep. Leslie C. Arends, Apr. 15, 1958, Box 2, all BB MSS.

20. BBDO, "How an Advertising Agency Works" (1954), 7, 10, Box 76, BB MSS; BB to Walter C. Carpenter, Jr., May 19, 1955, ibid.

21. BBDO *Newsletter*, Aug. 1959, Box 142; BBDO International Client List, Oct. 10, 1962, Box 7; James S. Milloy to BB, Oct. 27, 1947, Box 43, all BB MSS; *Editor & Publisher*, Feb. 23, 1957, 10; clippings, *The Advertiser*, March 1957; and "BBD&O Says It Didn't Plan Eisenhower Show," *New York Journal-American*, Dec. 27(?), 1957, both A7/3, BBDO; Martin Mayer, *Whatever Happened to Madison Avenue? Advertising in the '90s* (Boston: Little, Brown, 1991), 219–220; e-mail, Marcia Kamien to author, Jan. 6, 2002. Mayer speculated—wildly—that the austerity might be traced to the sufficiency of Barton's status as a "lay preacher of American capitalism" or because he was simply "cheap."

22. Memorandum, BB to Brower, Nov. 7, 1952, Box 78; clipping, *Chicago Defender*, Dec. 27, 1952, Box 28, both BB MSS; anonymous source.

23. BB to William Benton, Apr. 14, 1941, Box 123, BB MSS.

24. BB to Philip LeBoutellier, Oct. 3, 1951, Box 93, ibid.; e-mail, Robert D. Barton to author, Jan. 22, 2005.

25. Anonymous report of dinner with Willkie at Irita Van Doren's, Jan. 16, 1941, President's Secretary's File: Willkie, *President Franklin D. Roosevelt's Office Files,*

1933–1945 (Bethesda: University Publications of America, 1994), Part 4 (Subject Files), microfilm Reel 45, frame 0788.

26. Barton strove to build financial support for Dennis. BB to Harry Elmer Barnes, July 1, 1948; BB to Dennis, Oct. 1, 1948.; BB to Ernest T. Weir, May 17, 1951, all Box 17, ibid.

27. BB to Henry R. Luce, Mar. 4, 1941, Box 40, BB MSS.

28. BB to Raymond Moley, May 14, 1943, Box 110, BB MSS; BB to Henry Luce, Apr. 5, 1943, Box 40, ibid.

29. BB, "Post-War Book," second rewrite, 40–42, 106, 108, 142–145, 164, Box 134, BB MSS.

30. Henry Morton Robinson to Dick Simon, Jan. 12, 1943; BB to Burton Rascoe, Feb. 8, 1943; Ken McCormick to BB, Feb. 16, 1943; BB to McCormick, Feb. 18, 1943, all Box 110; D. L. Chambers to BB, Apr. 15, 1943, Box 105; BB to Chambers, Apr. 19, 1943, ibid.; Paul Palmer to BB, Mar. 25, 1943; M. L. Schuster to BB, Jan. 20, 1943; BB to Raymond Moley, May 14, 1943; BB to Chambers, Jan. 19, 1944; Louise MacLeod to Chambers, Apr. 3, 1944, all Box 110, all BB MSS.

31. BB to Charles A. Beard, Nov. 24, 1947, Box 42; BB to Ernest Gruening, Oct. 6, 1949, Box 1; BB to Sidney J. Weinberg, Jan. 11, 1951, Box 15; BB to John B. Beasley, Dec. 22, 1950, Box 91; BB to Gardner Cowles, May 11, 1950, Box 97, all BB MSS. On the cold war thinking of prewar isolationists, see Justus D. Doenecke, *Not to the Swift: The Old Isolationists in the Cold War Era* (Lewisburg, Pa.: Bucknell University Press, 1979).

32. His party, said Thomas, had failed to qualify for a place on the ballot. BB to Norman Thomas, July 10, 1950; Thomas to BB, July 12, 1950, both Box 60, Norman Thomas MSS, New York Public Library.

33. Barton blamed this trend on "the Government's battalions of press agents and subservient columnists." Clipping, BB column, "'Stand by the President,'" n.d. (October 1950), Box 91, BB MSS.

34. Barton and O'Connor were friendly. *Chicago Tribune*, May 13, 1936, 35; Fried, "Voting Against the Hammer and Sickle," 103–104.

35. BB to Dewey, Sept. 13, 1946, Box 17; BB draft, untitled, "WE Republican members of Congress . . ." (1945), Box 9; Dewey to BB, Sept. 17, 1946, Box 17; Eugene Lyons to BB, Nov. 18, 1948, Box 40; Eugene Lyons memo, "Redbaiters, Inc.," n.d. (1948), ibid., all BB MSS.

36. BB to Gardner Cowles, May 11, 1950, Box 97; BB memo re "General Eisenhower," July 14, 1952, Box 19; BB memorandum to Tax Cumings et al., June 16, 1950, Box 75; BB to John Hooper, Dec. 7, 1953, Box 28, all BB MSS.

37. BB, Jr., to BB, n.d. (ca. May 1954), Box 6, ibid.; clipping, BB, "What's Television Doing to Us?" *Pictorial Review*, October 1954, Box 36, John Francis Neylan Papers, Bancroft Library, University of California, Berkeley; BB memo, "Good People Get Mad About the Wrong Things," n.d. (1951), Box 140, BB MSS.

38. Jack Wren handled clearance for BBDO and its sponsors' programs. BB to Paul R. Milton, Feb. 3, 1954, Box 43; BB diary entry, Sept. 26, 1951, Box 149, both BB MSS; John Cogley, *Report on Blacklisting*, II, *Radio-Television* ([New York]: Fund for the Republic, 1956), 23, 60, 90, 115–121.

39. Memo, J. D. Danforth to BB et al., Aug. 1, 1953, Box 75; BB to U.S. Board of Parole, Aug. 28, 1950, Box 37; BB to Ellis Lardner, Aug. 10, 15, 1950, ibid., all BB MSS.

40. BB to Ward Greene, Nov. 29, 1945, Box 90, BB MSS; "A Businessman's Doubts on Government Spending," *Fortune*, February 1942, 136ff.; clipping, *New York Daily News*, Nov. 16, 1949, Box 121, BB MSS.

41. BB to J. J. Nance, July 15, 1942, Box 118; BB to Grace E. Billings, Aug. 30, 1951, Box 92; BB to Ralph H. Grieves, Aug. 10, 1951, ibid.; BB to Hon. Charles A. Eaton, Oct. 25, 1948, Box 19; "In memory of Jose Ortega y Gasset," n.d. (1955), Box 50; BB to Edwin F. Daikin, May 27, 1947, Box 15, all BB MSS.

42. "A Businessman's Doubts on Government Spending," 184; clipping, *New York Daily News*, Nov. 16, 1949, A8/5, BBDO.

43. BB to Henry Allen, Nov. 7, 1941, Box 124; *Denvertising*, n.d. (Nov. 1953); identical passages in "Bruce Barton Appeals to Industrialists in Drive," *Detroit Free Press*, Sept. 28, 1946, 3; and "Community Chest speech by Bruce Barton," n.d. (1953), all Box 120, BB MSS.

44. BB to D. L. Chambers, June 1, 1953, Box 105; BB to Carroll P. Newton, Aug. 22, 1944, Box 49, both ibid.

45. *New York Times*, Jan. 10, 1950, 10.

46. BB to William Benton, June 6, 1947, Box 7; BB to Paul G. Hoffman, July 3, 1951, Box 92; BB column, n.d. (ca. May 14, 1950), Box 91; BB to Harry Elmer Barnes, June 1, 1949, Box 120, all BB MSS. See Ellis, *Essays in War-Time* (Boston: Houghton Mifflin, 1917).

47. Press release, BB speech to Proprietary Association, "The War and After the War," May 19, 1942, Box 174, Roy Howard MSS; clippings, *Chicago Daily News*, May 20, 1949, Box 120, BB MSS; Robert C. Ruark, "Russkie-Rouser," *New York World-Telegram*, Mar. 1, 1949, ibid.

48. Clipping, *Seattle Post-Intelligencer*, Jan. 13, 1948, Box 124; draft, "Tomorrow," n.d. (ca. Apr. 21, 1950), Box 90; clipping, *Buffalo News*, Oct. 26, 1956, Box 123; speech material with BB to Harvey Firestone, Apr. 16, 1959, Box 20, all BB MSS.

49. BBDO, "One Million New Television Viewers Every Three Weeks," Apr. 4, 1950; BBDO Television Research Bulletin #143, both A4/3, BBDO; memo, BB to Fred Barrett et al., Apr. 9, 1957, Box 119, BB MSS; *Editor & Publisher*, June 15, 1957, 78.

50. BBDO, "The First 100 Years," 37, 39, 44–45, 47, 51, 52; memo, BB to Bob Foreman, Apr. 2, 1956, Box 78, BB MSS; Kent Anderson, *Television Fraud: The History and Implications of the Quiz Show Scandals* (Westport, Conn.: Greenwood, 1978), 35–36, 78; BB to N. R. Sutherland, Jan. 28, 1957, Box 79, BB MSS.

51. De Witt and Lila Wallace, publishers of *Reader's Digest*, were Barton's good friends. "Brower of BBDO," *Fortune*, Mar. 1958, 67; sheets listing annual agency highlights, 1937–1966, n.d., A7/3, BBDO; reprint, Harry W. McMahan, "BBDO Is 'Best' Three Out of Four Times—What Makes It Tick?" *Advertising Age*, July 17, 1964, ibid.

52. The hero of *The Man in the Gray Flannel Suit* was actually in public relations. BB to Rev. Robert J. McCracken, June 9, 1958, Box 41, BB MSS; AFO, remarks at stockholders' annual meeting, Feb. 25, 1956, A3/5, BBDO. For another rebuttal to advertising's critics, see *The Huckster's Revenge* (New York: Thomas Nelson & Sons, 1959) by Fred Manchee, retired treasurer of BBDO.

53. BB, "Are We Biting Off More Than We Can Chew?" *Reader's Digest*, December 1948, 45–48; BB to Gardner Cowles, May 27, 1949, Box 97, BB MSS.

54. BB, "The Fallacy of the Atlantic Pact," *Look*, Sept. 13, 1949, 32, 35, 38. See Thomas G. Paterson, ed., *Cold War Critics: Alternatives to American Foreign Policy in the Truman Years* (Chicago: Quadrangle Books, 1971).

55. BB to Ward Greene, June 10, Nov. 3, 1949; Greene to BB, Sept. 15, 1949, and attachment, all Box 90; BB to Bruce Bliven, Nov. 23, 1954, Box 9; BB to Eugene Pulliam, Sept. 16, 1949, Box 90; BB to Elliot Bell, Sept. 17, 1948, Box 7; BB, Jr., to BB, Oct. 17, 1949, Box 6, all BB MSS; *Time*, Oct. 24, 1949, 82. Typescripts of columns are in Box 127, BB MSS.

56. Ward Greene to BB, July 14, 1955; BB to Greene, July 18, 1955; BB to Pearl Buck, Oct. 20, 1955, all Box 90, BB MSS.

57. BB to Greene, June 10, 1949, Box 90; BB to Henry Luce, Dec. 11, 1942, Box 89, both ibid. Among other assets, Pete brought the perspective of a younger generation.

58. BB to Louise Locke, Jan. 27, 1957, Box 29; BB to D. L. Chambers, July 12, 1935; Chambers to BB, July 15, 1935; BB to Chambers, Jan. 3, 1949, Sept. 8, 15, 1952, all Box 105, ibid.

59. Herman Ziegner to BB, Aug. 10, 1955, and Feb. 24, 1956, Box 105; D. L. Chambers to BB, May 6 and June 8, 1959; BB to Chambers, May 25 and June 5, 1959; notes on *The Man Nobody Knows* attached to Ross G. Baker to BB, June 2, 1955, all Box 105, BB MSS.

60. Indeed, a small religious house that published a reprint of this version unknowingly claimed: "The style and language used in this book represents [*sic*] the voice of America in the 1920s." Editor's Note in *The Man Nobody Knows* (Stone Mountain, Ga.: GA Publishing, 1998).

61. BB to Louise Locke, Jan. 17, 1957, Box 39; De Witt Wallace to BB, Feb. 16, 1965, Box 144; "Copies sold to 3–1–59," list attached to D. L. Chambers to BB, n.d., Box 105, all BB MSS.

62. BB to D. L. Chambers, June 24, 1954; Chambers to BB, Dec. 24, 1953, and June 17, 1954, all Box 105, BB MSS.

63. BB to BB, Jr., Dec. 9, 1941, Box 6; BB to Mark W. Cresap, May 21, 1942, Box 14, both ibid.

64. *Washington Post*, Oct. 27, 1944, 6; June 13, 1948, S12; BB to Zilpha Lloyd, Dec. 15, 1944, Box 39; BB to BB, Jr., Feb. 11, 1944, Box 6; BB to Jacob Billikopf, Nov. 1, 1946, Box 8, all BB MSS; *New York Times Book Review*, May 19, 1957, VII, 2; e-mail, Robert D. Barton to author, Jan. 22, 2005. She also wrote the novel *Shadow of the Bridge* (New York: Duell, Sloan and Pearce, 1950).

65. BB to Mr./Mrs. Randall Barton, Apr. 10, 1947, Box 6; BB to Margaret A. Hogan, Nov. 3, 1955, Box 145; BB to Otto McFeely, June 2, 1960, Box 41; BB to Zilpha Lloyd, Dec. 8, 1943, and Dec. 5, 1945, Box 39, all BB MSS; *Time*, Oct. 11, 1963, 23.

66. BB to James Milloy, Nov. 9, 1951, Box 43, BB MSS; *New York Times*, Nov. 21, 1951.

67. BB to Martin Flavin, Apr. 15, 1952, Box 101, BB MSS; BB to Thomas Dreier, July 25, 1960, Box 18, ibid.; BB, "After a Long Illness," *Reader's Digest*, Apr. 1952, 1–3.

68. BB to Joseph Jacobs, June 29, 1953, Box 21; BB to E. E. Calkins, Apr. 20, 1959, Box 10; BB to Henry Doorly, Dec. 19, 1960, Box 3; BB to Otto McFeely, Feb. 20, 1956, Box 41, all BB MSS.

69. Barton traveled with her as well. BB to Mary Hood, Sept. 17, 1952, Box 81; BB to Louis R. Lurie, Oct. 8, 1956, Box 40; BB to Henry Deschampsneufs, Oct. 31, 1956, Box 55, all BB MSS.

70. One reviewer compared her to James Joyce's "Molly Bloom" in her influence on the literary set. *New York Times*, July 24, 1967, 24; Sept. 28, 1989, D22; Dec. 29, 1996, SM38; Burton Bernstein, *Thurber: A Biography* (New York: Dodd, Mead, 1975).

71. Daily Diary, Apr. 30, Sept. 17, Oct. 14, 1959; Sept. 8, 1960; Apr. 21–22, 1961, Box 147; Arends-BB correspondence, Box 2, both BB MSS. MacLeod may have kept the diary.

72. BB to L. B. Swift, July 27, 1949, Box 80; BB to Carl Wahlstrom, Nov. 28, 1956, Box 103; BB to Harry Ames Putnam, July 5, 1956, ibid., all BB MSS. Webster Barton Beatty became a dentist, and his children, to whom Barton extended help and endearment for years, also flourished. See Box 9, BB MSS.

73. Barton gave Randall power-of-attorney around 1960. *New York Times*, Dec. 13, 1962, 5; Sept. 30, 1963, 29; *Time*, Oct. 11, 1963, 123; Randall Barton to Robert S. Bray, Feb. 8, 1967, Box 144, BB MSS.

74. BB to Henry H. Allen, Jan. 7, 1943, Box 11; BB to Rev. George A. Buttrick, May 18, 1928, Dec. 18, 1931, Nov. 16, 1937, all Box 42; BB to Mrs. Henry H. Jackson, Dec. 16, 1942; BB to Ted Speers, Apr. 16, 1948, June 21, 1954, Feb. 6, 1956; Speers to BB, Jan. 6, 1949; BB to Mrs. Claude E. Forkner, May 26, 1952, all Box 11, all BB MSS.

75. Clipping, *New York Herald Tribune*, Jan. 23, 1942; BB, memo to Dewey, June 22, 1944, both Box 17; BB, memo to Herbert Brownell, Jr., July 12, 1944, Box 9, all BB MSS; BB to Dewey, Aug. 24, 1944, Oct. 11, 1944, Box 12, Series 4, Dewey Papers; BB to Dewey, Sept. 26, 1944, Box 3, Series 10, ibid.

76. BB to Brownell, Oct. 30, 1945 (with attachment), June 28, 1948, Box 9, BB MSS; BB to Dewey, Feb. 20, July 2, 1948, Box 3, Series 10, Dewey Papers; BB to W. H. Lawrence, Nov. 4, 1959, Box 17, BB MSS; Richard Norton Smith, *Thomas E. Dewey and His Times* (New York: Simon and Schuster, 1982), 512.

77. BB to Harry Darby, Feb. 20, 1961, Box 35; BB to Paul J. Carter, Apr. 10, 1952, Box 5; BB to Edward J. Bermingham, June 17, 1952, Box 8; BB to Eugene C. Pulliam, July 29, 1952, Box 55, all BB MSS.

78. BB to Stewart J. Alsop, July 9, 1958, Box 1; BB to Duffy, Sept. 15, 22, 23, and ca. Sept. 19, 1952, all Box 19, ibid. BBDO was offered the GOP's campaign advertising in 1936 and 1940 but turned it down. BB to Account Executives, Apr. 7, 1942, Box 5, ibid.

79. Bates "loaned" Reeves to BBDO for the campaign. Kathleen Hall Jamieson, *Packaging the Presidency: A History and Criticism of Presidential Campaign Advertising*, 3rd ed. (New York: Oxford University Press, 1996), 42, 86–87; Craig Allen, *Eisenhower and the Mass Media: Peace, Prosperity, and Prime-Time TV* (Chapel Hill: University of North Carolina Press, 1993), 130–131; Vance Packard, *The Hidden Persuaders* (New York: Pocket Books, 1958 [David McKay, 1957]), 166.

80. Packard, *Hidden Persuaders*, 160 and chap. 17, passim. On advertising and politics, see Lizabeth Cohen, *A Consumers' Republic: The Politics of Mass Consumption in Postwar America* (New York: Alfred A. Knopf, 2003), 331ff.; Robert V. Westbrook, "Politics as Consumption: Managing the Modern American Election," in Fox and Lears, *Culture of Consumption*, 145–173; and Jensen, "Armies, Admen, and Crusaders," 33–50.

81. *New York Times*, Dec. 27, 1957, 4. For another hostile Truman reference to BBDO, see ibid., Nov. 22, 1959, 53.

82. Reeves to Ben Duffy, Nov. 13, 1952, Box 29, Reeves MSS; clipping, *New York Herald Tribune*, June 4, 1953, A7/3, BBDO; memo, Ben Duffy to BB et al., Apr. 27, 1954, Box 18, BB MSS; *New York Times*, Jan. 9, 1963, 15.

83. BB to Brownell, Nov. 17, 1952, Box 9; BB to "Mike" Cowles, Jan. 17, 1956, and Jan. 28, 1958, Box 13; BB to Leslie C. Arends, Nov. 12, 1958, Box 2, all BB MSS.

84. BB to James Milloy, Dec. 19, 1950, Box 43; BB to Sen. George W. Malone, May 10, 1948, Box 42; BB to Margaret A. Hogan, Nov. 3, 1955, Box 145, all BB MSS; BBDO News Letter, Jan. 7, 1943, A8/5, BBDO. His service on State Street's board began in 1943.

85. MacLeod to Mayor William O'Dwyer, Aug. 16, 1948, Box 48, BB MSS; *New York Times*, May 23, 1931, 13.

86. Henry N. Flynt to BB, Sept. 18, 1947, Box 15; Frank [Boyden] to MacLeod, Aug. 24, 1965, Box 144; program, "Dedication: The Bruce Barton Dormitory, Deerfield Academy," Nov. 11, 1962, Box 16; BB to DeWitt Wallace, May 17, 1957, Box 41; BB to Harvey M. Rice, June 10, 1959, ibid.; Wallace to BB, Feb. 16, 1965, Box 144, all BB MSS.

87. Tribute, "Betsey Alice Barton, 1917–1962," Box 146; BB to Margaret Hogan, Nov. 3, 1955, Box 145; clippings, *New York Herald Tribune*, June 11, 1954, and *New York Journal-American*, June 18, 1959, Box 31, all ibid.; *New York Times*, June 22, 1951, 27; BB to Thomas D'Arcy Brophy, n.d. (1954), Box 27, Brophy MSS. It was mostly Barton's name that the United Negro College Fund mobilized. In the late 1950s he rejected their idea of titling a promotional booklet *The Colleges Nobody Knows*. "The Reminiscences of Dr. William J. Trent, Jr." (1981), Columbia Oral History Research Office, 84.

88. BB to E. E. Calkins, Apr. 20, 1959, Box 10, BB MSS.

89. BB to John Farrar, June 20, 1951, Box 46; *The Advertiser*, Feb. 1950, Box 46; BB to Everett R. Clinchy, Jan. 29, 1957, ibid., all BB MSS.

90. *New York Times*, Jan. 16, 1957, 40; Feb. 13, 1961, 34; *Printers' Ink*, Feb. 9, 1961, 54; Charles W. Cole, honorary degree citation (1957), Box 1, BB MSS.

91. Brower, *Me, and Other Advertising Geniuses*, 17–19; *New York Times*, July 9, 1957, 19; BB to Anne Hard, Apr. 11, 1961, Box 25; MacLeod to Dr. Irvine H. Page, Aug. 22, 1957, Box 4; BB to Dr. Francis S. Hutchins, Nov. 28, 1960, Box 7; BB to Dr. George F. Cahill, Oct. 14, 1957, Box 10; BB to Randall Barton, Oct. 29, 1957, Box 6; BB to Charles H. Bell, Dec. 30, 1957, Box 77, all BB MSS.

92. BB to Earnest E. Calkins, Apr. 20, 1959, Box 10; BB to Philip J. Kelly, Dec. 13, 1961, Box 35; BB to Charles H. Brower, Nov. 3, 1961, Box 9, all BB MSS; Brower, *Me, and Other Advertising Geniuses*, 19.

93. BB to Milton Lomask, Jan. 27, 1961, Box 39; desk diaries, 1959–1961, Box 147, both BB MSS.

94. *New York Times*, Feb. 9, 1959, 31; Aug. 18, 1959, 28; Feb. 8, 1960, 60.

95. BB to John Cowles, Jan. 8, 1960, Box 13; T. O. Griessemer to Lewis G. Harriman, Apr. 29, 1957; Hugh Moore to John W. Straub, July 29, 1960; Moore to BB, Sept. 22, 1961, all Box 53, all BB MSS; *New York Times*, Mar. 20, 1960, 32; Aug. 27, 1961, E5; *Washington Post*, Nov. 18, 1960, 10.

96. Daily Diary, 1961 passim, Feb. 24, Aug. 13, Aug. 21, 1962; Aug. 22, 1963; March 25, 1964, Box 147; MacLeod to Robert Gould, Nov. 9, 1964, Box 144; MacLeod to Ray Henle, Apr. 20, 1964, Box 29, all BB MSS.

97. Diary, Dec. 23, 1964 and 1964–1965 passim, Box 147; MacLeod to John L. Blair, June 29, 1966, Box 144; MacLeod to Florence B. Brown, Nov. 14, 1966, ibid., all BB MSS; photos in A8/5, BBDO.

98. *New York Times*, July 6, 1967, 1, 35; July 25, 1967, 16; Memorandum, "Jan" to "Jack," n.d. (ca. July 5, 1967), A8/5, BBDO; Brower, "The Man Everybody Knew," July 10, 1967, ibid.

99. *New York Times*, July 6, 1967, 1, 35; *Washington Post*, July 8, 1967, 12; *Newsweek* (July 17, 1967), 79; clipping, London *Times*, July 7, 1967; Cooke, "Moses of Advertising," *Manchester Guardian*, July 7, 1967, both A8/5, BBDO.

9. LEGACY OF AN ADMAN

1. Fox, *Madison Avenue Goes to War*, 3; BB pamphlet, "Here Is the Lever, Archimedes," quoted in Montgomery, "Bruce Barton," 63.

2. Josiah Strong, *Our Country*, Jurgen Herbst, ed. (Cambridge: Belknap Press, 1963; orig. ed. 1886), 146. Barton's suggestions to President Coolidge for his 1926 AAAA speech echo Strong closely (see page 127).

3. Stephen Richard Shapiro, "The Big Sell—Attitudes of Advertising Writers About Their Craft in the 1920s and 1930s" (Ph.D. dissertation, University of Wisconsin, 1969), 272, 297.

4. "Every advertising campaign," she suggested, "is a sort of private planned economy." Woodward, *It's an Art* (New York: Harcourt, Brace, 1938), 81–82.

5. BB to "Everybody in BBDO NY," Dec. 15, 1952, A8/5, BBDO; conversations with several former BBDO employees. For his discomfort with the runaway size and power of modern corporate capitalism, see Shapiro, "The Big Sell," 285–286.

6. BB to DeWitt Wallace, Nov. 16, 1954, Box 70, BB MSS.

7. BB, "Introduction to Schick Shaver Presentation," Apr. 18, 1949, Box 78, BB MSS.

8. "Bruce Barton said, on October 12, 1944 . . . ," A11/3, BBDO.

9. "Advertising: Word Man," *Newsweek*, July 17, 1967, 79; Harford Powel, Jr., "As You Were—III," *Advertising & Selling*, Aug. 29, 1935, 36.

10. Lears, "From Salvation to Self-Realization: Advertising and the Therapeutic Roots of the Consumer Culture, 1880–1930," in Fox and Lears, eds., *Culture of Consumption*, 5.

11. Ribuffo, "Jesus Christ as Business Statesman"; Montgomery, "Bruce Barton"; MacLeod to Col. Joseph R. Meacham, Apr. 1, 1964, Box 144, BB MSS. Warren Susman suggested greater success by Barton in maintaining an integrated outlook. "Culture Heroes: Ford, Barton, Ruth," in Susman, *Culture as History*, 122–131.

12. BB to Dr. Hubert S. Howe, May 15, 1931, Box 30, BB MSS.

13. See, e.g., Richard M. Huber, *The American Idea of Success* (New York: McGraw-Hill, 1971), 196–209; John Cawelti, *Apostles of the Self-made Man* (Chicago: University of Chicago Press, 1965).

14. Donald Meyer, *The Positive Thinkers* (Garden City, N.Y.: Doubleday, 1965 [Doubleday Anchor, 1966]).

15. Osborn, *Your Creative Power: How to Use Imagination* (New York: Charles Scribner's Sons, 1949).

16. BB, "Quick Starters," in *On the Up and Up* (Indianapolis: Bobbs-Merrill, 1929), 72; Harford Powel, Jr., "As You Were—III," *Advertising & Selling*, Aug. 29, 1935, 36.

17. "Something New in Annual Reports. A Report to Policyholders by a Policyholder, Bruce Barton" (1944), Box 33, BB MSS; BBDO News Letter, Nov. 16, 1935, A8/5, BBDO.

18. Susman, "Culture Heroes," 123; clipping, "Barton's Answer," *Country Newspaper Advertising*, February 1928, A8/5, BBDO; BB, "Grantland Rice," July 13, 1954, Box 59, BB MSS.

19. Clipping, Tex McCrary and Jinx Falkenburg, "New York Close-up," *New York Herald Tribune*, Sept. 12, 1949, Box 41, BB MSS.

20. *New York Times*, May 1, 1938, 5; Oct. 14, 1938, 5.

21. BB to W. H. Johnson, Dec. 17, 1932, Box 42, BB MSS.

22. *American Magazine*, Apr. 1928, 16–17; BB to J. Norton Brennan, Apr. 12, 1957, Box 50, BB MSS.

23 BB to W. H. Johnson, Dec. 17, 1932; Box 42; BB to William R. Baker, Jr., July 13, 1954, Box 18, both BB MSS.

24. BB to Orrin E. Dunlap, Jr., Nov. 21, 1931, Box 49, ibid.

25. BB article, n.d. (ca. 1931?), quoted in William Kniffin, "Repose Sadly Missing in Modern Existence," clipping, n.d., Box 99, BB MSS.

26. Memorandum, BB to Duffy et al. June 29, 1954, Box 18, BB MSS. Cf. Powel, *The Virgin Queene*.

27. Excerpt from *Space & Time*, Apr. 12, 1939, Box 18, BB MSS.

28. Advertising Federation of America, "Why We Spend $10 Billion a Year in Advertising," Nov. 1959, Folder 5, Box 5, Brophy MSS.

Index

Pease, Otis, 107
Perkins, George W., 95, 212
Perkins, Maxwell, 90, 251 n17
Pershing, Gen. John J., 43
Petrie, Flinders, 202, 207
Peyser, Rep. Theodore A., 159–160, 169
P. F. Collier & Son, 28–30, 36, 242 n24
Pickford, Mary, 168
Planned Parenthood Federation, 222
Population control, BB interest in, 208, 222
"Positive thinking," BB and, 36–37, 136–138, 209, 228, 230
Powel, Harford, Jr., 76, 79, 90, 233, 254 n50, 267 n61; authors *The Virgin Queene*, 106
Pratt, Rep. Ruth Baker, 159
Preachers' sons: in advertising, 73–74; BB on, 14–15
President's Organization on Unemployment Relief (POUR), 138
Printers' Ink (trade journal), 50, 52, 156, 220
Progressive Era, 12, 23, 25, 50, 207; BB disillusion with reform, 114–115
Prothero, Stephen, 88
Prothro, James W., 107
Pryor, Arthur, Jr., 76–77
Pure Food and Drug Act, 148, 172, 175
Puritanism, 11, 86–87, 88, 91, 92, 96, 109, 118, 119, 122, 250 n4

Radio: BB on potential of, 76, 80; BBDO role in, 53, 76–77, 146; role in politics, 115, 116, 117, 123, 133, 191
Reader's Digest, 64, 203, 210–211, 213
Redbook, 78
Reagan, Ronald W., 210
Reeves, Rosser, 194, 218
Republican National Committee, 132–133, 157, 193
Revlon, 210
Ribuffo, Leo, 107, 238 n15, 252 n19
Rice, Grantland, 87, 231
Rich, Rep. Robert, 215
Riesman, David, 121

Robbins (Tenn.), 3, 7–8
Rockefeller, John D., Jr., 64
Rockefeller, Nelson A., 219, 264 n6
Rogers, Will, 113
Roosevelt, Eleanor, 202, 222
Roosevelt, Franklin D., 115, 123, 129, 131, 132, 134, 137, 138, 153, 157, 159–192 passim, 201; attacks BB, 189–192; BB low opinion of, 152; BB praise for, 137, 138, 152–153; BB and third-term issue, 185, 188–189
Roosevelt, Theodore, 95, 163
Rorty, James, 147–148
Ruth, Babe, 77

Salvation Army, 39
Saturday Evening Post, 59, 61
Schlink, F. J., 68, 71–72
Schweitzer, Albert, 113
Scribner, Charles, 90, 251 n17. *See also* Charles Scribner's Sons.
Seldes, George, 137, 162
Seldes, Gilbert, 100
"Service," as BB theme, 33, 35, 71, 93–94, 96, 100, 123, 148, 228, 232
Seversky, Maj. Alex de, 204, 207
Shawmut Congregational Church (Boston), 8–9
Siddall, John M., 30–31, 78
Simpson, Kenneth, 160, 185, 186–187, 193
Sloan, Alfred P., 62, 64
Small-town life, BB idealization of, 14, 35, 71, 91–92, 94, 96, 230–231
Smith, Al, 111, 128–129, 131, 250 n4
Smith, Fred, 186
Smith, Rep. Robert, 215
Social Gospel, 23, 26–28, 33–34
Socony Vacuum Oil (Standard Oil of New York), 59, 233
Sorokin, Pitirim, 207
Sousa, John Philip, 77
Spargo, John, 115
Speers, Rev. Theodore, 216
Spencer, Herbert, 207
Spengler, Oswald, 207

A NOTE ON THE AUTHOR

Richard M. Fried was born in Milwaukee, Wisconsin, and studied at Amherst College and Columbia University, where he received a Ph.D. in American history. He has been a senior Fulbright lecturer and is now professor of history at the University of Illinois at Chicago. His other books include *Nightmare in Red: The McCarthy Era in Perspective*; *Men Against McCarthy*; and *The Russians Are Coming! The Russians Are Coming!: Pageantry and Patriotism in Cold War America*. Mr. Fried is married with two children and lives in Glen Ellyn, Illinois.